# TESI GREGORIANA

## Serie Teologia

—— 18 ——

T0126825

SEÁN CHARLES MARTIN

# PAULI TESTAMENTUM
## 2 Timothy and the Last Words of Moses

EDITRICE PONTIFICIA UNIVERSITÀ GREGORIANA
Roma 1997

*Vidimus et approbamus ad normam Statutorum Universitatis*

Romae, ex Pontificia Universitate Gregoriana
die 14 mensis decembris anni 1994

R.P. Prof. UGO VANNI, S.J.
Prof. JOSEPH SIEVERS

ISBN 88-7652-739-7

© Iura editionis et versionis reservantur

**PRINTED IN ITALY**

**GREGORIAN UNIVERSITY PRESS**
Piazza della Pilotta, 35 – 00187 Rome, Italy

Multas per gentes et multa per aequora uectus
aduenio has miseras, frater, ad inferias,
ut te postremo donarem munere mortis
et mutam nequiquam alloquerer cinerem,
quandoquidem fortuna mihi tete abstulit ipsum,
heu miser indigne frater adempte mihi.
Nunc tamen interea haec prisco quae more parentum
tradita sunt tristi munere ad inferias
accipe fraterno multum manantia fletu,
atque in perpetuum, frater, aue atque uale.

Catullus, Poem CI


*To the memory of*
*Kevin Francis Martin*
*January 26, 1952 — February 2, 1990*

# ACKNOWLEDGEMENTS

A work of this sort is not accomplished without the help and encouragement of many people. My debts to those who are listed here can never be fully repaid.

Most Reverend *Thomas Tschoepe*, retired Bishop of Dallas, during whose episcopate I began this study; Most Reverend *Charles V. Grahmann*, Bishop of Dallas, during whose episcopate I completed this work; Most Reverend *Joseph A. Fiorenza*, Bishop of Galveston-Houston, whose interest in this project has been encouraging; Rev. *Ugo Vanni, SJ*, Pontifical Gregorian University, under whose direction this book took shape, and who patiently endured my slow growth as a biblical theologian, not to mention my halting attempts to speak Italian; Prof. *Joseph Sievers*, Pontifical Biblical Institute, whose helpful comments at the conclusion of this work improved it immeasurably; Rev. Msgr. *Charles W. Elmer*, S.T.D., Director, Casa Santa Maria, Rome; Rev. Msgr. *Glenn D. Gardner*, J.C.D., Vicar General, Diocese of Dallas; Rev. Msgr. *Robert C. Rehkemper*, former Vicar General, Diocese of Dallas, and presently pastor, All Saints Church, Dallas; Rev. *Ramón Alvarez*, former Chancellor, Diocese of Dallas, and presently pastor, St. Pius X Church, Dallas; Rev. Msgr. *Donald F. Zimmerman*, pastor, Christ the King Church, Dallas; Rev. Msgr. *Donald L. Fischer*, pastor, St. Joseph Church, Richardson; Rev. *John J. Libone*, pastor, St. Elizabeth Ann Seton Church, Plano; Br. *Randal Riede, CFX*, Librarian, North American College, Rome; *Laura Olejnik*, Librarian, Cardinal Beran Library, St. Mary's Seminary, Houston; *Alice Puro*, William Blakely Library, University of Dallas, Irving; Rev. Msgr. *Chester Borski*, Rector, St. Mary's Seminary; Rev. *Lou Brusatti, CM*, D. Min., Dean, University of St. Thomas School of Theology at St. Mary's Seminary; Rev. *Jack Gallagher, CSB*, S.T.D., Dean Emeritus; *Sandra Magie*, Ph.D., S.T.D., Assistant Dean; Sr. *Maria Pascuzzi, CSJ*, S.S.L.; Rev. *C. Anthony Ziccardi*, S.S.L.; Rev. *Bartholomew S. Winters*, S.T.D., University of St. Mary of the Lake — Mundelein Seminary; Prof. *Donna Orsuto*,

S.T.D., Director, Vincent Pallotti Institute for the Laity, Rome; Sr. *Juliana Miska*, Pontifical Institute «Regina Mundi», Rome; Rev. *Jared Wicks, SJ*, Dean, Faculty of Theology, Pontifical Gregorian University; Rev. *Roland Meynet, SJ*, Director, Tesi Gregoriana; *Carlo Valentino*, Pontifical Biblical Institute; Rev. *Jan Michael Joncas*, S.L.D., Associate Professor of Theology, University of St. Thomas, St. Paul, MN; Prof. *Deirdre Dempsey*, Ph.D., Assistant Professor of Theology, Marquette University, Milwaukee, WI; Rev. *Thomas J. Paprocki*, J.D., J.C.D., Chancellor, Archdiocese of Chicago; Rev. *Piotr Koziel*, St. Gertrude Church, Kingsville, *Gary Picou* and *John Robert Skeldon*, St. Mary's Seminary, for their help with the indices; *Brian Joseph and Clare Marie Martin*, Atlanta, for peaceful and productive days by the fireplace; *Pat and Sharon Zaby*, Dallas and Payne Springs, for their friendship and encouragement; and my *students* at the University of St. Thomas School of Theology at St. Mary's Seminary, the Pontifical Gregorian University, and the Pontifical Institute «Regina Mundi», all of whom have helped me to clarify my own thinking about the literature of the Bible.

## CHAPTER I

## Claims to Authority in 2 Timothy

### 1. Introduction: the problem of authority

Raymond Brown has observed that twin crises of authority faced Christians who lived in the last third of the first century: on the one hand, the apostolic witnesses to the life, ministry, death, and resurrection of the Lord had died; on the other hand, the churches were in the process of breaking away, if they had not already done so, from much of what had previously constituted authority in Judaism[1]. How to survive, how to maintain fidelity to the Lord and to the convictions of the apostles in new circumstances, how to cope with threats never envisioned by the apostles — these were the challenges facing the churches of the latter part of the first century.

The New Testament letters commonly referred to as the Pastoral Epistles[2], and widely regarded as deutero-Pauline[3], reflect those crises, and,

---

[1] R. E. BROWN, *The Churches*, 30.

[2] The honour of first having so designated 1 Tim, 2 Tim and Titus goes to P. ANTON, *Abhandlung der Pastoralbriefe*, 1753. See R. F. COLLINS, *Letters*, 88. However, as J. D. QUINN (*Titus*, 1) has noted, the terminology had its precedent in Thomas Aquinas, *Commentaria* 2.184D; *Super I Epistulam ad Timotheum, lectio ii in 1:3*.

[3] I am persuaded by the arguments of scholars like Martin Dibelius and Hans Conzelmann that the historical Paul was not the author of the Pastoral Epistles, and that, as a consequence, the Pastoral Epistles represent an instance of pseudonymous literature in the New Testament. See M. DIBELIUS – H. CONZELMANN, *The Pastoral Epistles*, 1-5; hereinafter Dibelius – Conzelmann; R. F. COLLINS, *Letters*, 88-131; R. A. WILD, «The Pastoral Epistles», 892-893; W. F. TAYLOR, «1-2 Timothy, Titus», 72. See also W. MARXSEN, *Introduction*, 199-216; N. PERRIN – D. DULING, *The New Testament*, 384-388; A. J. HULTGREN, *I-II Timothy, Titus*, 17; D. L. BARTLETT, *Ministry*, 153. To attribute positions advanced in the Pastoral Epistles to Paul, however much they may be in continuity with his own thought, strikes me as misleading (see BROWN, *The Churches*, 31, n. 45); on the other hand, to have to refer constantly in

what is more, proffer some resolutions to them. The crises reflected in the Pastoral Epistles are usually thought to have been precipitated by the presence of false teachers in the community[4], who propound «myths and endless genealogies» (1 Tim 1:4), against whom the Pastor mounts a polemic[5]. The reasons for that polemic, and the nature of the positions taken by the διδάσκαλοι have been the subject of much scholarly speculation[6]. Whether or not one agrees with Benjamin Fiore's contention

---

the course of this study to the author of the Pastoral Epistles as «the writer of the Pastoral Epistles» or some other circumlocution impresses me as a singularly infelicitous expedient. Following R. FULLER'S lead, («The Pastoral Epistles», 97-121), I call the author of 1 Tim, 2 Tim and Titus the Pastor, an expression which has the advantage of at once distinguishing the author of these letters from Paul himself and pointing to his own purposes in writing these letters.

[4] The Pastor names three of these teachers: Alexander (1 Tim 1:20), who is said to have made a shipwreck of his faith along with Hymenaeus (1 Tim 1:20; 2 Tim 2:17b), who himself is said to hold with Philetus (2 Tim 2:17b) that the resurrection is past already (2 Tim 2:18). They are not the only ones, apparently, who aspire to be teachers of the law (1 Tim 1:7): there are «certain others» (τινες: 1 Tim 1:19b) among whom (ὧν ἐστιν: 1 Tim 1:20; 2 Tim 2:17b) these men are to be numbered.

[5] See 1 Tim 1:3-7, 19b-20; 4:1-3, 7a; 6:3-5, 20b-21a; 2 Tim 2:14, 16-19, 23, 25b-26; 3:1-9; 4:3-4; Tit 1:10-16; 3:9-11.

[6] C. K. BARRETT («Pauline Controversies») maintains that the polemic in the Pastoral Epistles is not directed against any particular group: «Judaism, legalism, mythology and gnosis are lumped together in a way that suggests rather that the author was concerned to omit no heresy he had heard of than that he wished, or was able, to analyze sub-divide, and classify» (240-241); he wonders if such teaching was characteristic of «a new Judaism, a gnosticizing Judaism» (242). For a similar point, see H. KOESTER. *Introduction, Vol 2: History and Literature*, 304. Koester sees the polemic against the διδάσκαλοι as typical of the genre of the testament, which usually contains some predictions about the difficulties which will be experienced in the «last days»; thus he thinks that the letter does not intend to describe any particular group within the community at which 2 Tim was directed, especially since the Pastoral Epistles as a whole, and 2 Tim in particular, do not furnish any detailed refutation to the teachings of the διδάσκαλοι; the descriptions of the false teachers have, rather, «the character of catch-words that point to typical phenomena of heresy in general» (304). In the fight against the διδάσκαλοι, the Pastoral Epistles «are designed to be a handbook, a manual for the church leader, enabling him to identify heresies of whatever kind, and to reject them without having to enter into a discussion of subtle theological points» (304). See also P. H. TOWNER, «Gnosis and Realized Eschatology», 95-124.

Among those scholars who think that the polemic in the Pastoral Epistles was directed against a particular group, the opinions range across the spectrum of possibilities. R. M. GRANT (*Gnosticism and Early Christianity*) maintains that the myths and genealogies were Gnostic accounts of the origin of the universe (161). Dibelius – Conthe nature of the polemical situation envisioned in the letters is unclear[7],

---

zelmann argue, on the basis of similar polemics waged by Irenaeus (*Adv. haer.* I 30.9) that the opponents advocated some type of «early Jewish or Judaizing forms of Gnos ticism» (17). And while they caution that «it is impossible to identify the particular heresy attacked here with one of the Gnostic sects known to us» (66), they nevertheless maintain that «it is clear that the image of Paul is dominated [...] by anti-Gnostic tendencies in the Pastoral Epistles» (66). J. L. HOULDEN (*The Pastoral Epistles*) sees in the myths and genealogies a reference to «the speculative, luxuriant, even vertiginous theological and cosmological constructions which came to their full flowering among the Gnostic sects of the second century» (55). J. DEWEY («1 Timothy») holds that the references to genealogies, speculation, and knowledge suggest Gnostic Christian groups (354). R. FULLER («The Pastoral Epistles») concludes that the teaching of the opponents typifies «an early form of Gnosticism which is largely, though eclectically Jewish in character» (106). P. DORNIER (*Les Épîtres Pastorales*) holds that the position of the heretics in the Pastorals represents a stage in the evolution of a heterodox Judaism towards Gnosticism (16). J. N. D. KELLY (*Commentary*) holds that «the most obvious characteristic of the heresy is its combination of Jewish and Gnostic ingredients», (11) and that the heresy advocated by the false teachers is «best defined as a Gnosticizing form of Jewish Christianity» (12). W. F. TAYLOR («1 – 2 Timothy, Titus») thinks that «the opponents seek to combine into one religion Pauline Christianity, more specifically Jewish Christian thought, and emerging Gnostic positions» (74). R. J. KARRIS (Background and Significance») does not attempt to root the propagation of the myths and genealogies in any specific Jewish teaching, but simply describes it as «esoteric» (563). W. LOCK (*Pastoral Epistles*, 8) and C. SPICQ (*Saint Paul*, I, 99-102) both think that the reference to «endless genealogies» probably alludes to rabbinic speculations about Old Testament *haggada*. R. P. MARTIN («1, 2 Timothy and Titus») holds that the interest of the false teachers «centered in a speculative treatment of the OT linked with an elaborate cosmological theory by which the origin of the universe was explained» (1238).

[7] B. FIORE, *The Function of Personal Example*, 3. See also R. M. KIDD, *Wealth and Beneficence*, who holds that «the hints of an over-realized eschatology, of myths and antitheses and genealogies, and of dietary asceticism are certainly tantalizing to the interpreter. But they were not necessarily any more than tantalizing to their original auditors either – "speculations" that "tickle the ear"» (97). But R. J. KARRIS («Background and Significance») holds that even though many of the charges against the teachers of falsehood are stereotyped, stock accusations, and have their antecedents in the quarrel between the philosophers and the sophists dating back to the time of Plato (551), a careful and critical probing of the polemic can yield «significant results about the teaching of the opponents» (562). He finds that the opponents are Jewish teachers of the law (1 Tim 1:7; Tit 3:9), who teach Jewish myths (1 Tim 1:4, 4:7; 2 Tim 4:4; Tit 1:14) and genealogies (1 Tim 1:4; Tit 3:9), forbidding marriage and enjoining abstinence from food (1 Tim 4:3; perhaps Tit 1:15). Some teach that the resurrection has already occurred (2 Tim 2:17-18) and apparently enjoy some degree of success among the womenfolk (2 Tim 3:6). See R. J. KARRIS, «Background and Significance», 563.

one must admit the legitimacy of his impatience with a scholarly procedure which proceeds «from the hints of a crisis in teaching and belief, to a designation of a likely historical situation, and from there to a characterization of the [Pastoral] letters»[8]. And while he recognizes the fact that the polemic against the false teachers is a consistent feature of all three letters, he suggests that, as a feature, it may be part of a constellation of formal elements characteristic of another type of literature, namely, Greco-Roman epistolary exhortation literature[9].

Fiore's work has been well received: Robert J. Karris mentions how «refreshing and exciting [it is] to read through a work which assumes an interpretive matrix different from and more fruitful than the commonly adopted ones of "early catholicism" and "threat of gnosticism"»[10]. And Hans Dieter Betz praises Fiore for «setting the Pastorals in their proper literary tradition»[11], and concludes from his reading of Fiore's study that «just as the Socratic Epistles present a later Cynic version of Socratic ideals, so the Pastoral Epistles with their image of Paul differ from the authentic letters of the apostle, creating a later form of Paulinism»[12]. Without detracting from the justice of their observations, I nevertheless maintain that there may be another, better interpretive matrix, to use Karris' term, and another, more proper literary tradition, to use Betz's, within which to view the theological strategies of the Pastor. If the problem facing the churches of the latter part of the first century is one involving a lapse of authority, then the solution for those churches must also involve a claim to authority — either the reaffirmation of some ancient authority, or the construction of some new authority, or some sort of combination of the two.

It would be well, at this juncture, to define the limits of this inquiry. This study will examine the claim to authority in 2 Tim, the last of the three Pastoral Epistles[13], by comparing what purport to be Paul's last words to his disciple, Timothy, to the words reputed to have been spoken by Moses to his successors before his death. Moses was, of course, the authority *par excellence* in Jewish estimation; and while what

---

[8] B. FIORE, *The Function of Personal Example*, 3.

[9] B. FIORE, *The Function of Personal Example*, 3, 101-163.

[10] R. J. KARRIS, «Review», 134-135.

[11] H. D. BETZ, «Review», 335-337.

[12] H. D. BETZ, «Review», 337.

[13] see J. D. QUINN, «Timothy and Titus, Epistles to», 564; ID., *Titus*, 21; and G. W. KNIGHT, *The Pastoral Epistles*, 10, 54.

are supposed to have been his final words are found in the Book of Deuteronomy, the mysterious circumstances which attended his death, and the fact that the place of his burial was otherwise unknown, occasioned the development of certain legends which may be found in what Geza Vermes has called the «rewritten Bible»[14]. C. T. R. Hayward defines the «rewritten Bible» as

> a series of post-biblical Jewish writings which, by re-presenting and re-drafting original books of scripture, seek to interpret and expound those books for particular purposes. The authors/compilers of such rewritten texts present their work as if they were biblical books, and thereby seem to claim for them an authority approaching, if not actually equal to, that of scripture itself[15].

Hayward includes a variety of literary phenomena under the rubric of the «rewritten Bible»: the targumim and the literature of the Qumran community are both, as far as he is concerned, examples of the kind[16]. Interesting as the targumim are and worthy as they may be of study in their own right[17], I shall not consider them in this study, owing to limitations on size and length, and a desire to confine this study to the literature of the Greek-speaking world wherein 2 Tim was written. For this same reason, I have also excluded from consideration in this study the literature of Qumran, since the majority of the texts which have been recovered were written in Hebrew or in Aramaic[18].

The same factors which lead to the exclusion of literature written in Hebrew or Aramaic also require that the Septuagint be employed in this study as the text of the Old Testament[19]. For Greek-speaking peoples of the first century, the Hebrew original of the Scriptures would have

---

[14] G. VERMES, *Scripture and Tradition in Judaism*, 95; ID., «Bible and Midrash», 199-231.

[15] C. T. R. HAYWARD, «Rewritten Bible», 595-596.

[16] C. T. R. HAYWARD, «Rewritten Bible», 596-598.

[17] See M. MCNAMARA, «Targums», 856-861; C. T. R. HAYWOOD, «Targum», 671-673; P. S. ALEXANDER, «Targum, Targumim», 320-331.

[18] J. A. FITZMYER, *Responses to 101 Questions*, 15-16.

[19] All citations of the LXX are taken from A. RAHLFS, ed., *Septuaginta*. For a critical evaluation of the legends surrounding the origin and purpose of the Greek translation of the Pentateuch, as well as a brief examination of the translation strategy employed in the LXX, see E. J. BICKERMAN, *Jews*, 101-116. See also P. LAMARCHE, «La Septante», 19-36. For a more comprehensive study of the place of the Septuagint in antiquity, see M. HARL – G. DORIVAL – O. MUNNICH, *La Bible grecque*.

been incomprehensible; a Greek translation of the Law, the Prophets, and the Writings would have provided their sole point of entry into the religious heritage of the Chosen People. Moreover, as C. H. Roberts reminds us, the LXX was itself regarded as an inspired work, to which the legends in the Letter to Aristeas regarding its origins testify[20]. But while there are no lack of scholarly studies of the Hebrew text in which Moses figures so prominently, serious analyses of the Septuagint are rather less numerous[21]. Thanks, however, to the persistence of narrative phenomena like plot, character, and theme, all of which survive the transformation wrought by the translation of the text from Hebrew into Greek, one may be permitted to employ analyses which base themselves on the Hebrew text of the narrative in order to understand the Greek.

Despite his reservations about the usefulness of the term «rewritten Bible», Daniel J. Harrington includes the *Testament of Moses*, along with Pseudo-Philo's *Liber Antiquitatum Biblicarum* and Josephus's *Jewish Antiquities*, in his list of works which «take as their literary framework the flow of the biblical text itself and apparently have as their major purpose the clarification and actualization of the biblical story»[22]. Such efforts of clarification and actualization are virtually by definition popular, and may be rooted in the homiletic traditions of early Judaism[23]. James L. Kugel has identified some purposes which may have motivated the production of the «rewritten Bible»: aside from the need to clarify obscure turns of phrase owing to linguistic shifts, and the desire to reconcile seeming contradictions in the various provisions of the Torah, authors of this sort of literature seem to have been motivated by the desire to impose order on what Kugel calls «the messiness of history»[24]. Cultural shifts which came in the wake of political changes seemed to call into question the age-old assurance that history had a plan, a plan which was dictated by the will of God:

> To put words in the mouth of an angel, or of a long-dead patriarch or sage, as many second-century and later writers do, is to accomplish precisely the

---

[20] C. H. ROBERTS, «Books in the Graeco-Roman World», 50.

[21] One new multi-volume commentary which takes as its subject the LXX is *La Bible d'Alexandrie*, Paris 1986-1994. The translation of the Pentateuch into French is now complete, and additional volumes are promised over the course of the next few years.

[22] D. J. HARRINGTON, «The Bible Rewritten (Narratives)», 239.

[23] See H. W. ATTRIDGE, *The Interpretation of Biblical History*.

[24] J. L. KUGEL, *Early Biblical Interpretation*, 11-106.

same extension of biblical history into the present. For in having a figure from «back then» (the God of biblical history — or his angel — who knows the arrangement of all things, or some ancient worthy solidly planted «back then» when the Divine Plan was clear) speak about current events and recent history, the author manages to make the present day too savor of the biblical world[25].

For the author of 2 Tim, Paul was just such a figure, an ancient worthy solidly planted «back then» when the Divine Plan was clear. And if the unknown author of the *Testament of Moses*[26], along with Philo's *Life of Moses*[27], Pseudo-Philo's *Liber Antiquitatum Biblicarum*[28], and Josephus's *Jewish Antiquities*[29], retold the ancient story of Moses' last words in order to let the great Mediator of the Torah speak to their contemporaries, so, too, does the Pastor bring Paul back from the dead, and permit him to speak again to another generation. Thus, along with the account in Deuteronomy, it will be to the last words of Moses in these works that 2 Tim will be compared.

Another limitation of this study must be addressed, namely the choice of 2 Tim alone as a subject of study. Michael Prior has recently drawn attention to the distinctiveness of 2 Tim. He notes that, alone of the three Pastoral Epistles, 2 Tim contains a thanksgiving period (2 Tim 1:3-5); furthermore, 2 Tim, unlike 1 Tim and Titus, makes no provision for the appointment to various ministries in the community, nor does the letter raise any sort of anti-Jewish polemic. These phenomena, among others, lead Prior to conclude that 2 Tim is not pseudepigraphical; rather, it constitutes a private letter of Paul to Timothy, written in the expectation of his imminent release from prison in Rome, and with the purpose of urging a reluctant Timothy to join him in the next stage of his missionary endeavors in Spain[30].

---

[25] J. L. KUGEL, *Early Biblical Interpretation*, 47.

[26] Hereinafter, *TM*. The Latin text and English translation of the *TM* is taken from J. TROMP, *The Assumption of Moses*.

[27] Hereinafter, *VM*. All references to the *VM* will be taken from the LCL edition.

[28] Hereinafter, *LAB*. The Latin text of the *LAB* is taken from D. J. HARRINGTON – J. CAZEAUX – C. PERROT – P. M. BOGAERT, *Pseudo-Philon: Les Antiquités Bibliques*; the English translation is that of D. J. HARRINGTON, «Pseudo-Philo: A New Translation», 297-377.

[29] Hereinafter, *JA*. All references to the *JA* will be taken from the LCL edition.

[30] M. PRIOR, *Paul the Letter-Writer*.

Following Michael Prior's lead, Jerome Murphy-O'Connor has recently challenged the critical consensus whereby the Pastoral Epistles are viewed as a single, undifferentiated whole, a consensus represented by Spicq's summary judgement: «toutes les trois sont du même style, contiennent la même doctrine, visent les mêmes tendances hérétiques, supposent à peu près les mêmes conditions de temps et de lieux»[31]. Murphy-O'Connor detects some thirty differences between 2 Tim, on the one hand, and 1 Tim and Titus, on the other, in literary style, in Christology, notions of ministry, the concept of the Gospel, and the nature of the false teaching combatted in the letters; and he claims that so many differences pose a major problem for the hypothesis of the literary unity of the Pastorals. He freely admits that some differences are more significant than others, but he maintains that on the basis of his investigation it does not seem possible that 2 Tim should have been composed by the author of 1 Tim and Titus. Unlike Prior, however, he does not conclude from these differences that 2 Tim should necessarily be included among the Pauline *homologoumena*[32].

To go from noting some differences among the letters to positing a different author for 2 Tim, as both Prior and Murphy-O'Connor do, is, in my view, to make a rather large leap, one after which I am not prepared to follow. But those differences do provide a sufficient rationale, to my mind, for studying 2 Tim in its own right. Consequently, this study will confine itself to a consideration of 2 Tim, and not the Pastoral Epistles as an undifferentiated whole. But insofar as the polemic against Hymenaeus (1 Tim 1:20; 2 Tim 2:17b), Philetus (2 Tim 2:17b), and Alexander (1 Tim 1:20) which is directed against those who, along with these three teachers, occupy themselves with «myths and endless genealogies» (μύθοις καὶ γενεαλογίαις ἀπεράντοις: 1 Tim 1:4; see also 1 Tim 4:7; 2 Tim 4:4; Tit 1:14, 3:9), controversies (ζητήσεις: 1 Tim 6:4; 2 Tim 2:23; Tit 3:9), disputes about words (λογομαχίας: 1 Tim 6:4; λογομαχεῖν: 2 Tim 2:14) and «profane chatter» (βεβήλους κενοφωνίας: 1 Tim 6:20; 2 Tim 2:16) is common to all three letters, it will be necessary to refer to the other Pastoral Epistles. It may be, for instance, that the claims to authority advanced on behalf of the putative author and the putative addressee of 2 Tim apply, *mutatis mutandis*, to the putative author and putative addressees of 1 Tim and Titus. But that is a claim which must be investigated elsewhere.

---

[31] C. SPICQ, *Saint Paul*, I, 31.

[32] J. MURPHY-O'CONNOR, «2 Timothy», 403-418.

## 2. The issue of authority: the letter collection

The first implicit claim to authority, according to Jerome D. Quinn, involved sending not one letter in the name of Paul, but a *collection* of letters. Quinn has noted both the classical and the biblical precedents for such a collection and drawn attention to the implicit claim to authority present in such collections:

> [t]he collection offered an authoritative message from the past, a message from a significant personality, a message containing (at least in the judgement of the collectors) observations whose significance was meant to transcend the setting presupposed by the text. The collected letters thus came as a «prophecy» from the past to a new generation[33].

According to Quinn, regardless of whether any of the Pastoral Epistles enjoyed an individual preëxistence, at least since the second century, and perhaps as early as the first, they were always read as a collection[34]. Moreover, as Quinn recognizes, the original addressees in such collections «tend to sink below the historical horizon while the author (genuine or putative) remains the polestar around which the new public revolves»[35]. Quinn's claim that the Pastoral Epistles were always read as a collection rests on his reading of the manuscript evidence: since the Pauline letters seem to have been arranged according to length, the Pastoral Epistles

> appear to mark a new beginning within the extant Pauline codices because 1 Timothy is noticeably longer than 2 Thessalonians. This marks, in all probability, the seam where two 2nd-century collections of Pauline letters were joined: a collection of letters to churches (at times including Hebrews, as in P[46] and the archetype of B) and a smaller collection of Pauline letters addressed to individuals (also arranged in almost every extant codex with the longest first and Philemon, the shortest, last[36].

Yet, as Quinn himself recognizes, the letters were in all probability composed on one or more scrolls: the process by which they came to be organized in codices «has its repercussions for every hypothesis about the origin and purpose of these letters»[37], which is to say that the authority

---

[33] J. D. QUINN, «Timothy and Titus», 564; ID., *Titus*, 8; ID., «Parenesis», 496.

[34] J. D. QUINN, «Timothy and Titus», 562; ID., *Titus*, 3, 8.

[35] J. D. QUINN, «Timothy and Titus», 564; ID., *Titus*, 8.

[36] J. D. QUINN, «Timothy and Titus», 562; ID., *Titus*, 3.

[37] J. D. QUINN, «Timothy and Titus», 563; ID., *Titus*, 2-3.

of the letters *qua* collection can be verified only from the earliest date to which the manuscript evidence can be assigned.

So far no scroll has come to light which contains any of the Pastoral Epistles. The oldest papyrus in which any of the Pastoral Epistles may be found is P[32], which is in codex-form, and which contains Titus 1:11-15; 2:3-8; it is usually dated to around 200 CE[38]. The oldest uncial manuscript in which any of the Pastoral Epistles may be found is ℵ, a fourth century codex which contains the entirety of the New Testament[39]. And though the Pastoral Epistles are listed together in the Muratorian Canon (c. 200 CE)[40], along with Philemon, as having been written by Paul «out of affection and love» (*pro affectu et dilectione, Frag. Mura.* 60-61) and as being «held sacred in the esteem of the Church catholic for the regulation of ecclesiastical discipline» (*in honorem tamen ecclesiae catholicae in ordinationem ecclesiasticae disciplinae sanctificatae sunt, Frag. Mura.* 61-63), the principle which seems to have governed the grouping of 1 Tim, 2 Tim, Titus, and Philemon together is the most obvious one: that each letter was written to an individual, and not to a church. Neither the manuscript evidence nor the Muratorian Canon, of themselves, provide evidence that by the end of the second century the Pastoral Epistles were circulating as a letter collection, with the implicit claim to authority with which Quinn would like to invest them.

It does not seem possible, then, to recover the intention of the Pastor from the manuscript evidence or from early lists of the Pauline letters. Quinn's argument in favor of the authority of the letters *qua* collection rests on evidence which, however instructive it may be for the early history of the interpretation of the Pastoral Epistles, fails to shed much light on the individual letters themselves, or on the purposes for which they were composed. One may argue with equal justification and by the same means for the authority of the Pauline *homologoumena* as a collection, and still shed no light on the purposes for which, say, Romans was written. Hence, one must search elsewhere for a solution to the crisis of authority.

---

[38] B. METZGER, *Text*, 250.

[39] B. METZGER, *Text*, 42.

[40] For a convenient discussion of the vexed question of authorship, date and provenance of the Muratorian Canon, see B. METZGER, *Canon*, 191-201. The Latin text of the Muratorian Canon is taken from C. KIRCH, *Enchiridion*, 95-96. An English translation is found in B. METZGER, *Canon*, 305-307.

### 3. The issue of authority: the direct references to Moses

Another, more clearly verifiable way in which the Pastor stresses the authority of the putative author of 2 Tim is through an intricate set of references to narratives in which the person of Moses figures prominently. Alert readers of 2 Tim have long recognized the direct references to Old Testament narratives in the letter. While E. Earle Ellis notes only one quotation from the Old Testament in 2 Tim[41], and one instance in which, perhaps, two Old Testament texts are alluded to[42], A. T. Hanson observes, on the other hand, four instances in which the author of 2 Tim makes use of the Scriptures[43].

### 3.1 *Numbers 16:5 at 2 Tim 2:19*

Both scholars agree, however, along with every other major commentator of 2 Tim[44], that in the assertion that «God's firm foundation stands» (ὁ μέντοι στερεὸς θεμέλιος τοῦ θεοῦ ἔστηκεν: 2 Tim 2:19), the Pastor makes a direct reference to Num 16:5: «The Lord knows who are his» (Ἔγνω κύριος τοὺς ὄντας αὐτοῦ). The text may be found in an episode in Num 16:1-40 involving the revolt of Abiram, Dathan, and Korah against Moses and Aaron. In that account, whose redactional history Martin Noth has explicated as the joining together of at least two narratives, united by the theme of rebellion[45], one narrative, featuring Dathan and Abiram as Moses' opponents, can be distinguished from its context with «comparative ease», according to Noth, and probably comes from the Yahwist strand of the Pentateuch[46]. The other narrative, which belongs to P[47], centers on the question of whether Korah, a Levite, is equal to Aaron in dignity and authority (Num 16:8-11, 16-24a,

---

[41] 2 Tim 2:19 (Num 16:5 and, perhaps, Is 26:13). See E. E. ELLIS, *Paul's Use*, 152.

[42] 2 Tim 4:14 (Ps 61:13; Prov 24:12): neither of these allusions, it must be noted, are manifestly intentional, according to E. E. ELLIS, *Paul's Use*, 154.

[43] 2 Tim 2:19 (Is 28:16, Num 16:5, Is 52:11 combined with Lev 24:16); 3:8 (a *haggada* originally based on Ex 8:18-19); 3:11 (Ps 34:19); 4:16-18 (Ps 22). See A. T. HANSON, *The Pastoral Epistles*, 140; ID., «The Use of the Old Testament», 203-219.

[44] See Dibelius – Conzelmann, 112; W. LOCK, *Pastoral Epistles*, 100; C. SPICQ, *Saint Paul*, II, 760; J. L. HOULDEN, *The Pastoral Epistles*, 122.

[45] M. NOTH, *Numbers*, 118-131.

[46] M. NOTH, *Numbers*, 121.

[47] P. J. BUDD, *Numbers*, 181.

35-40)[48]. Noth maintains that Moses and Aaron are representative figures in this account of the Jerusalem priesthood. Behind the account as it stands, he claims, lies the memory of a party, represented by Korah, in opposition to the Jerusalem priesthood, which demands a share in its special privileges[49]. In a similar fashion, Conrad L'Heureux holds that the story served as a way of settling controversies which arose in the post-Exilic period, and limiting whatever claims those Levites who claimed descent from Korah were putting forward on their own behalf[50]. Likewise, Philip Budd argues that the story of Korah reflects power struggles within post-Exilic Judaism, and that Korah represents Levitical opposition to the priestly hierarchy proposed by the settlers from Babylon[51]. Baruch A. Levine is rather less confident about the possibility of linking a traditional account, such as we have here, to a particular historical situation. Nevertheless, he is willing to admit the possibility that the episode masks a rivalry in the post-Exilic priesthood[52]. But whatever uses the narrative might have served in the communities for which they were originally preserved is less relevant to this discussion than the uses to which this story is put in the argument of 2 Tim.

What is of interest in the allusion to the story of the rebellion of Korah, Dathan, and Abiram is the theme of challenge to the authority of the divinely appointed leaders; the three rebels, along with two hundred and fifty followers, accuse Moses and Aaron of having exalted themselves above the assembly of the Lord. Moreover, they claim that «all the congregation are holy, every one of them, and the Lord is among them» (ὅτι πᾶσα ἡ συναγωγὴ πάντες ἅγιοι καὶ ἐν αὐτοῖς κύριος: Num 16:3). The rebels' complaint against Moses and Aaron strikes a distinctly egalitarian note, one which is founded on a conviction that no one group within the assembly can lay claim to a special privilege not

---

[48] M. NOTH (Numbers, 121) allows that this narrative may itself be woven from two different accounts of a rebellion led by Korah: one strand of the story features Korah as the leader of 250 «well-known men» (אַנְשֵׁי־שֵׁם: Num 16:2; ἄνδρες ὀνομαστοί: LXX Num 16:2); the other strand depicts Korah as the spokesman of Levitical opposition (Num 16:8-11).

[49] M. NOTH, Numbers, 123-125.

[50] C. L'HEUREUX, «Numbers», 86; see also R. R. HUTTON, «Korah», 101.

[51] P. J. BUDD, Numbers, 189.

[52] B. A. LEVINE, Numbers 1–20, 430.

accorded the others because no one group possesses the Lord any more fully than another.

In the allusion to the rebellion of Korah, Dathan, and Abiram in 2 Tim, the Pastor establishes a kind of analogy: Korah, Dathan, and Abiram are likened to Hymenaeus and Philetus, «who have swerved from the truth» (οἵτινες περὶ τὴν ἀλήθειαν ἠστόχησαν: 2 Tim 2:18), while, by implication, Paul and Timothy are likened to Moses and Aaron. In the episode as it is related in Numbers, the authority of the hereditary Aaronide priesthood is vindicated by the miraculous death of the rebels (Num 16:31-35). At the same time, the analogous relationship between the Mosaic characters and the Pauline characters serves to underscore the latters' divine right to exercise authority in the community. The allusion to the rebellion of Korah, Dathan, and Abiram thus constitutes the Pastor's oblique reply to the opponents in 2 Tim and is tantamount to a threat of destruction: should Hymenaeus and Philetus persist in their «profane chatter» (βεβήλους κενοφωνίας: 2 Tim 2:16), they will meet the same end as those who presumed to rebel against Moses and Aaron.

### 3.2 *Jannes and Jambres at 2 Tim 3:8-9*

In a similar fashion, the Pastor predicts the downfall of those who are «lovers of self, lovers of money, proud, arrogant, abusive [...] holding the form of religion but denying the power of it» (φίλαυτοι, φιλάργυροι, ἀλαζόνες, ὑπερήφανοι, βλάσφημοι [...] ἔχοντες μόρφωσιν εὐσεβείας τὴν δὲ δύναμιν αὐτῆς ἠρνημένοι: 2 Tim 3:2-5) by likening these opponents to Jannes and Jambres. These two figures are identified in subsequent legends with the otherwise nameless φαρμακοί of Ex 7:11 and 9:11, the magicians at Pharaoh's court who were unable to prevail against the power exhibited by Moses and Aaron: «As Jannes and Jambres opposed Moses, so these men also oppose the truth, men of corrupt mind and counterfeit faith; but they will not get very far, for their folly will be plain to all, as was that of these two men» (ὃν τρόπον δὲ Ἰάννης καὶ Ἰαμβρῆς ἀντέστησαν Μωϋσεῖ, οὕτως καὶ οὗτοι ἀνθίστανται τῇ ἀληθείᾳ, ἄνθρωποι κατεφθαρμένοι τὸν νοῦν, ἀδόκιμοι περὶ τὴν πίστιν· ἀλλ' οὐ προκόψουσιν ἐπὶ πλεῖον· ἡ γὰρ ἄνοια αὐτῶν ἔκδηλος ἔσται πᾶσιν, ὡς καὶ ἡ ἐκείνων ἐγένετο: 2 Tim 3:8-9).

Knight notes the parallel offenses of Jannes and Jambres, on the one hand, and Timothy's opponents, on the other. Both offenses are characterized by a form of the verb ἀνθίστημι: Jannes and Jambres opposed (ἀντέστησαν) Moses; the false teachers oppose (ἀνθίστανται) the truth. But while the opposition of the sorcerers in Exodus was directed against a person, the opposition of the false teachers in 2 Tim is directed against the truth itself: «even though in the first instance a person is opposed and in the second the truth is opposed, the two episodes are analogous in that opposition to Moses was really opposition to the truth of Moses' message»[53]. One may wish to extend the logic of Knight's observation: in 2 Tim, opposition to the truth is signified by opposition to a person, in this case, the bearer of the Pauline heritage.

Dibelius — Conzelmann and Lock have both indicated the literature in which Jannes and Jambres make their appearance[54], the earliest of which is the *Damascus Document* V.17-19, though Pietersma and Lutz remind us that the earliest Greek language reference to the pair is here in 2 Tim[55]. No commentator suggests that the author of 2 Tim knew the *Damascus Document*, much less the pseudepigraphical work known as *The Book of Jannes and Jambres*; all assume that the legend was in the process of development, and that the *Damascus Document*, *The Book of Jannes and Jambres*, and 2 Tim 3:8-9 represent differing stages of that development, an assumption which I think is justified[56]. Yet no commentator has pursued the question of why the Pastor should make a comparison between the opponents depicted in the 2 Tim and the legendary opponents of Moses and Aaron[57].

I contend that the allusion to the rebellion of Korah, Dathan, and Abiram through the citation of Numbers 16:5 and the mention of Jannes and Jambres deliberately introduce into the argument of 2 Tim a reference to the figure of Moses. The theme of challenge to the authority of the community's leader which is common to both stories is, of course, immediately relevant to the polemic against the νομοδιδάσκαλοι in the Pastoral Epistles. More to the point, however, the allusions set up

---

[53] G. W. KNIGHT, *The Pastoral Epistles*, 435.

[54] *Damascus Document* V.17-19; Pliny, *Hist. Nat.* 30.2.11. See Dibelius — Conzelmann, 117, for a complete listing of citations in literature later than the Pastoral Epistles. See also W. LOCK, *Pastoral Epistles*, 107. A. T. HANSON, *Studies*, has traced the legend of Jannes and Jambres and posited some link with Wisdom 15:18–16:1.

[55] A. PIETERSMA — R. T. LUTZ, «Jannes and Jambres», 427.

[56] See A. PIETERSMA — R. T. LUTZ, «Jannes and Jambres», 430-431. See also J. H. CHARLESWORTH, *The Old Testament Pseudepigrapha*, 70.

[57] Dibelius — Conzelmann (117) explicitly deny a typology of the wilderness generation in the Pastoral Epistles, and thus any intentional comparison of any of the figures in 2 Tim to any of the principals of the Old Testament narrative of the escape from Egypt found in the Pentateuch. Such an outright denial seems unjustified, in my opinion.

a kind of implicit analogy between Paul, Timothy, and «the faithful men who will be able to teach others also» (2 Tim 2:2) on the one hand, and Moses, Aaron, and those who have received the divine commission to lead the community of faith, on the other. By likening Paul and his heirs to Moses and Aaron, the Pastor has endowed them with a kind of authority which is divine in its origin and irresistible in its appeal.

## 4. The issue of authority: the indirect references to Moses

The Mosaic analogy is further reinforced by the series of indirect references to narratives involving Moses. Few critics, however, have made much of these indirect references to the Old Testament in 2 Tim. The reference to the laying on of hands at 2 Tim 1:6, for instance, when it has occupied the attention of the major commentators at all, has done so only in respect to questions involving, for instance, the manner and mode of ordination in the early church, and the apparent contradiction between this passage and 1 Tim 4:14, where in the context of an exhortation not to neglect «the gift you have» (μὴ ἀμέλει τοῦ ἐν σοὶ χαρίσματος), Paul reminds Timothy of how and when he first received the gift: «which was given to you by prophetic utterance when the council of elders laid their hands upon you» (ὃ ἐδόθη σοι διὰ προφητείας μετὰ ἐπιθέσεως τῶν χειρῶν τοῦ πρεσβυτερίου)[58]. Here, of course, it is Paul who lays hands upon Timothy: «I remind you to rekindle the gift of God that is within you through the laying on of my hands» (ἀνα-μιμνῄσκω σε ἀναζωπυρεῖν τὸ χάρισμα τοῦ θεοῦ, ὅ ἐστιν ἐν σοὶ διὰ τῆς ἐπιθέσεως τῶν χειρῶν μου: 2 Tim 1:6).

### 4.1 The laying on of hands

Dibelius − Conzelmann indicate the relevant passages in the New Testament in which the laying on of hands serves as a means of transmitting the Spirit for those who do not yet possess it[59], and J. N. D.

---

[58] So, for instance, W. LOCK, *Pastoral Epistles*, 54, 85; C. SPICQ, *Saint Paul*, II, 708, 722-730; Dibelius − Conzelmann, 70-71, 98; A. T. HANSON, *The Pastoral Epistles*, 94, 121; J. L. HOULDEN, *The Pastoral Epistles*, 89, 111; R. F. COLLINS, *Letters*, 110; R. P. MARTIN, «1, 2, Timothy and Titus», 1240; G. W. KNIGHT, *The Pastoral Epistles*, 208-209, 370-371; J. MURPHY-O'CONNOR, «2 Timothy», 411.

[59] Not connected with baptism: Acts 8:17; during baptism: Acts 19:6 and Heb 6:2; at an installation: Acts 6:6 and 13:3. See Dibelius − Conzelmann, 70, n. 4. See also J. L. HOULDEN, *The Pastoral Epistles*, 89.

Kelly and Robert A. Wild have both drawn attention to the allusions to Deut 34:9 and Num 27:18-23 and the laying on of hands upon Joshua by Moses[60], Spicq has noted these parallels, and has remarked that «le contexte général des Pastorales invite à comprendre l'*épithésis* de Paul et des Anciens comme une reproduction du geste de Moïse — transmettant au nom de Dieu à Josué son autorité sur le peuple de Dieu — et faisant de Timothée le représentant de l'Apôtre et le chef de la communauté ecclésiale»[61]. Yet he does not undertake a detailed investigation of the possible meaning of the imposition of hands in 2 Tim in the light of this Mosaic precedent.

### 4.1.1  The laying on of hands in Deuteronomy 34:9

J. Roy Porter has analyzed the Biblical references to the succession of Joshua, and concludes that the model for Joshua's succession to Moses is the transmission of the royal office from one king to another[62]. In effect, the notice of Joshua's succession to the office formerly occupied by Moses is, in this case, the Priestly redactor's retrojection of monarchical practices onto the wilderness narratives. With respect to the Hebrew text of the installation notice of Deut 34:9, he notes that it is his possession of the רוּחַ חָכְמָה which causes the Israelites to render obedience to Joshua; and that, moreover, חָכְמָה is closely associated with kingship[63]. Without rejecting Porter's primary thesis, namely, that the pattern of succession depicted here is after the manner of the Israelite monarchy, I wonder if his specific analysis of Deut 34:9 is supportable.

Structurally, the text is bipartite: v. 9a has Joshua as its subject and v. 9b has the children of Israel as its subject. Each of the two clauses is likewise bipartite: the first colon of v. 9a indicates Joshua's state after the death of Moses, and the second colon indicates the action which has brought about this state of being. Grammatically, the two cola of the clause are linked with a causal conjunction: Joshua possesses the spirit

---

[60] J. N. D. KELLY, *Commentary*, 106; R. A. WILD, «The Pastoral Epistles», 898.

[61] C. SPICQ, *Saint Paul*, II, 735.

[62] J. R. PORTER, «The Succession of Joshua», 102-132. He discerns two basic blocks of material: Num 27:12-23 and Deut 34:9, in connection with which Num 32:28 and 34:17 have also to be considered; and Deut 31:1-8, 14f, 23 and Josh 1:1-9, with which Deut 1:38, 3:21f, 28 are clearly connected (103). The relevance of the second block of passages with respect to the succession of Timothy will be more apparent in the discussion of 2 Tim 2:1.

[63] J. R. PORTER, «The Succession of Joshua», 128.

of knowledge *because* (כִּי/γὰρ) Moses has laid his hands upon him. In a similar fashion, v. 9b is divided into two cola, linked to each other by ו/καί, which functions here as a coördinate conjunction; the first colon describes the obedience of the children of Israel: they «hearkened unto him» (וַיִּשְׁמְעוּ אֵלָיו/καὶ εἰσήκουσαν αὐτοῦ). The second colon further specifies their obedience by the manner in which it was effectuated, namely, by doing «as the Lord had commanded Moses» (כַּאֲשֶׁר צִוָּה יהוה אֶת־מֹשֶׁה/ καθότι ἐνετείλατο κύριος τῷ Μωυσῇ). Hence, the cola of 9b offer an example of synthetic parallelism, wherein the second colon of a verse explains or develops some element of the first[64].

Thus, the effects of the laying on of hands are, really, two-fold: (1) Joshua comes into possession of the «spirit of knowledge»[65]; and (2) the children of Israel render obedience to Joshua, not so much, it should be noted, because he possesses the «spirit of knowledge», but because Moses has laid his hands upon him. To say, then, as Porter does, that the children of Israel obey Joshua because he possesses the «spirit of knowledge» is to confuse cause and effect. Joshua commands obedience because he is the successor to Moses. And he is the successor of Moses because Moses has laid hands upon him.

A similar logic is at work in 2 Tim 1:6-7: Timothy is reminded «to rekindle the gift of God that is within you through the laying on my hands (ἐπιθέσεως τῶν χειρῶν μου); for God did not give us a spirit of timidity (πνεῦμα δειλίας) but a spirit of power and love and self-control». The language of laying on of hands, coupled with a mention of πνεῦμα in the one upon whom the hands are laid, suggests that the Pastor had the passage from Deuteronomy in mind. And, as in Deut 34:9, the effect of the laying on of hands, the «gift of God», (τὸ χάρισμα τοῦ θεοῦ) receives mention before its cause, the laying on of hands; in the following verse, the nature of that χάρισμα is further specified, first by a description of what it is *not*, «a spirit of timidity» (πνεῦμα δειλίας), and secondly, by a tripartite listing of what it is, «[a spirit] of power and love and self-control» (δυνάμεως καὶ ἀγάπης καὶ σωφρονισμοῦ). Hanson has noted the similarities between 2 Tim 1:6-9 and Rom 8:12-17: he sees a deliberate play on words in the transformation of Paul's «spirit of slavery» (πνεῦμα δουλείας: Rom 8:15) to the Pastor's «spirit of timidity»

---

[64] See R. ALTER, *The Art of Biblical Poetry*, 3-26; and L. ALONSO SCHÖKEL, *A Manual of Hebrew Poetics*, 48-61.

[65] See E. LOHSE, «χείρ», 428-429.

(πνεῦμα δειλίας: 2 Tim 1:7)[66]. Yet Hanson does not attempt to provide a rationale for the play on words, aside from the Pastor's general tendency to reconstruct Paul's thought «to fit his own circumstances»[67]. In the light of the Moses/Paul analogy, the reasons for that paronomasia become clear: the Pastor's language is reminiscent of Moses' exhortation to Joshua in Deut 31:8b: «Fear not, neither be afraid» (μὴ φοβοῦ μηδὲ δειλία). This particular text, as Porter has noted, is part of the two basic blocks of tradition respecting Joshua's appointment to office[68]. The transformation of Pauline language through the use of the vocabulary of δειλία so that it echoes Deut 31:8 can hardly have been anything other than deliberate, and reinforces the comparison of Moses and Joshua, on the one hand, to Paul and Timothy, on the other.

As if the laying on of hands were not enough of a bond, Timothy's possession of this tripartite χάρισμα provides an additional link to Paul, since the gift which God has given «us» (ἡμῖν: 2 Tim 1:7), that is, both Timothy and Paul, is an identical spirit. I do not think that ἡμῖν refers to Christians in general[69], or that it gives evidence here of Paul's «kindly tact», softening an otherwise harsh statement by including himself as potentially timid[70]. Houlden, who holds that the tripartite listing of power, love, and self-control constitute the specific content of τὸ χάρισμα given by God[71], seems to be closer to the mark, with, perhaps, one additional proviso: the gift is God's, to be sure; but the spirit is Paul's, and now, by virtue of the laying on of hands, Timothy's. Thus is a double bond established between Paul and his successor.

### 4.1.2 The laying on of hands in Numbers 27:18-23

While scholars like A. Graeme Auld have stressed the similarities between Num 27:18-31 and its equivalent in Deut 34:9[72], several differ-

---

[66] A. T. HANSON, *The Pastoral Epistles*, 29, 121; see also J. L. HOULDEN, *The Pastoral Epistles*, 110; and Dibelius – Conzelmann, who hold that «the relation to Rom 8:15 should not be considered merely accidental» (98).

[67] A. T. HANSON, *The Pastoral Epistles*, 28.

[68] J. R. PORTER, «The Succession of Joshua», 103.

[69] G. W. KNIGHT, *The Pastoral Epistles*, 371. His reason for so understanding ἡμῖν is based on his understanding of the phrase [πνεῦμα] δυνάμεως καὶ ἀγάπης καὶ σωφρονισμοῦ as the Holy Spirit.

[70] J. N. D. KELLY, *Commentary*, 159-160.

[71] J. L. HOULDEN, *The Pastoral Epistles*, 110.

[72] A. G. AULD, *Joshua, Moses and the Land*, 84.

ences from the notice in Deuteronomy immediately present themselves in the account as it is presently found in Numbers. First of all, the causal connection between the laying on of hands and Joshua's possession of spirit is reversed. If in the text from Deuteronomy, Joshua possesses the spirit *because* Moses laid his hands upon him, in Num 27:18, Moses is ordered by God to lay his hands upon Joshua who *already* has spirit within him[73]. It is as though Joshua's possession of spirit qualifies him for the laying on of hands. Secondly, Joshua seems to occupy a subordinate position to that of Eleazar, the priest. There is a more or less explicit suggestion that Joshua will not function as the sole successor to Moses: just as Joshua must appear «before» (ἔναντι, ἐναντίον) Eleazar (vv. 19, 21a, 22b) and the assembly (vv. 19b, 19c, 22c), so both Joshua and Eleazar will make enquiry of the Urim «before» (ἔναντι) the Lord (v. 21b). Indeed, it is fair to say that Joshua is here made to submit to the approval of the priest[74], and that it is only in concert with Eleazar that he may enquire of the Lord's will through the use of the Urim[75].

The priestly origin of this section is clear, according to George Buchanan Gray[76]. And, in fact, the style of this passage, even in its Greek translation, is «grandly paratactic»[77]. In contradistinction to the installation notice from Deut 34:9, this priestly text from Numbers might well be referred to as the directions for an installation ceremony[78], for the use of the future tense in vv. 19, 20, and 21 has an imperative, or perhaps better, a prescriptive sense, suggesting an action which is to be repeated periodically[79]. Moreover, the notice in vv. 22-23 that Moses

---

[73] J. BLENKINSOPP, *The Pentateuch*, 231-232.

[74] C. L'HEUREUX, «Numbers», 91.

[75] M. NOTH, *Numbers*, 215.

[76] G. B. GRAY, *Commentary on Numbers*, 399; P. J. BUDD, *Numbers*, 305.

[77] The phrase is Robert Alter's, who uses it to characterize the prose style of the Hebrew text of the Priestly creation account. See R. ALTER, *The Art of Biblical Narrative*, 142.

[78] See J. R. PORTER, «The Succession of Joshua», 107-108, whose analysis of the Hebrew text indicates that the *Pi'ēl* of the root צוה indicates admission to a clearly defined office, be it that of a king (1 Kgs 2:1, 1 Chr 22:6), a judge (2 Chr 19:9), or an officer in a public works project (1 Chr 22:17). In all cases save the reference in 1 Kgs 2:1, the LXX translates צוה by ἐνετείλατο, the third person singular aorist of the verb ἐντέλλομαι. In Num 27:19, וְצִוִּיתָה is rendered by ἐντελῆ in the LXX, the second person future of ἐντέλλομαι, though in Num 27:23, וַיְצַוֵּהוּ is rendered by συνέστησεν.

[79] See F. BLASS – A. DEBRUNNER, *A Greek Grammar of the New Testament*, 178, § 349. Hereinafter Blass – Debrunner.

abided by these prescriptions «as the Lord ordered Moses», (καθάπερ
συνέταξεν κύριος τῷ Μωυσῇ) highlights not only Moses' obedience to
the directives of the Lord, but also what may be called his paradigmatic
function: Moses provides here a model for the choice and installation of
his successor. It is in these ceremonial interests, along with Joshua's
submission to Eleazar's priestly authority mentioned above, that the
priestly origin of this passage manifests itself [80].

Noth comments that what is to be understood by the הוֹד in the Hebrew text of v. 20, a portion of which is communicated from Moses to
Joshua through the laying on of hands, and which the LXX translates as
δόξα, «cannot be said with any certainty», but must «describe something
effective and perhaps even visible»[81]. Unique in the Hexateuch, הוֹד appears elsewhere in the Hebrew Scriptures to signify the majesty of the
king[82], and is translated there, as here, by δόξα[83]. The use of the partitive מִן[84] in the Hebrew text of Numbers doubtless indicates, as Noth
and others have suggested, that only a portion of the הוֹד of Moses, and
not its entirety, is to be transferred to Joshua; and that as a result,
Joshua's relationship with the priest Eleazar will differ from that of
Moses, so that Joshua will have need of a mediator in a way that Moses
did not[85]. The Greek text of Numbers accomplishes the same end
through the use of a partitive genitive: «And you will give some of your
glory to him» (καὶ δώσεις τῆς δόξης σου ἐπ' αὐτόν: Num 27:20a)[86].

Whatever the original signification of הוֹד/δόξα was, and however
great or small a portion Joshua receives, the transference of the הוֹד/δόξα
from Moses to Joshua through the laying on of hands permits him to
command an identical obedience from the Israelites[87]. Indeed, as D. T.
Olson points out, the laying on of hands in Numbers underscores «the

---

[80] P. J. BUDD, *Numbers*, 308.

[81] M. NOTH, *Numbers*, 215.

[82] G. B. GRAY, *Commenary on Numbers*, 402.

[83] see MT Ps 21:6 ‖ LXX Ps 20:6; 1 Chr 29:25; Dan 11:21.

[84] See P. JOÜON, *A Grammar of Biblical Hebrew*, Part Three: *Syntax*, 489.

[85] M. NOTH, *Numbers*, 215; for a similar point, see G. B. GRAY, *Commentary on Numbers*, 402; D. T. OLSON, «Numbers», 204.

[86] See Blass – Debrunner, 90-91, § 164.

[87] For an evaluation of the differences involved between the imposition of one hand and the laying on of two hands in the Old Testament, see R. PÉTER, «L'imposition des mains», 48-55.

essential continuity between the two leaders»[88]. The point could not have been lost on those for whom 2 Tim was originally written. Just as Paul could command obedience from his congregations[89], so can his legitimate successor.

Kelly thinks that «ordination or appointment to office in the apostolic Church was modelled on the contemporary Jewish rite for the ordination of rabbis»[90], a practice which «in turn found its inspiration in Joshua's ordination» as described in the texts from Deuteronomy and Numbers[91]. Thus, for Kelly, the references in 2 Tim 1:6 are not directly to the biblical texts, but rather to a ritual ostensibly based on those texts. Eduard Lohse has contrasted the ritual of rabbinic ordination with the laying on of hands connected with institution to office in the Pastoral Epistles, and suggests that the Spirit's crucial rôle in deciding who is to be selected as a minister of the Word in the Christian community, as well as the place of prayer in the Christian rite, provide the most telling differences between the rituals of the two faiths[92].

Yet the choice of a successor through the laying on of hands by the one who is approaching the end of his life, whatever else it may say about the manner by which ministers in the early church were empowered to undertake their apostolate, let alone its relation to the rituals of rabbinical ordination, cannot fail to have been understood by the Pastor's audience as an allusion to the last days of Moses. The image presented in 2 Tim 1:6 is of a latter-day Moses, Paul, authorizing his legitimate successor, Timothy, in a way which unmistakably assigns the latter a rôle in the community analogous to that of Joshua. Timothy is thereby endued with Pauline authority certainly, but also that of Moses and his successor.

## 4.2 The «Servant of the Lord»

The title «servant of the Lord» (δοῦλος κυρίου: 2 Tim 2:24), used to designate one who is supposed to be «kindly to everyone, an apt teacher, forbearing, correcting his opponents with gentleness» (ἤπιον εἶναι πρὸς

---

[88] D. T. OLSON, «Numbers», 204.

[89] See 1 Cor 4:16-21; 2 Cor 2:9; 7:13b-16; 10:1-6; Gal 5:7-10; Phil 2:12; Phlm 21.

[90] J. N. D. KELLY, Commentary, 106. See also C. ROWLAND, Christian Origins, 232.

[91] J. N. D. KELLY, Commentary, 106; see also E. LOHSE, «χείρ», 429.

[92] E. LOHSE, «χείρ», 433; see also C. SPICQ, Saint Paul, II, 725-726.

πάντας, διδακτικόν, ἀνεξίκακον, ἐν πραΰτητι παιδεύοντα τοὺς ἀντιδιατιθεμένους: 2 Tim 2:24b-25a), is, as A. T. Hanson has recognized, a
*hapax legomenon* in the New Testament[93], and is generally acknowledged by most scholars to be rooted in the *Weltanschauung* of the Hellenistic world[94]; or, when it is identified as an allusion to an Old Testament text, it is thought to refer to one or another of the prophetic texts.
Thus, Lock[95] and Kelly[96] both think that the reference to the δοῦλος
κυρίου in 2 Tim 2:24 is to the Song of the Suffering Servant in Isaiah.
The difficulty with this contention is that nowhere in the LXX translation
of Isaiah does the entire syntagm δοῦλος κυρίου occur[97]. Thus, it does
not seem very likely that the Pastor intended such a reference.

In the LXX, the syntagm δοῦλος κυρίου occurs three times, twice in
reference to the death of Joshua, the servant of the Lord (Josh 24:30,
Judg 2:8) and once in reference to Moses, the servant of the Lord (2
Kgs 18:12 ‖ 4 Kgdms 18:12). Once in the Psalms (MT Ps 134:1 ‖ LXX
Ps 133:1) the plural syntagm οἱ δοῦλοι κυρίου occurs as part of a call
to prayer, referring probably to priests and other Temple personnel «who
stand in the house of the Lord, in the courts of the house of our God»
(οἱ ἑστῶτες ἐν οἴκῳ κυρίου, ἐν αὐλαῖς οἴκου θεοῦ ἡμῶν: LXX Ps 133:1;
see also LXX Ps 134:2)[98]. In all cases, the phrase translates the
Hebrew עֶבֶד יהוה or, as in the Psalm text, its plural עַבְדֵי יהוה. This
construct chain occurs relatively frequently in the Old Testament:
nineteen times in the singular[99] and five times in the plural[100]. Yet,

---

[93] A. T. HANSON, *The Pastoral Epistles*, 141.

[94] So C. SPICQ: «L'expression «esclave du Seigneur» [...] courante dans les religions
orientales et l'Ancien Testament, assimile les rapports du fidèle avec son Dieu à ceux
de l'esclave avec son maître [...] il n'a pas de volonté propre» (*Saint Paul*, II, 766).

[95] W. LOCK, *Pastoral Epistles*, 101.

[96] J. N. D. KELLY, *Commentary*, 190.

[97] In actuality, the LXX translates the Hebrew עֶבֶד of Isaiah in a variety of ways:
in Is 42:1, 49:6, 50:10 and 52:13 it is translated by παῖς, whereas in Is 49:3, 5, it is
rendered δοῦλος, and in Is 53:11, by the present participle δουλεύοντα.

[98] A. WEISER, *The Psalms*, 786. But see H. J. KRAUS, *Psalms 60–150*, 488, who
claims that the עבדי יהוה of the Hebrew text of Ps 134:1 (and which is translated as
οἱ δοῦλοι κυρίου in LXX Ps 133:1) may not necessarily refer to the priests who served
in the presence of Yahweh, since individual members of the OT cultic community also
called themselves servants.

[99] Deut 34:5; Josh 1:1, 13, 15; 8:31, 33; 11:12; 12:6; 13:8; 14:7; 18:7; 22:2, 4,
5; 24:29; Judg 2:8; 2 Kgs 18:12; 2 Chr 1:3; 24:6.

[100] 2 Kgs 9:7; Ps 113:1; 134:1; 135:1; Is 54:17.

more often than not, עֶבֶד יהוה is translated in the LXX as ὁ παῖς κυρίου (eight times)[101], and only occasionally as something else, such as ὁ θεράπων κυρίου (twice)[102], οἰκέτης κυρίου (once)[103], ὁ παῖς τοῦ θεοῦ (once)[104], or even ἄνθρωπος τοῦ θεοῦ (once)[105]. Three times the Hebrew text uses the title עֶבֶד יהוה as an epithet for Moses[106] while the corresponding text of the LXX refers to him by name only.

Karl Heinrich Rengstorf has noted that for the most part when the LXX translates עֶבֶד as παῖς, the reference is to slaves «in the sense of those who from the very first stand at the disposal of another», and that when δοῦλος is used, «the primary thought is that of the illegality and essential unreason of the service rendered»[107]. But this understanding of δοῦλος cannot be the case in the reference to Moses in 2 Kgs 18:12 or Joshua in Josh 24:30 and Judg 2:8. Nor can this be the meaning intended in the call to prayer in Ps 133. Indeed, as Rengstorf recognizes, the עבד/δοῦλος word-group was also used to describe the relationship between any ancient king and his subjects since it «expresses with singular force both the extreme of power demanded and exercised on the one side and the extreme of objective subjection and subjective bondage present and experienced on the other». What is more, this political usage, according to Rengstorf, «provides the assumptions on which the [word-group] can be adopted into [Israel's] language of worship [...] [and] the relationship of dependence and service in which man stands to God». Such theological usage «always implies the exclusive nature of the relationship, whether we think of [...] עֶבֶד or [...] δοῦλος». Hence, «those men in the history of Israel who have satisfied the divine claim on them in an outstanding and exemplary manner are given the honorary title of δοῦλοι». Those who have so satisfied the divine claim, according to Rengstorf, include Moses and Joshua, as noted above, as well as Abraham (Ps 104:42), Isaac (Dan 3:35), David (Ps 88:4), the prophets (4 Kgdms 17:23 ‖ 2 Kgs 17:23), and the people of Israel in the person of Jacob (Is 48:20)[108].

---

[101] Josh 1:13; 11:12; 12:6; 13:8; 18:7; 22:2; 22:5; 2 Chr 1:3.
[102] Josh 8:31, 33.
[103] Deut 34:5
[104] Josh 14:7.
[105] 2 Chr 24:6.
[106] Josh 1:1, 15; 22:4.
[107] K. H. RENGSTORF, «δοῦλος», 266.
[108] K. H. RENGSTORF, «δοῦλος», 266-268.

But we must note here that in none of the instances which Rengstorf cites, with the exception of Moses and Joshua, does the LXX refer to the principals involved by the title δοῦλος κυρίου. Abraham is «his servant» (τὸν δοῦλον αὐτοῦ) in Ps 104:42, Isaac is «your servant» (τὸν δοῦλόν σου) in Dan 3:35, David is «my servant» (τῷ δούλῳ μου) in Ps 88:4, the prophets are «his servants» (τῶν δούλων αὐτοῦ) in 4 Kgdms 17:23, and the people of Israel in the person of Jacob in Is 48:20 are called «his servant» (τὸν δοῦλον αὐτοῦ Ιακωβ).

George W. Coats has investigated the use of various epithets to describe Moses in the Hebrew text: basing his work upon that of W. Zimmerli and J. Jeremias[109], he concludes that the title עֶבֶד יהוה in its various forms does not connote one single, limited office which is to be distinguished from other offices by a particular set of duties. Like Rengstorf, he holds that «the title is a general epithet available for describing traditionally famous and pious persons of the past»[110]. While this may be true of the Hebrew text of the Old Testament, the translators of the Septuagint seem to have restricted its reference to Moses and those who were thought to have been his successors – Joshua and the priests and Levites who staffed the Temple. Contrary to the claims of Rengstorf and Coats, the syntagm δοῦλος κυρίου in the LXX is more than an honorary title; it is, instead, a technical expression in the Greek translation of the Old Testament designating Moses and his heirs. That the Pastor should use such language with reference to Timothy cannot have been anything other than deliberate on his part. As in the case of the laying on of hands, the description of Timothy as a δοῦλος κυρίου endows Timothy with an authority divine in its derivation and compelling in its appeal.

### 4.3 The «Man of God»

Dibelius – Conzelmann say that δοῦλος κυρίου is reminiscent of «man of God» (ὁ τοῦ θεοῦ ἄνθρωπος: 2 Tim 3:17) and the vocative «Man of God» (Σὺ δέ, ὦ ἄνθρωπε θεοῦ: 1 Tim 6:11), and while they admit that this title comes from the Old Testament, especially 1 Kgs 2:27, Deut 33:1 and Ps 89:1, they explicitly deny that the author has in mind the image of the «man of God» which the Old Testament texts suggest[111].

---

[109] W. ZIMMERLI – J. JEREMIAS, *The Servant of God*. This work is itself a translation of the article Παῖς Θεοῦ, which appears in *TDNT* V, 654-717.

[110] G. W. COATS, *Moses*, 183.

[111] Dibelius – Conzelmann, 87.

George W. Knight thinks that ὁ τοῦ θεοῦ ἄνθρωπος is «a description that can apply to any Christian in general or to Timothy and any other Christian leader in particular»[112]. For Jerome Murphy-O'Connor, ὁ τοῦ θεοῦ ἄνθρωπος is the «one genuinely spiritual title» of the Christian minister in the Pastoral Epistles, though he does not attempt to trace its antecedents[113]. In fact, however, the title «man of God» (LXX: ἄνθρωπος τοῦ θεοῦ) as an epithet describing Moses occurs six times in the LXX, two instances of which (Deut 33:1 and Ps 89:1 [90:1]) Dibelius – Conzelmann note, but, in addition, Josh 14:6, 1 Chr 23:14, 2 Chr 30:16, and 2 Esd 3:2 ‖ Ezra 3:2. George W. Coats notes that of these six instances in which Moses is referred to by the epithet אִישׁ הָאֱלֹהִים, «man of God», two texts, namely Deut 33:1 and Ps 89:1 (90:1),

> are simply ascriptions for poems and thus tell little about the character of Moses or the shape of the image that portrays him. At most they suggest that Moses was a famous man who therefore might have been responsible for a poem, i.e., eligible for credit in the ascription of a pseudonymous poem. In these cases, the title indicates nothing more than a relationship between Moses and God[114].

Coats' point is well-taken, if these texts are taken in isolation from the rest of the Mosaic traditions enshrined in the Old Testament. But it is questionable whether the Pastor would have so read the Deuteronomic text in question or this particular psalm. Indeed, it is far more likely – virtually certain, in fact – that the Pastor would have regarded Moses as the actual author of the Blessing of Moses (Deut 33) and the meditation on the brevity of life which is Ps 89 (90). Coats' characterization of Deut 33 and Ps 89 (90) as pseudonymous poems reveals a hermeneutic which, however useful it may be in determining the process by which traditions and texts developed, does little to shed light on the subsequent history of the texts' interpretation, nor how the question of the texts' authorship was viewed by the Pastor.

With respect to three other references to Moses as אִישׁ הָאֱלֹהִים, Coats seems to be on surer ground. In 1 Chr 23:14, which delineates the divisions of the Levites, the sons of Moses, «the man of God», are numbered among the Levites. Coats maintains that the use of the title in this context is «a general element of the tradition, an epithet which [...] has

---

[112] G. W. KNIGHT, *The Pastoral Epistles*, 450.

[113] J. MURPHY-O'CONNOR, «2 Timothy», 408.

[114] G. W. COATS, *Moses*, 179.

no specific qualification for the Moses figure», since «in the contrast between the sons of Moses and the sons of Aaron, the Aaronides seem to
be the more highly exalted»[115]. But in the reference to Moses as «man
of God» in 2 Chr 30:16 and Ezra 3:2 he sees an attribution of authority
for the law by an appeal to the authority of Moses[116]. In both texts,
certain actions (the reinstitution of the Passover under Hezekiah in 2 Chr
30 or the restoration of the altar under Jeshua and Zerubbabel in Ezra
3) are justified by recourse to «the law of Moses, the man of God»
(כְּמִשְׁפָּטָם כְּתוֹרַת מֹשֶׁה אִישׁ־הָאֱלֹהִים/κατὰ τὴν ἐντολὴν Μωυσῆ ἀνθρώπου τοῦ
θεοῦ: 2 Chr 30:16) or «the things written in the law of Moses, the man
of God» (כַּכָּתוּב בְּתוֹרַת מֹשֶׁה אִישׁ־הָאֱלֹהִם: Ezra 3:2; κατὰ τὰ γεγραμμένα ἐν
νόμῳ Μωυσῆ ἀνθρώπου τοῦ θεοῦ: 2 Esd 3:2). This justification, according to Coats, has a two-fold character: it is (a) an appeal to Moses, (b)
who is known as a man of God, which suggests thereby that «Moses fa-
cilitates a final authority beyond himself [...] The authority of the law
resides in its origin in Moses. But in fact, Mosaic authority is valid because of its relationship with God»[117].

Given this background, it is hard to imagine that the Pastor's use of
the syntagm ὁ τοῦ θεοῦ ἄνθρωπος in 2 Tim 3:17 would have been an
«early sign of clericalism», as J. L. Houlden would have it[118]. Indeed,
the use of such language cannot have been anything other than deliberately referential, and the reference could not have been to anyone other
than Moses. Hence, the attribution of the epithet to the Christian minister and heir of Paul is an attempt to imbue him with that selfsame Mosaic authority.

### 4.4 *The exhortation to «be strong»*

Finally, in the admonition to «be strong in the grace that is in Christ
Jesus» (Σὺ οὖν, τέκνον μου, ἐνδυναμοῦ ἐν τῇ χάριτι τῇ ἐν Χριστῷ Ἰησοῦ:
2 Tim 2:1), the Pastor may be making an indirect reference to the repeated exhortation which appears in the farewell speech of Moses in
Deut 31. Here, Moses admonishes the people (31:6) and Joshua (31:7b,

---

[115] G. W. COATS, *Moses*, 179-180.

[116] G. W. COATS, *Moses*, 180.

[117] G. W. COATS, *Moses*, 180.

[118] J. L. HOULDEN, *The Pastoral Epistles*, 129.

23b) to «be courageous and strong» ('Ανδρίζου καὶ ἴσχυε)[119]. The indirect reference does not function in this instance, as in the cases of the titles δοῦλος κυρίου and ἄνθρωπος τοῦ θεοῦ, through a similarity in language; here, rather, the reference is accomplished through a similarity of situation and of structure. The similarity of situation plainly may be seen: the founding leader of the community is about to die, and he exhorts his successor not to shrink from the tasks which he will confront. As one might expect, a similar exhortation is found in the *TM* 10:15, «Therefore, you, Joshua, son of Nun, be strong. It is you, whom God has chosen to be my successor to his covenant». *LAB* 20:5 includes the exhortation to Joshua, «Be strong, and act manfully, because you alone are ruler in Israel» (*Confortare et viriliter age, quoniam tu solus in Israel principaberis*), though this exhortation, unlike those of Deuteronomy and the *TM*, is delivered not by Moses, but rather by the people (*Et dixerunt ad eum populi*: *LAB* 20:5). The *JA* describes no such farewell exhortation directed at Joshua alone: indeed, in Josephus' account, as in the installation ceremony recorded in Numbers 27:18-23, Joshua is not the sole successor to Moses; he is always paired with Eleazar, ὁ ἀρχιερεύς, as one of a pair who together inherit the mantle of Mosaic authority[120].

Following the analysis of N. Lohfink[121], J. Roy Porter has identified a tripartite structure for the installation formulae found in Deuteronomy: (A) encouragement of the person addressed, expressed in the Hebrew texts by the formula חֲזַק וֶאֱמָץ (Deut 31:7 [cf. v. 6], 23; as well as Josh 1:6, 7, 9), the first group of which is rendered in the LXX as ἀνδρίζου καὶ ἴσχυε while the second group is rendered by the equivalent expression ἴσχυε καὶ ἀνδρίζου; (B) statement of a task or function, introduced in the Hebrew text by כִּי אַתָּה (Deut 31:7, 23; Josh 1:6), which is translated as σὺ γάρ in the LXX; and (C) assurance of divine help, expressed

---

[119] M. WEINFELD, *Deuteronomy and the Deuteronomic School*, identifies Deut 31:1-6 as an example of a military oration, with the masc. plur. qal imperative חִזְקוּ וֶאֱמְצוּ (which recurs in v. 7b in the masc. sing. qal imperative חֲזַק וֶאֱמָץ) as an instance of the type of short rallying cry which typically punctuates the oration (45). If Weinfeld's analysis is correct, its relevance to the context in which this supposed example of military rhetoric occurs is far from established, since, as shall shortly be demonstrated, the purpose of the pericope seems not to rally the Israelites to war, but rather to install Joshua as the legitimate successor of Moses.

[120] see *JA* IV.186, 324, 326.

[121] N. LOHFINK, «Die deuteronomistische Darstellung», 32-44.

either in a double-member statement, as in Deut 31:8b and Josh 1:5, or in a single member statement, as in Deut 31:23, Josh 1:9, and Deut 3:22b[122]. Furthermore, though this formula receives «clear expression in the Deuteronomic tradition», according to Porter, «it is not itself confined to that tradition», but may be found in other strata of the Old Testament (for instance, 2 Sam 10:12; Hag 2:4; Ezra 10:4; 1 Chr 22:6-13, 16; 28:2-10, 20; 2 Chr 19:8-11; 32:6-8)[123]. The tripartite structure is not uniform in any of these additional texts Porter cites: sometimes, as in the texts from 1 and 2 Chr the statement of a task to be accomplished (B) precedes the exhortation to be brave (A). Nor is the language of exhortation uniform: the Hebrew texts cited by J. R. Porter always present some form of the verb חָזַק as the first of two imperatives joined by ו, which the LXX sometimes translates with some form of ἀνδρίζω[124], sometimes with some form of κραταιόω[125], and sometimes with some form of ἰσχύω[126] or κατισχύω[127]. The second of these two imperatives, however, varies widely: וְנִתְחַזַּק/καὶ κραταιωθῶμεν in 2 Sam 10:12, וַעֲשׂוּ/καὶ ποιεῖτε in Hag 2:4 (see also Ezra 10:4; 1 Chr 28:10; 2 Chr 19:11), וֶאֱמָץ/καὶ ἴσχυε in 1 Chr 22:13, and וֶאֱמָץ/καὶ ἀνδρίζου in 1 Chr 28:20 (see also 2 Chr 32:7). The formula, not to put too fine a point on it, is hardly formulaic[128].

The exhortation to «be strong» in 2 Tim 2:1, as I have already noted, does not make use of any of these expressions from the LXX. Yet the variety of expressions within the LXX itself argues that no single formula was imposed on writers working in this genre. The sense of standing fast, of being strong, courageous, and able to the appointed task is what is at issue here. The Pastor's choice of the imperative ἐνδυναμοῦ communicates this sense, especially since Paul had used a form of the verb in reference to himself, in Phil 4:13 (πάντα ἰσχύω ἐν τῷ ἐνδυναμοῦντί με), and in reference to Abraham, in Rom 4:20 (εἰς δὲ τὴν ἐπαγγελίαν τοῦ θεοῦ οὐ διεκρίθη τῇ ἀπιστίᾳ ἀλλ᾽ ἐνεδυναμώθη τῇ πίστει, δοὺς δόξαν τῷ θεῷ).

---

[122] J. R. PORTER, «The Succession of Joshua», 104-105.

[123] J. R. PORTER, «The Sucession of Joshua», 105-106.

[124] 2 Kgdms 10:12; 1 Chr 22:13.

[125] Ezra 10:4.

[126] 1 Chr 28:10, 20; 2 Chr 19:11, 32:7.

[127] Hag 2:4.

[128] This is the point made by D. MCCARTHY, *Institution and Narrative*, 183-186.

The second element as found in Lohfink's and Porter's analyses of the installation account, that of the statement of an assigned task introduced by the formula כִּי אַתָּה/σὺ γάρ, is echoed in the expression σὺ οὖν, τέκνον μου (2 Tim 2:1), which introduces the pericope 2:1-7. For Spicq, of course, the importance of the verse is found in its tone: «Conformément à sa coutume, lorsqu'il impose une prescription onéreuse, Paul l'accompagne d'un mot affectueux»[129]. Lock and Houlden both see in the expression a deliberate reference to 1:15-18: while Lock notes a contrastative sense in σὺ οὖν, so that Timothy receives an implicit warning *not* to be like «all in Asia [who] turned away from me, among them Phygelus and Hermogenes», (ἀπεστράφησάν με πάντες οἱ ἐν τῇ 'Ασίᾳ, ὧν ἐστιν Φύγελος καὶ Ἑρμογένης: 2 Tim 1:15)[130], Houlden stresses the comparative sense of the expression, so that, in effect, Timothy is urged to be like Onesiphorus (1:16-18)[131]. Knight allows for both a comparative and a contrastative sense for σὺ οὖν[132].

But in relating σὺ οὖν to 1:15-18, neither Lock, Houlden, nor Knight correctly apprehend the form of the pericope 2:1-7, and thereby miss the references to Old Testament installation accounts: σὺ οὖν introduces the assignment of a task, which is described by the aorist imperative παράθου. The task is the establishment of a chain of tradition: «and what you have heard from me before many witnesses entrust to faithful men who will be able to teach others also» (καὶ ἃ ἤκουσας παρ' ἐμοῦ διὰ πολλῶν μαρτύρων, ταῦτα παράθου πιστοῖς ἀνθρώποις, οἵτινες ἱκανοὶ ἔσονται καὶ ἑτέρους διδάξαι: 2 Tim 2:2).

Lock thinks that what Timothy is supposed to entrust to the faithful men, he has heard throughout Paul's ministry[133], though Dibelius – Conzelmann contend that the solemnity of the phrase «before many witnesses» (διὰ πολλῶν μαρτύρων) eliminates the possibility that the missionary preaching and teaching is what Timothy has heard and what he must pass on to others; rather, «the reference must be to [...] "ordination," which provided the occasion on which the "deposit" (παραθήκη) was transmitted to Timothy [...] Therefore, the act alluded to here is the

---

[129] C. SPICQ, *Saint Paul*, II, 737.

[130] W. LOCK, *Pastoral Epistles*, 93.

[131] J. L. HOULDEN, *The Pastoral Epistles*, 117; see also J. N. D. KELLY, *Commentary*, 172.

[132] G. W. KNIGHT, *The Pastoral Epistles*, 389.

[133] W. LOCK, *Pastoral Epistles*, 93; see also G. W. KNIGHT, *The Pastoral Epistles*, 390.

appointment of Timothy to his office»[134]. But whether the event on which Timothy has heard Paul is his ordination or not is probably irrelevant, insofar as the point of the sentence is communicated by the imperative «entrust», (παράθου). Michael Prior's contention that 2 Tim makes no provision for the appointment of various church ministries seems hardly supportable in the light of this verse[135]. The «faithful men» (πιστοὶ ἄνθρωποι) are, in fact, the chief ministers of the community, since the transmission of the Pauline tradition depends precisely upon their ability to teach others. That the charge to entrust to them the Pauline heritage comes at this point in the letter indicates, at least to my mind, that their appointment is of the highest importance, analogous to the task of leading the Chosen People into the Promised Land visited upon Joshua when he succeeded to Moses' office.

The third element common to installation accounts, that of the assurance of divine help, is to be found at the conclusion to this pericope: «Think over what I say, for the Lord will grant you understanding in everything» (νόει ὃ λέγω· δώσει γάρ σοι ὁ κύριος σύνεσιν ἐν πᾶσιν: 2 Tim 2:7). I do not think, as, for instance, Lock[136], Spicq[137], Kelly[138], and Hanson[139] do, that the promise of «understanding» (σύνεσις) refers here to some sort of divine guidance in persuading the Christian assembly to render monetary support to its leaders. To limit

---

[134] Dibelius – Conzelmann, 108; so, too, J. L. HOULDEN, *The Pastoral Epistles*, 117.

[135] M. PRIOR, *Paul the Letter-Writer*, 64.

[136] W. LOCK thinks that v. 7 is a *verbum sapienti*, and that the author of 2 Tim «did not think it wise to explain his allusion too explicitly» (*Pastoral Epistles*, 94).

[137] With reference to v. 7, C. SPICQ claims to recognize the delicacy of Paul whenever he deals with questions of money, leaving to Timothy's care the task of extricating the application from these parables (*Saint Paul*, II, 745).

[138] «With fine tact Paul leaves it to Timothy to discover for himself the deeper implications of his three parables, particularly, perhaps, the allusion to his honorarium from the community», J. N. D. KELLY, *Commentary*, 176. But to claim, as J. N. D. KELLY and C. SPICQ both do, that the relevance of the three parables is left to Timothy, is to admit, in effect, that one has no real idea as to what their relevance might be.

[139] «The author wishes to convey his instructions to church leaders that they have a right to expect financial support from the church. But, as the letter is probably going to be read out at the worship meeting of the local church, he does not wish to say so quite explicitly. He is therefore content to drop a broad hint, and does so in this verse», A. T. HANSON, *The Pastoral Epistles*, 130.

the applicability of this promise to a prudent sense of how best to elicit appropriate financial support from the Christian congregation seems to miss the point of the exhortation to «share in suffering» (συγκακοπά- θησον) and thereby to trivialize the message of the pericope.

For the assurance of divine help is preceded by an exhortation to share in Paul's own suffering, which, though certainly parenetic[140], serves also to strengthen the identification of Timothy with Paul, as Spicq has recognized on the basis of the similarity of language in 2 Tim 1:8b, 12: «l'assimilation de Timothée à Paul est remarquable: tout deux ont reçu le même charisme, ont à endurer les mêmes souffrances (1:7-8), à garder le même dépôt (vv. 12, 14)»[141]. The three illustrations which follow the parenesis, the soldier, the athlete, and the farmer, are commonplaces in the diatribe, though here, as most commentators recognize, the immediate literary precedent is most probably 1 Cor 9:7, 24-27[142]. That identification of literary precedent is doubtless responsible for the (mis)interpretations of 2 Tim 2:3-6 which see in the rewards accruing to the soldier, athlete, and farmer a justification for the Christian leader's *honoraria*. For what is more important than the supposed similarities are the differences between 2 Tim 2:3-6 and 1 Cor 9:7, 24-27.

In 1 Cor 9, as Wendell Willis has recognized, Paul is elaborating an argument for the renunciation of rights, using as an illustration his own practice of refusing financial support from the Corinthian community[143]. From vv. 4-14, he advances a series of twelve rhetorical questions encompassing ten arguments in favor of the right of financial support[144]. It is here that Paul brings forward three illustrations from everyday life, the soldier, the vineyard keeper, and the shepherd. Harry Nasuti notes that in all three illustrations, the recompense is the outcome of the activity in which the person engages, obvious enough in the cases of the shepherd and the vineyard keeper, but also including the soldier, who is fed from the spoils of war. «The dominant thrust of all these

---

[140] see Dibelius – Conzelmann, 107-108; J. L. HOULDEN, *The Pastoral Epistles*, 116.

[141] C. SPICQ, *Saint Paul*, II, 738.

[142] Dibelius – Conzelmann, 108; C. SPICQ, *Saint Paul*, II, 739-740; J. N. D. KELLY, *Commentary*, 174-176; J. L. HOULDEN, *The Pastoral Epistles*, 117; A. T. HANSON, *The Pastoral Epistles*, 129-130; KNIGHT, *The Pastoral Epistles*, 392-395.

[143] W. WILLIS, «An Apostolic Apologia?», 33-48.

[144] W. WILLIS, «An Apostolic Apologia?», 35.

examples», comments Nasuti, «is not simply that one is recompensed for one's work. Rather, one is also recompensed from one's work, in the sense that one receives a share of that which one does. One is not simply rewarded with an external reward. There is instead an intrinsic connection between one's activity and one's recompense»[145]. A similar significance may be said to underlie the illustration of the athlete in vv. 24-27, though here, as Orr and Walther recognize, the argumentation is more obviously *ad maius*[146]. The effect of this rhetorical plan, claims Willis, «would have been very arresting for the first hearers who, after the listing of the reasons why Paul should be supported, would most likely anticipate his "accounts due" statement»[147]. Such a statement, of course, never comes, since the point of the passage is to establish so strong a case for the exercise of rights, that the subsequent renunciation of them becomes all the more remarkable. The relevance to Paul's demand that the «strong» of Corinth renounce their right to eat the εἰδωλό-θυτα so that the «weak» might not be scandalized makes 1 Cor 9 something other than an excursus[148] or an interruption[149].

It seems hardly likely that after the Apostle himself should have expended so much rhetorical effort to illustrate his own renunciation of his community's financial support, his epigone should then use the same imagery in the service of an argument which advances precisely the opposite thesis. For, if Lock, Spicq, Kelly, and Hanson are right, 2 Tim 2:4-6 justifies the very practice which Paul himself was at such pains to renounce. It seems more likely that the imagery of soldier, athlete, and farmer are employed in 2 Tim 2:4-6 as examples of those whose work involves hard work and suffering.

In addition to differences in argumentative content, 1 Cor 9:1-27 differs from 2 Tim 2:1-7 in its rhetorical style. The rhetorical approach Paul adopts in 1 Cor 9 involves adopting elements of the diatribal style of argumentation, including the posing of rhetorical questions which expect an affirmative answer (vv. 1, 4-5, 8b)[150], and those which expect

---

[145] H. P. NASUTI, «The Woes of the Prophets», 250.

[146] W. F. ORR – J. A. WALTHER, *I Corinthians*, 243. Herinafter Orr – Walther.

[147] W. WILLIS, «An Apostolic Apologia?», 35.

[148] See, for instance, the treatment of 1 Cor 9:1-27 as an excursus in Orr – Walther, 235-243.

[149] H. CONZELMANN, *I Corinthians*, 151.

[150] οὐ and οὐ μή are used with questions which expect an affirmative response. See Blass – Debrunner, 220, § 427.2

a negative answer (vv. 8a, 9b)[151], or those which are introduced by the elliptical phrase «what then» (τίς οὖν: v. 18), or the (somewhat hectoring) question «do you not know?» (οὐκ οἴδατε: vv. 13, 24). Abraham J. Malherbe admits that a definition of the diatribe is fraught with difficulty, but calls it a «popular philosophical treatment of an ethical topic [which] has the practical aim of moving people to action rather than reflection»[152]. The earliest diatribes were chiefly characterized by a dialogue between the speaker and a fictive opponent, and frequently featured questions and counter-questions, the latter designed to wear the fictive opponent down. The speaker frequently exhibited impatience with his fictive opponent, and answered him in short sentences typified by a simple syntax and containing parallel elements[153]. Günther Bornkamm mentions that the diatribe was a means of teaching used by preachers in Hellenistic synagogues:

> It propounded philosophic, moral, or religious ideas without long-winded deductions or purely speculative arguments, and deliberately avoided elevated technical language [...] [The diatribe made] reader and hearer partners in a conversation [...] never for a moment losing sight of them[154].

Part of Paul's debt to the synagogue of his youth can be seen in his use of rhetorical devices adapted from classical learning by these synagogue preachers. These same methods of argumentation would have been familiar to the intended recipients of 1 Corinthians, whether they were converts from paganism, in which case they would have learned them as part of their literary and cultural inheritance, or whether they were converts from Judaism, in which case they would have acquired a familiarity in the same fashion Paul did[155].

Stanley Kent Stowers has sought to advance the notion that Paul made use of classical rhetorical devices in order to present his theological agenda, and that this agenda cannot be understood apart from these de-

---

[151] μή and μήτι are used when a negative response is expected. See Blass – Debrunner, 220, § 427.2.

[152] A. J. MALHERBE, *Moral Exhortation*, 129.

[153] A. J. MALHERBE, *Moral Exhortation*, 129-130.

[154] G. BORNKAMM, *Paul*, 9.

[155] See M. HENGEL, *The Hellenization of Judaea in the First Century after Christ*, 55-56.

vices[156]. But even as Paul made use of these devices and rhetorical strategies, he also adapted them: the larger ambassadorial purposes behind any of Paul's letters doubtless influenced the selection of certain conventions of the diatribal dialogue and the omission of others (e.g., the frequent impatience with which the teacher regards his interlocutor[157], the censorious tone[158], the abusive language[159], etc.) all of which would have served to alienate the very people on whose support Paul was counting and whose welfare he was trying to ensure.

Any sort of diatribal element, adapted or original, however, is entirely absent from 2 Tim 2:1-7. Indeed, it is fair to say that the elements of the diatribe are altogether lacking in 2 Tim. One looks in vain for a rhetorical question in 2 Tim, either one expecting an affirmative response, or one expecting a negative response, or one introduced by the phrases τίς οὖν or οὐκ οἴδατε. The absence of these elements, so characteristic of Paul's argument in 2 Cor 9, leads one to the conclusion that the Pastor had other purposes in mind than alluding to the Corinthian correspondence in 2 Tim 2:4-6.

Those other purposes are found in the close approximation to the literary form of the installation account. For it seems clear, in light of the pattern identified by Porter, and Lohfink before him, that the assurance of divine presence and help which is so characteristic of installation accounts in the Old Testament is here represented in 2 Tim 1:7 by a pledge of the Lord's help in understanding. The Pastor wishes to endow Timothy and those who look to him as a predecessor and a model (the πιστοὶ ἄνθρωποι of v. 2) with the legitimacy of heirs, and perhaps, in view of the polemic against the νομοδιδάσκαλοι, with the legitimacy of sole heirs.

To sum up what has been discovered thus far: the Pastor likens Paul to Moses, using both direct and indirect references to Old Testament texts in which Moses is prominently featured, thereby endowing the Apostle to the Gentiles with the authority of the one through whom the Law was given to Israel. In a similar fashion, Timothy is compared, both explicitly and implicitly, to the figure of Joshua, Moses's successor, thereby conferring upon him the mantle of legitimacy. Those who

---

[156] See, for instance, S. K. STOWERS, *The Diatribe*; ID., «Paul's Dialogue», 707-722; ID., «Social Status», 59-82; ID., «Diatribe», 190-193.

[157] A. J. MALHERBE, *Moral Exhortation*, 130.

[158] S. K. STOWERS, «Paul's Dialogue», 713.

[159] A. J. MALHERBE, *Moral Exhortation*, 130.

are named as opponents to Paul and Timothy are equated with the legendary enemies of Moses, and thereby robbed of any claim on their part to be the legitimate heirs of the Pauline legacy. Yet these references, direct and indirect alike, do not exhaust the claims for authority made on behalf of the putative author of 2 Tim.

## 5. The Issue of Authority: The Authority of the *Testamentum Pauli*

Another way in which the Pastor underscores the stature of the putative author of the letters is by employing the testamentary form in 2 Tim, a form which, as Helmut Koester has recognized, gives to the letter an irrefutable kind of authority. Koester's contention is that the choice of the testamentary genre was deliberate on the part of the author of 2 Tim, since «whoever speaks in his own testament no longer needs to be defended, because he is already one of the "ancient" people – in this case a revered martyr – whose authority is beyond question»[160]. Indeed, it is William S. Kurz's contention that testaments and farewell addresses exercise a particular appeal over those who hear or read them: «the last words before the departure of a loved one take on special significance for those remaining behind. Since the moment of death reveals to each person what is ultimately important, and the seemingly important becomes insignificant in the face of death, the last words of those facing death take on special importance for guiding those left behind. These final directives emphasize concerns which in view of their death they considered to be of special moment for future followers»[161]. Anitra Bingham Kolenkow writes that «testaments were viewed as authoritative because no person would be expected to tell an untruth at the hour of death/judgment, nor would the dying person fail to give children both goods and truth (or warning)»[162].

The testament was a popular genre in the Second Temple period, as Kolenkow and others have recognized[163]. James H. Charlesworth's

---

[160] H. KOESTER, *History and Literature*, 300.

[161] W. S. KURZ, *Farewell Addresses*, 16.

[162] A. B. KOLENKOW, «The Literary Genre "Testament"», 259.

[163] A. B. KOLENKOW, «The Literary Genre "Testament"», 259; X. LÉON-DUFOUR, «Jésus devant sa mort», 150-153. See also S. J. D. COHEN, *From the Maccabees*, who holds that testaments, like other paraphrases of Scripture, originated as expressions of folk piety (211-212).

recent edition of the Old Testament Pseudepigrapha[164] includes nineteen documents which bear the name «testament», and which purport to be the solemn last words of certain legendary figures from Israel's past[165]. According to Kolenkow, the genre of the testament, which she describes as «the last words of a great man given just before he dies», served «primarily as a vehicle for literature forecasting the future [in which] a patriarch receives visions or knowledge of heaven»[166]. Kolenkow's description of the testament is based on her survey of the content of farewell discourses in Gen 49, Deut 33, Philo's *VM*, the *TM*, 1 Enoch 91-94, the *Vita Adae et Evae* 25-29, and the *Testament of Levi*[167]. John J. Collins has adduced several formal criteria whereby the testament can be recognized: it is, first of all, «a discourse delivered in anticipation of death;» secondly, the speaker «is typically a father addressing his sons or a leader addressing his people or his successor»; thirdly, while the actual discourse is delivered in the first person, it is usually framed by a narrative which describes in the third person «the situation in which the discourse is delivered and ends with an account of the speaker's death»[168]. Although a narrative framework is absent in 2 Tim, because of its epistolary genre, it is still possible, I hold, to speak of the letter as an example of the testament.

## 5.1 *2 Tim as Paul's testament:* Status Quaestionis

The testamentary character of 2 Tim has long been recognized by scholars: Lock follows Bengel in identifying 2 Tim as the «Testamentum Pauli et cygnea cantio», but for Lock, the primary interest of 2 Tim is in its presentation of the portrait of the ideal Christian minister, specifically, «the Christian teacher face to face with death, with his work

---

[164] J. H. CHARLESWORTH, ed., *The Old Testament Pseudepigrapha*.

[165] The *Testament of the Twelve Patriarchs* (i.e., what purport to be the last words of the twelve sons of Jacob: Reuben, Simeon, Levi, Judah, Issachar, Zebulon, Dan, Naphtali, Gad, Asher, Joseph, and Benjamin); the *Testament of Job*; the *Testament of the Three Patriarchs* (i.e., what are presented as the final utterances of Abraham, Isaac, and Jacob); the *Testament of Moses*; the *Testament of Solomon*; and the *Testament of Adam*. See *OTPs* I, 771-995, for introductory notes, bibliographies, and translations.

[166] A. B. KOLENKOW, «The Genre Testament», 57.

[167] A. B. KOLENKOW, «The Genre Testament», 59-64.

[168] J. J. COLLINS, *The Apocalyptic Imagination*, 102.

finished»[169]. And though he suggests that as a testament 2 Tim ought to be compared with the farewell of Moses in Deut 31:1-8, his commentary never pursues this comparison systematically, nor does he examine the literary form of the testament.

It is on the basis of 2 Tim 4:6-8 that Spicq classifies the letter as a testament, which explains, as far as he is concerned, «l'intense affection qu'elle exprime à Timothée, la vivacité des exhortations, la façon dont l'Apôtre se met en avant, les retours sur son passé, l'exemple de son comportement qu'il propose au Pasteur d'Éphèse»[170]. The closest parallel in biblical literature to this Pauline testament is the farewell speech of Jesus in the Fourth Gospel, which possesses «le même sérénité, une psychologie de victoire, une certitude de gloire céleste, le même souci de transmettre à des disciples les dernières volontés du mourant»[171]. Spicq's concern here, as elsewhere in his two volume commentary, is to prove the authenticity of the Pastoral Epistles, that they were actually written by the historical Paul: hence, for Spicq, «aucun autre passage du *corpus* paulinien ne porte une marque plus évidente de son authenticité»[172]. His efforts here, then, are not so much literary — what are the typical conventions of the testament, and how are those conventions used in 2 Tim? — as they are historical — is the voice of 2 Tim the voice of Paul?

In a seminal article, Johannes Munck has analyzed the «discours d'adieu», or farewell address, and has isolated a number of elements which commonly appear in examples of the kind[173]. While there are several examples of the farewell address in the literature of the Old Testament[174], the genre appears much more frequently in the literature

---

[169] W. LOCK, *Pastoral Epistles*, 79.

[170] C. SPICQ, *Saint Paul*, II, 803.

[171] C. SPICQ, *Saint Paul*, II, 803

[172] C. SPICQ, *Saint Paul*, II, 803.

[173] J. MUNCK, «Discours d'adieu», 155-170.

[174] He cites the farewell of Jacob in Gen 47:29–50:14, the leave-taking of Joshua in Josh 23:1–24:32, the final speech of Samuel in 1 Sam 12, the last words of David in 1 Kgs 2:1-9 and 1 Chr 28:1–29:28, and the whole of Deuteronomy, which purports to be a single speech of Moses. J. MUNCK, «Discours d'adieu», 154-155. Whether the entirety of Deuteronomy should be so cited remains, perhaps, to be seen.

of late Judaism[175]. In farewell addresses of the intertestamental period, the following elements appear:

> 1) un personnage de l'A. T. faisant ses adieux soit parce que qu'il doit être enlevé au ciel, comme Esdras, Enoch, ou Baruch, soit qu'il va mourir. Il réunit autour de lui sa famille ou tout le peuple pour leur donner un suprême et définitif enseignement; 2) le trait le plus courant, c'est que celui qui s'en va exhorte ses descendants ou prédit ce qui arrivera s'ils suivent ses exhortations et observent la loi ou, au contraire s'ils désobéissent [...] 3) moins courant est le cas où celui qui va mourir raconte sa vie, de laquelle il tire des exhortations morales auxquelles sa personne sert de modèle ou d'exemple pour mettre en garde [...] 4) il est également rare que les paroles d'adieu contiennent une prophétie relative à la destinée du peuple dans les derniers temps [...] Mais les textes les plus intérressants comme parallèles aux passages du N. T. sont ceux qui contiennent aussi les deux derniers motifs car ils forment un tableau apocalyptique. Celui qui va mourir insiste sur l'importance de sa propre personne et il prédit les temps difficiles qui surviendront après sa mort[176].

In his analysis of 2 Tim, Munck concludes that the letter is, in fact, a farewell address since it contains

> 1) un enseignement définitif avant la mort de l'apôtre; 2) des exhortations qui 3) placent Timothée en face de Paul comme en face du maître et martyr modèle; 4) une prédiction relative aux faux docteurs, qui sont pourtant parfois décrits comme étant déjà apparus[177].

And if, says Munck, within those communities for which the intertestamental farewell addresses were directed, the principal aim was to present moral exhortation[178], the appearance of the genre of the farewell address within early Christianity is marked by the twin appearance of

---

[175] Tob 14:3-11; 4 Esdras 14:18ff.; 2 (Syriac Apocalypse of) Baruch 76ff.; 1 Enoch 91:1-19. 1 Macc 2:49-70 (the farewell of Mattathias), 2 Macc 6:30 (the last words of Eleazar), and 2 Macc 7:1-42 (the final speeches of the seven brothers and the mother) all lack the element of prediction. J. MUNCK, «Discours d'adieu», 157.

[176] J. MUNCK, «Discours d'adieu», 159.

[177] J. MUNCK, «Discours d'adieu», 163.

[178] J. MUNCK, «Discours d'adieu», 168-169. Yet I am not entirely convinced that the principal aim of the farewell address in the intertestamental period was hortatory: it may well have been, as I shall demonstrate below, that the farewell address and the testament alike sought to bring the religious heritage to bear on a contemporary crisis.

heresy and institutionalized ministries[179]. Hence the concern in the Pastoral Epistles for the qualifications of those who aspire to the office of bishop (1 Tim 3:2-7; Tit 1:7-9), presbyter (1 Tim 5:17-22; Tit 1:5-6; 2:2), widow (1 Tim 5:3-16), or deacon (1 Tim 3:8-13).

Munck is right, I think, to have identified elements of the genre of the farewell address in 2 Tim; but he does not take into account the difference between a farewell address, on the one hand, and a testament, on the other. The farewell address, as the examples which Munck himself adduces prove, is always found embedded in a larger narrative. The testament, on the other hand, is free-standing, and while it may *imply* a narrative about the one who delivers the testament (or, better, imply its eventual readers' knowledge of that narrative), it does not contain any (or much) narrative material *about the speaker himself*. The *TM*, for example, which purports to be the last words of Moses, and which presents a «predictive delineation of the history of the [Jewish] people from their entrance into Canaan until the end of days»[180], nevertheless makes no reference, direct or indirect, to the narrative of Moses' birth and upbringing, his encounter with Yahweh at the burning bush and his conflict with Pharaoh. The sole mention of the escape from Egypt and the wandering in the wilderness comes at 3:10-12 when, after a period of apostasy and idolatry, the tribes of Israel

> will remember me, each tribe saying to the other, and each man to his neighbor: «Is it not this, the things which Moses formerly testified to us in his prophecies? Moses, who suffered many things in Egypt and in the Red Sea, and in the desert during forty years. And having testified, he also called on heaven and earth to be witnesses lest we should transgress his commandments which he had mediated to us?» (*TM* 3:10-12).

The only other personal reference comes at 1:14, wherein Moses describes himself as one who was designed and devised by God, one «who (was) prepared from the beginning of the world, to be the mediator of his covenant», a reference which, however much theological importance it may assign to the rôle of Moses in salvation history, can hardly be said to give very much information about him. David L. Tiede has correctly noted that «what is said or revealed by the prophet Moses in

---

[179] «La mort des apôtres marque la venue de Antéchrist. Telle était la pensée de l'Église primitive. La mort des apôtres marque l'apparition de l'hérésie. C'est pourquoi il faut se réunir autour du ministère». J. MUNCK, «Discours d'adieu», 169.

[180] J. PRIEST, «Testament of Moses», 919.

the [TM] is of primary interest to the author. Moses' identity and history are only the backdrop for these revelations»[181].

Yet, the importance of Moses' last words as they are found in the TM cannot be understood apart from the narratives found in, or at least based upon the books of Exodus, Numbers, and Deuteronomy[182]. Indeed, the authority of these last words is dependent upon the readers' prior knowledge of those narratives which rehearse the birth and upbringing, life, career and death of Moses, whether those narratives be found in the canonical Scriptures or in the «rewritten Bible». And if the focus of the testament, as Anitra Bingham Kolenkow has recognized, is to provide a forecast of the future, written in the name of a patriarch, in which the description of a future judgement provides an impetus for remaining among or joining up with the righteous[183], the narrative energies of the testament are expended, so to speak, in the service of that forecast of the future. By the same token, the authority of the words which purport to be Paul's own in 2 Tim is dependent upon a prior understanding of Paul's rôle as κῆρυξ καὶ ἀπόστολος καὶ διδάσκαλος. In comparison to the TM, 2 Tim seemingly gives far more personal information about its putative author; but in actuality, the personal information supplied is really very sparse. We are told, for example, that Paul was appointed a «preacher and apostle and teacher» (κῆρυξ καὶ ἀπόστολος καὶ διδάσκαλος: 2 Tim 1:11), but when and where and under what circumstances this appointment came is never stated in 2 Tim. The consequence of this appointment, however, is made abundantly clear:

---

[181] D. L. TIEDE, «The Figure of Moses», 86.

[182] S. A. NIGOSIAN («Moses As They Saw Him») calls the traditional accounts of the life of Moses found in the canonical Scriptures «sacred biography», which he distinguishes from «historical biography». The latter seeks «to establish a core of historically verifiable facts or episodes», (344) whereas sacred biography's essential characteristic is the revelation of «an understanding of the sacred through a particular individual who represents a special relationship with the sacred during the course of history», (344). Moreover, he says, the construction of a sacred biography is usually confined to the followers of the individual whose life is thought so to reveal the operations of the sacred in history, and is compiled «from either oral traditions or previously segmented narratives, or both», (344). While Nigosian wants to analyse the life of Moses as it can be reconstructed from the Torah/Pentateuch, the logic of his line of analysis demands that episodes from the life of Moses which are found in the Old Testament represent «previously segmented narratives», which are subsequently compiled in the sacred biographies of the «rewritten Bible».

[183] A. B. KOLENKOW, «The Genre Testament», 57.

«and therefore I suffer as I do» (δι' ἣν αἰτίαν καὶ ταῦτα πάσχω: 2 Tim 1:12). Indeed, it is fair to say that every successive personal element supplied in 2 Tim simply specifies the manner in which Paul suffers. Thus, Paul has been abandoned by «all who are in Asia, among them Phygelus and Hermogenes» (ἄντες οἱ ἐν τῇ Ἀσίᾳ, ὧν ἐστιν Φύγελος καὶ Ἑρμογένης: 2 Tim 1:15; see also 2 Tim 4:10-12). Thus is he grateful to Onesiphorus who «was not ashamed of my chains» (καὶ τὴν ἅλυσίν μου οὐκ ἐπαισχύνθη: 2 Tim 1:16) and thus for the sake of the gospel, he tells Timothy, «I am suffering and wearing fetters like a criminal» (ἐν ᾧ κακοπαθῶ μέχρι δεσμῶν ὡς κακοῦργος: 2 Tim 2:9). Thus does Paul remind Timothy of «my teaching, my conduct, my aim in life, my faith, my patience, my love, my steadfastness, my persecutions, my sufferings, what befell me at Antioch, at Iconium, and at Lystra, what persecutions I endured; yet from them all the Lord delivered me» (Σὺ δὲ παρηκολούθησάς μου τῇ διδασκαλίᾳ, τῇ ἀγωγῇ, τῇ προθέσει, τῇ πίστει, τῇ μακροθυμίᾳ, τῇ ἀγάπῃ, τῇ ὑπομονῇ, τοῖς διωγμοῖς, τοῖς παθήμασιν, οἷά μοι ἐγένετο ἐν Ἀντιοχείᾳ, ἐν Ἰκονίῳ, ἐν Λύστροις, οἵους διωγμοὺς ὑπήνεγκα καὶ ἐκ πάντων με ἐρρύσατο ὁ κύριος: 2 Tim 3:10-11).

Most memorably, Paul describes his present circumstances: «For I am already on the point of being sacrificed; the time of my departure has come. I have fought the good fight, I have finished the race, I have kept the faith» (Ἐγὼ γὰρ ἤδη σπένδομαι, καὶ ὁ καιρὸς τῆς ἀναλύσεώς μου ἐφέστηκεν. τὸν καλὸν ἀγῶνα ἠγώνισμαι, τὸν δρόμον τετέλεκα, τὴν πίστιν τετήρηκα: 2 Tim 4:6-7). And in a similar, though less elegiac tone, Paul writes, «At my first defense no one took my part; all deserted me. May it not be charged against them! But the Lord stood by me and gave me strength to proclaim the message fully, that all the Gentiles might hear it. So I was rescued from the lion's mouth» (Ἐν τῇ πρώτῃ μου ἀπολογίᾳ οὐδείς μοι παρεγένετο, ἀλλὰ πάντες με ἐγκατέλιπον· μὴ αὐτοῖς λογισθείη· ὁ δὲ κύριός μοι παρέστη καὶ ἐνεδυνάμωσέν με, ἵνα δι' ἐμοῦ τὸ κήρυγμα πληροφορηθῇ καὶ ἀκούσωσιν πάντα τὰ ἔθνη, καὶ ἐρρύσθην ἐκ στόματος λέοντος: 2 Tim 4:16-17). All of these seemingly personal details serve to contribute to the understanding of Paul's suffering.

Lewis R. Donelson has touched upon the issue of the authority of the Pastoral Epistles and the portrait of Paul in the Pastoral Epistles by arguing that the image of Paul in the letters functions as an inductive paradigm in such a way that Paul's life provides the pattern for all subsequent Christians. And if, in 1 Tim, that paradigm is of the converted heretic or sinner, in 2 Tim, Paul is described as the abandoned leader who remains faithful to his calling. Thus, for Donelson, 2 Tim was written to console church leaders «who have lost out to the heretics in the battle for the allegiances of the church»[184]. It is, of course, beyond dispute that 2 Tim depicts Paul as one who is bereft of companionship: 2 Tim 1:15 and 4:10 bear ample witness to that aspect of the portrait of Paul. But I think it is quite another thing to conclude from that facet of the implied portrait of Paul to the very purpose for which the letter was written. Donelson is right, however, to have recognized the paradigmatic quality of the portrait of the abandoned but still faithful leader that is the Paul of 2 Tim. His case might have been strengthened, however, had he considered the testamentary character of 2 Tim.

Dibelius – Conzelmann recognize that in 2 Tim, «the personal elements become prominent to a remarkable extent»[185]. These personal elements have a parenetic function in the letter insofar as they establish Paul as an example of suffering in the hope that Timothy as well as those who seek to live a Christian life will be encouraged to put up with similar suffering[186]. In their commentary on 2 Tim 3:1-9, they recognize motifs deriving from the form of the farewell address, and citing the analysis of Johannes Munck, they explicitly identify 2 Tim as the testament of Paul[187]. And they attribute the presence of information about certain persons, be those persons Paul, Timothy, Titus, or any of the other principals mentioned in 2 Tim, to an interest in the story of the apostle's life at the time during which the Pastoral Epistles were being composed. «It seems plausible», they hold, «that the formation of legends about Paul had already begun»[188]. Such legends, like the apocryphal *Acts of Paul*, focus attention on those places in Paul's missionary journeys which receive scant attention in the canonical book of Acts[189]. Yet, they do not pursue OT and intertestamental parallels, nor do they explore the theological implications of the choice of the testamentary genre.

J. L. Houlden believes that the chief purpose of the personal details in 2 Tim is «to give vivid color to an edifying portrait of Paul, the heroic leader of the Church's early days»[190]. Likewise, Lewis R.

---

[184] L. R. DONELSON, «The Structure of Ethical Argument», 110.

[185] Dibelius – Conzelmann, 7.

[186] Dibelius – Conzelmann, 7, 128.

[187] Dibelius – Conzelmann, 115.

[188] Dibelius – Conzelmann, 127-128.

[189] Dibelius – Conzelmann, 128.

[190] J. L. HOULDEN, *The Pastoral Epistles*, 131.

Donelson holds that such personal notes «first of all provide verisimilitude to the [Pastoral] letters»[191]. But David G. Meade has noted that in the Pastoral Epistles, personal information about Paul is given not primarily for its historical or occasional value (or for verisimilitude), but for its paradigmatic, theological value. This paradigmatic use of these personal elements need not detract from the historical value of such information: indeed, he goes on to say, a great deal of it may be accurate. But the point of such information, in Meade's view, is to present Paul as a model of discipleship, the ὑποτύπωσις (1 Tim 1:16; 2 Tim 1:13) after whom believers are to model themselves. Paul's life as ὑποτύπωσις, claims Meade, «serves to establish the parameters of legitimate Christian experience»[192]. Meade's identification of the paradigmatic function of the personal elements in 2 Tim does not explain, however, why those personal elements should be subsumed under the rubric of suffering, nor why subsequent generations of believers should take suffering as their pattern or model of legitimate Christian experience. It may be, as I shall shortly demonstrate, that the portrait of Paul as one who suffers is an integral part of the Pastor's larger strategy to present the Apostle to the Gentiles as a latter-day Moses.

Jerome Quinn's posthumous commentary on the Letter to Titus contains an introduction to the Pastoral Epistles as a whole[193]. Owing, perhaps, to the circumstances under which his study was published, and the fact that the companion commentary on 2 Tim still awaits publication, the testamentary nature of 2 Tim receives only the briefest mention in his general introduction[194]. In occasional articles, Quinn mentions the testamentary character of 2 Tim, usually in relation to its parenesis; but this testamentary character is assumed, and never analyzed[195].

Alone of all the contemporary critics, Michael Prior denies that 2 Tim is a testament or a *discours d'adieu*. Based on his understanding of the meaning of the words σπένδομαι and ἀνάλυσις in 2 Tim 4:6, Prior concludes that, far from expressing Paul's expectation of his imminent death, 2 Tim is, in reality, a manifestation of confidence in his imminent

---

[191] L. R. DONELSON, «The Structure of Ethical Argument», 111.

[192] D. G. MEADE, *Pseudonymity and Canon*, 124-125.

[193] J. D. QUINN, *Titus*, 1-22. This introduction is substantially the same as his article «Timothy and Titus, Epistles to», 560-571.

[194] J. D. QUINN, *Titus*, 9.

[195] See, for instance, «Parenesis», 495-501; ID., «The Pastoral Epistles on Righteousness», 231-238.

release, a call for Timothy to persevere in spite of his own suffering, and a summons to Rome[196].

Benjamin Fiore's thorough study of the function of personal example in the Pastoral Epistles mentions the testamentary character of 2 Tim in passing, and though he provides an analysis of the traditional form of the testament, this part of his investigation confines itself to a consideration of the testaments in the Socratic letter collection, e.g., *Eps.* 6 and 27. He does not consider examples of the form as it may be found in the Old Testament or the intertestamental literature[197]. Hence the Mosaic resonances of the testamentary form in 2 Tim are entirely neglected.

The next three chapters of this study will attempt to set 2 Tim in what I believe to be its proper literary tradition, and the one which provides the best interpretive matrix by which to understand the formal elements of the *Testamentum Pauli*, namely, the story of the dying Moses found first of all in the Book of Deuteronomy, but also in those traditions concerning his last words which are found in examples of the «rewritten Bible».

---

[196] M. PRIOR, *Paul the Letter-Writer*, 61-90, 91-112, 113-139, 154-163. One notes, in this context, the rather lukewarm reception accorded Prior's book by, for example, L. T. JOHNSON («Review», 339-341) for whom the word studies which form the crux of Prior's argument against the testamentary character of 2 Tim «strike the reader as perhaps not totally *ad rem*». (341).

[197] B. FIORE, *The Function of Personal Example*, 4; 161-163; 216, n. 91; 229, n. 175. Indeed, he deliberately excludes from consideration the literature of the Jewish milieu, owing to limitations of space (24, n. 67).

CHAPTER II

## The Figure of Moses in First Century Judaism

The importance of Moses to the various religious groups within first century Judaism, including Christianity, can hardly be underestimated[1]. First century readers of the narratives in which Moses appears would scarcely have granted von Rad his thesis that the stories of the Old Testament in which Moses figures are not stories of Moses at all, but rather stories of God[2]. Nor would they have made much of Martin Noth's contention that «in the historical consciousness of Israel [Moses] never attained the significance that one would expect him to have attained in view of his present role in the Pentateuch»[3]. And it is doubtful if they could have fully agreed with David Aune's supposition that «the focus of the final version of the Pentateuch woven together by editors is the presentation and explication of the Torah, *to which the career of Moses is essentially tangential*»[4]. To say, as Aune does, that the career of Moses is «essentially tangential» to the Pentateuch would have struck first century readers as something close to nonsense, inasmuch as one of the books of the Pentateuch, namely Deuteronomy, purports to be a speech delivered by Moses in anticipation of his own death, and, indeed, is the only book in the Pentateuch explicitly ascribed to Moses («And Moses wrote the words of *this law* [τοῦ νόμου τούτου] in a scroll, and gave it to the priests» Deut 31:9, emphasis mine). Noth's contention respecting Moses' supposed insignificance would have seemed even to first century Christians as gratuitously obtuse insofar as they could refer

---

[1] For an evaluation of the question of the varieties of Judaism during the first century and the relation of the period's literary remains to these various religious groups, see M. E. STONE, *Scriptures, Sects and Visions*.

[2] G. VON RAD, *Moses*, 8-9; see also D. M. BEEGLE, *Moses*, 347-348.

[3] M. NOTH, *A History of Pentateuchal Traditions*, 156.

[4] D. E. AUNE, *The New Testament in Its Literary Environment*, 39. Emphasis mine.

to the Scriptures themselves by the name of Moses[5]. And while it is undoubtedly true that certain of the «historical credos» which von Rad has identified[6], and which summarize Israel's faith in Yahweh as the Lord of History, could identify God's mighty acts without explicit reference to Moses (Deut 6:20-25; 26:5-10), it is another question altogether whether such «historical credos» ever constituted the nuclei from which subsequent narratives developed[7], or, indeed, whether they were ever meant to serve as a comprehensive summary of Israel's faith, in the way, say, that the Nicene Creed is meant to provide such a summary for Christians[8].

---

[5] See, for example, 2 Cor 3:7-16, where in vv. 7 and 13, the historical Moses is evidently meant, whereas in v. 15, the *Scriptures* of which Moses was thought to be the author is meant: «Yes, to this day whenever Moses *is read* a veil lies over their minds» (ἀλλ᾽ ἕως σήμερον ἡνίκα ἂν ἀναγινώσκηται Μωϋσῆς κάλυμμα ἐπὶ τὴν καρδίαν αὐτῶν κεῖται). J. A. FITZMYER («Glory Reflected») thinks that the pericope was probably composed by Paul for another occasion, and later inserted into its present position in 2 Corinthians (632). See also Acts 15:21, where Moses is said to have «had in every city those who *preach* him, for he *is read* every sabbath in the synagogues» (Μωϋσῆς γὰρ ἐκ γενεῶν ἀρχαίων κατὰ πόλιν τοὺς κηρύσσοντας αὐτὸν ἔχει ἐν ταῖς συναγωγαῖς κατὰ πᾶν σάββατον ἀναγινωσκόμενος). This elliptical reference to the Scriptures by their supposed author is probably an extension of the usage found in Neh 13:1/2 Esdras 23:1, wherein the prohibition against the entry of the Ammonites and the Moabites into the congregation is read «in the book of Moses» (בְּסֵפֶר מֹשֶׁה/ἐν βιβλίῳ Μωυσῆ).

[6] G. VON RAD, «The Form-Critical Problem of the Hexateuch», 1-27; ID., *Genesis*, 13-24.

[7] See J. P. HYATT, «Ancient Historical Credo in Israel», who subjects G. von Rad's thesis to a searching critique, and who holds instead that the so-called «ancient short historical credo» is a «late summary of traditions rather than a very early nucleus of traditions» which «appears to be largely a product of the seventh century or early sixth century BC» (159). In a similar fashion, M. WEINFELD, *Deuteronomy and the Deuteronomic School*, argues on the bases of style and theology that the passage is not an ancient credo, but rather «that the author of Deuteronomy reworked ancient formulae and incorporated them in his own liturgical composition» (34). In *Moses and the Deuteronomist*, R. POLZIN argues that in the attempt to establish a date for the ancient historical credos, von Rad uncritically adopted the historiographical axiom that «the shorter a genre representative is, the older it probably is», a procedure which in Polzin's view is «questionable» and even «invalid» (14).

[8] D. McCARTHY (*Institution and Narrative*, 319) has made the telling point that while «men have fought over verbal changes in creeds because they express basic beliefs, [there is] no evidence that they did so over the variations in the speeches called "creeds" in modern Old Testament scholarship».

I do not discount the value of studies like those of von Rad or Noth, which attempt to establish the process by which the Book of Deuteronomy as it presently exists came into being. Such diachronic approaches to the study of the literature of the Old Testament have contributed much to the contemporary understanding of the history of Israel and the development of its religious institutions and practices. Indeed, the diachronic and synchronic approaches to the biblical text need not be seen as mutually exclusive: as Robert Polzin has noted, «a scholarly understanding of biblical material results from a *circular* movement that begins with literary analysis, then turns to historical problems, whose attempted solution then furnishes refinements and adaptations of one's literary critical conclusions»[9]. That having been said, the point of departure in this investigation is not diachronic but synchronic, which is to say that my purpose here is not to analyse the biblical texts in an attempt to reconstruct the history of their composition; rather, I will take as my task in this section an investigation of those literary structures which present themselves as the consequence of the historical process which von Rad, Noth, and others have taken such pains to describe. In this respect, the approach taken here is what Meir Sternberg has termed «discourse-oriented analysis», which is to be distinguished from «source-oriented inquiry», and which, as he puts it, «sets out to understand not the realities behind the text but the text itself as a pattern of meaning and effect»[10]. Consequently, while I rely on the pioneering studies of scholars like von Rad and Noth, and will have occasion to cite their work from time to time in this section of the study, my literary analysis in this investigation will diverge considerably from theirs.

George W. Coats rightly notes that the term «literary analysis» does not refer to a uniform methodological operation: in addition to questions of authorship and *traditionsgeschichte*, Coats holds that a literary analysis of a Biblical narrative needs must concentrate on questions respecting the style and artistic merit of a text[11]. This is *not* part of the agenda of this investigation: my purposes here are analytic, not appreciative and aesthetic[12]. The primary purpose in this chapter of the investigation is

---

[9] R. POLZIN, *Moses and the Deuteronomist*, 6.

[10] M. STERNBERG, *The Poetics of Biblical Narrative*, 15.

[11] G. W. COATS, *Moses*, 27.

[12] Even so thoroughly literary a critic as N. FRYE (*The Great Code*) has decried the tendency of some literary critics to conceive of their task as primarily appreciative; for Frye, aesthetic evaluation is «a minor and subordinate function of the critical process,

to see how the stories of the last words and death of Moses present themselves in the biblical narrative as the literary tradition from within which to understand what purport to be the last words of Paul in 2 Tim. Consequently, I am interested in the way in which first century readers — including the Pastor — would have understood the figure of the dying Moses. The underlying methodological presupposition is that the literary structures in the biblical stories which take as their subject the figure of the dying Moses would have been detectible to readers in the first century, readers who did not share, it need hardly be said, the twentieth century preoccupation with questions concerning the origin and development of religious practices reflected in the literature of the Old Testament.

A number of studies of the figure of Moses in the literature of the New Testament have begun with at least some of these presuppositions in mind[13]. To date, however, no study has yet appeared which ex-

---

at best an incidental by-product, which should never be allowed to take priority over scholarship» (xvi). For a perceptive review of *The Great Code*, see P. J. CAHILL, «The Unity of the Bible», 404-411, who maintains that Frye «has made a very good case for the primacy of the literary operation in understanding the Bible. This emphasis on critical reading implies that *the outcome of literary criticism is not to uncover external decoration or ornamentary form [...] but to disclose that the theological and religious meaning of the Bible is inextricably bound up with its literary character*» (409, emphasis mine).

[13] In the Anglo-Saxon world, B. W. BACON («The "Five Books" of Moses») set the agenda for a whole generation of scholars in his analysis of Mosaic typology in the Gospel of Matthew. Other important studies of Mosaic imagery in the Matthean Gospel include W. D. DAVIES, *The Setting of the Sermon on the Mount*; R. H. GUNDRY, *The Use of the Old Testament in Matthew*. U. LUZ (*Matthew 1 – 7*) questions many of Bacon's fundamental contentions (i.e., the division of the Gospel into five «books», [43-44]), though he does allow for a deliberate recall of Mount Sinai in the setting for the Sermon on the Mount (224). W. A. MEEKS' 1965 doctoral dissertation at Yale University (*The Prophet-King*) investigated the figure of Moses in the Old Testament, in the writings of Philo and Josephus, in the Apocrypha and Pseudepigrapha, the Qumran texts, the rabbinic *haggada*, and the Samaritan and Mandaean sources as a way of establishing the proper interpretive matrix for understanding the figure of Jesus as prophet and king in the Fourth Gospel. M. R. D'ANGELO's 1976 doctoral dissertation at Yale University (*Moses in the Letter to the Hebrews*) examined the image of Moses in the letter to the Hebrews, analysing, among other things, first century traditions concerning the exemplary fidelity of Moses in the effort to explicate the parenetic uses to which the author of the Hebrews puts the figure of Moses. Like the Matthean scholars, both Meeks and D'Angelo concerned themselves with the *Christological* uses to which the figure of Moses was put in the Fourth Gospel and the letter to the Hebrews. D. P.

amines the traditions of Moses' last words as an interpretive matrix for understanding what the Pastor presents as the last words of Paul in 2 Tim. The topic of Moses' last words was a popular one in the first century, and by no means one which was subjected to a uniform treatment: a variety of traditions concerning the last words of Moses can be recovered through an analysis of the literature which survives from that era. The principal source for understanding how the figure of the dying Moses would have been viewed in the first century community of which the Pastor was a member is, of course, the Greek text of Deuteronomy itself. But in addition to Deuteronomy, traditions concerning the last words of the dying Moses are found in Philo's *VM*, as well as in the *JA* of Josephus, the Pseudo-Philo's *LAB*, and in the otherwise anonymous *TM*. Insofar as these works differ from the biblical texts themselves, either through omission of certain details, or by addition of others, they offer the scholar an opportunity to chart the ways in which the biblical narratives themselves were understood by the authors of these respective works and the communities to which these authors directed their efforts[14].

## 1. Foundations: the Deuteronomic portrait of Moses

The point of embarkation for this examination of the figure of the dying Moses as a prototype of the dying Paul is the book of Deuteronomy, which presents itself as Moses' valedictory address to Israel[15]. The por-

---

MOESSNER («Paul and the Pattern of the Prophet like Moses»), however, has analysed the career of Paul in the Acts of the Apostles, and concludes that Luke has presented Paul, along with Stephen, according to the pattern of the Prophet like Moses of Deut 18:15-18. More recently, G. W. COATS (*Moses*), whose work I have already had occasion to cite, has undertaken a full-length study of the heroic significance of Moses in the Hebrew text of the Pentateuch and Hexateuch with a brief set of references to the uses to which that heroic conception of Moses was put in the New Testament. And, most recently of all, D. C. ALLISON (*The New Moses*) has examined the typological uses to which the figure of Moses is put, not just in the Gospel of Matthew, but also in the presentation of figures like Gideon and Josiah within the literature of the Old Testament, Jesus, Peter and Paul within the literature of the New Testament, and, outside the Bible proper, figures as diverse as Hillel, Gregory Thaumaturgis, and Benedict of Nursia.

[14] See, for instance, J. H. CHARLESWORTH, «Biblical Interpretation», 66-78; S. J. HAFEMANN, «Moses in the Apocrypha», 80, 101-104.

[15] G. VON RAD, *Studies in Deuteronomy*, 11, 70; ID., *Deuteronomy*, 12, 28; M. WEINFELD, *Deuteronomy 1 – 11*, 4-6.

trait of Moses which appears in Deuteronomy is, as Patrick Miller, among others, has observed, «obviously the result of a complex stream of tradition, story, and legislation whose final shape is more readily discernible than the process by which it came into being»[16]. Miller made his observation, of course, with the Hebrew text of Deuteronomy in mind; but what may be said of the Hebrew text of Deuteronomy may be said *a fortiori* of the Greek text. It is that «final shape» of the portrait of the dying Moses as it presents itself in the Greek text of Deuteronomy which shall be the concern of this section of the investigation.

While the actual report of Moses' death and burial is found in Deut 34:5-12, the reader of Deuteronomy is reminded that Moses' days are soon coming to an end at 31:2, 14, 16, 27, 29; 32:49-50; 33:1. Consequently, one may identify the last four chapters of Deuteronomy as those in which the figure of the dying Moses is depicted. The dying Moses appears under various aspects in these last four chapters: he is a prophet, insofar as Deuteronomy explicitly identifies him as one (34:10) and shows him predicting what will befall his people after his death (e.g., 31:27-29 and 33:1-29); he is a law-giver, insofar as Deuteronomy encompasses legislation attributed to him (e.g., 31:10-13); and he suffers on behalf of his people, insofar as his death is linked in Deuteronomy to the disobedience of the wilderness generation (32:51).

J. R. Porter has held that of all the categories which have been proposed to understand the figure of Moses, «the most inclusive and the one that best explains most features in the Pentateuchal portrait of Moses would seem to be that of the [...] Davidic monarch of the pre-exilic period»[17]. A first century reader of Deuteronomy might not have agreed with Porter; he or she is more likely to have viewed Moses as a figure *sui generis*. It is true that Philo certainly saw Moses as the great exemplar of kingship in the *VM*, as Porter recognises and as we shall shortly see; yet it is also true that Philo seems to have done so with encomiastic purposes in mind[18]. Even he felt constrained to organise his presentation of the life of Moses not only around his accomplishments as king (βασιλεύς), but also his achievements as law-giver (νομοθέτης), as high priest (ἀρχιερεύς), and as prophet (προφήτης)[19]. More-

---

[16] P. D. MILLER, «Moses My Servant», 245. See also J. BLENKINSOPP, *The Pentateuch*, 178.

[17] J. R. PORTER, *Moses and Monarchy*, 8.

[18] J. R. PORTER, *Moses and Monarchy*, 8, n. 8.

[19] See *VM* I.334.

over, Josephus does not apply the term βασιλεύς to Moses in the *JA*, preferring to identify him as the general, chief, leader, or commander-in-chief (στρατηγός) of the Israelites[20], their νομοθέτης[21], or, once, as the προφήτης[22]. The author of the *LAB* likewise applies a number of different titles to Moses, calling him a «shepherd» (*pastore*: 19:3), a «judge» (*iudice*: 19:3), «prophet» (*prophetas*: 53:8) «first of all the prophets» (*primus omnium prophetarum*: 35:6) and God's «servant» (*servo*: 20:2, *minister*: 30:1; *famulus*: 30:2; 47:1; 53:2, 8, 10; 57:2; 58:1), «friend» (*amicus*: 23:9; 24:3; 25:3; 25:5) and «beloved» (*dilectus*: 32:8). In the *TM*, Moses is called, conventionally enough, «mediator» (*arbiter*: 1:14; 3:12), «lord» (*domine*: 11:4, 9, 14, 19), and «great messenger» (*magnus nuntius*: 11:17b), but more curiously, «the holy and sacred spirit» (*sanctum et sacrum spiritum*: 11:16b), «the worthy one before the Lord» (*dignum Domino*: 11:16b), «the trusted one in everything» (*fidelem in omnia*: 11:16c), «the divine prophet for this world» (*divinum per orbem terrarum profetem*: 11:16d), «the perfect teacher for this earth» (*consummatum in saeculo doctorem*: 11:16e), and most exotically of all, «the versatile and inscrutable lord of the word» (*multiplicem et incompraehensibilem dominum verbi*: 11:16c). It seems safe to say that in the first century, Moses could be thought of in a variety of ways, under a variety of titles, and according to a variety of categories.

Thus, while Porter may well be justified in positing a royal understanding of the figure of Moses at the time during which Israel was ruled by the succession of Davidic kings, by the first century such an interpretation of the significance of Moses seems to have vanished, along with the successors to David. It seems justifiable, therefore, in attempting to recapture how the Pastor might have read the narrative of Deuteronomy, to consider the figure of Moses as a prophet, a law-giver, and a sufferer. Before these various aspects of the figure of Moses can be examined, however, a preliminary question has to be faced, namely, the justifiability of considering the Book of Deuteronomy as a narrative.

## 2. Status Quaestionis: Deuteronomy as a narrative

Scholarly studies of Deuteronomy in this century have been dominated by the pioneers of the diachronic approach to Old Testament literature

---

[20] *JA* III.12, 67, 78, 102; IV.165, 194.

[21] *JA* III.180; IV.322, 329.

[22] *JA* IV.329.

and their epigones; consequently, most contemporary scholars have concerned themselves with historical questions like the process by which the book as we now have it came to be[23], or the relationship between the Deuteronomic law and the reforms of Josiah[24], or between the Deuteronomic law and the other law collections of the Pentateuch[25]. Indeed, before they even begin to undertake their analysis of Deuteronomy, most contemporary scholars seem to presume that the work's sole purpose is legal, even if some, like Anthony Phillips, qualify that preconception with phrases like «preached law»[26]. Yet even Calum Carmichael in his study of the laws of Deuteronomy recognises the importance of the formal setting for the laws, namely, the Mosaic valediction, and the putative authorship of the work, namely, that of Moses[27].

## 2.1 *Paradigms for understanding Deuteronomy*

Scholarly investigations of the narrative character of Deuteronomy have been few. Nearly a century ago, for instance, S. R. Driver asserted that Deuteronomy consisted of three discourses, and recognised that these discourses may be said to comprise three elements: the historical element, the legislative element, and the parenetic element. Of these three, Driver contended that the parenetic element was the most important, and that the other two were entirely subservient to it: the historical element, as Driver viewed it, served a didactic purpose, and the legislative element was employed by the author of Deuteronomy «as a vehicle for exemplifying the principles which it is the main object of his book to enforce»[28].

What Driver did not examine, however, was the narrative phenomenon of the putative authorship of Moses himself − indeed, he went to

---

[23] See, for instance, S. R. DRIVER, *Deuteronomy* (hereinafter, Driver); E. W. NICHOLSON, *Deuteronomy and Tradition*; A. D. H. MAYES, *Deuteronomy*, 34ff.; J. BLENKINSOPP, «Deuteronomy», 94-109; R. NELSON, «Deuteronomy», 209-234.

[24] Driver, li-lxv.

[25] Driver, iii-xiv; G. VON RAD, *Studies in Deuteronomy*, 25-36; J. G. McCONVILLE, *Law and Theology*.

[26] A. PHILLIPS, *Deuteronomy*, 7. See also G. VON RAD, «Deuteronomy», 835, who uses the term «preached commandments», and to whom Phillips probably owes the expression «preached law».

[27] C. M. CARMICHAEL, *The Laws of Deuteronomy*, 30-31.

[28] Driver, xix.

some pains to disprove it[29] – which is absolutely essential to the parenetic ends of Deuteronomy. The parenetic elements which Driver was
right to identify as primary receive their rhetorical force from the fact
that it is Moses himself who delivers them: they are not a set of abstract
principles; they are exhortations delivered by a man on the very brink
of death. But in Driver's confusion of the authorship of Moses as a narrative phenomenon and the authorship of Moses as an historical fact, or
what one might better term as a kind of confusion of Moses as character
with Moses as author, and in his dismissal of what he thought was the
Mosaic authorship of Deuteronomy, he failed to account for the persua-
siveness of the parenesis which suffuses Deuteronomy.

Driver's discursive understanding of Deuteronomy has cast a long
shadow. Thus Joseph Blenkinsopp, whose work in the *NJBC* represents
a kind of consensus among the majority of contemporary Catholic biblical scholars in America, asserts that Deuteronomy consists of three
separate addresses with a series of appendices, displaying the following
macrostructure[30]:

| | | |
|---|---|---|
| I. | 1:1 – 4:49 | First Address |
| II. | 5:1 – 11:32 | Second Address |
| III. | 12:1 – 26:15 | The Law Book |
| IV. | 26:16 – 28:69 | Conclusion to the Giving of the Law |
| V. | 29:1 – 30:20 | Third Address |
| VI. | 31:1 – 34:12 | Last Will, Testament, and Death of Moses |

The immediate difficulty with this discursive understanding of Deuteronomy's structure is that it tends not to take sufficiently seriously the
narrative character of the entire work, thereby reducing the last four
chapters to appendices. Indeed, Nicholson goes so far as to divorce the
last four chapters of the work from Deuteronomy proper, claiming that
they belong to the Pentateuch «as a whole»[31]. Moreover, Blenkinsopp,
like Driver before him, and like those who similarly resolve the structure of Deuteronomy, fails to account thereby for the rhetorical force

---

[29] Driver, xxiv-lxxvii.

[30] J. BLENKINSOPP, «Deuteronomy», 95-96; see also, with minor variations, Driver,
i; E. W. NICHOLSON, *Deuteronomy and Tradition*, 18-19; A. PHILLIPS, *Deuteronomy*,
1; A. D. H. MAYES, *Deuteronomy*, 108-109, 371-414; R. NELSON, «Deuteronomy»,
209.

[31] E. W. NICHOLSON, *Deuteronomy and Tradition*, 22.

and the parenetic value of the «preached law» which is found in Deutero-nomy.

Another paradigm has been suggested for understanding the structure of Deuteronomy, namely the covenant formulary. As early as 1938, von Rad had inquired into the structure of the Book of Deuteronomy, and concluded from its arrangement of homily, laws, sealing of covenant, blessings, and curses that the literary structure of Deuteronomy reflected the procedures of a formal cultic ceremony of covenant renewal[32]. He claimed in 1947 that the origins of the Deuteronomic movement were to be found in the Levites[33], a supposition which was rejected *inter alia* by Moshe Weinfeld[34]. G. von Rad's primary intuition respecting the covenantal form of Deuteronomy was ratified, however, by George E. Mendenhall's ongoing research into the structure of Hittite suzerainty treaties, first published in 1954[35], which led Mendenhall to identify six characteristic elements of the treaty[36]:

(1) Preamble, which identifies the covenant giver;
(2) Historical retrospect, which places the relationship between the signatories on a basis other than sheer force;
(3) Presentation of the stipulations outlining the obligations of the signatories, which obligations were, for the vassal, usually very specifically stated, including, for instance, the amount of tribute which must be paid yearly, but which, for the overlord, were rather less definite, requiring him only to treat his vassal decently;
(4) Provisions for the deposit of the text and for its public reading, the place of which was usually in the sacred shrines of the chief gods of the vassal's land;
(5) Invocation of the divine witnesses to the treaty, the intention of which was, apparently, that both the overlord's gods and the vassal's gods should be aware of the vassal's oath, especially since they would be the ones to take vengeance, should the vassal break his oath;
(6) Series of blessings and curses, which provided the sanctions for breaking the oath, and the promise of certain goods which will come from keeping it.

---

[32] G. VON RAD, *The Problem of the Hexateuch*, 1-78.

[33] G. VON RAD, *Studies in Deuteronomy*,

[34] M. WEINFELD, «Deuteronomy: The Present State of Inquiry», 252.

[35] G. E. MENDENHALL, «Covenant Forms in Israelite Tradition», 66-87.

[36] G. E. MENDENHALL, «Covenant», 714-715; ID. – G. A. HERION, «Covenant», 1180-1182. A convenient collection of Hittite treaties in translation may be found in A. GOETZE, trans., «Hittite Treaties», 201-206; 529-530.

Subsequent investigations into the treaties of Esarhaddon ratified the fundamental insight respecting the prevalence of the literary tradition of covenant writing, while at the same time acknowledging important differences between the various types which have survived to this day[37]. According to this line of analysis, the structure of the central section of Deuteronomy (Deut 4:44 – 28:68) reflects the structure of the suzerainty treaty in the following fashion: chapters 5 – 11 represent the historical-parenetic prologue; Deut 12:1 – 26:15 contains the stipulations which govern the relationship between Yahweh and Israel and which bind Israel to Yahweh; Deut 26:16-19 contains the invocation-adjuration; and, finally, Deut 28:1-46 contains the blessings and curses typical of the ancient Middle Eastern treaties[38]. The literary form of the treaty did not perfectly reproduce itself within Deuteronomy: the appeal to the gods as divine witnesses, as Delbert Hillers has noted, «hardly lent itself to use within Israel»[39], though the Song of Moses (Deut 32:2-43) itself functions as a witness (μαρτύριον: Deut 31:19; μαρτυροῦσα: Deut 31:21) against the future apostasy of the Israelites.

Even more recently, Klaus Baltzer's investigations in to the form and function of the covenant formularies in Israelite, Jewish, and early Christian writings have persuaded him that Deuteronomy evidences close relationships with the covenant formulary. According to Baltzer's reading of the historical and literary evidence, a change in Israel's leadership necessitated a reconfirmation of the covenant relationship between Israel and Yahweh. The testament of the dying leader, be it that of Moses or David, comprises the elements of the normal covenant formulary with one important difference: the blessings and curses of the covenant formulary become in the testament a series of promises and threats.[40]

Starting from an entirely different set of concerns with respect to the literary structures of Deuteronomy, Duane L. Christensen has identified a five-part concentric design to Deuteronomy, which may be charted as follows:

A    Outer Frame: A Look Backwards (Deut 1 – 3)
  B    Inner Frame: The Great Peroration (Deut 4 – 11)
    C    Central Core: Covenant Stipulations (Deut 12 – 26)

---

[37] M. WEINFELD, «Traces of Assyrian Treaty Formulae in Deuteronomy», 417-427.

[38] D. McCARTHY, *Treaty and Covenant*, 186.

[39] D. R. HILLERS, *Covenant*, 52.

[40] K. BALTZER, *The Covenant Formulary*, 68, 137.

B'    Inner Frame: The Covenant Ceremony (Deut 27 – 30)
A'    Outer Frame: A Look Forwards (Deut 31 – 34)

According to Christensen's analysis, the figure of Joshua, who appears only in Deut 3, 31, and 34, ties together the three chapters, thus enabling the reader to see a single document in his «Outer Frame»[41]. In a similar fashion, the two parts of the «Inner Frame» are linked by the references to curses and blessings connected with cultic ceremonies on Mount Gerizim and Mount Ebal. Thus the heart of Deuteronomy, according to Christensen's reading of the structures, would be found in what he calls the «Central Core», Deut 12 – 26, the Deuteronomic law code[42]. Crucial to Christensen's analysis of the structure of Deuteronomy is his contention that the work is best explained as a didactic poem, and was intended to be recited publicly with musical accompaniment in the course of Israel's liturgical celebrations[43]. Basing his research in part on the work of the French musicologist, Suzanne Haïk-Vantoura, who holds that the Masoretic accentual system preserves the ancient method of musical notation from the Second Temple period[44], in part on the system of counting *morae*[45], and in part on the metrical theories of Jerzy Kurylowicz[46], Christensen claims that Deuteronomy is a musical composition, and that its concentric structure is typical of ancient liturgical expressions, ancient musical compositions, and ancient epic literature. Deuteronomy, claims Christensen, combines elements of all three[47].

---

[41] D. L. CHRISTENSEN, *Deuteronomy 1 – 11*, xli; ID., *A Song of Power*, 9. He seems to have been influenced in his understanding of the structure of Deuteronomy by M. NOTH, *A History of Pentateuchal Traditions*, 12-18, who held that Deut 1–3 with 31:1-8 constituted a Deuteronomistic framework for Deut 4:44–30:20, and evidenced a concern for the succession of Joshua.

[42] D. L. CHRISTENSEN, *Deuteronomy 1 – 11*, xli; ID., *A Song of Power*, 9.

[43] D. L. CHRISTENSEN, *Deuteronomy 1 – 11*, lx.

[44] S. HAÏK-VANTOURA, *The Music of the Bible Revealed*.

[45] D. L. CHRISTENSEN, *Deuteronomy 1 – 11*, lviii; ID., *A Song of Power*, 10.

[46] J. KURYLOWICZ, *Studies in Semitic Grammar and Metrics*. For a somewhat skeptical review of Kurylowicz's «syntactical-accentual» approach to Hebrew metrics, comparing it with the syllable-counting method of F. M. Cross and D. N. Freedman, as well as an application of the two methods to Deut 33:7-29 and Jer 12:3-9, see T. LONGMAN, «A Critique of Two Recent Metrical Systems», 230-254.

[47] D. L. CHRISTENSEN, *Deuteronomy 1 – 11*, lx-lxi; ID., *A Song of Power*, 10-11.

Whatever else one may think of Christensen's fundamental contention respecting the musical character of Deuteronomy, this aspect of his analysis seems ultimately to possess archaeological interest only: it is a «source-oriented inquiry» in different clothing, which may hold relevance only for those who might be interested in the original conditions under which Deuteronomy was proclaimed in Israel, a factor that he seems to recognise[48]. For even if Deuteronomy, like the Homeric epics, was originally oral poetry set to music, by the first century it had become, like the *Iliad* or the *Odyssey*, a literary artifact − a written text, in other words, not a performance piece. Moreover, to Greek-speaking Jews of the Diaspora, Deuteronomy was a text known only in translation. It does not help our understanding of how Greek-speaking first century readers of Deuteronomy would have grasped the work-in-translation to know that some five or six centuries earlier the original work was sung in the public gatherings of Israel.

On the other hand, Christensen's understanding of the structure of Deuteronomy is not entirely without merit: the virtue of his five-part concentric design is that it permits him to perform a «discourse-oriented» analysis; he takes seriously the present form of the text of Deuteronomy. In addition, his analysis relates the discourses which Moses delivers to the narrative in which they are presently found. For it is that narrative which provides the setting from within which the laws of Deuteronomy receive their parenetic force. Thus, Deuteronomy may be more properly analysed as a five-part narrative comprising three extended speeches, which adapts the literary form of the treaty or covenant, and which derives its parenetic value from the fact that the central character of the narrative is the speech-maker.

## 2.2 *Narrative point of view*

Having established the need to examine the narrative structure of Deuteronomy, the issue with which this study must next concern itself is that of the narrative point of view, an issue which has been raised in a particularly acute form by Robert Polzin[49]. While the figure of Moses dominates the narrative of Deuteronomy, and his is the primary point of view from which the events related therein are told, not every reference to Moses is in the first person. Indeed, there are 32 third person references

---

[48] D. L. CHRISTENSEN, *Deuteronomy 1 − 11*, lxii.

[49] R. POLZIN, *Moses and the Deuteronomist*; ID., «Deuteronomy», 92-101.

to Moses, most of which are found in the peripheries of Deuteronomy[50]. Basing his analysis on the difference between reported speech and reporting speech[51], Polzin has attempted to distinguish between the voice of Moses and the voice of the narrator in the Hebrew text of Deuteronomy, a distinction echoed by Cécile Dogniez and Marguerite Harl in their study of the Greek text of Deuteronomy[52]. And while Polzin confines the words of the narrator to a mere fifty-six verses (1:1-5; 2:10-12, 20-23; 3:9, 11, 13b-14; 4:41 – 5:1a; 10:6-7, 9; 27:1a, 9a, 11; 28:69; 29:1a; 31:1, 7a, 9-10a, 14a, 14c-16a, 22-23a, 24-25, 30; 32:44-45, 48; 33:1; 34:1-4a; 5-12)[53], he assigns to the narrator far more importance than these fifty-six verses might lead one to conclude. For Polzin, the most obvious but least important function of the narrator's words is to situate the words of Moses in a particular context[54]. Thus, for instance, the first «speech» of the narrator in Deut 1:1-5 serves to locate the words of Moses in space: «on this side of the Jordan in the desert towards the west near the Red Sea, between Paran, Tophol, and Lobon, and Aulon, and the goldworks» (πέραν τοῦ Ιορδάνου ἐν τῇ ἐρήμῳ πρὸς δυσμαῖς πλησίον τῆς ἐρυθρᾶς ἀνὰ μέσον Φαραν, Τοφολ καὶ Λοβον καὶ Αυλων καὶ Καταχρύσεα)[55], and time: «in the fortieth year, on the first day of the eleventh month» (καὶ ἐγενήθη ἐν τῷ τεσσαρακοστῷ ἔτει ἐν τῷ ἐνδεκάτῳ μηνὶ μιᾷ τοῦ μηνὸς). Beyond this *overt* function, as Polzin calls it, lies what one is tempted to call the *covert* function of the narrative voice, namely, to identify itself as the sole, authentic interpreter of Moses' words[56]. This covert function of the narrative voice tends to relativise the importance of the voice of Moses himself, and to exalt

---

[50] LXX Deut 1:1, 3, 5; 4:41, 44, 45, 46; 5:1; 27:1, 9, 11; 29:1; 31:1, 7, 9, 10, 14, 22, 23, 24, 30; 32:44, 45, 48; 33:1, 4; 34:1, 5, 7, 9, 10, 12.

[51] R. POLZIN, *Moses and the Deuteronomist*, 18-19.

[52] C. DOGNIEZ – M. HARL, *Le Deutéronome*, 77. Hereinafter Dogniez – Harl.

[53] R. POLZIN, *Moses and the Deuteronomist*, 29.

[54] R. POLZIN, *Moses and the Deuteronomist*, 30; ID., «Deuteronomy», 93.

[55] It is important to note, for the sake of accuracy, that the LXX differs from the Hebrew text with respect to the details of place, which reads: «beyond the Jordan in the wilderness, in the Arabah over against Suph, between Paran and Tophel, Laban, Hazeroth, and Dizahab» (בְּעֵבֶר הַיַּרְדֵּן בַּמִּדְבָּר בָּעֲרָבָה מוֹל סוּף בֵּין־פָּארָן וּבֵין־תֹּפֶל וְלָבָן וַחֲצֵרֹת וְדִי זָהָב: Deut 1:1). Such differences in detail, while interesting from the point of view of textual criticism and the history of biblical translation, do not detract from the essential point Polzin is endeavouring to make, namely, that the function of the narrative voice here is locative.

[56] R. POLZIN, *Moses and the Deuteronomist*, 30-31.

the authority of the narrator at Moses' expense, indeed, to present itself as the fulfillment of the Lord's promise in Deut 18:15-18 to raise up another prophet like Moses[57].

It is unlikely that first century readers so would have understood the narrative point of view in the Book of Deuteronomy. Philo, for instance, does not seem to have made any distinction between the narrative voice and that of Moses: in the *VM*, for instance, one of the wonders with which he credits Moses is the ability to have foreseen the circumstances of his own death and burial, and to have revealed them:

> For when he was already being exalted and stood at the very barrier, ready at the signal to direct his upward flight to heaven, the divine spirit fell upon him and he prophesied with discernment while still alive the story of his own death; told ere the end how the end came; told how he was buried with none present, surely by no mortal hands but by immortal powers; how also he was not laid to rest in the tomb of his forefathers but was given a monument of special dignity which no man has ever seen; how all the nation wept and mourned for him a whole month and made open display, private and public, of their sorrow, in memory of his vast benevolence and watchful care for each one of them and for all (*VM* II.291).

Here, Philo assumes that Moses was the author of the entirety of the Book of Deuteronomy and, as such, must also be responsible for those elements of the narrative which depict his death, elements which, of course, Polzin assigns to the narrator. Hence Philo's contention that as wonderful as the prophecies concerning the twelve tribes are (θαυμάσια μὲν οὖν ταῦτα: *VM* II.290), those concerning his own death are «most wonderful» (θαυμασιώτατον: *VM* II.290).

Josephus' description of the death of Moses in the *JA*, based as is that of Philo on the narrative in Deuteronomy, likewise assumes that Moses is the author of the «sacred books» (ἱεραῖς βίβλοις) in which the story of his death is found:

> And, while he bade farewell to Eleazar and Joshua and was yet communing with them, a cloud of a sudden descended upon him and he disappeared in a ravine. But *he has written of himself in the sacred books* that he died, for fear that they should venture to say that by reason of his surpassing virtue he had gone back to the Deity (*JA* IV.326, emphasis mine).

Even more explicitly than Philo, Josephus thinks that Moses is himself responsible for the account of his own death. Philo allows that Moses

---

[57] R. POLZIN, *Moses and the Deuteronomist*, 35-36; ID., «Deuteronomy», 97.

prophesies (προφετεύει: *VM* II.291) his own death; Josephus claims that he actually writes it (γέφραφε: *JA* IV.326). In neither case, however, do either of these first century authors consider the possibility that someone else should have been responsible, either by prophecy, or by the act of writing, for the account of Moses' death. Polzin's distinction between a narrative voice in Deuteronomy and a voice proper to Moses himself thus imposes a reading of the evidence which is foreign to both Philo and Josephus, and which, in any case, was not observed by these two first century authors.

An additional weakness in Polzin's analysis is evident in his treatment of other passages which in his estimation belong to the narrator (2:10-12, 20-23; 3:9, 11, 13b-14), and which he characterizes as «pedantic explanatory remarks»[58]. Less polemically, Moshe Weinfeld refers to these passages as «archaeological notes»[59]. But neither Polzin nor Weinfeld attempts to account for the presence of these remarks or notes. It seems to me that they constitute a way of linking the events related in the narrative to the legendary past, during which giants roamed the land, but also to the present, which preserves the remains of those giants, here, the bed or sarcophagus of Og[60], the king of Bashan (see Deut 3:11). Thus does Moses' first discourse speak to each generation which listens to it: they are invited to marvel at their good fortune to have inherited a land which had once been the dominion of superhuman figures, one of whom had been overcome by Moses himself.

Moreover, what Polzin would dismiss as «pedantic explanatory remarks» introduce into the narrative of Deuteronomy the theme of displacement and replacement. So, for instance, the descendants of Esau displace the Horites in Seir (2:12, 22), and the Ammonites displace the Zamzummim (2:20-21), and the Caphtorim displace the Avvim (2:23): the history of displacement and replacement serves as a kind of foreshadowing of the activity of displacement and replacement in which the Israelites themselves will engage, an activity which is sanctioned by God himself, not just for the Israelites, but also for the Ammonites (2:21b) and the descendants of Esau (2:22). Ultimately, of course, the Israelites themselves will be displaced, first by the succeeding generations (as

---

[58] R. POLZIN, *Moses and the Deuteronomist*, 31; ID., «Deuteronomy», 94.

[59] M. WEINFELD, *Deuteronomy 1 – 11*, 161, 164, 183,

[60] P. CRAIGIE (*Deuteronomy*) translates עֶרֶשׂ as «sarcophagus». See Dogniez – Harl, 130, who allow that κλίνη, like עֶרֶשׂ, may be translated by «sarcophagus».

Moses is replaced by Joshua), and finally, by their enemies as they are scattered among the nations (4:25-31).

## 2.3 *Direct address in Deuteronomy*

From the perspective of a literary-critical, synchronic approach to the question of Moses' character as presented in the narrative of Deuteronomy, no single set of factors are more important than (1) the fact that the book adopts as its primary voice that of Moses himself, and (2) the fact that Moses habitually addresses himself personally to his auditors as «you»[61]. The first factor means that the events and the predictions related therein are filtered through the mediation of Moses. He is the «I» (אָנֹכִי, ἐγώ) of Deuteronomy[62]. Even Polzin holds that

---

[61] For purposes of this study, it makes little difference whether the «you» envisioned in the discourses delivered by Moses in Deuteronomy are singular or plural. Important studies have attempted to distinguish the sources of Deuteronomy on the basis of «singular» and «plural» sources: see, for instance, H. MITCHELL, «The Use of the Second Person in Deuteronomy», 61-109; G. VON RAD, *Studies in Deuteronomy*, 11, n. 1; G. M. DE TILLESSE, «Sections "tu" et sections "vous" dans le Deutéronome», 29-87 or C. T. BEGG, «The Significance of the *Numeruswechsel*», 116-124; but, along with C. M. CARMICHAEL, *The Laws of Deuteronomy*, 30-31; N. LOHFINK, *Das Haupt-gebot*, 239ff.; D. McCARTHY, *Treaty and Covenant*, 158, n. 2; and M. WEINFELD, *Deuteronomy 1–11*, 15, I am convinced that not all the interchanges of second-person singular and plural in Deuteronomy can be so explained. According to Weinfeld, «the change may simply be a didactic device to impress the individual or collective listener, or it may reflect the urge for literary variation» (15). More to the point, it is unlikely that the first-century reader of Deuteronomy would have concerned himself or herself with questions of source; he or she would doubtless have considered the whole of Deuteronomy to be a production of Moses himself.

[62] Some interesting phenomena present themselves: of the 51 verses in which אָנֹכִי appears in the Hebrew text of Deuteronomy, only 6 refer to God (5:6, 9, 31; 18:18; 31:18; 32:40) the remaining instances have Moses as their antecedent (4:1, 2, 8, 22, 40; 5:1, 5; 6:2, 6; 7:11; 8:1, 11; 10:13; 11:8, 13, 22, 26, 27, 28, 32; 12:11, 14, 28; 13:1, 19; 15:5, 11, 15; 19:7, 9; 24:18, 22; 27:18, 22; 27:1, 4, 10; 28:1, 13, 14, 15; 29:13; 30:2, 8; 31:2, 27; 32:46. Similar phenomena may be adduced of the Greek text of Deuteronomy: of the 53 verses in which ἐγώ occurs, only 8 refer to God (5:9, 31; 18:19; 31:18, 21; 32:39, 40, 49); the remainder are references to Moses (4:1, 2, 8, 22, 40; 5:1; 6:2, 6; 7:11; 8:1, 11; 10:13; 11:8, 13, 22, 26, 27, 28, 32; 12:11, 14, 28; 13:1, 19; 15:5, 11, 15; 19:7; 24:18, 20; 27:1, 4, 10; 28:1, 13, 14, 15; 29:13; 30:2, 8, 11, 16; 31:2, 27; 32:46), except for 7:17, in which the antecedent is a fearful Israelite.

the principal role of Moses, as seen in the Book of Deuteronomy, is hermeneutic: he is the book's primary declarer (*maggîd*) and teacher (*mᵉlammed*) of God's word. He not only declares what God has said, he teaches or interprets what the divine words mean for Israel. And he is pictured as doing so in an authoritative manner that was consonant with the status he is pictured as enjoying within the Israelite community[63].

We are a long way from Aune's conception of the rôle of Moses as «essentially tangential». Far from being peripheral to the presentation and explication of the Torah in the book of Deuteronomy, Moses is indispensable to it. Indeed, of the fifty-three verses cited above in which the Mosaic ἐγώ appears, ἐντέλλομαι occurs in thirty-six[64]. Thus has von Rad illuminated an important aspect of the portrait of Moses as he appears in Deuteronomy:

His real office was to pass on to Israel, in the form of a proclaimed word, the word of Jahweh which had been addressed to himself. In Deuteronomy Jahweh still speaks to Israel through the medium of Moses [...] The most impressive corroboration of this all-embracing mediating office of proclamation is of course the fact that the corpus of Deuteronomy is put in the form of the words of Moses (and so not of Jahweh) spoken to Israel[65].

The second factor, Moses' direct address to his auditors, means that in such an interpretative scheme, the reader is put in the same position as the participants in the events and the predictions: indeed, the narrative envisages that Moses addresses himself not only to the Israelites gathered in solemn assembly in the land of Moab, but also to «those who are not here with you today» (καὶ τοῖς μὴ οὖσιν μεθ' ἡμῶν ὧδε σήμερον: Deut 29:14). In this way, the reader becomes the «you» of the narrative; and Moses becomes his or her leader just as surely as he is the leader of the Israelites. Patrick D. Miller has identified this «future-oriented» feature of the Deuteronomic portrait of Moses as part of the concern «for the passing on of the tradition to the next generations, who will not have seen the fire and heard the voice, nor experienced the Lord's provision

---

[63] R. POLZIN, *Moses and the Deuteronomist*, 10.

[64] 4:2, 40; 6:2, 6; 7:11, 17; 8:1, 11; 10:13; 11:8, 13, 22, 27, 28; 12:11, 14, 28; 13:1, 19; 15:5, 11, 15; 19:7; 24:18, 20, 22; 27:1, 4, 10; 28:1, 13, 14, 15; 30:2, 8, 11, 16.

[65] G. VON RAD, *Old Testament Theology*, Vol 1: *The Theology of Israel's Historical Traditions*, 294.

and discipline along the journey, nor heard Moses' exposition of God's will»[66].

There are two seemingly contradictory implications to this arrangement. On the one hand, the readers as «you» are transported back to this crucial moment in Israelite history: the readers recall, as though they themselves were present on the plains of Moab, the events which Moses summons his auditors to remember. The readers, so to speak, dwell in the past. On the other hand, the predictions of future blessing or future woe which Moses makes take on an immediate relevance to the readers: their «present» is the «future» envisaged in the narrative, as in Deut 4:25-31. Thus do the readers confront their own present circumstances. What is more, the authority of Moses and his heirs is undergirded when the readers are able to recognise in their present circumstances the fulfillment of ancient predictions (see Deut 18:21-22).

This paradoxical double focus on the past and the present accounts for much of the rhetorical complexity of Deuteronomy. Readers of Deuteronomy are tugged, as it were, in two directions – backward, to contemplate the *magnalia Dei*, and forward, to anticipate the blessings (and the woes) promised by God[67]. As they travel backward in time, they encounter Moses, whose words about the future seem to refer to their contemporary situation, an encounter which sends them forward in time, back to their own present-day circumstances, there to await the future judgement of God. And regardless of whether that future judgement is one of weal or woe, the authority of Moses is vindicated.

## 3. Moses as prophet in Deuteronomy

The predictive function undertaken by Moses is closely allied to his rôle in Deuteronomy as a prophet. So, for instance, in Deut 31:3-6, after the first announcement of his death, Moses predicts the conquest of the Promised Land:

> The Lord your God who goes before you shall destroy these nations before you, and you shall inherit them: and it shalll be Joshua who goes before your face, as the Lord has spoken. And the Lord your God shall do to them as he did to Seon and Og, the two kings of the Amorites, who were beyond

---

[66] P. D. MILLER, «Moses My Servant», 246.

[67] This contention accords with McCarthy's understanding of the problem of the *Numeruswechsel* in Deuteronomy: «the plural points more to historical memory, the singular to involvement by means of parenesis» (*Treaty and Covenant*, 158, n. 2).

the Jordan, and to their land, as he destroyed them.   And the Lord has delivered them to yo; and you shall do to them as I charged you.  Be courageous and strong; fear not, neither be cowardly nor afraid before their face (ἀνδρίζου καὶ ἴσχυε, μὴ φοβοῦ μηδὲ δειλία μηδὲ πτοηθῇς ἀπὸ προσώπου αὐτῶν: Deut 31:3-6).

The speech serves to encourage the Israelites, and thus is hortatory in intent, as Dogniez – Harl recognise[68]. Hence the translators of the LXX employ the imperative ἀνδρίζου καὶ ἴσχυε in v. 6. But the exhortation to «be manly and strong» is effective precisely insofar it follows on the predictions about which Moses speaks in the future tense regarding the activities of God (vv. 3, 4, 6) and of Joshua (v. 3): God *will destroy* the nations and Joshua *will lead* the people; *therefore* be manly and strong. The promise of future benefits serves as a motive for present virtue.

It should be noted here at the outset of this discussion of the prophetic rôle of Moses in Deuteronomy that the term προφήτης occurs only nine times in the LXX text of Deuteronomy[69], each time translating the Hebrew word נָבִיא; and of those nine verses in the LXX, only three refer to the figure of Moses: Deut 18:15 and 18 both refer to the promise of God to raise up another prophet like Moses; and Deut 34:10, the encomium of Moses which concludes Deuteronomy, claims that «οὐκ ἀνέστη ἔτι προφήτης ἐν Ισραηλ ὡς Μωυσῆς, ὃν ἔγνω κύριος αὐτὸν πρόσωπον κατὰ πρόσωπον».

## 3.1 *Deuteronomy 18:15-19*

Within the greater organizational scheme of Deuteronomy, the divine promise to raise up another prophet like Moses is part of Deut 16:18 – 18:22, a legislative unit which deals with the functions and duties of those who bear office in the theocracy envisioned by Deuteronomy[70]. These officials include the judge (16:18 – 17:13), the king (17:14-20), the Levitical priest (18:1-8), and the prophet (18:9-22).

The section on the prophet commences with a series of prohibitions which enjoin the Israelites against the use of any of the various forms of magic which were employed by their pagan neighbours, and which

---

[68] Dogniez – Harl, 309-310.

[69] Deut 13:2, 4, 6; 18:15, 18, 19, 20, 22; 34:10.

[70] So Driver, 199-320; A. D. H. MAYES, *Deuteronomy*, 261-283; J. BLENKINSOPP, «Deuteronomy», 103.

utilized figures otherwise well known in the ancient world like the diviner (μαντευόμενος μαντείαν: 18:10), the omen-taker (κληδονιζό- μενος: 18:10), the augurer (οἰωνιζόμενος: 18:10), the sorcerer (φαρμα- κός: 18:10) and the enchanter (ἐπαείδων ἐπαοιδήν: 18:11)[71]. E. J. Bic- kerman notes the careful use of language in the LXX and its restriction of the term μάντις and its cognates to heathen soothsaying in the effort to distinguish prophetic service to the Lord from the activities of the pagans[72]. Dogniez – Harl mention that the Greek text of Deuteronomy renders even more strongly than the Hebrew original the fierce opposi- tion between pagan fortune-telling and Hebrew prophecy, thanks to the use of the adversative δέ in 18:14. This strict prohibition against any form of mantic divination or necromancy is what will distinguish Israel from her neighbours[73].

It is only after these manifold forms of soothsaying have been ex- cluded from Israel that the promise of another prophet like Moses is given in verses 15-19[74]. I have already had occasion to mention Robert

---

[71] Dogniez – Harl (50-51) note that the Hebrew original of vv. 10-11 lists eight forms of divination and magic prohibited to the Israelites: the translators of the LXX have rendered קֹסֵם קְסָמִים as μαντευόμενος μαντείαν, מְעוֹנֵן as οἰωνιζόμενος, and מְנַחֵשׁ as κληδονιζόμενος. Both μαντεία and οἰώνισμα were terms well known in Greek-speaking circles for mantic practices; the third term, formed from the noun κληδών, is otherwise unattested, but seems to mean making a prediction on the basis of a noise or an understood word. מְכַשֵּׁף and חֹבֵר חָבֶר, both referring to forms of magic, are rendered by φαρμακὸς and ἐπαείδων ἐπαοιδήν respectively. The last three Hebrew expressions, וְשֹׁאֵל אוֹב וְיִדְּעֹנִי וְדֹרֵשׁ אֶל־הַמֵּתִים, probably all designate forms of necromancy or consultation of the spirits of the dead (if that is, in fact, what the enigmatic term אוֹב means), but are modified in their meaning by the translators of the LXX. The first expression is translated by the Greek word ἐγγαστρίμυθος, literally, «one who speaks with one's womb», and may refer to the possession of an interior voice. The translators of the LXX have modified the meaning of the second Hebrew expression to mean «an observer of prodigies» (τερατοσκόπος). The third Hebrew phrase is rendered literally as «one who questions the dead» (ἐπερωτῶν τοὺς νεκρούς).

[72] E. J. BICKERMAN, Jews, 114.

[73] See G. VON RAD, Deuteronomy, who notes that in the distinction between mantic practices, on the one hand, and the exercise of the prophetic office, on the other, Deuteronomy is demanding «an undivided commitment, without any reinsurance by consulting strange gods, spirits of the dead, etc., to the conditions of fellowship with God» (123).

[74] These particular verses have been the object of a great deal of speculation in the centuries since they were first composed, but it is not the purpose of this section of the study to examine the subsequent interpretation of these verses. The promise to raise up

Polzin's interpretation of the promise to raise up another prophet like Moses: according to Polzin, the «prophet like Moses» is the narrator of Deuteronomy himself, who, by relating the story of Moses' exploits, establishes himself as the one foreseen in Deut 18:15ff, and dons the mantle, so to speak, of Mosaic authority[75]. But this interpretation is too subtle, in my view, and imposes upon the text a reading which is ultimately anachronistic: it is unlikely that the author of Deuteronomy would have subscribed to twentieth century notions like the difference between reported speech and reporting speech.

There are two points to be made about the divine promise to raise up a prophet like Moses: the first point is that the promise occurs twice, the first time directly from Moses to the people (18:15), and the second time, as a reminiscence of the episode at Choreb, in which as a response to the people's fear of God, the promise comes from the Lord himself to Moses (18:18). Structurally, each mention of the promise involves two parties, a speaker who uses the first person singular (ὡς ἐμὲ refers to Moses in v. 15; the Lord is the subject of the verb ἀναστήσω in v. 18) and an audience who is addressed in the second person singular (σου and σοι are references to the people in v. 15; σέ refers to Moses in v. 18). This parallel set of grammatical structures invites the reader to see a kind of functional parallel: what the Lord is to Moses, Moses is to the people. As a prophet, he speaks for the Lord. But the functional parallel is not perfect: Moses' word of promise alone is not enough, which is to say that he does not speak independently of the Lord. Thus so important a promise like the one to raise up a prophet like himself cannot issue from Moses alone: it must have some sort of divine warrant. Hence the need for a second mention of the promise issuing from the Lord himself, which undergirds and guarantees, as it were, the first.

The second point to be made about the promise in Deut 18:15-19 is that within the narrative of Deuteronomy, the promise to raise up another prophet like Moses is an example of «future-oriented» speech. When Moses speaks in vv. 15-16, the promise is directed to «you» (σύ), ostensibly, the Israelites who were with Moses «in Choreb in the day of the assembly» (ἐν Χωρηβ τῇ ἡμέρᾳ τῆς ἐκκλησίας: 18:16) but, in actuality,

---

a prophet like Moses appears twice in the New Testament, Acts 3:22-26 and Acts 7:37. See Ch 5, §1.4.2 below for a discussion of the form and function of these references. For a list of patristic citations regarding the interpretation of Deut 18:15, 18, see Dogniez – Harl, 230-231.

[75] R. POLZIN, *Moses and the Deuteronomist*, 35-36; ID., «Deuteronomy», 97.

the present-day audience who have identified themselves with the Israelites. As the previous discussion about direct address in Deuteronomy has
indicated, first century readers of Deuteronomy would have seen such
a promise as directed particularly to themselves, and thus either would
have awaited in their own time the realization of the promise (e.g., the
expectation of «the prophet» reflected in John 1:21b), or else recognised
in their own time its fulfillment (e.g., Jesus, in the community to which
the sermons in Acts 3:12-26 and 7:2-53 were directed). This understanding of the «future-orientation» of Deut 18:15-19 accords well with the argument urged by A. D. H. Mayes, whose reading of the Hebrew text of
Deuteronomy follows that of Steuernagel, and who understands the
Hiph'il imperfect form of the verb קום in a distributive sense (i.e., that
God will raise up a prophet from time to time), thereby determining the
meaning of the promise in such a way that it becomes

> a general reflection on the history and the significance of prophecy in Israel,
> in which the prophets are understood in relation to Moses and legitimated
> through connection of their proclamation with the law that was given through
> him[76].

Mayes' understanding of the legitimation of prophecy through its connection with the Mosaic law corresponds with Blenkinsopp's contention
that in Deut 18:15-18 not only is Moses understood as a prophet, but
prophecy is redefined as Mosaic[77]. What Mayes' reading of the promise excludes, however, is the interpretation of the promise in its
singular sense, namely, that God will raise up a particular individual
who will be like Moses, into whose mouth he will place his word.

We shall see that the Pastor seems to have understood Paul as the singular fulfillment of the promise to raise up a prophet like Moses[78].
There is a certain sweet irony in the fact that Paul, great opponent of the
Law in his own lifetime, should be posthumously presented in 2 Tim in
the likeness of the one through whom the Law was first given.

## 3.2 *Deuteronomy 34:10-12*

The second explicit identification of Moses as prophet comes in the
concluding encomium of Deuteronomy 34:10-12. If the function of Deut

---

[76] A. D. H. MAYES, *Deuteronomy*, 282.

[77] J. BLENKINSOPP, *The Pentateuch*, 235.

[78] See below, Ch 5, § 1.1.

18:15-19 is to stress the similarity of «the prophet like Moses» to his great predecessor, the function of this statement is to stress Moses' incomparability. A. D. H. Mayes notes that the presentation of Moses in 34:10 «stands in some conflict with 18:18, and can scarcely derive from the same hand»[79]. He concludes that the encomium is the contribution of a post-Deuteronomistic editor, who combined the Deuteronomistic work with the Tetrateuch[80]. Driver, on the other hand, while admitting that at least part of the encomium was the work of another author, claimed that the two passages were not inconsistent with one another, since the comparison in Deut 18:15, 18) involving the use of «like» (כמו, in the Hebrew text and ὡς, ὥσπερ in the corresponding verses of the LXX) in Driver's view expresses similarity, not equality[81]. The divine promise to raise up a prophet «like» Moses, then, does not exclude the incomparability of Moses himself.

The position of this encomium in the narrative of Deuteronomy is important: it is, so to speak, the «last word» on Moses, and may be understood as a summary of all that the figure of Moses means in the Book of Deuteronomy and to the community of Israel. Structurally, the encomium consists of three elements: (1) a statement of the incomparability of Moses, consisting in the fact that the Lord knew him face to face (ὃν ἔγνω κύριος αὐτὸν πρόσωπον κατὰ πρόσωπον: 34:10), (2) the first of two specific notices of Moses' incomparability, this one mentioning «all the signs and prodigies» (πᾶσι τοῖς σημείοις καὶ τέρασιν) which Moses wrought in Egypt (34:11), and (3) the next one of which mentions the «great wonders and the mighty hand which Moses displayed before all Israel (τὰ θαυμάσια τὰ μεγάλα καὶ τὴν χεῖρα τὴν κραταιάν, ἃ ἐποίησεν Μωυσῆς ἔναντι παντὸς Ισραηλ: 34:12).

George W. Coats identifies the claim in 34:10 that Moses alone is known by God πρόσωπον κατὰ πρόσωπον as an element of his heroic greatness, precisely because such an intimate relationship between God and a human being had not been known before Moses, and would not be known again[82]. Without denying Coats his thesis of Mosaic heroism, it seems arbitrary, in my opinion, for Coats to consider such intimacy as a particular expression of heroism. Moses' heroics are expressed by

[79] A. D. H. MAYES, *Deuteronomy*, 413.

[80] A. D. H. MAYES, *Deuteronomy*, 47, 413-414.

[81] Driver, 425.

[82] G. W. COATS, «Legendary Motifs», 37.

the author of this encomium, it seems to me, in his conduct before the Egyptians and his great wonders for his own people.

There is, accordingly, a double focus to this concluding encomium in Deuteronomy: Moses is great, first of all, because of the exploits done in the face of his enemies in Egypt, and, secondly, because of those accomplished on behalf of his people. We shall see, when we turn to the analysis of the figure of Paul as he appears in the implied narrative of 2 Tim, that there is a similar double focus to his greatness, and a similar attention paid to his conduct before his enemies as well as his care for his people[83].

## 3.3 *Review of scholarship*

Thus, despite the relative paucity of explicit references to the prophetic rôle of Moses in Deuteronomy, it is not inappropriate so to view the person of Moses. Certainly, both contemporary readers of Deuteronomy as well as the ancients have done so. Quite apart from these two passages which explicitly ascribe the title prophet to Moses, the portrait of Moses which emerges in the last four chapters of Deuteronomy depicts the dying Moses undertaking the functions traditionally discharged by the prophet. He announces the word of the Lord (31:1, 3); he calls the people to obedience (31:10-13); he predicts future blessings if they do obey (32:46-47), and future woes if they do not (31:29); he even engages in the traditional prophetic lawsuit (32:1-43). True, none of his speeches in these four chapters are prefaced by the traditional prophetic preamble «thus says the Lord»[84], but the narrative context makes it clear that the message he announces is one which he received from the Lord[85].

---

[83] See 2 Tim 2:10; 4:17; and below, Ch 5, § 1.1.2.

[84] The Hebrew expression כֹּה אָמַר יהוה is generally rendered τάδε λέγει κύριος in the LXX (e.g., Ex 7:17, where Moses threatens Pharaoh that the waters of the Nile will be changed into blood; see also 2 Sam 12:7; Amos 1:6, etc.). Occasionally, there are variant translations of the prophetic preamble, such as οὕτος λέγει κύριος (eg., Is 37:33; Jer 14:10) or, more simply still, εἶπεν κύριος (e.g., Amos 1:3).

[85] God commands, for instance, that Moses «write the words of this song and teach it to the sons of Israel» (καὶ νῦν γράψατε τὰ ῥήματα τῆς ᾠδῆς ταύτης καὶ διδάξετε αὐτὴν τοὺς υἱοὺς Ισραηλ: Deut 31:19) and Moses carries out the command immediately (Deut 32:1-43). In a similar fashion, Moses' prediction of the future transgressions of the people in Deut 31:29 should be seen as a summary statement of the more detailed prediction of future transgression which the Lord makes in Deut 31:16-21.

Patrick Miller maintains that the certain features of the Mosaic portrait in Deuteronomy are «consonant with the prophetic experience and understanding as we see it elsewhere», especially in the book of the prophet Amos. In particular, he sees in Moses' function as an intercessor a reflection of his prophetic rôle, and identifies three features which the image of Moses as prophetic intercessor has in common with Amos as intercessor (Amos 7:1-3): (1) both figures appeal to God's mercy despite an extensive pattern of rebelliousness on the part of the people; (2) both figures appeal to various aspects of God's character, i.e., his faithfulness; and (3) both figures succeed in changing God's mind, a result which is startling, says Miller, since it cuts against the grain of our understanding of God as beyond change[86].

It seems to me, first of all, that Miller's understanding of the immutability of God owes rather more to Plotinus than it does to the prophets. Moreover, those features which Miller claims as common to both Moses and Amos are also ones shared by other figures identified as prophets in the literature of the Old Testament: one notes in this context, for instance, James Muilenburg's observation that Samuel plays the part of intercessor between God and the people at the gathering of «all Israel» at Gilgal (1 Sam 12:1-25), that, indeed, in 1 Samuel he is presented as a second Moses[87]. Despite these shortcomings in his presentation, Miller nevertheless has identified an important facet of the prophetic dimension of the figure of Moses in Deuteronomy. We shall see that the intercessory function of Moses' prophetic rôle is an important factor in the presentation of the figure of Moses in the $TM$[88], and, in addition, may well have influenced the Pastor's depiction of the dying Paul in 2 Tim[89].

True to his concerns for the process by which the Book of Deuteronomy was formed, von Rad thought that the prophetic dimension of the figure of Moses owed something to the circumstances under which the work originated. Even though he held that Deuteronomy had originated in Levitical circles[90], he contended that insofar as the book demonstrated an affinity with the thought of the prophets, it was because «the faith of that time had the phenomenon of prophecy so strongly stamped

---

[86] P. D. MILLER, «Moses My Servant», 251.

[87] J. MUILENBURG, «Form and Structure», 360-364.

[88] See $TM$ 11:11, 14, 16-19.

[89] See 2 Tim 1:3, and below, Ch 5, § 1.1.

[90] G. VON RAD, *Deuteronomy*, 24-25.

upon it that it would be rather surprising if so broadly based a presentation of the faith had been able to escape this contemporary influence»[91].

E. W. Nicholson, on the other hand, makes a claim for the direct prophetic origin of Deuteronomy, contending that the work emerged from the teachings of the prophetic party in northern Israel[92]. He adduces three factors in particular to support his case: first of all, both Deuteronomy and the northern prophets share a common concern for the observance of covenant law, for the sacral institution of holy war, and for charismatic leadership at the expense of the institution of kingship[93]; secondly, Nicholson sees several points of contact between Deuteronomy and the prophecies of Hosea, especially in the references to God's love for Israel (Deut 7:7-8; Hos 11:1)[94]; thirdly, Nicholson thinks that Deuteronomy's portrayal of Moses as a covenant mediator betrays the book's northern origin, where such an office would have been held by a prophet who proclaimed the covenant law to the people[95].

R. E. Clements, however, raises the objection to Nicholson's thesis that although Deuteronomy speaks favourably of the prophets as a whole, «the rôle that it ascribes to them hardly gives them a very magisterial position. They are [...] little better than soothsayers and diviners»[96]. Clements holds that respectful and admiring of the prophets though the authors of Deuteronomy may have been, the Deuteronomists were not prophets themselves: «[t]hey do not speak in the manner of prophets, and they consistently interpret the rôle of the prophets in a very distinctive way. They make them out to be educationalists and national reformers, and they display almost nothing of the highly articulate prophetic speech forms»[97]. These are telling objections, and

---

[91] G. VON RAD, *Studies in Deuteronomy*, 69; see also *Deuteronomy*, 25. This conjecture respecting the original circles in which Deuteronomy developed was not one with which Weinfeld, for instance, was willing to agree, preferring instead the supposition that Deuteronomy was composed by court scribes or wise men between the reigns of Hezekiah and Josiah. See M. WEINFELD, *Deuteronomy and the Deuteronomic School*, 158ff.; ID., «Deuteronomy – The Present State of Inquiry», 253-254.

[92] E. W. NICHOLSON, *Deuteronomy and Tradition*, 58ff.

[93] E. W. NICHOLSON, *Deuteronomy and Tradition*, 47-50.

[94] E. W. NICHOLSON, *Deuteronomy and Tradition*, 70.

[95] E. W. NICHOLSON, *Deuteronomy and Tradition*, 76-79.

[96] R. E. CLEMENTS, *Deuteronomy*, 78.

[97] R. E. CLEMENTS, *Deuteronomy*, 78.

Clements is probably correct in warning scholars against the temptation to identify the authors of Deuteronomy with any single professional class in ancient Israel: «[w]e can best think of a "Reforming Party" with members drawn from more than one group of leading citizens»[98].

But whether Deuteronomy originated among the Levites of the Judaean countryside, as von Rad thought, or in northern prophetic circles, as Nicholson thinks, or even among the «Reforming Party» of Israel's élite, as Clements thinks, is less important for the purpose of this study than the fact that, in the first century, Moses was viewed as a prophet. That first century view of Moses rests on an understanding of two great discourses from the Book of Deuteronomy in which Moses implicitly speaks as a prophet. Those two discourses are the Song of Moses (Deut 32:1-43) and the Blessing of Moses (Deut 33:1-29).

### 3.4 *Deuteronomy 32, the Song of Moses*

Form-critical considerations have long moved scholars to recognise that the Song of Moses, Deut 32:1-43, is an interpolation into the Book of Deuteronomy[99], though for the purposes of this discussion, when the Song was composed is less important than the fact that here it is placed on the lips of Moses himself. First century readers would doubtless have seen in the Song an expression of Moses' prophetic gifts if for no other reason than he speaks therein of what will befall the Israelites as a result of their infidelity. If the depiction of an Israel beset by hunger (v. 24) and the sword (v. 25), abandoned by God (v. 20) and sent into exile (v. 26), were not sufficiently sobering, the fact that it is Moses who draws the picture makes the prospect all the more somber: the seriousness of the message is heightened by the status of the messenger. Any examination of the prophetic image of Moses in Deuteronomy, then, must analyse the Song of Moses, together with its influence on the subsequent literature, especially the legends of the last words of Moses which survive from the first century.

---

[98] R. E. CLEMENTS, *Deuteronomy*, 79.

[99] See, for instance, Driver's long discussion regarding the date of the Song to the age of Ezekiel and Jeremiah, i.e., *ca.* 630 B.C.E. (345-348). But O. EIßFELDT, *The Old Testament*, basing his estimation on the character of the enemies who beset Israel in the Song of Moses, dates the Song to the mid-eleventh century B.C.E. W. F. ALBRIGHT, («Some Remarks on the Song of Moses», 339-346), suggests on the basis of archaic morphology and vocabulary that the Song should be dated to a period not later than the tenth century B.C.E. (346).

A number of scholars have acknowledged that the Song of Moses is a typical form of prophetic speech, namely, the prophetic lawsuit or רִיב[100]. But James R. Boston, who adopts Weinfeld's hypothesis of a scribal origin for Deuteronomy[101], claims that the Song of Moses owes much to the royal wisdom traditions[102]. Certainly, there are motifs in the Song of Moses which resemble those of the didactic psalms[103]: the exordium which calls upon heaven and earth as witnesses (vv. 1-3) is reminiscent of the invocation of the teacher which is so characteristic of wisdom literature in general, and didactic wisdom poetry in particular[104]. This is followed by a statement of praise for God's fidelity and justice (v. 4), after which the Song moves towards its indictment of Israel (v. 5-6), which is expressly condemned for its lack of wisdom: «Do you thus recompense the Lord, foolish and unwise people?» (ταῦτα κυρίῳ ἀνταποδίδοτε οὕτω, λαὸς μωρὸς καὶ οὐχὶ σοφός: 32:5). Israel's faithlessness is contrasted to the goodness of God by means of an historical retrospect, which rehearses God's actions on behalf of Israel (vv. 7-15a), juxtaposing them with Israel's abandonment of God (vv. 15b-18). The influence of the wisdom tradition may be felt here, too: frequently, historical events become examples for instruction in wisdom

---

[100] See, for example, H. B. HUFFMON, «The Covenant Lawsuit»; J. HARVEY, «Le "Rib-pattern", réquisitoire prophétique»; G. E. WRIGHT, «The Lawsuit of God»; C. WESTERMANN, *Basic Forms of Prophetic Speech*. An important dissenting voice to the critical consensus that the Song of Moses represents an example of the prophetic lawsuit is that of G. E. MENDENHALL, «Samuel's Broken *Rîb*», who holds that, far from being a covenant lawsuit, the Song of Moses is a prophetic oracle responding to the destruction of Shiloh (66), which was composed by the prophet Samuel (68). But whether the Song is a lawsuit or an oracle is less important for the purposes of this study than the fact that it is an expression of prophetic consciousness.

[101] See M. WEINFELD, «Deuteronomy — The Present State of Inquiry», 253-257.

[102] J. R. BOSTON, «The Wisdom Influence», 198-202.

[103] For a complete explanation of the characteristics of the didactic psalm, see H. J. KRAUS, *Psalms 1–59*, 58-60. Over forty years ago, in his work with the Hebrew text of the Song, P. Skehan thought the writer deliberately designed his composition on an alphabetic pattern of 69 verses, that is, three times the number of letters in the Hebrew alphabet from א to ת with the letter פ added again at the end to close the cycle. Such alphabetic designs are frequently found in wisdom psalms, as, for example, Ps 119. See P. SKEHAN, «The Structure of the Song of Moses». Interesting and ingenious as his theory is, the alphabetic pattern which he identified is entirely absent, of course, from the Greek text of the Song.

[104] J. R. BOSTON, «The Wisdom Influence», 198; H. J. KRAUS, *Psalms 1–59*, 60.

literature, as in Ps 78 with which the Song of Moses has many affinities[105]. God punishes them (vv. 19-26) by means of their enemy, the «no-nation» (οὐκ ἔθνει: v. 21), but then turns against the «no-nation» (vv. 27-42). Finally, the Song ends with a peroration (vv. 43), inviting the heavens (οὐρανοί), the angels (ἄγγελοι), and the Gentiles (ἔθνη) to rejoice in God.

The evidence which Boston adduces in favour of his thesis is persuasive, but it does not invalidate the claim that the Song of Moses may be seen as a particular expression of the prophetic gifts of Moses. Even Boston himself seems to recognise this, and cautions against drawing too sharp a line between the wise man and the prophet[106].

A literary analysis of the Song reveals that at the heart of the poem is a two-part scheme: after the prefatory material which functions as a kind of invocation (vv. 1-7), the Song sounds its first primary theme, the recital of *what has happened* (vv. 8-19). This section is itself divided in two, with the first retrospective relating what God has done for Israel (vv. 8-15a), which is here referred to as «the beloved» (ὁ ἠγαπημένος: v. 15), a term which translates the Hebrew יְשֻׁרוּן, a word which evidently derives from יָשַׁר, to be straight or right[107]. The second retrospective recounts Israel's unfaithful response (vv. 15b-18). 32:19-20 constitute the transition to the second great theme of the Song, the prediction of *what will happen* «in the last days» (ἐπ' ἐσχάτων), a transition which is signalled by a shift to the future tense: «I will turn away my face from them, and will show what will happen to them in the last days» ('Αποστρέψω τὸ πρόσωπόν μου ἀπ' αὐτῶν καὶ δείξω τί ἔσται αὐτοῖς ἐπ' ἐσχάτων: 32:20a). This predictive section is divided in three, with the first prediction foretelling what punishments will befall Israel (vv. 20b-26), the second predicting what vengeance will be taken against the «no-

---

[105] See H. J. KRAUS, *Psalms 60–150*, 59.

[106] J. R. BOSTON, «The Wisdom Influence», 202.

[107] M. J. MULDER, *TDOT*, 472-477, s.v. יְשֻׁרוּן. H. W. F. GENESIUS, (*Hebrew and Chaldee Lexicon*, 376; s.v. יְשֻׁרוּן) thought that perhaps יְשֻׁרוּן might have been a diminutive for יִשְׂרָאֵל. G. VON RAD (*Deuteronomy*) admitted the need for further elucidation of the meaning of the term, but was certain that it was an honourable title for Israel (199). Whatever specific meaning the term might have had in Hebrew, it is clear that the translators of the LXX thought it had something to do with being beloved. Indeed, Dogniez – Harl contend that the Greek participle ἠγαπημένος modified the motif of Israel's privilege in such a way that for the translators of the LXX it was not Israel's rectitude but God's love which made Israel his Chosen People (329).

nation» (vv. 27-35), and the third prophesying the eventual vindication of Israel (vv. 36-42). The Song ends with a coda of praise (vv. 43)[108].

The literary organisation of the Song thus may be charted as follows:

|      |                                                   |             |
|------|---------------------------------------------------|-------------|
| I.   | Prefatory Material                                | 32:1-7      |
| II.  | First Theme: *what has happened*                  | 32:8-18     |
|      | A.  God's actions                                 | 32:8-15a    |
|      | B.  Israel's response                             | 32:15b-18   |
| III. | Transition: the Lord's response                   | 32:19-20a   |
| IV.  | Second Theme: *what will happen*                  | 32:20b-42   |
|      | A.  Israel's punishment by the «no-nation»        | 32:20b-26   |
|      | B.  God's vengeance upon the «no-nation»          | 32:27-35    |
|      | C.  Israel's vindication                          | 32:36-42    |
| V.   | Coda                                              | 32:43       |

The bipartite narrative of *what has happened* and *what will happen* outlined in the Song implies an understanding of God and of human history which has been enormously influential: we shall see, when we turn to the *LAB* and the *TM* that the three-fold predictive scheme of punishment, vengeance, and vindication controls the prophetic understanding of Israel's destiny as it is enunciated in those two works.

## 3.5 *Deuteronomy 33, the Blessing of Moses*

Since, in Philo and Josephus, no single utterance of Moses was cited more frequently as an example of Mosaic prophecy than the Blessing of Moses found in Deut 33[109], it seems appropriate to examine that work

---

[108] Dogniez – Harl call it a «final acclamation» (340).

[109] Despite (or perhaps, precisely because of) the obscurity of the Blessing of Moses, both in the Hebrew original and in the Greek text of Deuteronomy, the work was thought of by Philo and Josephus as an example of prophecy. In the *VM*, for instance, Philo alludes to a series of prophecies Moses makes when he is at the point of death: «Then, indeed, we find him possessed, no longer uttering general truths to the whole nation but prophesying to each tribe in particular the things which were to be and hereafter must come to pass» (τότε δὴ κατασχεθεὶς οὐκέτι συλλήβδην ἀθρόῳ παντὶ τῷ ἔθνει θεσπίζειν ἔοικεν ἀλλὰ καὶ κατὰ μέρος ἑκάστῃ φυλῇ τὰ μέλλοντα γενέσθαι καὶ αὖθις ἀποβησόμενα: *VM* II.288). On the other hand, in his treatise on φιλανθρωπία, Philo seems to have understood the Blessing of Moses as a series of benedictions and supplications on behalf of his people: «Then after accomplishing the preparations for his departure he did not set out for his new home until he had honoured all the tribes of his nation [numbering twelve] with the concent of his benedictions, mentioning the founders of the tribes by name [...] What he had himself he gave them ready for their use, what he did not possess, he supplicated God to grant them, knowing that though

at this juncture. From a form-critical perspective, the Blessing of Moses is a collection of formerly independent sayings about each of the tribes[110]. Each of the tribes of Israel, Simeon excepted, receives some sort of mention in the Blessing, and the literary form of each saying, as von Rad recognised, is one in which «the characteristics and distinctive features of a tribe are conveyed in general sayings of praise or blame»[111]. But even so resolute a practitioner of the historical-critical method as von Rad recognises that whatever the original settings for the individual blessings might have been, the poem in its present narrative context now represents the final words of the dying Moses, and as such, «is much more than an empty wish. [The Blessing] contains creative words which are able to shape the future»[112]. This future orientation of the Blessing is largely a function of its literary form: verbs in the future tense predominate, and the grammatical mood is largely subjunctive.

Formally, the Blessing is tripartite: 33:1-5 constitute, as Driver recognised[113], an introduction or exordium to the individual blessings (vv.

---

the fountains of his grace are perennial they are not free for all, but only to suppliants: (εἶθ' ἑτοιμασάμενος τὰ πρὸς ἔξοδον οὐ πρότερον ἐστείλατο τὴν ἀποικίαν ἢ τὰς τοῦ ἔθνους φυλὰς ἁπάσας εὐχαῖς ἐναρμονίοις [ἀριθμῷ δώδεκα] γεράραι διὰ τῆς τῶν φυλάρχων κατακλήσεως [...] ἃ μὲν αὐτὸς εἶχεν, ἐξ ἑτοίμου διδούς, ἃ δὲ μὴ κέκτητο, τὸν θεὸν ἱκετεύων παρασχεῖν, εἰδὼς τὰς τῶν χαρίτων αὐτοῦ πηγὰς ἀενάους μὲν οὔσας, οὐ πᾶσι δ' ἀνειμένας, ἀλλὰ μόνοις ἱκέταις: De Virtutibus 77-79).

The distinction between prophecy and benediction does not seem to have been an exclusive one in the first century, however, for in a similar fashion Josephus understands the Blessing of Moses as both a prophecy and a blessing: «When Moses, at the close of life, had thus spoken, and, with benedictions (μετ' εὐλογίας), had prophesied (προφητεύσαντος) to each of the tribes the things that in fact were to come to pass, the multitude burst into tears, while the women, too, with beating of the breast, manifested their emotion at his approaching death» (JA IV.320). As in the VM, it is clear that here Josephus has Deut 33 in mind, since Moses prophesies to «each of the tribes» (ἑκάστῃ τῶν φυλῶν) what is to come; moreover, since he couples the expression «with benedictions» (μετ' εὐλογίας) with the verb «had prophesied» (προφητεύσαντος), it is also clear that, like Philo, he thinks of Deut 33 as both a prophecy and a blessing. In both Philo and Josephus, as we shall see, the ability of Moses to predict what will happen is a particular manifestation of his prophetic gifts. Here, however, it has become clear that prediction does not exhaust the prophetic gifts of Moses. To bless is evidently for both Philo and Josephus an exercise of the prophetic rôle.

[110] O. EIßFELDT, The Old Testament, 228-229.

[111] G. VON RAD, Deuteronomy, 205. See also Driver, 385.

[112] G. VON RAD, Deuteronomy, 205.

[113] Driver, 385.

6-25), and vv. 26-29 constitute the general conclusion. Following von Rad[114], Duane Christensen thinks that the introduction and conclusion to the Blessing was originally an independent, two-stanza hymn which the arranger of Deuteronomy 33 used to frame the individual blessings[115]. The two stanzas, that is, the introduction and the conclusion to the Blessing, are tied together by another mention of the «beloved one» (ἠγαπημένῳ: v. 5; θεὸς τοῦ ἠγαπημένου: v. 26), which here, as in the Song of Moses (Deut 32:15), evidently refers to Israel.

This introduction itself comprises an *incipit*, a recapitulative summary, and a prediction. 33:1 constitutes the *incipit* of the blessing, identifying Moses as the bestower of the blessing, the Israelites as its beneficiaries, as well as providing a temporal reference to the narrative setting, namely before Moses' death (πρὸ τῆς τελευτῆς αὐτοῦ). Moses is referred to in this *incipit* as «the man of God» (ἄνθρωπος τοῦ θεοῦ: 33:1), as has already been noted in connection with the discussion of the indirect references to Moses in 2 Tim. In the larger narrative context of Deuteronomy, this title exercises a summary function, referring not so much to any particular facet of Moses' relationship to God, or to any particular office he occupies in the community; rather, the title ἄνθρωπος τοῦ θεοῦ sums up in one compact phrase the totality of the Mosaic ministry: to his community, he represents God, and to God, he represents his community[116]. A similar summary sense seems to be at work in 2 Tim 3:17. Within the immediate narrative context of the Blessing of Moses,

---

[114] G. VON RAD, *Deuteronomy*, 205.

[115] D. L. CHRISTENSEN, «Two Stanzas of a Hymn in Deuteronomy 33», 382-389. Christensen detects a concentric design in the Hebrew text of Deut 33:2-4 which he outlines as follows (388):

A    YHWH's March of Conquest from the Southland (2-3c)
  B    He upholds the pronouncements entrusted to you (3d)
  B'   His Torah is your heritage (4)
A'   YHWH's reign in Jeshurun (5)

Likewise, he sees a concentric design to Deut 33:26-29a (388):

A    There is no god like «El» (26)
  B    He is a refuge (27a)
  B'   He is a warrior/deliverer (27b-28)
A'   There is no people like Israel, a people delivered by YHWH (29a)

Interesting and persuasive as these analyses are, they are, ultimately, of little help in the understanding of the Greek text of Deuteronomy 33, given the wide divergence of the Greek from the Hebrew original.

[116] For a summary of how the title was understood by the Fathers, see Dogniez – Harl, 343.

however, the title ἄνθρωπος τοῦ θεοῦ takes on a more specific connotation: since here the man of God is at the point of death, his words of blessing concerning those who will survive him take on a prophetic character.

33:2-4 constitute a recapitulative summary. Dogniez – Harl admit that these verses in Hebrew constitute some of the most difficult and obscure passages in all of the Pentateuch, with rare words and elliptical turns of phrase[117]. It must be admitted that the Greek version does not lack obscurity, not so much because of its vocabulary as for its shifting pronominal references. The implicit subject of «he said» (εἶπεν) in 33:2 is, presumably, Moses, since he is the subject of the preceding verse. Thus, all that follows purports to issue from the mouth of Moses. Likewise, the implicit subject of «has appeared» (ἐπέφανεν) in 33:2 must be the Lord, since he is the subject of the preceding verb «is come» (ἥκει). The Lord continues as the subject of the next two succeeding verbs, «has hasted» (κατέσπευσεν, 33:2) and «spared» (ἐφείσατο, 33:3a), until 33:3b when, thanks to a shift from the third person to the second («*your* hands» χεῖράς σου), the reference becomes obscure. Here, the second person possessive σου must refer to the Lord, since it is hardly likely that the «sanctified ones» (οἱ ἡγιασμένοι) should be under (ὑπό) any other hands save those of the Lord, given the synonymous parallel structures which liken the people of 33:3a (τοῦ λαοῦ) to the holy ones (οἱ ἡγιασμένοι) of 33:3b. In a similar fashion, σέ in 33:3c must also refer to the Lord, since οὗτοι refers to the holy ones who are under (ὑπό) the one so addressed.

The obscurity brought on by shifting pronominal references is compounded in 33:3d-4: «and he received of his words the law which Moses charged us, an inheritance to the assemblies of Jacob» (καὶ ἐδέξατο ἀπὸ τῶν λόγων αὐτοῦ νόμον, ὃν ἐνετείλατο ἡμῖν Μωυσῆς, κληρονομίαν συναγωγαῖς Ιακωβ). The implicit subject of ἐδέξατο cannot be the Lord, even though the Lord is the subject of the previous verse; the subject of ἐδέξατο must be Moses, even though the putative speaker of the Blessing is Moses himself, and even though Moses is explicitly named in 33:4. The introduction of the first person plural pronoun in the dative, ἡμῖν, serves only to complicate the matter further. Under ordinary circum-

---

[117] Dogniez – Harl, 343. W. F. ALBRIGHT («Remarks on the Song of Moses», 346) has characterised the language of the Blessing of Moses as «replete with extreme archaisms», a characteristic which renders the usual complications of exegesis and interpretation even more problematic.

stances, such a usage might well serve as an indication of the speaker of the Blessing. But this cannot be so, since the *incipit* has already named Moses as the speaker.

There is another possible antecedent for ἡμῖν in 33:4a, namely the congregation at which the Blessing is directed. Ugo Vanni's studies of liturgical dialogue in the Book of Revelation have drawn attention to the various literary phenomena typical of liturgical dialogue: these phenomena include the alternation of proclamation and response, repetition of *verba dicendi* attributed to different subjects, and a shift from the second person to the first[118]. While not all of these phenomena are present in this pericope, the various shifts in person, coupled with the *incipit* of 33:1 which may function here as a proclamatory form, suggests the possibility of a liturgical setting for the Blessing of Moses. Anthony Phillips even goes so far as to identify the specific liturgical occasion on which the Blessing might have been recited originally, namely, the enthronement festival[119]. By the first century, however, such festivals had long ago fallen into disuse, and the liturgical occasion must have altered considerably. I have already mentioned the double focus of the entirety of the Book of Deuteronomy in its attention to the present and future audiences which hear the word. Given the attention which Deuteronomy displays towards these audiences, ἡμῖν may well refer to those who hear the proclamation of the Blessing, and who appropriate the promises of the Blessing to themselves, on whatever liturgical occasion this proclamation may have occurred.

Despite the obscurities brought on by the shifting pronominal references, it seems clear that what is being described in 33:2-4 is the whole of what we have come to call the Exodus-event, meaning by that term the escape by the Sea, the wanderings in the desert, and the bestowal of the Law at Sinai[120]. This recapitulative summary provides the theological rationale for the blessings which follow in the same way, for instance, that the first three chapters of the Book of Deuteronomy provide the historical rationale for the exhortation of 4:1-40[121]: the

---

[118] See U. VANNI, «Un esempio di dialogo liturgico», 453-467; ID., *L'Apocalisse*, 101-114; ID., «Liturgical Dialogue», 348-372.

[119] A. PHILLIPS, *Deuteronomy*, 227.

[120] See F. M. CROSS, *Canaanite Myth and Hebrew Epic*, 156, who holds, however, that the introduction to the Blessing of Moses rehearses only the march from Sinai northward, which is to say the Conquest proper.

[121] R. E. CLEMENTS, *Deuteronomy*, 34.

wonders which God has accomplished in the past are but a preface to what he will accomplish in the future[122].

The shift from the recapitulative summary of 33:2-4 to the prediction of 33:5 («And he shall be prince with the beloved one, when the princes of the people are gathered together with the tribes of Israel:» καὶ ἔσται ἐν τῷ ἠγαπημένῳ ἄρχων συναχθέντων ἀρχόντων λαῶν ἅμα φυλαῖς Ισραηλ) is signaled by a change to the future tense. The meaning of the verse, apart from the question of the adequacy of the translation of יְשֻׁרוּן by ἠγαπημένῳ, is obscured by the problem of the shifting pronominal reference here, too. It is not at all clear what the implicit subject of ἔσται is supposed to be. The choices should probably be limited to two: Moses, since he is the subject of the antecedent clause, or the Lord, since he is the subject of the previous sentence[123]. It is not necessary here, however, to choose between these alternatives: whatever the original significance of the verse in Hebrew was[124], the transformation from a converted Qal imperfect third masculine singular (וַיְהִי בִישֻׁרוּן מֶלֶךְ: «thus he became king of his darling», [NAB]; «there arose a king in Jeshurun», [NRSV]; «there was a king in Jeshurun», [NJB]) to a future indicative in the LXX (Καὶ ἔσται ἐν τῷ ἠγαπημένῳ ἄρχων: «and he will be prince with the beloved«) renders a completely different significance to the verse, and not just because of the translation of יְשֻׁרוּן by ἠγαπη-μένῳ, but, more particularly, because an historical observation (what *has* happened) has been transformed into a statement about the future (what *will* happen).

The blessings of each of the tribes follow the introduction of 33:1-5. Eight of the blessings directed to the individual tribes are characterised by the following structure: the tribe is identified by an *adscriptio* in the dative case (τῷ Λευι, 33:8; τῷ Βενιαμιν, 33:12; τῷ Ιωσηφ, 33:13; τῷ Ζαβουλων, 33:18; τῷ Γαδ, 33:20; τῷ Δαν, 33:22; τῷ Νεφθαλι, 33:23; τῷ Ασηρ, 33:24), followed by the verb εἶπεν («he said») and then the speci-

---

[122] For a discussion of the question of the literary unity of Deut 4, as well as its relation to the first three chapters of Deuteronomy, see C. T. BEGG, «The Literary Criticism of Deut 4, 1-40»; A. D. H. MAYES, «Deuteronomy 4».

[123] Dogniez – Harl (343-344) provide a convenient summary of the targumic, rabbinic, and patristic readings of the verse.

[124] There is good reason, in view of the anti-monarchical bias which pervades the whole of Deuteronomy, and the symbolic rôle which Moses plays as a source of alternative authority, to think that Deut 33:5 originally pointed to a time when someone else – God or Moses – reigned over Israel. See R. E. CLEMENTS, *Deuteronomy*, 37-38.

fic words of blessing. By contrast, the blessing directed to Judah is introduced by a demonstrative *incipit*: καὶ αὕτη Ιουδα, 33:7; and the blessings directed to Reuben (33:6), and Ephraim and Manasseh (33:17) lack any sort of introductory formulae. Some of the blessings are quite brief[125]; others are rather more lengthy[126]. Mayes draws attention to the following characteristics[127]: the sayings which comprise the Blessing sometimes personify the tribe in its eponymous ancestor[128]; sometimes it is the tribe itself which stands in the foreground[129]; sometimes the blessings are strongly Yahwistic[130]; but some of the sayings reflect no religious content whatsoever[131].

The blessing of Reuben (Deut 33:6) may be characterised as more of a wish than a blessing *per se*[132]. Specifically, the wish is for numerical augmentation: «Let Reuben live and not die, and let him be many in number» (ζήτω Ρουβην καὶ μὴ ἀποθανέτω καὶ ἔστω πολὺς ἐν ἀριθμῷ). Such a wish, whatever its historical foundation[133], doubtless reflects the theological conviction that the promises extended to the people as a whole through the patriarchs, specifically the promise of numerous descendants to Abraham (Gen 15:1-6; 17:1-8; 22:17), to Isaac (Gen 26:2-5, 24) and to Jacob (Gen 28:13-15; 35:9-12) should also embrace a particular segment of the people, here the tribe of Reuben.

The blessing of Judah (Deut 33:7) is formally a prayer for help from the Lord: «Hear, Lord, the voice of Judah, and visit his people» (εἰσάκουσον, κύριε, φωνῆς Ιουδα, καὶ εἰς τὸν λαὸν αὐτοῦ εἰσέλθοισαν), followed by a guarantee of divine aid: «His hands shall contend for him, and you shall be a help from his enemies» (αἱ χεῖρες αὐτοῦ διακρινοῦσιν αὐτῷ, καὶ βοηθὸς ἐκ τῶν ἐχθρῶν αὐτοῦ ἔσῃ). What kind of help is being

---

[125] For example, Reuben (33:6), which comprises only 10 words in Greek, or Dan (33:22), which comprises only 12 words.

[126] For example Levi (33:8-11), and Joseph (33:13-17).

[127] See A. D. H. MAYES, *Deuteronomy*, 397.

[128] For example, vv. 8 (Levi), 12 (Benjamin), 22 (Dan), 24 (Asher).

[129] For example, vv. 6 (Reuben), 7 (Judah), 13 (Joseph), 18 (Zebulon), 20 (Gad), 23 (Naphthali).

[130] For example, vv. 7 (Judah), 8 (Levi), 12 (Benjamin), 13 (Joseph), 21 (Gad), 23 (Naphthali).

[131] For example, vv. 22 (Dan), 24 (Asher).

[132] G. VON RAD, *Deuteronomy*, 205.

[133] Driver thinks that the blessing reflects a time when Reuben lacked political importance and suffered from dwindling numbers (395).

sought here is a matter of some dispute. Driver hesitantly admitted the
possibility that the prayer may have been one for reunion between Judah
and the Northern tribes after the rupture under Jeroboam, but he admitted that «our ignorance of the *exact* circumstances under which the
Blessing was composed naturally precludes us from being confident that
it is the correct one»[134]. Phillips, on the other hand, rejects this
possibility, and allows as the prayer may reflect Judah's inability to participate in the sacral gatherings of the pre-monarchical confederacy[135].
In fact, however, the inability to fix a specific reason for help being
sought allows the prayer to be used on a variety of occasions; by the
same token, the guarantee of divine help becomes applicable to virtually
any situation.

The blessing of Levi (Deut 33:8-11) is one of the lengthiest of all the
blessings, and gives, as Driver recognised, a general picture of the rights
and privileges of the tribe of Levi, specifically, the giving of Torah
(33:10a), and the offering of incense (33:10b)[136]. Formally, the blessing of Levi may be said to be composed of three sections: the first section (33:8-9) rehearses the tribe's accomplishments; the second section
(33:10) lists the tribe's duties; the third section (33:11) implores the
Lord's aid against the tribe's enemies. Whatever the specific events were
which are alluded to in the first section[137], it seems clear that Levi is
being commended here for its fidelity: «he kept your oracles, and observed your covenant» (ἐφύλαξεν τὰ λόγιά σου καὶ τὴν διαθήκην σου
διετήρησεν: Deut 33:9). As a result, the Levites become the authentic
interpreters of the law to Israel and officiate at its liturgies (Deut 33:10).
The prayer for the tribe of Levi (Deut 33:11) is so generally phrased
that it does not permit one to assign a particular occasion on which the
Levites might have needed divine help. This generality, of course, lends
itself to virtually any situation.

The blessing of Benjamin (Deut 33:12) characterises the tribe as «beloved» (ἠγαπημένος, here translating the Hebrew יְדִיד), thus linking in

---

[134] Driver, 307. G. VON RAD (*Deuteronomy*, 206) made a similar, and equally
hesitant, suggestion.

[135] A. PHILLIPS, *Deuteronomy*, 228.

[136] Driver, 402-403.

[137] G. VON RAD (*Deuteronomy*, 206) is not surprised that allusions here to historical
events cannot be squared with any of the accounts in the Pentateuch, since «reminis-
cences are revived here which were still current in Israel when the saying was composed».

the LXX the fortunes of this particular tribe with the destiny of Israel as a whole which is enunciated in the introduction (33:1-5) and the conclusion (33:26-29) to the hymn. The specific claim on Benjamin's behalf, namely, that «the beloved shall dwell in confidence, and God overshadows him always, and he rested between his shoulders» (ἠγαπη-μένος ὑπὸ κυρίου κατασκηνώσει πεποιθώς, καὶ ὁ θεὸς σκιάζει ἐπ' αὐτῷ πάσας τὰς ἡμέρας, καὶ ἀνὰ μέσον τῶν ὤμων αὐτοῦ κατέπαυσεν: Deut 33:12) lacks any limiting historical specificity, and thus, like the other blessings directed to Judah and Levi, is applicable to a variety of situations.

The blessing of Joseph (Deut 33:13-17), like that of Levi, is lengthy in comparison to the other blessings. Much of the blessing is taken up with a description of the agricultural bounties which come to the tribe of Joseph (vv. 13-16a)[138]; the sole hope which is expressed in the blessing is that «the things pleasing to him that dwelled in the bush come on the head of Joseph, and on the crown of him who was glorified above his brothers» (καὶ τὰ δεκτὰ τῷ ὀφθέντι ἐν τῷ βάτῳ ἔλθοισαν ἐπὶ κεφαλὴν Ιωσηφ, καὶ ἐπὶ κορυφῆς δοξασθεὶς ἐν ἀδελφοῖς: Deut 33:16b). Here again, a certain vagueness in the blessing permits a universal applicability.

The blessing of Ephraim and Manasseh (Deut 33:17) hardly make any claim at all upon God, except insofar as the mention of the «ten thousands» (μυριάδες) of Ephraim and the «thousands» (χιλιάδες) of Manasseh represent a wish for tribal growth, like the blessing of Reuben. What is notable about this double blessing of the half-tribes is the theromorphic imagery it employs: «his beauty is as the first-born of the bull; his horns the horns of the unicorn: with them he shall thrust the nations at once, even from the ends of the earth» (πρωτότοκος ταύρου τὸ κάλλος αὐτοῦ, κέρατα μονοκέρωτος τὰ κέρατα αὐτοῦ· ἐν αὐτοῖς ἔθνη κερατιεῖ ἅμα ἕως ἐπ' ἄκρου γῆς: Deut 33:17a). The purpose of such imagery is undoubtedly military, as Driver contended[139].

The blessings of Zebulon and Issachar (Deut 33:18-19), like those of Ephraim and Manasseh, are linked: to bless someone in his «going out» (ἐξοδία) is, as Driver noted, to bless a man's whole activity and enter-prise[140]; to bless someone in his tents (ἐν τοῖς σκηνώμασιν αὐτοῦ) is

---

[138] Thus, G. VON RAD (*Deuteronomy*) thinks of the blessing of Joseph as a fertility blessing (207).

[139] Driver, 407.

[140] Driver, 408.

to wish domestic security. Hence the blessing to Zebulon and Issachar is comprehensive in its nature, predicting military success («they shall utterly destroy the nations», ἔθνη ἐξολεθρεύσουσιν: v. 19a), religious fervour («and you shall call men there, and there offer the sacrifice of righteousness», καὶ ἐπικαλέσεσθε ἐκεῖ καὶ θύσετε θυσίαν δικαιοσύνης: v. 19a), and material prosperity («for the wealth of the sea shall suckle you, and the markets of those who dwell by the sea-coast», ὅτι πλοῦτος θαλάσσης θηλάσει σε καὶ ἐμπόρια παράλιον κατοικούντων: v. 19b).

The blessing of Gad (Deut 33:20-21), like the blessing of Ephraim and Manasseh and that of Dan, employs theromorphic imagery. To liken Gad here to a lion is to stress the strength of the tribe in military affairs. The rest of the blessing seems to connect the military prowess of Gad with the just division of the land among the tribes. Such apportionment of the land seems to have been the occasion for the praise of God in v. 21b: «the Lord worked righteousness, and his judgement is with Israel» (δικαιοσύνην κύριος ἐποίησεν καὶ κρίσιν αὐτοῦ μετὰ Ἰσραηλ).

G. von Rad characterises the blessing of Dan (Deut 33:22) as «colour-less»[141]; certainly, it is one of the briefest of all the tribal blessings. It likewise employs theromorphic imagery, here the lion's whelp (σκύμνος λέοντος); indeed, the blessing exhausts itself in the comparison of Dan to the lion's whelp. Such animal imagery was probably deployed to the same military end as that in the blessings of Ephraim and Manasseh and Gad.

The blessing of Naphtali (Deut 33:23) seems to be the least specific of all the tribal blessings in its reference. To say that Naphtali has «the fulness of good things» (πλησμονὴ δεκτῶν) and to pray that the tribe «be filled with the blessing from the Lord» (ἐμπλησθήτω εὐλογίαν παρὰ κυρίου) is to say no more than a kind of general prayer for prosperity. The promise that Naphtali «shall inherit the lake and the south» (θάλασ-σαν καὶ λίβα κληρονομήσει) is doubtless a reference to the traditional homeland of the tribe[142].

The blessing of Asher (Deut 33:24-25), like those directed to Reuben, Ephraim, and Manasseh, is a wish for numerical augmentation («Asher is blessed with children», εὐλογητὸς ἀπὸ τέκνων Ασηρ: v. 24a), though here, seemingly, the wish has been granted. In addition, the theme of augmentation recurs in the wish «As your days, so your strength» (καὶ ὡς αἱ ἡμέραι σου ἡ ἰσχύς σου: v. 25b), which Driver suggested meant

---

[141] G. VON RAD, *Deuteronomy*, 208.
[142] Driver, 413.

that Asher's strength should be maintained as time wears on, instead of diminishing with the onset of old age[143].

Given the diversity in form, in length, and in content alike, a good case can doubtless be made for the independent origin of each of these sayings[144]. But the genetic question is less compelling than the interpretive question: how would a first century reader of Deuteronomy, especially the Pastor, have understood the Blessing of Moses? The specific answer to that question must wait until we can consider the interpretation of these last words of Moses in the work of Philo and Josephus, but a preliminary response can be framed at this juncture. The kinds of benefits – military success against one's enemies, religious piety, commercial and agricultural prosperity, security in the land, strength in numbers, and length of days – which are promised to the tribes in the Blessing of Moses are such that Israel might lay claim to them at any stage of its history. These are the sorts of blessings which an inhabitant of the Jerusalem of Solomon, or that of Uzziah, or that of Ezra, or that of Herod or Josephus might justifiably wish for himself and his contemporaries. Hence their widespread appeal. The Blessing of Moses thus lends itself by the universality of its promises to a reappropriation by each generation of believers. The putative author of this Blessing would then be seen by these subsequent generations as one who foresaw their needs, and endowed them with hope for the future.

## 4. Moses as law-giver in Deuteronomy 31 – 34

The second aspect under which the figure of Moses may be analysed in the last four chapters of the Book of Deuteronomy is that of the law-giver. Given the constraints of the narrative with which the author of Deuteronomy is working, the last four chapters of Deuteronomy give relatively little evidence of Moses the law-giver: a dying man is hardly going to deliver himself of legal dicta. Yet the image of Moses as law-giver is not entirely absent from Deut 31 – 34. There are, in fact, two passages which depict the law-giving functions of Moses.

---

143 Driver, 415.

144 G. VON RAD, *Deuteronomy*, 205.

## 4.1 *Deuteronomy 31:9-13*

The first mention of Moses' law-giving functions in the last four chapters of Deuteronomy comes in Deut 31:9-13:

> And Moses wrote the words of this law (τὰ ῥήματα τοῦ νόμου τούτου) in a book and gave it to the priests the sons of Levi who bear the ark of the covenant of the Lord, and to the elders of the sons of Israel. And Moses charged them in that day, saying «After seven years, in the time of release, in the feast of tabernacles, when all Israel come together to appear before the Lord your God, in the place which the Lord shall choose, you shall read this law before all Israel in their ears, having assembled the people, the men, and the women, and the children, and the stranger that is in your cities, that they may hear, and that they may learn to fear the Lord your God; and they shall hearken to do all the words of this law. And their sons who have not known shall hear, and shall learn to fear the Lord your God all the days that they live upon the land, into which you go over Jordan to inherit it (Deut 31:9-13)[145].

Driver followed Delitzsch in supposing that the reference behind the expression «the words of this law» (τὰ ῥήματα τοῦ νόμου τούτου: Deut 31:9) is not to Deuteronomy as we have it, «but to its kernel, the legal code of which the existing book is its parenetic expansion»[146]. Craigie, on the other hand, holds out the possibility that the reference may be to the entirety of the Book of Deuteronomy[147]. The disagreement over the question of reference, it seems to me, is misdirected: the point the authors of Deuteronomy want to make here is not so much *what part* of the law Moses wrote, but the fact that *Moses* wrote the law.

E. W. Nicholson thinks that perhaps this passage reflects the actual practice of the covenant renewal ceremony[148]. J. A. Thompson holds that the giving of the law to the priests reflects the normal practice in the

---

[145] This passage has excited a great deal of comment among those scholars who take as their field of interest the reconstruction of the religious practices and institutions of ancient Israel, and specifically, the history of Israelite priesthood: the issue at stake is whether Deuteronomy recognises a distinction between Levites and priests. See, for example, J. G. McCONVILLE, *Law and Theology*, 137f., 143, 181. Interesting as this question is, it is for the purpose of this study ultimately irrelevant, insofar as first century readers are likely to have projected their own understanding of the relationship of Levites to priests onto the text of Deuteronomy.

[146] Driver, 335.

[147] P. CRAIGIE, *Deuteronomy*, 370.

[148] E. W. NICHOLSON, *Deuteronomy and Tradition*, 22, 45.

ancient Near East: at the conclusion of a treaty the suzerain handed over a copy of the treaty to be lodged in the sanctuary of the vassal under the care of the priests[149]. According to this paradigm, Moses represents the suzerain, and the vassal, Joshua[150]. But this understanding of the report fails to take into account the larger purposes of Deuteronomy, which posits a suzerain-vassal relationship between the Lord and Israel, not Moses and Joshua.

It is not necessary for the purposes of this study to recover the original paradigm which informs this passage. It is likely that a first century reader would have understood that to have written the law is the central exercise of the law-giving function; to have confided this law to «the priests the sons of Levi» (τοῖς ἱερεῦσιν τοῖς υἱοῖς Λευι) and the elders of the sons of Israel (τοῖς πρεσβυτέροις τῶν υἱῶν Ισραηλ) is to have ensured its preservation. Likewise, to have issued directives for the periodic proclamation of the law is here, like the writing of the law and the making of provisions for its preservation, a further exercise of the law-giving function.

In effect, these three actions of writing, preserving, and proclaiming amount to the promulgation of the law, the equivalent in an oral culture of its publication in a book-based culture. The periodic proclamation of the law serves, according to the scheme set forth in Deuteronomy, as the primary means whereby the Israelites come to know the full extent of the obligations visited upon them through their obedience to the law[151]. Indeed, to listen to the proclamation of the law is the first act of obedience to its mandates. That the writing of the law, the making of provisions for its preservation, and the giving of directions for its periodic proclamation are attributed to Moses indicates that for the first century reader, if not for the authors of Deuteronomy, Moses is the law-giver *par excellence*.

### 4.2 *Deuteronomy 32:44b-47*

The other mention of law-giving functions proper to Moses comes at the conclusion of the Song of Moses (Deut 32:1-43):

---

[149] J. A. THOMPSON, *Deuteronomy*, 290-291. See also P. CRAIGIE, *Deuteronomy*, 370-371.

[150] J. A. THOMPSON, *Deuteronomy*, 291.

[151] P. CRAIGIE, *Deuteronomy*, 371.

And Moses went in and spoke all the words of this law in the ears of the people, he and Joshua the son of Naue. And Moses finished speaking to all Israel. And he said to them «Take heed with your heart to all these words which I testify to you this day, which you shall command your sons to observe and do all the words of this law. For this is no vain word to you (ὅτι οὐχὶ λόγος κενὸς οὗτος ὑμῖν); for it is your life (ὅτι αὕτη ἡ ζωὴ ὑμῶν), and because of this word you shall live long upon the land (καὶ ἕνεκεν τοῦ λόγου τούτου μακροημερεύσετε ἐπὶ τῆς γῆς) into which you go over Jordan to inherit it» (Deut 32:44b-47).

In contradistinction to Deut 31:9-13, which depicts the law-giving activities of Moses in a functional way, showing a concern for preservation, proclamation and promulgation, this passage is largely parenetic. The sole mention of a law-giving function comes in v. 44b where Moses is said to speak «all the words of this law in the ears of the people» (καὶ ἐλάλησεν πάντας τοὺς λόγους τοῦ νόμου τούτου εἰς τὰ ὦτα τοῦ λαοῦ). The purpose of this mention seems to be summary; that is to say, all of that which has preceded this verse may be summed up in it. Of itself, however, the verse does not shed any further light on the way in which Moses is presented as a lawgiver in Deuteronomy.

But the parenesis which follows this summary mention, while ostensibly calling the Israelites to a greater reverence for the law, nevertheless reveals some important dimensions of the figure of Moses as lawgiver. The exalted language by which Moses refers to the law in the exhortation (οὐχὶ λόγος κενός: «no vain word», and αὕτη ἡ ζωὴ ὑμῶν: «it is your life») testifies not only to the regard with which the law itself is held in Deuteronomy, but also to the status of the lawgiver himself. What Moses commands is life itself, and furthermore, is capable of bestowing life: «because of this word you shall live long upon the land» (καὶ ἕνεκεν τοῦ λόγου τούτου μακροημερεύσετε ἐπὶ τῆς γῆς: Deut 32:47b).

Patrick Miller has observed that while Deuteronomy underscores Moses' rôle as law-giver, the act of transmitting the law in Deuteronomy is primarily a teaching task: «[t]he Lord *tells* or *speaks* all the commandments, the statutes, and the ordinances to Moses, who in turn *teaches* them»[152]. This law-giving/teaching task has, in Miller's view, two dimensions: on the one hand, it is directed to the present generation, seeking «at every turn to convey, explain, and also turn the heart to

---

[152] P. D. MILLER, «Moses My Servant», 246.

respond to the divine instruction, to follow the way that is set forth»[153]. On the other hand, it is also directed to future generations: Moses orders his auditors to teach their children and their children's children (Deut 4:9-10; 6:7, 21-25; 31:3) both in the family (6:7) and in the sacral gatherings of the whole people (31:10-13)[154]. The exhortation in Deut 32:46 to «Take heed with all your heart to all these words, which I testify to you this day, which you shall command your sons, to observe and do all the words of this law», gives evidence of the two audiences, present (ἐγὼ διαμαρτύρομαι ὑμῖν σήμερον: «I testify to *you* this day») and future (ἐντελεῖσθε τοῖς υἱοῖς ὑμῶν: «you shall command *your sons*»), to which Deuteronomy's Moses directs his parenesis, and is, then, a particular expression of the law-giving/teaching task.

Moreover, here, in distinction to the first report of law-giving activity on the part of Moses, Joshua takes part in the recitation of the Law. Joshua's participation in the recitation of the law is a tangible sign that he is the appointed successor of Moses; indeed, this report of Joshua's activity is the first action he undertakes after his commission in Deut 31:7-8, 14-15, 23. Klaus Baltzer identifies in this episode of the transition from the leadership of Moses to that of Joshua the effort to establish a pattern of succession which would be viewed by subsequent generations as the norm, or at the very least the goal for which to strive[155]. We shall see, when we turn to 2 Tim, that the succession to Paul by Timothy through the laying on of hands functions as a similar norm or model according to which subsequent generations are supposed to operate.

## 5. The suffering Moses in Deuteronomy 31 – 34

There is, in addition, another dimension to the portrait of Moses in Deuteronomy: Moses as one who suffers[156]. The basis for this claim rests on several passages, all of which offer reasons for Moses' failure to enter the Promised Land: Deut 1:37 depicts the Lord telling Moses that he shall not enter the Promised Land «because of you» (δι' ὑμᾶς), that is, those who are listening to this speech; 3:26 recounts the Lord's

---

[153] P. D. MILLER, «Moses My Servant», 247.

[154] P. D. MILLER, «Moses My Servant», 247-248.

[155] K. BALTZER, *The Covenant Formulary*, 68, 72, 82-83.

[156] G. VON RAD, *Old Testament Theology*, I, 294; see also P. D. MILLER, «Moses My Servant» 251.

denial of Moses' request to see the Promised Land «because of you» (ἔνεκεν ὑμῶν); Deut 4:21 describes Moses as saying that the Lord was angry with him «because of your words» (עַל־דִּבְרֵיכֶם) as the Hebrew text puts it, or «because of the things said by you» (περὶ τῶν λεγομένων ὑφ' ὑμῶν), according to the LXX. In all three instances, Moses' failure to enter to Promised Land is linked to some sin on the part of his people, and in all three instances, the Lord's anger at his people is, as it were, deflected from its original object, and settles on Moses.

Deuteronomy is curiously reticent, however, to assign any fault to Moses himself for his failure to enter the Promised Land. To this reticence one may contrast the story of the waters of Meribah found in Numbers 20:2-13, in which it is Moses' lack of faith which moves the Lord to forbid him entry into the land. In that account, Moses and Aaron are commanded to speak to the rock so that it will provide water for the congregation and their cattle. Instead, Moses strikes the rock twice with his rod, and earns a rebuke from the Lord: «Because you have not believed in me to sanctify me before the children of Israel, therefore you shall not bring this congregation into the land which I have given them» (καὶ εἶπεν κύριος πρὸς Μωυσῆν καὶ Ααρων Ὅτι οὐκ ἐπιστεύσατε ἁγιάσαι με ἐναντίον υἱῶν Ισραηλ, διὰ τοῦτο οὐκ εἰσάξετε ὑμεῖς τὴν συναγωγὴν ταύτην εἰς τὴν γῆν, ἣν δέδωκα αὐτοῖς: Num 20:12).

The closest Deuteronomy comes to assigning any personal responsibility to Moses for his failure to enter the Promised Land comes in Deut 32:48-52:

> And the Lord spoke to Moses in this day, saying «Go up to the mount Abarim, this mountain Nabau which is in the land of Moab over against Jericho, and behold the land of Canaan which I give to the sons of Israel: and die in the mount where you go up, and be added to your people; as Aaron your brother dies and was added to his people. Because you disobeyed my word among the children of Israel, at the waters of strife at Kades in the wilderness of Sin, because you did not sanctify me among the sons of Israel. You shall see the land before you, but you shall not enter into it» (Deut 32:48-52).

We may note that there is a shift from the singular (vv. 49-50) to the plural (v. 51) and back again to the singular (v. 52) in the course of this passage. The singular verbs all refer to Moses and frame, as it were, the plural verbs. I have drawn attention to the alternating singular and plural references because determining their antecedents is crucial for understanding Deuteronomy's attitude towards the failure of Moses to enter the Promised Land. The set of plural verbs comes in v. 51: «Because you disobeyed my word among the children of Israel, at the waters of the strife of Kades in the wilderness of Sin; because you did not sanctify me among the sons of Israel» (διότι ἠπειθήσατε τῷ ῥήματί μου ἐν τοῖς υἱοῖς Ισραηλ ἐπὶ τοῦ ὕδατος ἀντιλογίας Καδης ἐν τῇ ἐρήμῳ Σιν, διότι οὐχ ἡγιάσατέ με ἐν τοῖς υἱοῖς Ισραηλ). Who has disobeyed (ἠπειθήσατε)? Who has failed to sanctify (οὐχ ἡγιάσατε)?

An earlier generation of scholarship would have seen the alternation between singular and plural verbs as evidence of different sources from which the authors of Deuteronomy drew. Thus, according to this line of analysis, the plural verbs simply point to the community's awareness of its own sinfulness. From the point of view of Meir Sternberg's «discourse-oriented analysis» however, the text as it presently stands indicates that those who have disobeyed in failing to sanctify are Moses himself, along with Aaron. Moses and Aaron are likened to one another here in the circumstances of their deaths: Moses will die on a mountain (32:50a) and will be added to his people (32:50a) just as Aaron died on a mountain (32:50b) and was added to his people (32:50b). The parallel manner of their deaths suggest that both Moses and Aaron have to die for the same reason. Moses will die, just as Aaron has already died, because (διότι) both have sinned at Kades in the wilderness of Sin.

Coats tries to make a case for understanding the failure of Moses to enter the Promised Land as an instance of vicarious suffering[157]: he bases his argument upon that of Noth, who held that the Deuteronomic version of the story in which Moses fails to gain entry into the Promised Land because of his sin was not an innovation, but rather part of the received tradition to which the author of Deuteronomy felt bound, one which, furthermore involved a vicarious substitution of Moses for the people[158]. Consistent with his understanding of the figure of Moses as heroic, Coats claims that the element of vicarious suffering increases rather than diminishes the stature of Moses[159].

Not all scholars hold that this dimension of the portrait of Moses is present in the narrative of Deuteronomy. Mann maintains that «it is incorrect to interpret Moses' punishment as vicarious suffering»[160], and notes that the language of *biglal* in Deuteronomy indicates a suffering accomplished *because of* and not *in place of*. Moreover, for suffering to

---

[157] G. W. COATS, «Legendary Motifs», 39.

[158] M. NOTH, *A History of Pentateuchal Traditions*, 170, 479.

[159] G. W. COATS, «Legendary Motifs», 39.

[160] T. W. MANN, «Theological Reflections», 486.

be redemptive, it must in some way benefit those on whose behalf one is suffering, something which Mann finds lacking in the narrative of Deuteronomy[161].

In any case, it may well be in the motif of Moses' suffering, vicarious or not, that the Pastor found another likeness to Paul. Certainly, Paul's suffering looms large in 2 Tim; indeed, the suffering of Paul is virtually all the reader learns about the Apostle to the Gentiles in 2 Tim.

---

[161] T. W. MANN, «Theological Reflections», 486-487.

CHAPTER III

## The last words of Moses in Philo and Josephus

The various legends concerning the last words of Moses which have
survived from the first century, regardless of the language in which
these legends were ultimately preserved, Greek or Latin, arose thanks
to a conviction within the Jewish community of the Second Temple period that theirs was a «postclassical age», as Shaye J. D. Cohen puts it:

> it was their duty to collect, venerate, and study the works of their great
> ancestors. This tendency ultimately yielded the Bible and the idea that classi-
> cal prophecy was no longer alive. On the other hand, the sense that they
> could no longer compete with their past, because their ancestors were giants
> and they themselves were but dwarves, impelled them to express their
> literary creativity in new forms: apocalypses, testaments, romances, his-
> tories, poems, hymns, oracles, translations, paraphrases, commentaries, and
> others[1].

The figure of Moses makes his appearance in virtually all of these expressions of literary creativity, as one might expect. In an age convinced
of the paradigmatic value of the past, the greatest figure of Israel's past
is bound to be the subject of much of its literary activity, and the object
of much of its theological speculation.

In this respect, it is good to recall T. L. Donaldson's reminder of the
importance of the figure of Moses to the various religious groups of first
century Judaism:

> The Samaritans refused to acknowledge any prophet but Moses, «the great
> Prophet». The Pharisees claimed that their oral tradition had been given to
> Moses at Sinai along with the written law. The Qumran sect saw themselves
> as the reconstitution of the true covenant community in the wilderness and
> looked for the appearance of the eschatological prophet like Moses in their

---

[1] S. J. D. COHEN, *From the Maccabees*, 213.

midst. Both Philo and Josephus, attempting to win a hearing for Judaism in the Roman world, pressed the figure of Moses into the service of their apologetic aims. It is likely that the Sadducees as well appealed to the authority of Moses in the rejection of oral tradition [...] Our sources for the Zealots are scanty, but in their resistance to foreign domination, emphasis on law observance [...] and penchant for prophet- and wilderness-symbolism [...] similar Mosaic-remnant themes may be at work [2].

In Donaldson's view, Moses was invoked as an authority figure to justify a variety of theological points of view, but common to them all is the attempt to draw a line in such a fashion that «a division was to be made between the righteous and sinners within Israel, and each felt that its group was at the heart of the true people of God»[3]. We shall see that a similar use is made of the figure of Paul in 2 Tim.

Two major works in which Moses was invoked as an authority, both of which were preserved in the Greek in which they were originally written, survive from the first century. Philo's *De Vita Mosis* and the *Jewish Antiquities* of Josephus both depict the figure of Moses in such a way that the authors of each of these works are able to comment on the issues facing the audiences to which each of them directed their literary efforts. And since these issues varied from the Alexandria of Philo's audience to the Roman audience for whom Josephus wrote, the portrait of Moses which emerges in each of these works varies considerably, too.

## 1. Philo, *De Vita Mosis* II.288-292

Philo of Alexandria, also known as Philo Judaeus, was a prominent member of the Jewish πολίτευμα of Alexandria[4]. Philo is best known today for his allegorizing treatment of the Old Testament using the categories of Greek philosophy[5]. About the man himself, as Samuel Sandmel notes, relatively little can be said[6]. He is thought to have been

---

[2] T. L. DONALDSON, «Moses Typology», 40-41.

[3] T. L. DONALDSON, «Moses Typology», 38.

[4] A. N. SHERWIN-WHITE, *Roman Society and Roman Law*, 185. See also E. M. SMALLWOOD, *The Jews under Roman Rule*, especially Chapter 10: «Jews in Egypt and Alexandria».

[5] See P. TREVES, «Philon», 822-823; D. WINSTON, «Philo», 287-290; R. M. BERCHMAN, «Philo of Alexandria», 726-727.

[6] S. SANDMEL, *Judaism and Christian Beginnings*, 280; ID., *Philo of Alexandria*, 11-12; ID., «Philo», 4.

born between 25 and 20 BCE, and he is presumed to have died by the middle of the first century CE[7]. His family was both prominent and wealthy[8]: Goodenough reasoned that the family must have enjoyed several generations of wealth, since in the ancient world, family fortunes and family connections such as the ones possessed by Philo and his relatives were rarely acquired rapidly[9], and Sandmel argues from the voluminousness of his literary production that Philo must have had ample private means to support the necessary leisure to sustain so great an output[10].

If Jerome (*De viris illustribus* 11) may be believed, Philo was from a priestly family[11]. Priest or not, Philo himself seems to have taken an active rôle in the life of his community, at least from time to time, since he served as part of an embassy to Rome in 39 to protest the treatment of the Jews of Alexandria under the administration of Flaccus[12]. He was probably by this time already an old man, as passing references to his age in the *De Legatione* seem to indicate[13]. Sandmel judiciously

---

[7] S. SANDMEL, «Philo», 3-4.

[8] The family included among its members the wealthy Alexander Lysimachus, Philo's brother, *alabarch* of the Jewish πολίτευμα of Alexandria who is reported to have paid for the gold and silver plating of the Temple gates in Jerusalem, as well as the notorious Tiberius Julius Alexander, Philo's nephew, who is described as «a renegade from the ancestral faith» (M. E. HUBBARD, «Tiberius Julius Alexander», 1072); he was appointed procurator governor of Judaea (*ca.* 46-48), in which capacity he executed the sons of Judah the Galilean; during the siege of Jerusalem, he was present with Titus as general staff officer. See also E. M. SMALLWOOD, *The Jews Under Roman Rule*, 257-259; P. BORGEN, «Judaism in Egypt», 1068.

[9] E. R. GOODENOUGH, *Introduction to Philo Judaeus*, 2.

[10] S. SANDMEL, *Philo of Alexandria*, 12

[11] For a measured estimation of the evidence supporting Jerome's statement of Philo's priestly descent, see D. R. SCHWARTZ, «Philo's Priestly Descent», who concludes on form-critical grounds that Jerome's report may be trusted, since «it is neither written the way a legend would be nor exploited as one» (170). Moreover, references to Philo's family and social status, his position in the Alexandrian Jewish community, his references to the priesthood and his appreciation of cultic service, along with the possibility that he might have been a Sadducee all taken together «tend to corroborate the attribution of priestly descent» (170).

[12] *De Legatione Ad Gaium*, 178ff.

[13] See *De Legatione* 1, wherein he refers to «we the aged» (ἡμεῖς οἱ γέροντες) and 182, wherein he professes alarm at what gives joy to his fellow ambassadors since he believes himself to possess a greater amount of good sense «in virtue of my age and my good education» (ἐγὼ δὲ φρονεῖν τι δοκῶν περιττότερον καὶ δι' ἡλικίαν καὶ τὴν

estimates that while it is possible that the whole of his life was characterised by this kind of active leadership of the πολίτευμα, it is more likely
that he was a solitary scholar, admired by his contemporaries, though
read by few of them[14].

This paucity of biographical material, however, need not stand in the
way of an informed reading of his work, however difficult it may be to
relate that work to the circumstances of his life. His literary output was
prodigious: Robert M. Berchman, following the traditional custom, classifies Philo's writings into four groups: (1) historical and apologetical,
(2) expository on the books of Moses, (3) allegorical on Genesis, and (4)
philosophical[15]. David Winston, on the other hand, divides the Philonic
corpus into three groups: (1) historical or apologetic, (2) philosophical,
and (3) exegetical[16]. The *VM* falls, according to either system of
classification, into the first group, though one doubts, in view of the
sometimes conflicting aims between historical accounts and apologetical
literature, the usefulness of creating a category which contains them
both. We shall see, when we undertake a literary analysis of the *VM*,
that there may well be a more satisfactory classification of the *VM* which
takes into account its peculiar characteristics[17].

## 1.1 *Date, provenance, and original language*

Assigning a specific date for the *VM* is somewhat problematic, given
the difficulty of establishing anything more than a general chronology of
the life of Philo. Indeed, trying to arrange the entire Philonic corpus
chronologically is virtually an impossible exercise, though an earlier
generation of scholarship usually contented itself with the assertion that
Philo's philosophical works preceded those of a more exegetical character, an assertion that has been subsequently abandoned[18]. A partial relative chronology may be posited insofar as Philo mentions the *VM* in
his treatise on φιλανθρωπία:

---

ἄλλην παιδείαν εὐλαβέστερος ἤμην ἐφ' οἷς ἔχαιρον οἱ ἄλλοι.)

[14] S. SANDMEL, «Philo», 5.

[15] R. M. BERCHMAN, «Philo», 726.

[16] D. WINSTON, «Philo», 288.

[17] For a review of various proposals according to which the writings of Philo ought
to be classified, and where the *VM* should be specifically assigned, see P. BORGEN,
«Philo of Alexandria», 117-118.

[18] D. WINSTON, «Philo», 288.

The next subject to be examined is humanity, the virtue closest akin to piety, its sister and its twin. The prophetic legislator who perhaps loved her more than anyone else has done, since he knew that she was the high road leading to holiness, used to incite and train all his subjects to fellowship, setting before them the monument of his own life like an original design to be their beautiful model. Now the actions which he performed from his earliest years to old age for the care and protection of each single man and of them all have been set forth already in two treatises in which I wrote about the life of Moses (ἐν δυσὶ συντάξεσιν, ἃς ἀνέγραψα περὶ τοῦ βίου Μωυσέως: *De Virtutibus* 51-52).

By the time Philo writes this treatise on the virtues, the *VM* was completed, though for how long is not able to be determined from this passage.

The *VM* also receives passing mention in *De Praemiis et Poenis* where Philo lauds Moses as a paragon of piety (εὐσέβεια):

Now all the virtues are virgins, but the fairest among them all, the acknowledged queen of the dance, is piety, which Moses, the teacher of divine lore, in a special degree had for his own, and through it gained a multitude of other gifts, which have been described in the treatises dealing with his life (ἅπερ ἐν τοῖς γραφεῖσι περὶ τοῦ κατ' αὐτὸν βίου μεμήνυται), four special rewards, the offices of king, legislator, prophet and high priest (*De Praemiis et Poenis* 53).

Here, too, it is clear that the *VM* antedates *De Praemiis*, though by how long one is not able to say. Jenny Morris thinks that both *De Praemiis* and *De Virtutibus* are appendices to Philo's larger exposition of the Law[19], which itself comprises the treatises *De Opificio Mundi*, *De Abrahamo*, *De Iosepho*, *De Decalogo*, and *De Specialibus Legibus* I-IV; but, while this supposition makes sense, it cannot be proven from internal references. Thus, with respect to the chronological placement of the *VM* within the larger Philonic corpus, we must satisfy ourselves with the minimal claim that Philo wrote this work before he undertook his treatises on the virtues and on rewards and punishments.

If it is difficult to place the *VM* within the Philonic corpus, it is even more difficult to place the Philonic corpus within a larger literary and theological context. Wayne A. Meeks has noted the difficulties associated with any investigation of Philo's thought: apart from its complexity, and a certain formlessness and repetitiveness, there is the larger problem

---

[19] J. MORRIS, «The Jewish Philosopher Philo», 851-853.

of determining when Philo is original and when he is representative of Alexandrian Judaism[20]. Meeks' point is well taken, but the «larger problem» which he raises may not admit, ultimately, of a solution, if for no other reason than that the literary remains of first century Alexandrian Judaism — Philo's work excepted — are very meagre indeed, and offer little grounds by which to make the judgement of originality[21].

As a member of the Jewish πολίτευμα of Alexandria, Philo's native language would have been Greek; indeed, there is some question whether he would have known any Hebrew at all[22]. Regardless of whether he did or did not have any Hebrew, he seems, in any case, to have been steeped in the language and thought-patterns of the LXX[23]. Sandmel characterises the style in which Philo composed as fundamentally *koine*, with touches of «the pretentious imitation of Athens that is customarily called Atticistic»[24]. Thomas M. Conley, on the other hand, questions the assumption on the part of scholars like Sandmel that Philo's «Atticism» represents an affected and artificial, even a decadent usage: Conley's analysis of the stylistic features of Philo's rhetoric, particularly his reliance upon the optative, indicates that his rhetoric is governed by the argumentative needs and intentions imposed by the audience to whom he was addressing himself [25]. There is evidence, Conley maintains, «that such usage was not only approved by Philo's contemporaries as polite language, but was expected of him»[26].

---

[20] W. A. MEEKS, *The Prophet-King*, 101.

[21] See B. L. MACK, «Philo and Exegetical Traditions», 227-271, esp. 241-249, wherein he makes some acute observations on the pre-Philonic Alexandrian traditions.

[22] S. SANDMEL, *The First Christian Century*, thinks that what little knowledge of Hebrew Philo displays «may well owe more to a *notarikon*, a list of biblical names with their attendant Hebrew etymologies, on which he drew», rather than any personal understanding of the language (113); ID., *Judaism and Christian Beginnings*, 281, 284. See also E. R. GOODENOUGH, *Introduction to Philo Judaeus*, 8. But C. K. BARRETT («The Interpretation of the Old Testament in the New») comments that while «Philo's expositions of Hebrew words do not inspire confidence in him as a Semitic philologist [...] his etymologies are no wilder than that of the rabbis, and in no way disprove knowledge of colloquial Hebrew» (383).

[23] E. R. GOODENOUGH, *Introduction to Philo Judaeus*, 9.

[24] S. SANDMEL, *Philo of Alexandria*, 15; ID., «Philo», 5.

[25] T. M. CONLEY, «Philo's Rhetoric», 347.

[26] T. M. CONLEY, «Philo's Rhetoric», 347.

## 1.2 *Literary analysis*

The *VM* recasts the stories of Moses' life and work which are scattered throughout the Pentateuch into one complete and continuous narrative. It may thus be seen as an example of the «rewritten Bible». Philo himself claims to retell the story of Moses as he has learned it, «both from the sacred books (βίβλων τῶν ἱερῶν), the wonderful monuments of his wisdom (θαυμάσια μνημεῖα τῆς αὐτοῦ σοφίας) which he has left behind him, and from some of the elders of the nation (ἀπὸ τοῦ ἔθνους πρεσβυτέρων)» (*VM* I.4). Despite his claim to have written a «life» (βίος) of Moses (*VM* I.1; II.292), it is clear that Philo's *VM* is not a biography of Moses in the modern sense, that is, an orderly account of its subject's life, arranged chronologically, with special attention to the important influences on its subject's development; rather, Philo has organised the matter of Moses' life thematically around his exploits as king (*VM* I), as law-giver (*VM* II.8-65), as high priest (*VM* II.66-186) and as prophet (*VM* II.187-291). This thematic organisation has provoked some exasperation from some of Philo's modern-day readers like F. H. Colson, who complains that

> Philo's arrangement of the life of Moses under the four heads of king, law-giver, priest, and prophet does, no doubt, serve for a logical basis to the work, but it leads him into many oddities. While the story of Moses as king or leader is carried on consistently to the end of Exodus 18, what next to the deliverance itself is the central point of the story, the theophany on Sinai, is entirely omitted; the account of Balaam and Balak, which has little to do with Moses himself, is given at disproportionate length, while the stories of the Red Sea and the manna and the golden calf are given twice over[27].

Such complaints assume an understanding of biography which expects the biographer to stick to the sources at his disposal, in this case, the biblical record, while at the same time recounting the life of his subject in an organised and logical fashion. According to Colson's standard, Philo has failed to write an adequate biography of Moses. But Colson's complaint betrays a failure to read Philo on his own terms and according to the authorial intention embodied in the literary form of the *VM* itself. Whatever else the *VM* may be, it is not a modern biography.

Another model has been proposed by which to understand the *VM*, one founded on certain presuppositions regarding the audience to which the work was aimed. Philo says at the very beginning of his work that

---

[27] F. H. COLSON, «General Introduction», *De Vita Mosis*, xv.

he intends to relate the story of «this greatest and most perfect of men» (ἀνδρὸς τὰ πάντα μεγίστου καὶ τελειοτάτου: *VM* I.1) in order to bring it «to the knowledge of such as deserve not to remain in ignorance of it» (καὶ γνώριμον τοῖς ἀξίοις μὴ ἀγνοεῖν αὐτὸν ἀποφῆναι: *VM* I.1). Those who «deserve not to remain in ignorance» of the life of Moses are never explicitly identified in the *VM*, but Goodenough, for instance, assumed that Philo meant to address himself to Gentiles, with the purpose of converting them[28]. The *VM* is thus an apologetic work in Goodenough's view, or at the very least seems to have been aimed, as Goodenough recognised, at people who would have been otherwise unfamiliar with the biblical narratives[29].

Sandmel, who holds along with Goodenough that the *VM* served as a kind of introduction to Philo's exposition of the Law found in treatises like *De Decalogo*, *De Specialibus Legibus*, and *De Virtutibus*[30], nevertheless does not think that the *VM* was composed for the purpose of converting Gentiles to Judaism[31]. But while he rejects Goodenough's claim that the *VM* was written with conversionist aims, he does allow for an «obliquely related missionary purpose», one directed towards secularised Jews, who were on the verge of leaving the Jewish community, or who, like Tiberius Alexander, had already made the break with the faith of their forebears[32].

It may not be possible, twenty centuries after the work was written, to reconstruct the *specific* audience for which Philo wanted to compose the *VM*. But neither Goodenough's contention that Philo sought to bring about the conversion of his Gentile readers nor Sandmel's insistence that the *VM* attempted to bring secularised Jews back into the fold of their ancestral faith, each of which assume an apologetic purpose for the work, attends to the rhetoric of praise which Philo employs in the *VM*.

Using rhetorical categories current in the handbooks with which Philo would probably have been familiar, Philip L. Schuler has proposed another classification than the usual biographical or apologetic category by which to understand the *VM*: his analysis of the literary remains of the first century, including the canonical gospels and the works of secular

---

[28] E. R. GOODENOUGH, «Philo's Exposition of the Law», 109-125.

[29] E. R. GOODENOUGH, «Philo Judeus», 796.

[30] E. R. GOODENOUGH, «Philo's Exposition of the Law», 109-125.

[31] S. SANDMEL, *Philo of Alexandria*, 49.

[32] S. SANDMEL, *Philo of Alexandria*, 47.

writers like Suetonius, Tacitus, and Lucian, as well as Philo's *VM*, leads him to understand all of these works as epideictic literature, and more specifically as examples of the encomium[33]. The encomium had as its objective the marshalling of examples from the life of an individual, the purpose of which was the demonstration of the individual's virtues so as to establish the basis for honor and memorial[34]. Thus, Philo states that he proposes to write his βίος because «Greek men of letters have refused to treat him as worthy of memory» (οὐκ ἐθελησάντων αὐτὸν μνήμης ἀξιῶσαι τῶν παρ' Ἕλλησι λογίων): his work will, presumably, redress the lapse on the part of the Greek men of letters, and demonstrate how very worthy of memory (μνήμης ἀξιῶσαι) Moses actually is.

The pattern by which an author occasionally organised an encomiastic treatment of his subject was topical[35], a pattern which, of course, Philo observes in his treatment of Moses' life according to his exploits as king, as law-giver, as priest, and as prophet. The topical arrangement of a life is recommended by Quintilian, for instance, when a more conventional chronological arrangement does not seem as suitable:

> Praise awarded to character is always just, but may be given in various ways. It has sometimes proved the more effective course to trace a man's life and deeds in due chronological order, praising his natural gifts as a child, then his progress at school, and finally the whole course of his life, including words as well as deeds. At times on the other hand it is well to divide our praises, dealing separately with the various virtues, fortitude, justice, self-control and the rest of them and to assign to each virtue the deeds performed under its influence (*Institutio Oratorica* III.vii.15).

The order of the topics by which Philo discusses Moses' life does not seem to have been accidental: to have lauded Moses' achievements as king first is to have drawn attention to those accomplishments which would have recommended him to the widest possible audience, Gentiles and Jews alike, since the office of king was one with which all peoples in the ancient world would have been familiar. Only after Philo has demonstrated how great a king Moses was in Book I of the *VM* does he turn to a consideration of his achievements as law-giver, as priest, and

---

[33] P. L. SCHULER, «Philo's Moses», 89.

[34] For a brief description of the encomium, see B. L. MACK, *Rhetoric and the New Testament*, 47-48.

[35] B. L MACK, *Rhetoric and the New Testament*, 48; P. L. SCHULER, «Philo's Moses», 92.

as prophet in Book II of the *VM*. These of Moses' life Philo considers to be «allied and consequent» (ἑπομένων καὶ ἀκολούθων: *VM* II.1) to his primary rôle as king.

Similarly, Philo's tendency to have embellished the *VM* with events not found in the Biblical narrative, however much it may offend modern sensibilities, is nevertheless a hallmark of the encomium. Aristotle, for instance, advises one who is composing an encomium to praise his subject, even if the achievement is of a type he is only likely to have accomplished:

> [W]e pronounce an encomium upon those who have achieved something. Achievements, in fact, are signs of moral habit; for we should praise even a man who had not achieved anything, if we felt confident that he was likely to do so (*Rhetoric* I.ix.33).

In keeping with Aristotle's advice, Philo's claim that Moses received an education in «arithmetic, geometry, the lore of meter, rhythm and harmony and the whole subject of music» (ἀριθμοὺς μὲν οὖν καὶ γεωμετρίαν τήν τε ῥυθμικὴν καὶ ἁρμονικὴν καὶ μετρικὴν θεωρίαν καὶ μουσικὴν τὴν σύμπασαν: *VM* I.23) from Egyptian teachers, while he was instructed in the rest of the «regular school course» (ἐγκύκλιον παιδείαν), presumably grammar, rhetoric, and logic, by Greek masters (*VM* I.23) may be seen, not as sheer invention on Philo's part, but rather as praise for an achievement which Moses is likely to have accomplished.

Hence both Goodenough's claim that the *VM* was written with the intention of bringing about the conversion of Philo's Gentile readers, as well as Sandmel's rejection of that thesis in favour of a reintegrationist claim on Philo's secularised contemporaries fail to understand the purpose of encomiastic literature, which is as much directed *ad intra*, to strengthen the commitments of those who are already convinced of Moses' virtues, as it is oriented *ad extra*, to bring about a change in attitude in those for whom Moses would have been virtually unknown. The supposition that the original audience for *VM* should have been limited to any particular group of people plays false with the nature of the encomium: the rhetoric of praise is, by its nature, inclusive, and the audiences for which the *VM* was written may be said to have been as diverse as the Greek-speaking population of first-century Alexandria itself. Here I find myself in substantial agreement with Peder Borgen, who holds that Philo's purpose in writing the *VM* was

> to show the divine calling of Moses and the Jewish people to worship God, to keep the Sabbath, and to serve the whole world. Philo expects that the

new (eschatological) order will come when all nations cast aside their ancestral customs and honour the laws of Moses alone (II.42-43). Thus the book was written to tell Gentile readers about the supreme law-giver whose laws they are to accept and honour. It was also to strengthen the Jews for their universal rôle. This dual purpose fits well the situation of the Jewish community of Alexandria in the period before Gaius Caligula, when Jews were actively penetrating the Greek community[36].

### 1.2.1 Moses as king and law-giver in Philo

Wayne Meeks contends that the fundamental purpose of the Philo's *VM* is to present Moses as an ideal king[37]. For Meeks, as for Goodenough before him[38], Philo presents Moses in the *VM* according to the lineaments of the ideal king with which the Gentiles would have been familiar[39]. In a justly celebrated study of Hellenistic monarchy, Goodenough had examined the predominant Hellenistic ideology of kingship, which viewed the ideal king as a νόμος ἔμψυχος, a living law[40]. Meeks holds that the transitional statements at *VM* I.334 and II.187 which indicate the divisions of the *VM* indicate «that the "offices" of legislator, priest, and prophet are really adjuncts to the primary office of king»[41]. Thus Philo writes at the conclusion of the first book of the *VM*:

> We have now told the story of Moses' actions in his capacity as king (κατὰ τὴν βασιλείαν). We must next deal with all that he achieved by his powers as high priest and legislator (ἀρχιερωσύνης καὶ νομοθετικῆς), powers which he possessed as the most fitting accompaniments of kingship (*VM* I.334).

The relationship between this Hellenistic ideology of kingship and Moses' law-giving is particularly evident in the *VM*:

> It is the king's duty to command what is right and forbid what is wrong. But to command what should be done and to forbid what should not be done is the peculiar function of law; so that it follows at once that the king is a living law (νόμον ἔμψυχον), and the law a just king (*VM* II.4).

---

[36] P. BORGEN, «Philo of Alexandria», 235.

[37] W. A. MEEKS, *The Prophet-King*, 107.

[38] E. R. GOODENOUGH, «Philo Judeus», 796.

[39] W. A. MEEKS, *The Prophet-King*, 108.

[40] E. R. GOODENOUGH, «The Political Philosophy of Hellenistic Kingship».

[41] W. A. MEEKS, *The Prophet-King*, 112.

The encomiastic usefulness of such a relationship is immediately obvious; to have presented Moses in the guise of a Hellenistic king would
have commended him to a reader for whom the Biblical narrative itself,
even in its Greek translation, would have been otherwise unknown.
Moreover, to those for whom the Biblical narratives were a familiar and
beloved element of their religious heritage, the presentation of Moses as
a Hellenistic king would have accomplished at least two aims: first of
all, the figure of Moses is thereby rendered in contemporary and thus
comprehensible terms; and secondly, as the figure of Moses is thus
exalted, so is the faith of which he is regarded as the primary exponent:
his glory redounds to his followers. In this respect, Philo's retelling of
the life of Moses accords with the intention of the Biblical narratives as
George Coats understands them; he contends that the Biblical narratives
intend to depict Moses in a way which says that the hero lived for the
sake of his people: «[i]t is to say, with a certain kind of humble pride,
that this man was the father of our people»[42].

Yet in so presenting Moses as a royal «living law», Philo has rung an
important change on one important strain of the Biblical narrative: Ex
20:1 and Deut 5:5 alike make clear that the Decalogue comes from God,
and not from Moses. In these passages, Moses is a legislator only by
courtesy, which is to say that he enunciates laws which God himself has
formulated. In the *VM*, by contrast, Moses is the νομοθέτης *par excellence*: Philo's claim is

> that Moses himself was the best of all law-givers in all countries (νομοθετῶν
> ἄριστος τῶν πανταχοῦ πάντων), better in fact than any who have ever
> arisen among either the Greeks or the barbarians, and that his laws are the
> most excellent and truly come from God, since they omit nothing that is
> needful [...] (*VM* II.12).

This claim for the superlativeness of Moses is based on two factors, according to Philo: first of all, Moses is himself a better law-giver than
any other; and secondly, his laws are comprehensive: «they omit nothing
that is needful» (μηδὲν ὧν χρὴ παραλιπόντες).

### 1.2.2 Moses as prophet in Philo

Philo's discussion of Moses' prophetic office involves a three-fold distinction between the types of prophecy. The first kind of prophecy is es-

---

[42] G. W. COATS, «The Moses Narratives», 43-44.

sentially interpretation: God speaks in his own person and the prophet serves as his interpreter (*VM* II.188). This first type Philo characterises as «too great to be lauded by human lips; scarcely indeed could heaven and the world and the whole existing universe worthily sing their praises», (*VM* II.191), and he excludes it from his discussion of prophecy. The second type of prophecy consists in the putting of questions to God by the prophet to which God replies (*VM* II.190). The third type of prophecy is more properly an exercise of the prophet himself: «God has given to him of his own power of foreknowledge (προγνωστικῆς δυνάμεως) and by this he will reveal future events» (*VM* II.190). The function of the third type of prophecy is predictive, and it is this third type of prophecy which dominates Philo's presentation of Moses. Hence, the Israelites hail Moses in the *VM* as «a true seer (ἀληθόμαντιν), an interpreter of God (θεοφράδμονα), and alone gifted with foreknowledge of the hidden future» (*VM* II.269).

Philo adduces several examples to demonstrate the prophetic gifts of Moses: the parting of the Red Sea (*VM* II.247-257), the production of manna (*VM* II.258-269), the episode of the golden bull (*VM* II.270-274), and the rebellion of Korah, Dathan, and Abiram, whom he does not identify by name (*VM* II.275-287). In the first and the last of these examples, the prophetic gifts of Moses manifest themselves in such a way that he alone is able to see the immediate future. So, for instance, at the shore of the Red Sea, as the Israelites despair of their future, fearing destruction at the hands of the Egyptians, Moses rallies them, urging them not to give into panic, since the destruction they envision will come, not to them, but rather to their enemies:

> The prophet, seeing the whole nation entangled in the meshes of panic, like a draught of fishes, was taken out of himself by divine possession and uttered these inspired words: «Alarm you needs must feel. Terror is near at hand: the danger is great. In front is a vast expanse of sea; no haven for a refuge, no boats at hand: behind, the menace of the enemy's troops, which march along in unresting pursuit. Whither can one turn or swim for safety? Everything has attacked us suddenly from every side – earth, sea, man, the elements of nature. Yet be of good courage, faint not. Stand with unshaken minds, look for the invincible help which God will send. Self-sent it will be with you anon, invisible it will fight before you. Ere now you have often experienced its unseen defence. I see it preparing for the contest and casting a noose round the necks of the enemy. It drags them down through the sea. They sink like lead into the depths. You see them still alive: I have a vision of them dead, and today you too shall see their corpses» (*VM* II.250-252).

Moses' speech to the Israelites is divided into two parts: in the first half
(*VM* II.251), he describes the parlous situation facing the Israelites.
Hemmed in from all sides, their predicament seems hopeless, and their
imminent destruction seems assured. The second half of his speech (*VM*
II.252), looks beyond the immediate crisis to the near future. It is in this
second half of his speech that Moses manifests his prophetic gift, which
has two aspects to it: he fore*sees* what others cannot detect, and he
fore*tells* what others cannot predict. Thus while the Israelites see nothing
but the sea before them and their enemies behind, Moses sees the
«invisible help which God will send» (προσδοκᾶτε τὴν ἀήττητον ἐκ θεοῦ
βοήθειαν: *VM* II.252). Similarly, the Israelites see the Egyptian troops
«still alive» (ἔτι ζώντων: *VM* II.252), Moses has «a vision of them dead»
(τεθνεώτων δ' ἐγὼ φαντασίαν λαμβάνω: *VM* II.252), a vision he promises
the Israelites will soon share. That *foresight* which constitutes the first
aspect of Moses' prophetic gift permits him to *foretell* what will befall
his people. Philo evidently intends this second aspect of the prophetic
gift to accomplish hortatory ends, since, having heard the speech, the
Israelites renew their hope: «So he spake with words of promise ex-
ceeding anything they could hope for» (καὶ ὁ μὲν ταῦτ' ἀπεφθέγγετο μεί-
ζονα ὄντα πάσης ἐλπίδος: *VM* II.253).

In a similar fashion, in Philo's version of the rebellion of Korah,
Abiram, and Dathan (*VM* II.275-287), Moses sees what others, the rebels in particular, cannot see, namely, the punishment for rebellion:

> I see the earth opened and vast chasms yawning wide. I see great bands of
> kinsfolk perishing, houses dragged down and swallowed up with their
> inmates, and living men descending into Hades (*VM* II.281).

No sooner does he see his vision than it comes about, a factor which
moves Philo to remark that «the quick succession of these punishments
and their magnitude in both cases clearly and widely established the
fame of the prophet's godliness (εὐσέβειαν), to the truth of whose
pronouncements God himself had testified» (*VM* II.284). It should be
noted that the structure of this episode does not reflect the distinction
between fore*seeing* an event and fore*telling* it; instead, this prophecy
resembles a «speech-act» in that it seems almost to bring about the very
event that it describes. In this sense, the destruction of Korah, Abiram,
and Dathan in the *VM* looks more like a curse than a prophecy.

The middle two episodes involving the appearance of manna (*VM*
II.258-269), and the episode of the golden bull (*VM* II.270-274) both
depict Moses' exercise of his prophetic gift as an instance of *in*sight,

which is to say that in these episodes, Moses' prophetic gifts are employed in the service of understanding the *meaning* of the events which are unfolding. Here, too, as in the episodes which bracket them, Moses alone possesses the insight permitting him to understand what is happening around him.

In Philo's retelling of the appearance of manna, Moses alone knows what to do (and what not to do) with what the *VM* calls «a celestial fruit in the form of dew, like millet grain» (καρπὸν αἰθέριον ἐν δρόσῳ κέγχρῳ παραπλήσιον: *VM* II.258):

> When Moses saw it, he bade them gather it, and said under inspiration: «We must trust God as we have experienced his kindnesses in deeds greater than we could have hoped for. Do not treasure up or store the food he sends. Let none leave any part of it over for the morrow» (*VM* II.258).

His prophetic insight enables him first, to see the manna as one more example of God's kindness, and second, to know that storing the manna is, in effect, failing to trust that God's kindness will always be forthcoming. When some of the Israelites attempt to save some of the manna for the next day, Moses becomes angry, not simply because of their disobedience, but because, «in their utter incapacity for learning, [they] actually disbelieved» (ἀλλὰ καὶ ἀπιστοῦσιν οἱ δυσμαθέστατοι πάντων: *VM* II.261). In Philo's view, the difference between what Moses understands and what the disobedient Israelites understand is equivalent to the difference between belief and unbelief. Philo could not have chosen a more pointed measure by which to distinguish Moses from the Israelites.

Similarly, when the manna rains down in a double portion on the sixth day (*VM* II.264) and not at all on the seventh day (*VM* II.268-269), Moses alone understands the significance of what is transpiring about him, realising that the long-forgotten Sabbath is about to be reinstituted:

> Moses, when he heard of this and also actually saw it, was awestruck and, guided by what was not so much surmise as God-sent inspiration (θεοφορη- θείς), made announcement of the Sabbath (*VM* II.264).

Philo is quick to note that the insight which Moses displays in this episode should not be confused with anything other than a prophetic inspiration which comes from God himself:

> I need hardly say that conjectures of this kind are closely akin to prophecies. For the mind could not have made so straight an aim if there was not also the divine spirit guiding it to the truth itself (*VM* II.265).

Philo attributes the same kind of God-sent inspiration to Moses when he orders the Levites to slaughter all who have offered sacrifice to the golden bull (*VM* II.270-274), though he is careful to note that the orders Moses gives «may be thought to resemble exhortations rather than oracular sayings» (καίτοι δόξαντα ἂν παραινέσεσιν ἐοικέναι μᾶλλον ἢ χρησ‐ μοῖς: *VM* II.270). Thus, when Moses sees that the Israelites have fallen into idolatry, he is transformed by the prophetic spirit which overtakes him:

> He therefore became another man, changed both in outward appearance and mind; and filled with the spirit (ἐπιθειάσας), he cried: «Who is there who has no part with this delusion nor has given to the no-lords the name of lordship? Let all such come to me» (*VM* II.272).

The prophetic charism which animates Moses here is one which keeps him faithful to God, but more than that, it moves him to summon others who are like-minded to separate themselves from the idolaters. These are the Levites, though, curiously, Philo never explicitly identifies the «one tribe» which answers his call.

> When Moses found them hot with rage and brimful of courage and resolution, he was more than ever possessed by the spirit (ἔτι μᾶλλον ἢ πρότερον θεοφορηθείς) and said: «Let each of you take his sword and rush through the whole camp, and slay not only those who are strangers to you but also the very nearest of your kinfolk. Mow them down, holding that to be a truly righteous deed which is done for truth and God's honour, a cause which to champion and defend is the lightest of labours» (*VM* II.273).

The first point to be noted about this passage is that the command to destroy those who have worshipped the golden bull is, like Moses' anger, the product of divine inspiration. Indeed, here Moses is «more than ever possessed by the spirit» (ἔτι μᾶλλον ἢ πρότερον θεοφορηθείς: *VM* II.273). This may be Philo's attempt to justify what might well have appeared to his contemporaries, particularly those who were not members of the πολίτευμα of Alexandria, as an act of barbarism. The second point to be noted is that the alacrity with which the Levites answer Moses' summons is the first sign of their likeness to Moses, insofar as they are similarly zealous for the Lord.

> So they slaughtered three thousand of the principal leaders in godlessness, without meeting any resistance, and thereby not only made good their defence against the charge of having been party to the shameless crime, but were accounted as the noblest of heroes and awarded the prize most suitable to their action, that is the priesthood (*VM* II.274).

If, as I have noted, the Levites resemble Moses first of all in their zeal for the Lord, their likeness to Moses is further strengthened when, as a reward for their obedience, both to God and to Moses, they are appointed priests. Thus, for Philo, the Mosaic office continues to be exercised in his own day by those who claim descent from these first priests.

### 1.2.3  The *Vita Mosis* and the Bible

With respect to the last *words* of Moses, Philo is really quite restrained in comparison to both the biblical narratives and other examples of the «rewritten Bible». He presents the last words of Moses according to a bipartite scheme. First of all, he claims that Moses becomes

> possessed by the spirit, no longer uttering general truths to the whole nation but prophesying to each tribe in particular the things which were to be and hereafter must come to pass. Some of these have already taken place, others are still looked for, since confidence in the future is assured by fulfillment in the past (*VM* II.288).

Philo characterises these prophecies as «oracles and inspired sayings» (λογίων καὶ χρησμῶν) and evaluates them as «wonderful» (θαυμάσια μὲν οὖν ταῦτα: *VM* II.290). It is evident that Philo has the Blessing of Moses in mind here: he insists that Moses prophesies to each of the tribes in particular, an insistence which unmistakably points to Deut 33. The fact that some of the things prophesied by Moses have not yet come to pass does not indicate for Philo a failure on either Moses' or God's part: they provide, instead, an occasion for confidence in the future (πίστις τῶν μελλόντων: *VM* II.288). What is important to note here, however, is that Philo is content merely to summarise the Blessing of Moses, and to praise Moses for having delivered it: he does not attempt to recast it in a form which permits him to comment on contemporary affairs. This differentiates him from his near contemporary, Josephus, as well as the anonymous authors of the *TM* and the *LAB*.

The second half of the bipartite final speech in the *VM* shows Moses prophesying his own death and burial:

> For when he was already being exalted and stood at the very barrier, ready at the signal to direct his upward flight to heaven, the divine spirit fell upon him and he prophesied with discernment while still alive the story of his own death; told ere the end how the end came; told how he was buried with none present, surely by no mortal hands but by immortal powers; how also he was not laid to rest in the tomb of his forefathers but was given a monument of special dignity which no man has ever seen; how all the nation wept and

mourned for him a whole month and made open display, private and public, of their sorrow, in memory of his vast benevolence and watchful care for each one of them and for all (*VM* II.291).

The first point to be noted about this second half of Moses' final speech is that Moses prophesies about himself and the manner of his death and burial. This is, again, a departure from the biblical narrative, in which the content of the final Mosaic prophecy is the future of the Chosen People, however generally that future might have been imagined. Thus the reader's attention is directed here in the *VM*, not to the destiny of the Chosen People themselves, but rather to the person of Moses. This emphasis on the person of Moses is in perfect keeping with the nature of the encomium, which, as we have noted, seeks to demonstrate the virtues of its subject, and how worthy of memory he is. Here, the immediate virtue being demonstrated is clearly his ability to prophesy.

There may be a suggestion, in addition, of Moses' serenity in the face of his own death: he himself does not mourn his passing, though «all the nation wept and mourned for him a whole month and made open display, public and private of their sorrow» (σύμπαν τὸ ἔθνος αὐτὸν ὅλον μῆνα δακρυρροοῦν ἐπένθησεν ἴδιον καὶ κοινὸν πένθος ἐπιδειξάμενον: *VM* II.291). The people's mourning stands in contrast to Moses' prophetic composure.

F. H. Colson has drawn attention to the essential fidelity with which Philo adheres to the narrative of Scripture in the *VM*[43]. Yet, unlike the biblical narratives, which depict the death of Moses in one of three fashions – as a consequence of the sin of both Moses and Aaron at Meribah in Kadesh (Num 27:12-14; Deut 32:48-52), or as a consequence of old age (Deut 31:1-2) or because his time had come, even though «his eye was not dim, nor his natural force abated» (οὐκ ἠμαυρώθησαν οἱ ὀφθαλμοὶ αὐτοῦ, οὐδὲ ἐφθάρησαν τὰ χελύνια αὐτοῦ: Deut 34:7)[44] – Philo depicts his end as a transformation:

Afterwards the time came when he had to make his pilgrimage from earth to heaven, and leave this mortal life for immortality, summoned thither by the Father Who resolved his twofold nature of soul and body into a single unity (ὃς αὐτὸν δυάδα ὄντα, σῶμα καὶ ψυχήν, εἰς μονάδος), transforming his whole being into mind pure as the sunlight (*VM* II.288).

---

[43] F. H. COLSON, «General Introduction», *De Vita Mosis*, xvii.

[44] See G. W. COATS, *Moses*, 148.

Meeks has noted the similarities between the portrayal of Moses' ascent at Sinai in the *Quaestiones et Solutiones in Exodum* and that of his death here in the *VM*[45], a similarity which has moved Burton L. Mack to posit a paradigmatic function for both events, thus understanding both the Sinai ascent and the death in Philo as varieties of mystic apotheosis[46]:

> But he who is resolved into the nature of unity, is said to come near God in a kind of family relation, for having given up and left behind all mortal kinds, he is changed into the divine, so that such men become kin to God and truly divine (*QE* ii.29)[47].

The similarities between Moses' ascent to Sinai and his death are striking and cannot have been anything other than deliberate on the part of Philo; thus Meeks and Mack are right to have recognised the parallel between the two events. Meeks goes so far as to claim that the «mystic ascent» at Sinai «is a kind of "realised eschatology"; the final ascension is a projection and fulfillment of the goal of the mystic ascent»[48]. But what Meeks fails to take under consideration in his reading of Philo's depiction of the death of Moses is the extent to which Philo has made use of the Platonic heritage.

### 1.2.4  The *Vita Mosis* and Plato

Philo's debt to Plato here is unmistakable in his depiction of Moses' death as a resolution of the δυάδα ὄντα of body and soul into a single μονάδος, a «mind pure as the sunlight» (νοῦν ἡλιοειδέστατον). David T. Runia contends that here Philo follows the well-known distinction between body (σῶμα), soul (ψυχή), and mind (νοῦς) found in the *Timaeus* 30b[49]. Moreover, the transformation of the dying Moses into a «mind pure as the sunlight» is probably a reference to the well-known Platonic analogy of the sun in Book Six of the *Republic*. In that celebrated passage, Plato likens reason to the sun in such a way that just as to

---

[45] W. A. MEEKS, *The Prophet-King*, 124.

[46] B. L. MACK, «*Imitatio Mosis*», 27-55.

[47] Both the *Quaestiones et Solutiones in Exodum* as well as its companion volume, *Quaestiones et Solutiones in Genesin*, survive in their entirety only in an Armenian translation of the Greek language original.

[48] W. A. MEEKS, *The Prophet-King*, 125.

[49] D. T. RUNIA, *Philo of Alexandria and the* Timaeus *of Plato*, 331.

see requires light, the best source of which is the sun, so to know requires reason:

> When [the soul] is firmly fixed on the domain where truth (ἀλήθεια) and reality (τὸ ὄν) shine resplendent it apprehends and knows them and appears to possess reason (*Republic* VI.508d).

Philo has not adopted Plato's analogy of the sun uncritically, however: for though he may owe a debt here to Plato, he owes greater one to his religious heritage. That religious debt moves him to transform the Platonic analogy. If Moses becomes νοῦν ἡλιοειδέστατον, «mind pure as the sunlight», it is because he has been so transformed by ὁ ὤν, «He who is», namely, God (Ex 3:14), not because he has gazed upon τὸ ὄν, «what is», namely, reality. Philo's use of the Platonic analogy of the sun serves to illustrate the «naturalness» of Moses' transformations, both at Sinai as well as at the moment of death: just as all people have implanted within them the capacity to reason, the right exercise of which leads them to a knowledge of the truth, so all people have implanted within them the capacity to know God, which capacity is fulfilled in their obedience to the Law. Philo's Moses remains even here, at the end of his life, the servant of the Almighty, and not Plato's Philosopher-King.

The freedom with which Philo departs from the narrative of Moses' death as it is found in the Scriptures extends to more than his use of Platonic imagery. Here one must attend not only to what Philo adds to his narrative, but to what he deletes. The survey of the Promised Land which figures so prominently in the biblical narratives (Num 27:12, Deut 32:49; 34:1-4) is altogether missing from the *VM*. One reason such a survey is missing may have to do with the audiences to whom Philo seems to have intended his work: whoever his readership was – potential Gentile converts to Judaism, as Goodenough contended, secularised Jews, as Sandmel holds, or literate inhabitants of Alexandria, Gentiles and members of the Jewish πολίτευμα alike, as I think – such people, living far from the Land of Israel, would hardly have been likely to appreciate a geographic survey of a country to which their ties would have been, at best, tenuous, and at worst, non-existent.

## 1.3 *Theological analysis*

The literary analysis of both the *VM* as a whole as well as that section which depicts his death in particular has demonstrated that one of the primary impulses which moves Philo throughout this two-volume treatise is the depiction of the life and death of Moses in terms which are comprehensible to the various communities to which Philo directed his work. The thematic organisation of the βίος, for instance, utilises categories which are immediately familiar to any contemporary of Philo, regardless of religious allegiances: pagan and Jew alike would have been familiar with the duties and accomplishments of a king, a law-giver, a high priest, or a prophet. The literary conventions of the encomium serve Philo's theological agenda, which is to portray Moses as a figure of universal appeal.

That theological agenda may be said to have three items. First of all, to have characterised the death of Moses in a way which is virtually identical with the way in which his ascent to Sinai is depicted is to have constructed a kind of enthymeme about obedience to the law which runs something like this: (1) Moses is united with God when he receives the law; (2) Moses is united with God when he dies; (3) those who obey the law will be similarly united with God when they die. This first item may be imagined to have appealed particularly to those for whom obedience to the law would have been particularly prized, namely, Philo's Jewish contemporaries. But we would be mistaken to think that the theme of obedience to the law would have been limited solely to first century Jews: death comes to all men and women, and the longing for union with God is nigh universal, as the prevalence of mystery cults in the first century attest[50]. To have linked the theme of obedience to the law to these universal experiences, as Philo does, is to have claimed a universal significance for that law.

The second item on Philo's theological agenda is more patently universal: to have marshalled certain Platonic categories and images by which to describe the death of Moses, however much it may depart from the Biblical traditions upon which Philo draws, was one of the means whereby Philo was able to enhance the significance of this «greatest and most perfect of men» (ἀνδρὸς [...] μεγίστου καὶ τελειοτάτου: *VM* I.1). These Platonic categories were thought to be accurate descriptions of the way in which reality is structured; so, when Philo marshals the analogy of the sun to describe Moses' transformation, he is claiming that Moses' experience is one which any reasonable person will recognise as authentic. Moreover, to have portrayed the ascending/dying Moses in terms of the analogy of the sun is, again, to have constructed a kind of enthymeme along the following lines: (1) all men and women long for the

---

[50] For an examination of the connection between the problem of mortality and the mystery cults in the ancient world, see W. BURKERT, *Ancient Mystery Cults*, 12-29.

truth; (2) Moses attains the truth through union with God; (3) all men and women will attain the truth through union with God.

The third item on Philo's theological agenda presents itself through the manner in which he has omitted certain details of the tradition. Unlike other first century narratives depicting the death of Moses, Philo does not exploit the prophetic opportunity provided in the tradition to comment on contemporary affairs. Indeed, as we have seen, he seems to have resisted the temptation to do so in his substitution of a summary statement at *VM* II.288 for some sort of detailed outline of events which would befall the Chosen People. The reason for his substitution lies, again, in the encomiastic nature of his work: the *VM*, as I have already noted, was directed at least in part to people who would have been otherwise unfamiliar with the biblical narratives themselves in which Moses figures; that dimension of the work is addressed *ad extra*. But the sort of prophecies which Deuteronomy depicts Moses as having delivered in his last hours are not «general truths to the whole nation», as Philo puts it; rather, Moses speaks «to each tribe in particular the things which were to be and hereafter must come to pass» (*VM* II.288). To have substituted a summary statement for those particular prophecies, as Philo does, however much he lauds them in the abstract, is to dismiss then as no longer relevant to the audience for whom he is now writing. It is fair to say, I think, that Philo has deliberately downplayed the *content* of the prophecies for which Moses was responsible, doubtless because their aim was too parochial for his encomiastic purposes. By so downplaying the content of Moses' last words, Philo has sought to universalise his message as a whole.

It seems clear that Philo has depicted Moses in a way which makes the great βασιλεύς καὶ νομοθέτης καὶ ἀρχιερεύς καὶ προφήτης comprehensible to the audiences to whom the *VM* was directed, however those audiences might have been composed, whether they encompassed Philo's Alexandrian, non-Jewish neighbours, as Goodenough thought, or Philo's fallen-away, secularised Jewish relatives like Tiberius Alexander, as Sandmel thinks, or even educated inhabitants of Alexandria, pagans as well as members of the Jewish πολίτευμα of Alexandria, as I think. He extols those accomplishments which would have commended Moses to his Alexandrian contemporaries, pagan and Jew alike, and he presents the manner of his death in such a way that Moses becomes an exemplary Everyman. In that respect, Philo's Moses is all things to all people.

## 2. Josephus, *Jewish Antiquities* IV.177-193; 312-314; 320-331

Thanks to his autobiography, the *Life*, much more may be known about the man Josephus than his older near-contemporary Philo. He reports that he was born in Jerusalem «the year Gaius Caesar became emperor» (τῷ πρώτῳ τῆς Γαΐου Καίσαρος ἡγεμονίας: *Life* 5), that is, 37-38 CE, into a priestly family, about which he takes considerable pride: «Different races base their claims to nobility on various grounds; with us a connexion with the priesthood is the hallmark of an illustrious line» (*Life* 1).

He took a leading rôle in the affairs of his people, starting out as a relatively young man of twenty-six with a mission to Rome to secure the release of some priests imprisoned there (*Life* 13-16). And while it is not my purpose here to rehearse the details of Josephus' life, it is important to note that the man's literary activities and his extensive public activities are closely linked; indeed, he seems to have engaged in the former in order to justify the latter. Thus, in the exordium to the *JA*, he claims to have written his *Bellum Judaicum* because «I was constrained to narrate it in detail in order *to refute those who in their writings were doing outrage to the truth*» (ἐβιάσθην ἐκδιηγήσασθαι διὰ τοὺς ἐν τῷ γράφειν λυμαινομένους τὴν ἀλήθειαν: *JA* I.4; emphasis mine). Similar passages occur in the *Life*[51], and in *Against Apion*[52].

### 2.1 *Date, provenance, and original language*

As an educated Palestinian Jew of the first century, Josephus would have known Hebrew and Aramaic, and, of course, he would have been schooled in the sacred literature of his people. This is undoubtedly what is meant by the claim in the *Life* 9 that as a fourteen year old boy, he won the acclaim of all for his love of letters. Similarly, in the epilogue to the *JA*, he asserts that «my compatriots admit that in our Jewish learning I far excel them (ἔχω γὰρ ὁμολογούμενον παρὰ τῶν ὁμοεθνῶν πλεῖστον αὐτῶν κατὰ τὴν ἐπιχώριον καὶ παρ' ἡμῖν παιδείαν διαφέρειν: *JA* XX.263). His accomplishments in Hebrew were, apparently, a source of no little pride to him.

He seems to have been somewhat more modest about his linguistic prowess in the Greek language:

---

[51] See, for instance *Life* 6.

[52] See, for example, *Against Apion* I.2; I.53ff.

I have also laboured strenuously to partake of the realm of Greek prose and poetry, after having gained a knowledge of Greek grammar, although the habitual use of my native tongue has prevented my attaining precision in the pronunciation. For our people do not favour those persons who have mastered the speech of many nations, or who adorn their style with smoothness of diction, because they consider that not only is such skill common to ordinary freemen but that even slaves who so choose may acquire it (*JA* XX.263-264).

Those strenuous labours in Greek do not seemed to have served him as well as his efforts with the learning of his own people: he admits in *Against Apion* I.50 that he needed to hire assistants (συνεργοί) to help him with the demands of the Greek language as he wrote his narrative of the Jewish Revolt of 66-70. Nevertheless, it is thanks to those strenuous labours, and to the help of the συνεργοί that Josephus writes his own version of the ancient stories of his people.

The *JA* represents the second of Josephus' great works. The first, the *Bellum Judaicum*, relates the events leading up to the First Jewish Revolt and Josephus' rôle in that affair. After having narrated the recent history in which he himself played so prominent a part, Josephus next turns to the distant past:

I had indeed ere now, when writing the history of the war, already contemplated describing the origin of the Jews, the fortunes that befell them, the great law-giver under whom they were trained in piety and the exercise of the other virtues (παιδευθέντες νομοθέτῃ τὰ πρὸς εὐσέβειαν καὶ τὴν ἄλλην ἄσκησιν ἀρετῆς), and all those wars waged by them through long ages before this last in which they were involuntarily engaged against the Romans. However, since the compass of such a theme was excessive, I made the *War* into a separate volume, with its own beginning and end, thus duly proportioning my work (*JA* I.6-7).

Josephus himself considered the work to be «a translation of our sacred books» (ἐκ τῶν ἱερῶν γραμμάτων μεθηρμήνευκα: *Against Apion* I.54), though the work may more aptly be described as a paraphrase rather than a translation, in other words, an example of the «rewritten Bible»[53].

---

[53] For a brief discussion of the collection of biblical books at Josephus' disposal, see S. Z. LEIMAN, «Josephus and the Canon of the Bible», 50-58.

## 2.2 *Literary analysis*

As L. L. Grabbe recognises, the *JA* has as its primary aim the presentation of the history of the Jewish people in as favourable a light as possible to those who would be otherwise unfamiliar with that history, in this case, Josephus' Graeco-Roman readership[54]. The *JA* thus represents an apologetic attempt to describe «the origin of the Jews, the fortunes that befell them, [and] the great law-giver through whom they were trained in piety and the exercise of the other virtues, and all those wars waged by them through long ages before this last» (*JA* I.6). What is interesting in this thumbnail description of the *JA* is the prominent place accorded to Moses in the scheme. He is the law-giver (νομοθέτη), as one might expect, but also the teacher from whom they learned «piety and the exercise of the other virtues» (εὐσέβειαν καὶ τὴν ἄλλην ἄσκησιν ἀρετῆς: *JA* I.6).

In an important series of articles, Louis H. Feldman has examined Josephus' presentation of Moses in the *JA* and has concluded that his intention in presenting Moses as the virtual embodiment of the Hellenistic virtues was apologetic, and that thus the work as a whole was directed primarily to non-Jews[55]. Indeed, as Samuel Sandmel has noted, apologetic concerns appear in practically every work to have issued from the hand of Josephus: he identifies two tasks of Jewish apologetics: (1) to demonstrate the compatibility of Judaism with the «worthy aspects» of Greek thought (preeminently the works of Plato and Aristotle), and (2) to stress the antiquity of Jewish civilisation and thought[56]. This second task of stressing the antiquity of Jewish civilisation and thought Josephus accomplishes first in the exordium of the *JA*:

> At the outset, then, I entreat those who will read these volumes to fix their thoughts on God, and to test whether our law-giver has had a worthy conception of his nature and has always assigned to him such actions as befit his power, keeping his words concerning him pure of that unseemly mythology current among others; albeit that, in dealing with ages so long and so remote, he would have had ample license to invent fictions. For he was born two thousand years ago, to which ancient date the poets never ventured to

---

[54] L. L. GRABBE, «Josephus», 366.

[55] L. H. FELDMAN, «Josephus' Portrait of Moses», 285-328; ID., «Josephus' Portrait of Moses: Part Two», 7-50; ID., «Josephus' Portrait of Moses: Part Three», 301-330.

[56] S. SANDMEL, *Judaism and Christian Beginnings*, 267.

refer even the birth of their gods, much less the actions or the laws of mortals (*JA* I.15-17).

In addition to the demonstration of the antiquity of the civilisation whose laws Moses gave, the exordium accomplishes a further purpose: to have located Moses in the distant past of two thousand years ago is to have placed him in an era even more ancient than that of the gods of the Gentiles; Moses is thereby greater than the gods, insofar as he existed before them. We shall see, in the course of our analysis of the *JA*, that one of the means by which Josephus demonstrates Moses' compatibility with the best of Hellenistic culture is by likening him to Socrates.

### 2.2.1 Moses as law-giver in Josephus

The most common title in the *JA* by which Josephus identifies Moses is ὁ νομοθέτης[57]. That five of these instances come in the introduction to the *JA* seems to indicate that this is the title by which Josephus intends his readers to view the whole of Moses' activities. Wayne Meeks notes how this title is already an accommodation of Moses' rôle in sacred history to Gentile sensibilities:

> [T]he mediation of the Torah is one of the essential characteristics of Moses in the rabbinic haggadah. Still the Rabbis would not call Moses the «law-giver» — only God *gave* the Torah, while it came «by Moses' hand». The usual title in Rabbinic writings is rather «Moses our master» (משה רבינו). To call Moses νομοθέτης, then, is already to adapt for Gentile understanding his primary rôle in Jewish sacred history[58].

This concern to present Moses using categories of thought which are intelligible to non-Jews explains why the term νομοθέτης appears so frequently in *Against Apion*, Josephus' most overtly apologetic work[59]. As I have already noted, a similar apologetic desire informs the preface to the *JA*:

---

[57] *JA* I.6, 15, 18, 20, 23, 24, 95, 240; III.180, 187; IV.6, 13, 150, 156, 263, 322; VIII.192; XI.77; XII.110; XVIII.264. See K. H. RENGSTORF, *A Complete Concordance to Flavius Josephus*, s.v. νομοθέτης. Moses is also the subject of the verb νομοθετέω in *JA* III.266, 267, 268, 317.

[58] W. A. MEEKS, *The Prophet-King*, 132.

[59] I. 316; II.75 (*noster legislator*) 145 (ὁ νομοθέτης ἡμῶν Μωυσῆς) 154, 156, 161, 165, 169, 173, 186, 209, 218, 237, 257, 279, 286, 290.

Now I have undertaken this present work, in the belief that the whole Greek-speaking world will find it worthy of attention; for it will embrace our entire ancient history and political constitution, translated from the Hebrew records. I had indeed ere now, when writing the history of the war, already contemplated describing the origin of the Jews, the fortunes that befell them, the great law-giver (νομοθέτη) under whom they were trained (παιδευθέν-τες) in piety and the exercise of the other virtues [...] (JA I.5-6).

If, for Philo, the law-giving functions of Moses are an expression of his kingly office, for Josephus, Moses' law-giving functions are an exercise of his teaching office. Meeks notes the distinctively Greek connection between legislation and παιδεία, a connection which does much to re-commend Moses to an audience otherwise unfamiliar with the narratives in which the figure of Moses appears[60]. Thus Josephus describes Moses here in terms which are as reminiscent of the teacher as they are of the law-giver:

Be it known, then, that the sage deemed it above all necessary, for one who would order his own life aright and also legislate for others, first to study the nature of God, and then, having contemplated his works with the eye of reason, to imitate so far as possible that best of all models and endeavour to follow it. For neither could the law-giver himself, without this vision, ever attain to a right mind, nor would anything that he should write in regard to virtue avail with his readers, unless before all else they were taught that God, as the universal Father and Lord who beholds all things, grants to such as follow him a life of bliss, but involves in dire calamities those who step outside the bounds of virtue (JA I.19-20).

Josephus' debt to Plato is evident here in his understanding of virtue as the imitation of the divine pattern[61]. The particular virtues which Moses wishes to promote in his readers, according to Josephus, are those which are appropriate to a religion which holds that there is but one God: indeed, the first thing Moses' readers will learn is that God is «the universal Father and Lord who beholds all things» (πάντων πατήρ τε καὶ δεσπότης ὁ θεὸς ὢν καὶ πάντα ἐπιβλέπων); only subsequently do they learn the way to a happy life:

our legislator [...] having shown that God possesses the very perfection of virtue (ἀκραιφνῆ τὴν ἀρετὴν ἔχοντα τὸν θεὸν), thought that men should

---

[60] W. A. MEEKS, The Prophet-King, 133.

[61] See Phaedo 27, 28.

strive to participate in it; and inexorably punished those who did not hold with or believe in these doctrines (*JA* I.23).

To call Josephus' law-giver a teacher is not to downplay his legislative functions: it is, however, to recognise that Josephus sought to present the figure of Moses as a law-giver in such a way that Moses would be intelligible and attractive to the audience for whom he, Josephus, was writing his own work.

### 2.2.2 The suffering and intercession of Moses

Josephus' depiction of the sufferings of Moses is not as prevalent in the *JA* as the image of the νομοθέτης which I have heretofore analysed. Nevertheless, it is not entirely absent, and merits some consideration, primarily because of its connection with another dimension of the traditions associated with Moses in the first century, namely, his power to intercede before God on behalf of his people.

The sufferings of Moses as they are presented in the *JA* seem to be, first of all, an expression of Moses' solidarity with his people. Thus, in Josephus' version of the incident at Marah (Exodus 15:22-25) which he relates in *JA* III.1-9, the people grumble because of the bitter water, and Moses suffers along with them:

> Moses, seeing their despondency and the indisputable gravity of the case — for this was no sound army, capable of meeting the stress of necessity with manly fortitude, but one whose nobler instincts were vitiated by a rabble of women and children, too feeble to respond to an oral admonition — Moses, I say, was yet in more serious straits, in that he made the sufferings of all his own (ἐν χαλεπωτέροις ἦν συμφορὰν τὴν ἁπάντων ἰδίαν αὑτοῦ ποιούμενος: *JA* III.5).

After the multitude comes to him, as Josephus puts it, «to procure for them some means of salvation» (ἐκπορίζειν αὐτοῖς ἀφορμήν τινα σωτηρί-ας: *JA* III.6), Moses intercedes before God:

> He therefore betook himself to prayer, entreating God to change that present evil property of the water and to render it drinkable. And, God having consented to grant that favour, he picked up the end of a stick that lay at his feet, cleft it in twain, lengthwise, and then, flinging it into the well, impressed upon the Hebrews that God had lent an ear to his prayers and had promised to render the water such as they desired, provided that they executed his orders with no remissness, but with alacrity (*JA* III.6-7).

The suffering of Moses and his intercessory functions are juxtaposed here; indeed, the latter follows hard upon the former. While the connection is never explicitly made, there is a sense in this episode that Moses' suffering and his capacity to intercede on behalf of his people are interrelated: it is as though Josephus wants his readers to understand that Moses' solidarity with his people, as expressed in his suffering along with them, moves him to come before God to plead on their behalf.

A similar juxtaposition of suffering and intercession informs the brief episode related in *JA* III.295-299. But, in this retelling of Numbers 11:1-34, Josephus rings some curious changes on his Biblical source. The Israelites have begun to complain about their condition, and, as Josephus puts it, «to reproach Moses for the trials which they had undergone on these peregrinations» (καὶ τὸν Μωυσῆν αἰτιᾶσθαι τῶν τε κατὰ τὴν ἀποδημίαν αὐτῷ πεπειραμένων: *JA* III.295):

> Amid this torrent of abuse showered upon the hero, there was yet one who admonished them not to be unmindful of Moses and what he had suffered for the salvation of all (καὶ τῶν πεπονημένων αὐτῷ περὶ τῆς κοινῆς σωτηρίας), nor to despair of God's aid (*JA* III.297).

Unlike the narrative in Numbers, which identifies two figures in the camp, namely Eldad and Medad, Josephus mentions only one, whose identity he never reports. And while in the narrative from Numbers, the content of the prophecies delivered by Eldad and Medad are never indicated, Josephus' version of the story specifies that the subject of the speech is none other than Moses and the hardships he had undergone (πεπονημένων) for the salvation of all (κοινῆς σωτηρίας). These alterations of the Biblical narrative cannot have been anything other than deliberate, and serve the purpose of reinforcing the connection between what Moses suffers and what benefits the people reap.

Josephus' version of the rebellion of Korah, Abiram, and Dathan (*JA* IV.14-58) posits a similar correlation between Moses' suffering and his intercessory powers. In his prayer for vindication (*JA* IV.40-50), Moses mentions the sufferings he has endured for the sake of his people:

> I, who had secured for myself a life of ease, through my prowess and at thy will, thanks too to what Raguel my father-in-law left me, abandoning the enjoyment of those good things, devoted myself to tribulations on behalf of this people. At first for their liberty, and now for their salvation, great are the toils that I have undergone, opposing to every peril all the ardour of my soul (*JA* IV.42).

Here, as above in *JA* III.297, the tribulations (ταλαιπωρίας) and the toils (πόνους) of Moses are directed towards securing the salvation (σωτηρί-ας) of the Israelites. And while Moses' intercessory functions do not figure explicitly in this passage, the fact that he is addressing God in this speech, asking God to avenge him against Korah, Abiram, and Dathan, not to mention the fact that the prayer is answered, and Abiram and Dathan are swallowed up by the earth (*JA* IV.51-53), while Korah is consumed by fire (*JA* IV.55-56), serves to establish the connection between the suffering of Moses and his powers of intercession.

The final mention of the sufferings of Moses comes after Moses has delivered himself of his first farewell address (*JA* IV.180-193): Josephus describes the reaction of those who hear him predict the loss of the Promised Land as the result of their rebelliousness:

> they were in tears and displaying deep regret for their general, alike remembering the risks which he had run and all that ardent zeal of his for their salvation, and despondent concerning the future, in the belief that they would never more have such a ruler and that God would be less mindful of them, since it was Moses who had ever been the intercessor (*JA* IV.194).

The scene as Josephus describes it places a great deal of emphasis on Moses' intercessory functions, and the peoples' anticipated suffering in the absence of those supplications before God. Like the passage in *JA* III.6-7, Moses' sufferings, here referred to as «the risks he had run» (κινδυνεύσειε: *JA* IV.194) are mentioned in conjunction with his willingness to serve as their intercessor (παρακαλοῦντα: *JA* IV.194).

To have noted the connection between the suffering of Moses and his rôle as intercessor in the *JA* is not to suggest that Josephus posits a causal relation between the two in such a way that God hears Moses' prayers on account of his suffering. Such a conception is foreign to Josephus, who is careful always to preserve the sense that God operates out of his own sovereign purposes. Nevertheless, the constant juxtaposition of suffering and intercession in these passages leads one to conclude that Josephus likely viewed both activities as signs of Moses' devotion to the Israelite people and a dedication to a divinely appointed task which is otherwise unparalleled in the history into which Josephus wishes to initiate his audience.

## 2.2.3  The death of Moses

The narrative of Moses' passing concludes Book IV of the *JA*. The reader is prepared for the scene by a series of speeches, the first of which is a valediction (*JA* IV.177-193) which Moses delivers «where today stands the city of Abile» (ὅπου νῦν πόλις ἐστὶν Ἀβίλη: *JA.* IV.176):

Comrades in arms and partners in this long tribulation, seeing that now, by God's decree and at the call of age, having completed a span of one hundred and twenty years, I must quit this life, and that in these coming actions beyond the Jordan I am not to be your helper and fellow-combatant, being prohibited by God, I have deemed it right even now not to renounce my zeal for your welfare, but to labour to secure for you the everlasting enjoyment of your good things and for myself an abiding memorial when you shall be endowed with a store of blessings yet better (*JA* IV.177-178).

This passage amounts to an exordium for the paranesis on obedience to the law which follows, a parenesis which parallels that of the Song of Moses in Deuteronomy. Moses is here presented in this exordium as one whose devotion to his duty and to his people is such that, even at the point of death, he is unwilling to renounce his obligations to his people, but continues to work on their behalf. This conception of Moses reminds one of Socrates, who is portrayed by Plato in the *Phaedo* as one whose devotion to his duty is such that he continues to teach even though he is about to die. The point would not have been lost on Josephus' first century audience: what Socrates was to the Athenians, Moses was to the Jews.

Following this exordium, Moses delivers an exhortation enjoining obedience to the law (*JA* IV.179-193). He announces the theme of the exhortation by issuing an invitation to the Israelites: «Come then, let me first propound the means whereby you may yourselves attain bliss and may bequeath to your children the possession of blessings for all eternity, and so depart from life» (φέρε οὖν ὑποθέμενος ὃν τρόπον ὑμεῖς τ' ἂν εὐδαιμονήσαιτε καὶ παισὶ τοῖς αὐτῶν καταλίποιτε κτῆσιν ἀγαθῶν ἀΐδιον [παραθέμενος] οὕτως ἀπέλθω τοῦ βίου: *JA* IV.179). To present obedience to the law as a means whereby personal happiness is to be achieved, as Josephus' Moses does here, is to present the law in the most favourable light possible. The bipartite parenesis which follows this invitation is organised according to two interrelated themes: first, God is the source of happiness for all humanity (*JA* IV.180-183); and second, obedience to the law and to the nation's leaders is a prerequisite for maintaining possession of the Promised Land (*JA* IV.184-193).

The second half of the parenesis, with its theme of possession of the land and the threat of its loss, is likely to have been understood by

Josephus' first century readers as having a poignant relevance. Moses here warns his auditors against insurrection:

> Never display towards these rulers the like of that wrath which you have oft-times dared to vent on me; for you know that my life has more often been imperilled by you than by the enemy. I say this with no intent to reproach you – at my exit from life I should be loath to leave you aggrieved by re-calling these things to mind, I who even at the moment when I underwent them refrained from wrath – but rather, that you may learn moderation for the future [...] and to prevent you from breaking out into any violence against those set over you (*JA* IV.188-189).

The warning against rebelliousness in the future takes its force from the reminder that, in the past, mutinous behaviour against Moses himself has characterised Israel's conduct towards its rulers. In that respect, the loss of the land which is consequent upon the outbreak of rebellion is itself inevitable:

> For, should you be carried away by it into a contempt and disdain for virtue, you will lose even that favour which you have found of God; and, having made him your enemy, you will forfeit that land, which you are to win, beaten in arms and deprived of it by future generations with the grossest ignominy, and, dispersed throughout the habitable world, you will fill every land and sea with your servitude (*JA* IV.190).

The condemnation of violence against «those set over you» (προεστηκό-τας), coupled with the prediction of the loss of the land, seems to function here as a *vaticinium ex eventu*, and would have been read by Josephus' contemporaries as a description of the situation facing the Jews in the aftermath of the First Jewish Revolt. The destruction of Jeru-salem along with its Temple is presented here in the *JA* as the divine punishment for having risen in rebellion. Thus does Josephus enable Moses to comment on contemporary affairs.

This farewell speech (*JA* IV.177-193) is not the only valediction in the *JA*. Following a paraphrase of the law (*JA* IV.196-301) and a summary of other ordinances (*JA* IV.302-311), Josephus provides Moses with another opportunity to speak directly to his people about what will trans-pire after his departure:

> Then, recounting all that he had done for the people's salvation in war and in peace, in compiling laws and cooperating to procure for them an ordered constitution, Moses foretold, as revealed to him by the Divinity, that, if they transgressed his rites, they would experience afflictions of such sort that their land would be filled with the arms of enemies, their cities razed, their

Temple burnt (ὡς ὅπλων τε αὐτοῖς πολεμίων πληρωθῆναι τὴν γῆν καὶ κατασκαφῆναι πόλεις καὶ τὸν νεὼν καταπρησθῆναι); that they would be sold into slavery to men who would take no pity on their misfortunes, and that their repentance would profit them naught amid those sufferings. «Howbeit», said he, «God who created you will restore these cities to your citizens and the Temple too; yet will they be lost not once, but often» (*JA* IV.312-314).

Here, the relevance to events which had transpired in Josephus' own lifetime, chief among them the destruction of cities and the burning of the Temple, is unmistakable: Moses' prophecy regarding the destruction of his people's cities and their Temple would have been understood by Josephus' contemporaries as an unmistakable allusion not only to the destruction of Jerusalem and its Temple under Nebuchadrezzar II in 587 BCE, but also to the events which had transpired in their own lifetime during the First Jewish Revolt, events in which Joseph himself had participated. Moreover, Moses' prophecy of destruction and restoration, «not once, but often», (οὐχ ἅπαξ ἀλλὰ πολλάκις) may well have been understood by Josephus and his contemporaries as a promise that the Second Temple eventually would be rebuilt.

But here, unlike the first valediction, the blame for these misfortunes is assigned to the people not because they have rebelled against their rulers, but rather because they have «transgressed his rites» (παραβάντες τὴν πρὸς αὐτὸν θρησκείαν), as Thackeray translates the phrase, though θρησκεία may be more generally understood as «religion»[62]. In this latter case, the sin of Israel which results in the destruction of Jerusalem and its Temple is not some sort of liturgical infraction, but a general neglect of the demands of the law which Josephus' Moses has just finished rehearsing.

Though there seems to be a kind of contradiction between the first valediction and the second insofar as Moses identifies two different sins – insurrection in the first, and religious transgression in the second – on account of which the Israelites will lose their land, their city, and their Temple, the point Josephus seems to want to make here is that the loss of land, city, and Temple is the just punishment for having sinned. *Which* sin has ultimately brought the Israelites to their present condition is less important for Josephus than the fact that *they have sinned*. It may well be that he considers insurrection to be a particular kind of religious

---

[62] H. G. LIDDELL – R. SCOTT, *A Greek-English Lexicon*, s.v. θρησκεία.

transgression, a kind of political symptom of a greater religious disorder.

Clearly, Josephus is indebted in both of these valedictions to the historical scheme outlined in Deut 4:23-31, a scheme characterised by a descent from covenant fidelity into idolatry (Deut 4:23-25), which is punishable by war and exile (Deut 4:26-28), before the Israelites can return to the Lord's mercy (Deut 4:29-31). Yet he does not adopt the scheme wholesale. Although the sin which earns the Israelites the punishment of their wars and exiles in Deuteronomy is idolatry, for Josephus, the sin is religious transgression in general and insurrection in particular. The substitution of idolatry (an action which is would not have been identifiable as sinful in a polytheistic culture) for insurrection (an action which would have been viewed by the Romans, at least, as particularly reprehensible) permits Josephus to translate the Deuteronomic scheme into terms which would have been more readily comprehensible to his non-Jewish readership. Israel deserves what has befallen it, according to Josephus, because it has rebelled against its legitimate rulers. Thus does he shift the responsibility for the destruction of Jerusalem from the Romans to the Jews.

The actual scene of Moses' passing in the *JA* commences with a display of mourning. Feldman has written about the differences between the Biblical announcement of the mourning connected with the death of Moses, and the scene as Josephus presents it; he notes that while in Deut 34:8, the Israelites mourn *after* Moses has died, in Josephus, their mourning *anticipates* his parting[63]:

> When Moses, at the close of life, had thus spoken, and, with benedictions, had prophesied to each of the tribes the things that in fact were to come to pass, the multitude burst into tears, while the women, too, with beating of the breast, manifested their emotion at his approaching death. Aye, and the children, wailing yet more, in that they were too feeble to suppress their grief, displayed an understanding of his virtues and grand achievements beyond their years. Yet in the thoughts of their hearts there was conflict between the grief of the young and of their seniors. For these, knowing of what a protector they were to be bereft, lamented for the future; while those, beside that cause for grief, had the sorrow that, ere they had right well tasted of his worth, it was their lot to lose him (*JA* IV.320-321).

---

[63] L. H. FELDMAN, «Josephus' Portrait of Moses: Part Three», 324.

Feldman attributes these differences to Josephus' desire to heighten the pathos of the incident in a way which would appeal to his (largely) pagan readership[64]. Indeed, Josephus heightens the pathos to so great an extent even Moses himself joins in the mourning:

> How extraordinary was this outburst of weeping and wailing of the multitude may be conjectured from what befell the law-giver. For he, who had ever been persuaded that men should not despond as the end approached, because this fate befell them in accordance with the will of God and by a law of nature, was yet by this conduct of the people reduced to tears (*JA* IV.322).

The poignancy of the departure scene is heightened in the movement to Mount Abaris, which amounts to a kind of funeral procession before the fact:

> On his advancing thence toward the place where he was destined to disappear, they all followed him bathed in tears; thereupon Moses, by a signal of his hand, bade those in the distance to remain still, while by word of mouth he exhorted those nearer to him not to make his passing a tearful one by following him. And they, deciding to gratify him in this also, to wit, to leave him to depart according to his own desire, held back, weeping with one another. Only the elders escorted him, with Eleazar the high priest, and Joshua the general (*JA* IV.323-324).

The funeral march proceeds in stages, and at various junctures along the way, groups of the mourners halt in the progression toward Mount Abaris − first the multitude, then those nearer to him, then the elders, and finally Eleazar and Joshua. This gradual separation of Moses from the mourners serves narratively to isolate the law-giver from among those who accompany him: Moses is, quite literally, set apart from his fellows. As a literary device, the isolation of Moses serves to draw attention to the unusual manner of his passing. It is likely, too, that Josephus' readers would have detected in Moses' exhortations to the mourners not to cry another resemblance to the passing of Socrates, who likewise urged his followers to refrain from weeping[65].

> But when he arrived on the mountain called Abaris − a lofty eminence situated over against Jericho and affording to those on its summit a wide view beneath of the best of the land of the Canaanites − he dismissed the elders. And, while he bade farewell to Eleazar and Joshua and was yet communing with them, a cloud of a sudden descended upon him and he disap-

---

[64] L. H. FELDMAN, «Josephus' Portrait of Moses: Part Three», 324.

[65] See *Phaedo* 117 D.

peared in a ravine. But he has written of himself in the sacred books that he died (γέγραφε δ' αὐτὸν ἐν ταῖς ἱεραῖς βίβλοις τεθνεῶτα), for fear that they should venture to say that by reason of his surpassing virtue he had gone back to the Deity (*JA* IV.325-326).

Like the account of Moses' death in Philo's work, that of Josephus seems to indicate that the death of Moses was unlike that of ordinary mortals, though, in distinction to that of Philo, the story in Josephus seems to involve a deception. Moses disappears into a ravine, covered by a cloud, but the official version in the «sacred books» (ἱεραῖς βίβλοις) is that he actually dies. Josephus seems to have wanted to account for the difference between the official version, on the one hand, and the legends current in the various denominations of Judaism, to which he bears witness, that Moses did not die at all, but was rather assumed into heaven[66].

Once Josephus concludes the narrative of Moses' passing, he sums up the significance of his life in a brief encomium:

> He lived in all one hundred and twenty years and was ruler for a third part of that time bating one month. He departed in the last month of the year, which the Macedonians call Dystros and we Adar, on the day of the new moon, having surpassed in understanding all men that ever lived and put to noblest use the fruit of his reflections. In speech and in addresses to a crowd he found favour in every way, but chiefly through his thorough command of his passions, which was such that he seemed to have no place for them at all in his soul, and only knew their names through seeing them in others rather than in himself. As general he had few to equal him, and as prophet none, insomuch that in all his utterances one seemed to hear the speech of God himself (*JA* IV.327-329).

Since this encomium comes at the close of the fourth book of the *JA*, it may be taken as a kind of summary statement, which recapitulates everything which Josephus considers to be important about Moses. Faithful to the narrative in Deuteronomy, Josephus mentions the mourning period of thirty days which followed the parting of Moses, even if he does embroider the grief of the Israelites: «So the people mourned for him for thirty days, and never were Hebrews oppressed by grief so profound as that which filled them on the death of Moses» (πενθεῖ μὲν οὖν αὐτὸν ὁ λαὸς ἐφ' ἡμέρας τριάκοντα, λύπη δὲ οὐκ ἄλλη κατέσχεν Ἑβραίους τοσαύτη τὸ μέγεθος, ὅση τότε Μωυσέος ἀποθανόντος: *JA* IV.330).

---

[66] See *VM* II.291.

And while Moses is here eulogised as one who surpasses in understanding every other human being (*JA* IV.328), and commended for speaking well (*JA* IV.328), the chief reason for which Josephus praises Moses is his «thorough command of his passions» (παθῶν αὐτοκράτωρ: *JA* IV.328), a tribute which might surprise someone whose knowledge of the Biblical narratives is first-hand. Yet for someone whose understanding of virtue is influenced by Stoic conceptions of ἀπάθεια and αὐτάρ-κεια, this presentation of Moses would have been at once familiar and attractive. Thus do apologetic considerations influence even a summary statement of Moses' significance.

It must be admitted, however, that Josephus does not entirely transform Moses into some sort of deutero-Socratic sage; Moses is here said to be a prophet without equal (προφήτης δὲ οἷος οὐκ ἄλλος: *JA* IV.329) in whom God spoke: «in all his utterances one seemed to hear the speech of God himself» (ὅ τι ἂν φθέγξαιτο δοκεῖν αὐτοῦ λέγοντος ἀκροᾶσθαι τοῦ θεοῦ: *JA* IV.329). Moreover, subsequent generations of believers come to know Moses through their study of the law, says Josephus: «[T]he very readers of his laws have sadly felt his loss, deducing from these the superlative quality of his virtue» (καὶ οἱ τοῖς νόμοις ἐντυγχά-νοντες αὐτοῦ δεινὴν ἐποιοῦντο τὴν ἐπιζήτησιν, τὸ περιὸν αὐτοῦ τῆς ἀρετῆς ἐκ τούτων λογίζομενοι: *JA* IV.331). This final image of Moses which Josephus provides for his readers directs them to contemplate the law which Moses gave his people, should they wish to come to know the virtue of the law-giver himself.

### 2.3 *Theological analysis*

Josephus' apologetic concerns govern his presentation of the life of Moses in general, and the passing of Moses in particular. His concern to present Moses in a way which renders him both accessible and attractive to an audience which does not have first-hand acquaintance with the narratives in which he appears or the laws he is purported to have given dominates the *JA*. Thus, as we have seen, in his command over his passions and in his devotion to his duty, Josephus' Moses bears a more than passing resemblance to Socrates. These apologetic concerns are two-pronged: first, they are meant, as Grabbe, Feldman, and Sandmel acknowledge, to demonstrate the superiourity of Jewish culture over that of the nations; beyond that, however, the apologetic concerns which undergird the *JA* are designed ultimately to bring about the conversion of Josephus' readers to the way of life which Moses and his followers lead.

There is, however, another concern which governs Josephus' portrayal of Moses, and that is the need to present a theological justification for the misfortunes which have befallen Israel, particularly those within the living memory of Josephus and his contemporaries. And here, surprisingly, Josephus does not attempt to exculpate Israel; on the contrary, he tends to assign to the Israelites the sole responsibility for their disasters, claiming that they are the just retribution of a just God for the wilful disobedience of his just laws. This concern to provide a theological justification for Israel's tragedy permits Josephus to speak to Jews and pagans alike. In the allusion to Deut 4:25-31 in both the first and the second valedictions, Josephus reminds his co-religionists that the loss of their land, their city, and their Temple is something for which Moses long ago provided as a punishment for their iniquities. In the substitution of insurrection for idolatry, especially in the first valediction, Josephus is able to speak to pagans in terms which are, if not religiously meaningful, at least politically meaningful, so that Israel is punished by its God for having rebelled against its Roman overlords.

CHAPTER IV

## Latin language legends of the last words of Moses

The works of Philo and Josephus survived from the first century, largely intact, and for the most part in their original Greek; so happy a fate did not befall the anonymous authors of the *Liber Antiquitatum Biblicarum* and the *Testament of Moses*. Whatever the original language of each of these works actually was, the literary efforts of their authors have been preserved only in their Latin translations. To a source-oriented scholar for whom the questions of derivation and influence are paramount, this situation presents some rather troublesome difficulties: how can one speak meaningfully about a narrative whose author is unknown and whose original text is now obscured by subsequent translation(s)? On the other hand, for the practitioner of discourse-oriented analysis, who views any narrative as «a pattern of meaning and effect»[1], the investigation of which is not necessarily limited by one's inability to determine author or original language, the survival of such narratives is testimony to the tenacity of narrative phenomena like plot, character, and thought, despite linguistic shifts and the vagaries of history. An analysis of these narrative phenomena will provide the starting-point for this investigation into the legends of the dying Moses.

## 1. Pseudo-Philo, *Liber Antiquitatum Biblicarum* 19:1-16

The *Liber Antiquitatum Biblicarum*, long thought to have been the work of Philo of Alexandria, is, in the opinion of Geza Vermes, a cate-chetical work, which retraces salvation history from Adam to Saul[2]. Daniel J. Harrington, who has done so much to bring this work to the attention of contemporary scholars, thinks that the original attribution of the work to Philo owes something to the impression that the work bears

---

[1] M. STERNBERG, *The Poetics of Biblical Narrative*, 15.

[2] G. VERMES, «La figure de Moïse», 88.

some similarities to the *JA* of Josephus, «and thus the work was attributed to Philo of Alexandria as the other great Jewish writer of antiquity known to Christian scribes»[3]. In fact, however, the author of the *LAB* is unknown, and his identification as «Pseudo-Philo» should not be interpreted as indicating any sort of affinity, literary, theological, or otherwise, with the Alexandrian exegete and philosopher.

## 1.1 *Date, provenance, and original language*

The traditional scholarly problems respecting the original setting of the *LAB*, especially with regard to the date of the work, are not easily settled in a summary statement. Unlike Philo of Alexandria or Josephus, both of whom left a relatively extensive set of works behind them, about which much may be learned through the comparison of one work to another within each author's corpus, the author of the *LAB* seemingly confined his efforts to this single work. And since the author of the *LAB* is otherwise unknown, appeals to his biography to explicate obscurities in his work is impossible. Hence, questions of the work's origin must be solved by recourse to internal evidence.

### 1.1.1 Problems in dating the *LAB*

In his highly influential monograph, James H. Charlesworth maintains that the *LAB* is pre-Christian and «roughly contemporaneous with New Testament writings»[4]. Apparent references to the Second Temple which «will be turned over into the hands of [the Israelites'] enemies, and they will destroy it, and foreigners will encircle it» (*Et post hec tradetur in manus inimicorum suorum et demolientur eum, et circumdabunt eum alienigene*: *LAB* 19:7) have led many scholars to conclude that the *LAB* was written sometime after 70[5]. Harrington, however, notes that the reference need not be confined to Titus' capture of Jerusalem, and that it could as easily refer to the capture of the city by Nebuchadnezzar, Antiochus Epiphanes, or Pompey[6]. Harrington further claims that the reference to decrees governing the holocaust offering which are binding «even unto this day» (*usque in hodiernum diem*: *LAB* 22:8) indicates that

---

[3] D. J. HARRINGTON, «Philo, Pseudo-», 344; ID., «Pseudo-Philo», 6.

[4] J. H. CHARLESWORTH, *The Old Testament Pseudepigrapha*, 42.

[5] C. DIETZFELBINGER, «Pseudo-Philo: Antiquitates Biblicae», 96.

[6] D. J. HARRINGTON, «Pseudo-Philo: A New Translation», 299.

the Temple was still standing at the time the *LAB* was written[7]. Thus, he would conclude that the *LAB* was written sometime before 70.

Yet, it must be noted that well after the destruction of the Temple, people were capable of writing about it as though it still stood[8]. Josephus's *Against Apion* provides a good example of this tendency. In this apologetic work, composed, in all probability after 93 CE[9], Josephus describes an edifice which had lain in ruins for more than twenty years. Yet he speaks of the Temple and its priesthood as though they were still extant:

> We have but one Temple for the one God (for like ever loveth like), common to all as God is common to all. The priests are continually engaged in His worship, under the leadership of him who for the time is head of the line. With his colleagues he will sacrifice to God, adjudicate in cases of dispute, punish those convicted of crime. Any who disobey him will pay the penalty as for impiety against God Himself (*Against Apion* II.193-195).

The assertion that «we have but one Temple for the one God» (Εἷς ναὸς ἑνὸς θεοῦ) is remarkable coming from a man whose rôle in the First Jewish Revolt – however ambivalent his attitude towards its timeliness, and however ambiguous his conduct during its course – allowed him to witness the destruction of Jerusalem and its Temple[10]. Yet the point Josephus seems to be making here is more theological than historical[11]. *Against Apion* is a work of apologetics, and the immediate context of Josephus's claims about the «one Temple» has to do with one of the four pillars of Judaism, namely, its monotheism:

> The universe is in God's hands; perfect and blessed, self-suffing and suffing for all, He is the beginning, the middle, and the end of all things.

---

[7] D. J. HARRINGTON, «Pseudo-Philo: A New Translation», 299, 332; ID., «Palestinian Adaptations», 245.

[8] For a brief survey of the ways in which the Temple was understood and appropriated among the various denominations of Judaism of the first century, both before and after its destruction, see J. A. OVERMAN – W. S. GREEN, «Judaism in the Greco-Roman Period», 1037-1054. For an analysis of the reaction of the Jewish population outside of Palestine to the destruction of the Temple, see M. GOODMAN, «Diaspora Reactions», 27-38.

[9] H. ST. J. THACKERAY, «Introduction», *The Life* and *Against Apion*, xiii.

[10] See D. M. RHOADS, *Israel in Revolution*, 7.

[11] G. VERMES («A Summary of the Law», 301-302) holds that *Against Apion* II.164-219 constitutes a summary of the Torah, and is one of the oldest Jewish theological syntheses, if not actually the earliest.

By His works and His bounties He is plainly seen, indeed more manifest than ought else; but His form and magnitude surpass our powers of description. No materials, however costly, are fit to make an image of Him; no art has skill to conceive and represent it. The like of Him we have never seen, we do not imagine, and it is impious to conjecture (*Against Apion* II.190-191).

Josephus's debt to the Psalter, especially Psalm 135:15-18 (LXX 134:15-18), and to wisdom literature, especially the polemic against idolatry found in Wisdom 13:1–15:17, is clear here; though he has softened the harshness of the traditional Israelite critique of the worship of the multitudinous gods of their pagan neighbors, and presented the Jewish doctrine of God positively. And since his God is «perfect and blessed [...] the beginning, the middle, and the end of all things» (παντελὴς καὶ μακάριος [...] ἀρχὴ καὶ μέσα καὶ τέλος οὗτος τῶν πάντων), the place where He is to be worshipped is likewise perfect and blessed. The «one Temple, one God» analogy, then seems to locate the Temple and its associated institutions in eternity. What is «perfect and blessed [...] the beginning, and the middle, and the end of all things» can never perish, even though it may be hidden from human sight for a time. Josephus's language here may indicate his own expectation, founded on his theological convictions, that before long the Temple would be restored to human sight and its priests would take up once again their traditional duties.

A similar contention may be advanced with respect to the attitude toward the Temple and its cultus which is found in the *LAB*. For Pseudo-Philo to speak of the place as though it were still standing is, *pace* Harrington, hardly strange[12]. Schürer holds that, traumatic as the destruction of the Temple was, «it was [...] a long time before the situation was accepted as definitive»[13]. And Neusner maintains that what was important for the subsequent unfolding of events was not the destruction of the Temple – that had happened before – but that the Temple was not eventually rebuilt. For Neusner, the failure in 135 CE on the part of Bar Kokbah's armies to retake the city and rebuild the Temple proved to be the turning point in Jewish religious sensibilities, provoking a complete revision of their heritage[14]. And even then, according to Jon D. Levenson's account, until the emergence of liberal Judaism in the nineteenth

---

[12] D. J. HARRINGTON, «Pseudo-Philo: A New Translation», 299.

[13] E. SCHÜRER, *History*, I, 523.

[14] J. NEUSNER, *Judaism in the Beginning of Christianity*, 43.

son's account, until the emergence of liberal Judaism in the nineteenth century, «the succession of the Jerusalem Temple by the synagogue was not regarded as final. Rather, the synagogue was seen as a temporary measure, although, sadly, a long-lived one, until the reconstruction of the Temple»[15].

In an attempt to sharpen the focus of the discussion of the dating of the *LAB*, Saul Olyan has recently examined the episode of the debate at the edge of the Red Sea in *LAB* 10:3. The crux of Olyan's thesis is that the tribes of Levi, Judah, Joseph, and Benjamin have the last word in their insistence on fighting with the Egyptians, and that Pseudo-Philo «highlights and favors the martial position even though it does not integrate well with the Exodus 14 narrative»[16]. He contends that Pseudo-Philo has given the Red Sea tradition a distinctly contemporary shape by evoking the issues and conflicts of the Jewish War of 66-70: the position advocated by the tribes of Reuben, Issachar, Zebulon, and Simeon, who recommend suicide rather than death at the hands of the Egyptians, alludes to the events at Gamala in 67 where the choice was suicide or certain death at the hands of an enemy; in a similar fashion, the strategy of surrender and voluntary enslavement advocated by the tribes of Gad, Asher, Dan, and Naphtali reflects the position of those who urged a peaceful resolution to the conflict with Rome. «Pseudo-Philo looks very much like a revolt sympathizer, perhaps connected to one of the war factions. The evidence suggests that he expanded and reshaped the older tradition of debate at the Reed Sea, drawing on the narrative of Ex 14 to do so; his version of the debate may have addressed directly the beleaguered and divided community during the Jewish War»[17].

The difficulty with Olyan's reading of the episode of the debate by the Red Sea is that it could apply with equal relevance to, say, the Maccabean Revolt of 167-164 BCE which did not attract universal support among the inhabitants of Israel (see 1 Macc 7:13), and which pitted one Jew against another (1 Macc 6:21-27; 7:5-7). Even those who joined in the rebellion differed among themselves over which strategy of resistance to adopt (see 1 Macc 2:31-41)[18]. Similar claims could be made with respect to internal divisions at the time of the first deportation to Babylonia (see 2 Kings 25:22-26; Jer 27:9-11). Olyan seems to have con-

---

[15] J. D. LEVENSON, «The Jerusalem Temple», 57.

[16] S. M. OLYAN, «The Israelites Debate Their Options», 84.

[17] S. M. OLYAN, «The Israelites Debate Their Options», 91.

[18] See S. J. D. COHEN, *From the Maccabees*, 30-31.

fused narrative relevance (the divisions among the Israelites are similar to those among the rebels) with authorial intention (the *LAB* was written to support the cause of the rebels). It does not seem possible, therefore, to conclude from the portrayal of the debate by the Red Sea that the *LAB* was written during the course of the Jewish Revolt of 66-70.

This is not to say that the *LAB* was not written in the first century. Indeed, there are compelling arguments for accepting Harrington's thesis that Pseudo-Philo wrote in the first century, the strongest of which being the nature of the biblical text used in the *LAB*[19]. My reservations with respect to Harrington's and Olyan's arguments alike are not with their conclusions, but rather with their methodology. Neither the argument from liturgical decree, specifically, the decrees implying a continuation of holocaust offering at the Temple (Harrington), nor the argument from analogy, specifically, the analogous situations of the Israelites at the edge of the Red Sea and the rebels of 66-70 (Olyan), are strong enough by themselves to establish a firm date by which the *LAB* may be said to have been completed. We had best content ourselves with rough approximations, and conclude, with Charlesworth, that the *LAB* is «roughly contemporaneous» with the writings of the New Testament. Any statement less roughly approximate is merely speculative.

### 1.1.2  Provenance of the *LAB*

Harrington's contention that the *LAB* originated in Palestine is well-argued and amply supported. Frederick J. Murphy has recently identified idolatry as the central theme of the *LAB*: «[i]n the narrative world of the *Biblical Antiquities*, idolatry symbolizes infidelity to God. It is a problem especially when Israel lacks good leaders and/or is in close contact with foreigners»[20]. While contact with foreigners and idolaters was a problem faced by Jews of the Diaspora also, it would have been felt as especially poignant by the inhabitants of the Promised Land. Murphy goes on to observe that Pseudo-Philo's choice of the pre-monarchic period as his subject is not without significance: «Choosing a section of the Hebrew Bible which has as a major theme the importance of proper leaders, but in which those leaders are neither monarchs nor priests, allows him to look back to a time in Israel's history when issues of

---

[19] See D. J. HARRINGTON, «The Biblical Text», 1-17.

[20] F. J. MURPHY, «Retelling the Bible», 286.

leadership concentrated on loyalty to God rather than genealogy»[21]. Such concerns are not untypical of Pharisaical Judaism, and accord well with the working hypothesis among contemporary scholars is that the thinking represented in the *LAB* is that of Pharisaic Judaism[22]. The argument Vermes advances against any sort of polemic opposing heretics or schismatics in the work of Pseudo-Philo, suggesting instead that the inspiration for the work is rooted in the questions a pious Jew might have had concerning the biblical narratives, implies a homiletic motive behind the *LAB*[23]. Thus it seems fair to conclude, as Perrot does[24]. that the provenance of the *LAB* is that of the synagogue.

## 1.1.3  Original language of the *LAB*

The *LAB* survives in a Latin translation of a work originally written in Hebrew, and subsequently translated into Greek from which the Latin translation was made[25]. It is thus a translation of a translation, and for that reason alone, if for none other, one must exercise caution in attri-

---

[21] F. J. MURPHY, «Retelling the Bible», 287.

[22] See, for example, A. J. FERCH, «The Two Aeons», and L. H. FELDMAN, «Josephus' *Jewish Antiquities* and Pseudo-Philo's *Biblical Antiquities*», 76. See also A. F. SEGAL, *Rebecca's Children*, who notes that the obligation to keep the rules of priestly purity, even by those Jews who were not from priestly families, was insisted upon by the Pharisees (125-126). Among these purity regulations was endogamy, the transgression against which is reflected in *LAB* 9:5; 18:13f; 21:1; 30:1; 44:7. With respect to the use of the term «Pharisee» to characterize a particular religious group within first century Judaism, A. SALDARINI («Pharisees») maintains that in the extant sources, no Jewish group refers to itself as Pharisees: «[t]he name Pharisees is a name used by outsiders, such as Josephus (taking the stance of a Hellenistic historian) and the New Testament» (300). One wonders how he accounts for Paul's use of the term in the Letter to the Philippians: «Though I myself have reason for confidence in the flesh also. If any other man thinks he has reason for confidence in the flesh, I have more: circumcised on the eighth day, of the people of Israel, of the tribe of Benjamin, a Hebrew born of Hebrews; as to the law a Pharisee, as to zeal a persecutor of the church, as to righteousness under the law blameless» (καίπερ ἐγὼ ἔχων πεποίθησιν καὶ ἐν σαρκί. εἴ τις δοκεῖ ἄλλος πεποιθέναι ἐν σαρκί, ἐγὼ μᾶλλον· περιτομῇ ὀκταήμερος, ἐκ γένους Ἰσραήλ, φυλῆς Βενιαμίν, Ἑβραῖος ἐξ Ἑβραίων, κατὰ νόμον Φαρισαῖος, κατὰ ζῆλος διώκων τὴν ἐκκλησίαν, κατὰ δικαιοσύνην τὴν ἐν νόμῳ γενόμενος ἄμεμπτος: Phil 3:4-6). Paul's language here is hardly that of an «outsider».

[23] G. VERMES, «La figure de Moïse», 88.

[24] C. PERROT, *Les Antiquités Bibliques*, II, 33-39.

[25] See P. WINTER, «Philo, Biblical Antiquities of», 796; D. J. HARRINGTON, «The Original Language», 503-514.

buting parallels in language to the biblical narratives which it retells, or to other examples of the «rewritten Bible». The fact that the work has undergone so many translations bears witness, in my opinion, to its popular character: the impulse which originally gave rise to a work like the *LAB* – to retell the Biblical stories to a people for whom the original texts, for whatever reason, were no longer sufficiently comprehensible – also gave rise to the effort to translate it into a language more accessible to its potential audience.

## 1.2 *Literary analysis*

Scott Hafemann has noted that of the sixty-five extant chapters of the *LAB*, eleven are devoted to the life and ministry of Moses[26], namely, chapters nine through nineteen. The figure of God's «friend», as he is called in *LAB* 23:9[27], thus dominates this first century narrative in a way that no other person does. Here, as in the other legends which survive from the first century, Moses may be understood according to several controlling images: as prophet, as law-giver, and as intercessor.

### 1.2.1 Moses as prophet in the *LAB*

While it is possible to maintain that Moses' prophetic activities are demonstrated every time he makes a prediction of what will befall his people after his death, as for instance in the farewell speech to the Israelites in *LAB* 19:1-5, such an assertion fails to take under consideration the full range of Moses' prophetic gifts in its implicit restriction of his prophetic activity to the predictive. For the *LAB*'s Moses does very little in the way of prediction, aside from foretelling that after his death, the Israelites will forsake his teachings, in consequence of which «God will be angry at you and abandon you and depart from your land» (*et irascetur Deus in vobis, et derelinquet vos, et discedet de terra vestra*: *LAB* 19:2). What follows the departure of the Lord from the land, namely, the subjection of Israel to its enemies, may be seen as the logical outcome of abandonment by God: without divine protection, this people must fall prey to its stronger neighbours. Important as these predictions

---

[26] S. J. HAFEMANN, «Moses in the Apocrypha», 95.

[27] «I remembered your fathers and sent Moses *my friend* and freed them from there, but their enemies I struck down (*memoratus fui patrum vestrorum et misi Moysen amicum meum, et liberavi eos inde, inimicos autem illorum percussi*: *LAB* 23:9; emphasis mine.)

probably were to the congregations for whom the *LAB* was originally destined, the prophetic office of Moses in the *LAB* is not exhausted by his
capacity to foretell what is to come.

Oddly, for a narrative in which Moses figures so prominently, he is
explicitly identified as a prophet only twice, and neither in a setting in
which he himself plays a part. In the first of these two instances, Moses
is called «first of all the prophets» (*primus omnium prophetarum*: *LAB*
35:6), not so much because he enjoys the ability to predict the future;
on the contrary, the *LAB* tends to restrict to God the capacity to foresee
what has yet to happen[28]. Rather, the *LAB* assigns the title «first of all
the prophets» to Moses because he «asked the Lord for a sign, and it was
given to him» (*petiit Dominum signum, et datum est ei*: *LAB* 35:6). The
title *primus omnium prophetarum* is given to Moses in the *LAB* by
Gideon, who wants a sign of his own as proof that God will guide him
in the battle against the Midianites. The nature of the sign which had
been vouchsafed to Moses is never specified in the *LAB*; Gideon's sign,
on the other hand, is water poured over a rock which becomes half
blood and half fire, «and the blood did not extinguish the water nor did
the fire consume the blood», (*et non extinxit ignem sanguis nec sanguin-
em ignis exussit*: *LAB* 35:7). Like the fleece of the canonical account in
Judges 6:36-40, the water serves, first of all, to authenticate to Gideon
himself his own call. Secondly, in the *LAB* as in Judges, the sign serves
as a kind of advance guarantee of success: if God is truly with Gideon,
he cannot fail against the Midianites. Gideon's sign of blood and water
serves to portend his eventual success, and is then, to a limited extent,
prophetic in the predictive sense of the term. In a similar fashion, the
otherwise unknown sign which Moses is said to have asked of God in
the *LAB* would have served the dual purpose of authentication and prediction of success.

The other episode in which Moses is also explicitly identified as a
prophet comes in the narrative of Samuel's call (*LAB* 53). God has
called out to Samuel while the boy slept, first in the voice of his master,
Eli (*LAB* 53:3), and next in the voice of his father, Elkanah (*LAB* 53:5).
The third time God calls to him, the boy recognises the voice of the
Lord, and God's first announcement is to tell him that

---

[28] See, for instance, the prophecy of the destruction of the Temple which God
makes in *LAB* 12:4, 19:7 or the prediction of the Israelites' future apostasy in *LAB*
13:9, 19:6.

> I have indeed enlightened the house of Israel in Egypt and have chosen for
> myself then as a prophet Moses my servant (*et elegi tunc mihi prophetam
> Moysen famulum meum*) and have done wonders through him for my people
> and have taken revenge on my enemies as I wished (*LAB* 53:8).

The paratactic structure of this divine announcement is deceptively simple: four clauses, linked together by *et*, each one introduced by a perfect
indicative active verb in the first person (*illuminavi, elegi, feci, vindi-
cavi*). But the parataxis here does not indicate four clauses of equal
weight; in fact, the second and the fourth clauses are parallel to the first
and the third in such a way that the election of Moses as prophet is a
specification of the way in which God has illumined Israel, and the re-
venge God takes on his enemies is a particular instance of the wonders
he has worked. In view of this structure, one may say that an important
dimension of Moses' prophetic office, according to the *LAB*, is to provide enlightenment for the house of Israel. In this respect, the function
of Moses as prophet is virtually indistinguishable from the function of
Moses as law-giver.

### 1.2.2  Moses as law-giver in the *LAB*

Paradoxically, the image of Moses as law-giver, like the image of
Moses as prophet, is virtually absent from those sections of the *LAB*
which relate the narrative of his activities. This is not to say that Moses
is presented without reference to the law: such a presentation would
have been impossible, given the nature of the *LAB* as «rewritten Bible».
What the *LAB* stresses is God's activity as a law-giver. Thus, after
Moses' father Amram determines neither to submit to Egyptian commands to kill all male children, nor to accede to Israelite proposals to ab-
stain from sexual contact lest children be born only to die (*LAB* 9:1-6),
God blesses Amram:

> Because Amram's plan is pleasing to me, and he has not put aside the cove-
> nant established between me and his fathers, so behold now he who will be
> born from him will serve me forever, and I will do marvelous things in the
> house of Jacob through him, and I will work through him signs and wonders
> for my people that I have not done for anyone else; and I will act gloriously
> among them and proclaim to them my ways. And I, God, will kindle for him
> my lamp that will abide in him, and I will show him my covenant that no
> one has seen. And I will reveal to him my Law and statutes and judgements,
> and I will burn an eternal light for him, because I thought of him in the days

of old, saying, «My spirit will not be a mediator among these men forever, because they are flesh and their days will be 120 years» (*LAB* 9:7-8).

The position of Moses *vis-à-vis* other human beings is privileged, and God accords him extraordinary blessings, thanks to his father's fidelity, including the revelation of the law, but for the author of the *LAB*, this blessing is extraordinary precisely because it is God's law which is revealed.

If in the *LAB*, Moses is not a law-giver *per se*, he is nevertheless the most authoritative interpreter of the law. His rôle in the *LAB* is to explain the law, as the episode involving the construction of the calf may serve to illustrate. Moses is on the mountain (*LAB* 12:2), and the people petition Aaron to construct gods for them, because they fear that Moses has been taken away from them. Aaron's reply communicates the illuminative function of Moses' activities as law-giver:

> And Aaron said to them, «Be patient. For Moses will come, and he will bring judgement near to us and will illumine the Law for us (*et legem illuminabit nobis*) and will explain from his own mouth the Law of God (*et superexcellentiam Dei exponet de ore suo*) and set up rules for our race», (*LAB* 12:2).

Here, Moses is presented as a kind of exegete, whose explanations are necessary to prevent the kind of misunderstanding which leads to infidelity. But the law which he expounds is always the law of God, and never the law of Moses. Thus *LAB* 19:1 speaks of «the words of the Law that God had spoken to them on Horeb» (*Et cepit manifestare eis verba legis, que locutus est eis in Oreb Deus*: *LAB* 19:1). *LAB* 19:6 shows God himself predicting that the Israelites will forget «*my Law*, by which I have enlightened them» (*et obliviscentur legem meam in qua illuminavi eos*: *LAB* 19:6). In *LAB* 19:9, Moses intercedes with God, and in a rehearsal of the events of the Exodus, reminds him that «you gave them the Law and statutes in which they might live and enter as sons of men» (*Et dedisti eis legem et iusticias, in quibus viverent et intrarent sicut filii hominum*: *LAB* 19:9). This insistence on the law of God as opposed to the law of Moses stands in marked contrast to the position taken by Josephus and Philo.

### 1.2.3 Moses as intercessor in the *LAB*

As in the other examples of the «rewritten Bible» which survive from the first century, the *LAB* places a great deal of emphasis on the intercessory powers of Moses before God. Those powers are depicted in several different episodes, the first of which comes after the Israelites have prevailed upon Aaron to fashion the molten calf (*LAB* 12:2-3). God tells Moses that because the Israelites have committed the sin of idolatry, he will abandon them: «And the race of men will be to me like a drop from the pitcher and will be reckoned like spittle» (*Et erit mihi hominum genus tamquam stillicidium urcei, et tamquam sputum estimabitur*: *LAB* 12:4). Moses' first reaction is to fall into a frenzy of painful anger:

> And his hands were opened, and he became like a woman bearing her first-born son who, when she is in labour, her hands are upon her chest and she has no strength to help herself bring forth (*LAB* 12:5).

His frenzy lasts only an hour, and he recovers, saying to himself, «And now, I will rise up and gird my loins, because even if they have sinned, what was declared to me above will not be in vain» (*Et nunc exsurgam et confortabo lumbos, quoniam si peccaverunt non in vano erunt que sursum enarrata sunt mihi*: *LAB* 12:6). Thus does Pseudo-Philo establish the basis upon which Moses' intercession is conducted: the promises that God extends to his people will not be vitiated by that people's disobedience. Moses' intercessory powers, then, are not the result of some innate capacity within himself; they come about thanks to God's fidelity to his people.

It is only after Moses suffers this painful frenzy that he destroys the calf, and prays for his people, using the traditional imagery of Israel as the vine which God himself has planted (Ps 80:9-17; Is 5:1-7; Jer 2:21).

> Therefore, if you do not have mercy on your vine, all things, Lord, have been done in vain, and you will not have anyone to glorify you. For even if you plant another vine, this one will not trust you, because you have destroyed the former one. For if you indeed forsake the world, then who will do for you what you say as God? And now let your anger be restrained from your vine; rather let what was said previously by you and what still must be said be done, and do not let your labour be in vain, and do not let your inheritance be pulled apart in humiliation (*LAB* 12:9).

The appeal which Moses mounts is so effective that God rescinds his decree of destruction: «And God said to him, «Behold I have been made merciful according to your words» (*Et dixit ei Deus: Ecce misericors factus sum iuxta sermones tuos*: *LAB* 12:10).

In this episode may be seen the same sort of juxtaposition of suffering and intercession that Josephus used[29], though here it is deployed to a different end. If in Josephus, the suffering of Moses is an expression of his essential unity with his people, here in the *LAB*, the suffering of Moses comes about for the opposite reasons. Moses is in pain here because his people have forsaken their God, and they have done so at precisely the same moment that he is in union with God on the mountain. He does not suffer *with* his people in this episode from the *LAB*, as he does in the *JA*: he suffers *because* of them. Indeed, one may claim here that if Moses' suffering is an expression of any kind of solidarity, it is an expression of solidarity with God, against whom the Isarelites have sinned in their idolatry.

In Pseudo-Philo's retelling of the story of the twelve spies based on the account in Num 13:1–14:38 (*LAB* 15:1-7), Moses' prayer saves his people. The Israelites have succumbed to despair, wondering if God has brought them to the wilderness that they might die: «And how does he bring us up so that we should fall upon the sword and our wives be taken into captivity» (*Et quomodo nunc elevat nos ut incidamus in rompheam, et mulieres nostre erunt in captivitatem? LAB* 15:4). God determines to punish the Israelites for their failure to believe the reports of Caleb and Joshua: «And now behold the days will come, and I will do to them as they wished, and I will cast forth their bodies in the wilderness» (*Et nunc ecce venient dies et faciam eis sicut voluerunt, et corpora eorum deiciam in heremo*: *LAB* 15:6). Moses' prayer for mercy is framed by two leading questions:

> Before you took the seed from which you would make man upon the earth, was it I who did establish their ways? Therefore let your mercy sustain us until the end, and your fidelity for length of days; for unless you had mercy, who would ever be born? (*LAB* 15:7).

Both questions assume a negative answer – Moses is not responsible for the fractious ways of the human race, and no one would ever be born in the absence of divine mercy – but the first question with its implicit answer seems to shift the responsibility for Israel's rebelliousness onto God himself who made them the way they are.

Moses' powers of intercession are also displayed in the second dialogue between himself and God (*LAB* 19:8-15) in which he ascends Mount Abarim and prays,

---

[29] *JA* III.1-9; 295-299; IV.40-50; 194.

> Behold I have completed my lifetime; I have completed 120 years. And now I ask, May your mercy with your people and your pity with your heritage, Lord, be established; and may your long-suffering in your place be upon the chosen race because you have loved them before all others (*LAB* 19:8).

The prayer for mercy (*misericordia*), and pity (*miseratio*), with which Moses begins his prayer, seems, at the outset, somewhat indefinite; the plea for «long-suffering in your place» (*longanimitas tua in loco tuo*), however, specifies the request: Moses is asking God to rescind the sentence of destruction for the Temple (*loco*). It is clear that this request is based on Moses' relationship with God:

> And you know that I was a shepherd. And when I fed the flock in the wilderness, I brought them to your mountain Horeb and then I first saw your angel on fire from the bush. But you called me from the bush, and I was afraid and turned my face. And you sent me to them and you freed them from Egypt, but their enemies you drowned in the water. And you gave them the Law and statutes in which they might live and enter as sons of men (*LAB* 19:9).

This retrospect accomplishes two purposes: on the one hand, to rehearse the history of a relationship is to establish a claim for the future of that relationship; what you have done for me in the past obliges you to do something for me in the future. If God has called Moses so that his people might be freed from Egypt, and they might receive the Law, God is bound not to abandon these selfsame people in the future. But the retrospect accomplishes a further purpose. Moses is portrayed herein as someone who is weak and even sinful: «I was afraid and turned my face» (*ego timui et declinavi faciem meam*: *LAB* 19:9). Implicitly, Moses is likened to the Israelites who are also weak and sinful; thus, if God called a weak and sinful man, so he can continue to protect a weak and sinful people:

> For who is the man who has not sinned against you? And unless your patience abides, how will your heritage be established, if you were not merciful to them? Or who will yet be born without sin? Now you will correct them for a time, but not in anger (*LAB* 19:9).

Here, as in *LAB* 15:7, Moses poses a series of questions, all of which assume a negative answer. There is no one who has not sinned against God. God's heritage (*hereditas* = Israel) cannot be established in the absence of his patience (*longanimitas*) and his mercy. No one will ever be born without sin. On the face of things, such questions, along with their assumed answers, could as well provide the rationale for the de-

struction of the nation as they could supply an argument for its preservation. The intercessory prayer, however, places the responsibility for Israel's continued welfare on God, though, paradoxically, the one who can
so intercede before God also bears some responsibility for Israel's
future. Indeed, in the final question, Moses' intercessory powers reveal
themselves to be so great that he can even intervene on behalf of generations yet to be born.

Moses' intercessory functions in the *LAB* are founded, ultimately, on
Pseudo-Philo's theology. God's promises have not been made in vain
(*LAB* 12:6), and the one who intercedes for his people may rely on
God's fidelity which he has established for length of days (*LAB* 15:7).
Insofar as suffering enters into Moses' intercessory rôle, it does so as a
tangible sign of Moses' own fidelity to God, and his dismay at his peo-
ple's propensity to forsake their God.

### 1.2.4  The death of Moses in the *LAB*

The farewell and death of Moses are found in the nineteenth chapter
of the *LAB*. An examination of the structure of *LAB* 19 based on an analysis of the speakers' rôles reveals the following arrangement:

I.   Dialogue 1
    A.   19:1-5        The farewell of Moses to his people
    B.   19:6-7        God's address to Moses
II.  Dialogue 2
    A.   19:8-9        The prayer of Moses
    B.   19:10a-d      The vision of the Promised land
    C.   19:10e-13     God's address to Moses
    D.   19:14-15      Dialogue concerning times
III. Narrative Conclusion
    A.   19:16a        The death and burial of Moses
    B.   19:16b-d      Cosmic mourning
    C.   19:16e        Recapitulation: the burial of Moses

As the outline makes clear, the farewell discourse of Moses in *LAB* 19,
strictly speaking, occupies only the first five of the sixteen verses which
narrate the last days of Moses, and may be characterized as testamentary
in character[30]. It is introduced by a brief narrative preface which
equates what follows to the Torah: «And [Moses] began declaring to

---

[30] See J. J. COLLINS, *The Apocalyptic Imagination*, 102.

them the words of the Law that God had spoken to them on Horeb»
(*LAB* 19:1b).

The farewell discourse proper is quadripartite in form:

1. 19:2a    Announcement of impending death
2. 19:2b-c  Prediction of apostasy and woes
3. 19:3     Prediction of Israel's call for a «shepherd like Moses»
4. 19:4-5   Solemn witness and blessing

Much of this schema is familiar to readers of Deuteronomy 31: the announcement of impending death is clearly based on Deut 31:2, and the
prediction of apostasy and the woes which are consequent upon it takes
its inspiration from Deut 31:16-18. Even the solemn witness is probably
inspired by the Lord's command to Moses to compose a song and teach
it to the Israelites «that this song may be a witness (עֵד/μαρτύριον) for
me against the people of Israel» (Deut 31:19).

But Pseudo-Philo has taken some liberties with his source: in the narrative as it is found in Deuteronomy, the prediction of future apostasy
and woes issues from the mouth of the Lord (Deut 31:16-18); here, of
course, it is Moses who makes the prediction. Furthermore, God predicts in Deuteronomy 31 that Israel will eventually admit «Because the
Lord my God is not with me, these evils have come upon me» (διότι οὐκ
ἔστιν κύριος ὁ θεός μου ἐν ἐμοί, εὕροσάν με τὰ κακὰ ταῦτα: Deut
31:17). In the *LAB*, by contrast, Israel's complaint refers not to the absence of *God* from the life of the community, but rather to the absence
of *Moses*: «Who will give us another shepherd like Moses or such a
judge for the sons of Israel to pray always for our sins and to be heard
for our iniquities?» (*Quis dabet nobis pastorem unum sicut Moyses aut
iudicem talem filiis Israel, qui in omni tempore oret pro peccatis nostris
et exaudiatur pro iniquitatibus nostris? LAB* 19:3b). Such alterations
cannot have been anything other than deliberate, and exhibit a surprising
tendency in the *LAB* to ascribe to the person of Moses attributes proper
to God in Deuteronomy.

Moses' farewell prediction of apostasy and its consequent woes would
have seemed especially chilling to Pseudo-Philo's first century readers:
to predict apostasy is bad enough, but Pseudo-Philo's Moses foretells
that «God will be angry at you and abandon you and depart from your
land» (*et irascetur Deus in vobis, et derelinquet vos, et discedet de terra
vestra: LAB* 19:2). In distinction to Josephus's Moses, who predicts in
his first valediction that the *people* will depart from the land (*JA*
IV.190), Pseudo-Philo's Moses predicts that *God* will leave the land. In

this, Pseudo-Philo is doubtless drawing upon the work of the prophet Ezekiel, who depicts the Lord's departure in stages from Jerusalem (Ez 10:1-22; 11:22-25) because of the sin of apostasy among the Israelites. Moreover, in the prediction that God will «bring upon you those who hate you, and they will rule over you» (*et adducet super vos odientes vos, et principabuntur vobis*: *LAB* 19:2), Pseudo-Philo's readers would have seen an unmistakable reference to the hated Roman occupation of their land[31].

Moses' prophecy of the misfortunes which will follow the Israelites' lapse into apostasy is reinforced by an even more specific prediction which issues from the mouth of God:

> But this people will rise up and not seek me, and they will forget my law, by which I have enlightened them, and I will abandon their seed for a time. Now I will show you the land before you die, but you will not enter it in this age lest you see the graven images with which this people will start to be deceived and led off the path. I will show you the place where they will serve me for 740 years (*Demonstrabo tibi locum in quo mihi servient annos DCCXL*). After this it will be turned over into the hands of their enemies, and they will destroy it, and foreigners will encircle it (*Et post hec tradetur in manus inimicorum suorum et demolientur eum, et circumdabunt eum alienigene*). And it will be on that day as it was on the day I smashed the tablets of the covenant that I drew up for you in Horeb; and when they sinned, what was written on them flew away. Now that day was the seventeenth day of the fourth month (*LAB* 19:6-7).

In contrast to the more general prophecy of Moses, this prediction is specific in the extreme: the «place» which God shows Moses at 19:7 (*locum*, behind which, presumably, is the Hebrew מָקוֹם, translated in the LXX as τόπος), is undoubtedly a reference to the Temple itself, since in Deuteronomy, מָקוֹם/τόπος had already become a *terminus technicus* for the Temple[32]. Here, of course, God shows Moses the Temple only to predict its eventual destruction, a destruction which is described in terms which are unmistakably reminiscent of the siege of Jerusalem by the Romans. The sin of apostasy which merits the destruction of the «place» is likened to the worship of the golden calf (Ex 32) insofar as the destruction of the Temple is likened to the smashing the tablets of the

---

[31] C. DIETZFELBINGER, «Pseudo-Philo», 96.

[32] See, for instance, Deut 12:5, 11, 14, 18, 21, 26; 14:23, 24, 25; 15:20; 16:2, 6, 7, 11, 15, 16; 17:8, 10; 18:6; 31:11.

covenant (*tabulas testamenti*: 19:7). To destroy the Temple is, in effect,
to break off covenantal relations between God and Israel.

The grim predictions of the Temple's destruction and the sundered
covenant are relieved, however, by the intercession of Moses which begins the second dialogue. The prayer displays the intercessory powers
of Moses, insofar as he pleads with God to mitigate the sentence of destruction. Moses' plea for mitigation begins with an historical retrospect
which recounts the call of Moses and the episode of the burning bush.
Although Moses was afraid (*ego timui*: *LAB* 19:9) and turned away from
God (*et declinavi faciem meam*: *LAB* 19:9), an expression which implies
an initial refusal to comply with the divine will, God nevertheless sent
him to his people and freed them from Egypt. Moses makes an analogi-
cal case for mercy here in the historical retrospect in such a way that
just as his own sinfulness did not prevent God from choosing him to
serve as an instrument of the divine will, so the iniquity of the Israelites
should not prevent God from sparing them. This argument from human
sinfulness alludes to the prayer of Solomon in 1 Kgs 8:46 with its frank
acknowledgement of the human propensity to immorality (*Quis est enim
homo qui tibi non peccavit*: *LAB* 19:9). Thus does the author of the *LAB*
heighten the importance of the figure of Moses by implicitly comparing
him to one of Israel's greatest kings, indeed, the builder of the Temple
whose destruction is now being prophesied.

In addition, Moses' appeal bears some similarity to Amos' plea for
mercy after his visions of Israel's devastation by locusts (Amos 7:1-2)
and fire (Amos 7:4): «How can Jacob stand? He is so small!» (Amos
7:2, 5). Like Amos, Pseudo-Philo's Moses cites the weakness of his
people as a reason for God's mercy. God's reply to this prayer for
mercy is not to rescind his threat of punishment, as he does in Amos
(Amos 7:3, 6), but rather to show Moses a vision of the land:

> Then the Lord showed him the land and all that is in it and said, «This is the
> land that I will give to my people». And he showed him the place from
> which the clouds draw up water to water the whole earth, and the place from
> which the river takes its water, and the land of Egypt, and the place in the
> firmament from which only the holy land drinks. And he showed him the
> place from which the manna rained upon the people, even unto the paths of
> paradise. And he showed him the measurements of the sanctuary and the
> number of the sacrifices and the signs by which they are to interpret the
> heaven. And he said, «These are what are prohibited for the human race
> because they have sinned against me», (*LAB* 19:10).

This display of the land is the equivalent, in the *LAB*, of the survey of the land found in Deut 34:1-4. It functions here, however, as a way of reassuring Moses, not to mention the readers of the *LAB*, that the eventuality which he, and they, fear most, namely, the sundering of the covenant thanks to the destruction of the «place», will not, in fact, happen. The earthly Temple may go the way of destruction, but the «place», that is, the privileged *locus* of divine presence has been removed to a different level. Now God is to be found at another series of «places:» the place from which the clouds draw up water to water the whole earth (*locum unde elevant nubes aquam ad irrigandum omnem terram*), and the place from which the river takes its water (*locum unde accipit fluvius irrigationem*), and the place from which only the holy land drinks (*locum firmamenti unde bibet sola terra sancta*), even the land of Egypt (*terram Egipti*). This first series of places suggest that God, as creator of the world, may be encountered anywhere in that world, even in the land of Egypt, from which Moses has liberated his people.

But the author of the *LAB* proceeds to identify another series of «places» wherein God may be encountered, these next being more cosmic in scale in comparison to the first series of places: «the place from which the manna rained upon the people» (*locum unde pluit manna populo*)[33], «the paths of paradise» (*semitas paradysi*), and, finally, «the measurements of the sanctuary and the number of the sacrifices and the signs by which they are to interpret the heaven» (*mensuras sanctuarii et numerum oblationum et signa in quibus incipiant inspicere celum*). To mention the measurements of the sanctuary in the context of these cosmic *loci* is to suggest that the Temple survives at some cosmic level of existence, despite its disappearance here below. God's «place», in other words, survived its destruction.

The reason for the preservation of the cosmic Temple, and the withholding of the divine wrath, is none other than Moses himself, who is likened herein to Noah:

> And now your staff with which these signs were performed will be a witness between me and my people. And when they sin, I will be angry with them

---

[33] H. JACOBSEN («Biblical Quotation») notes that the phrase *ostendit ei locum unde pluit manna populo* is probably best rendered «the place where he [God] rained down manna for the people» since *pluit* is not often used intransitively with a «personal» subject, (i.e., that which is falling), and since in the relevant Biblical parallels, all have manna as an object, not as a subject (62). Jacobsen may be granted his thesis without vitiating my own, which concerns itself with the meaning of *locum* here.

but I will recall your staff and spare them in accord with my mercy. And your staff will be before me as a reminder all the days, and it will be like the bow with which I established my covenant with Noah when he went forth from the ark, saying, «I will place my bow in the cloud and it will be for a sign between me and men that never again will the flood water cover all the earth», (*LAB* 19:11).

Not only is the Temple assigned a place in the cosmos, but so is the staff of Moses. The effect of so elevating the sign of Moses' office of leadership among the Israelites is to similarly elevate the one who occupies the office. Moses is given a cosmic status in the *LAB*.

The similarity between Pseudo-Philo's consolation for the loss of the Temple (the earthly «place» may be gone, but God's «place» in the cosmos remains) and that proposed by Josephus in *Against Apion* II.193-195 is instructive: while Josephus strongly implies that the by-now destroyed Temple still perdures in eternity, Pseudo-Philo makes of this insinuation an article of faith; it is God, after all who reveals the *loci* to Moses, and promises him that he and all else who have died will one day live in the heavenly sanctuary: «I will hurry to raise up you who are sleeping in order that all who can live may dwell in the place of sanctification I showed you» (*quoniam festinabo excitare vos dormientes, ut quem ostendi tibi locum sanctificationis in eo habitent omnes qui possunt vivere*: *LAB* 19:13).

What follows this revelation of the place is the revelation of the time:

And Moses said, «If I can make another request of you, Lord; according to your great mercy be not angry with me, but show me what amount of time has passed and how much remains». And he said to him, «There is honey, the topmost peak, the fullness of a moment, and the drop of a cup; and time has fulfilled all things. For four and a half have passed, and two and a half remain», (*LAB* 19:14-15).

Harrington proposes to amend the text from *Istic mel, apex magnus* («There is honey, the topmost peak») to *Stigma et apex manus* («An instant, the topmost part of a hand»)[34], an emendation which does little to clear up what was probably intended to be deliberate obscurity. What is clear is that Moses wants to know when the consummation of the divine plan will take place. The fact that an answer is given to him in such cryptic terms is probably a literary device which accomplishes two purposes: first, it serves notice to the readers of the *LAB* that this divine

---

[34] D. J. HARRINGTON, «Pseudo-Philo: A New Translation», 328.

consummation will occur at a time when they least expect it, since they cannot decipher the temporal notice; and second, it serves to enhance the status of Moses, who is able to decode the revelation. For after he receives the revelation of time, «he was filled with understanding and his appearance became glorious» (*repletus est sensu, et mutata est effigies eius in gloria*: *LAB* 19:16).

The depiction of the death of Moses in the *LAB* bears some similarities to the corresponding episode in the *VM*: like Philo, Pseudo-Philo depicts the moment of Moses' death as one of intellectual/mystical enlightenment, for it occurs after Moses is vouchsafed the revelation of place and time:

> And when Moses heard this, he was filled with understanding and his appearance became glorious (*repletus est sensu, et mutata est effigies eius in gloria*); and he died in glory according to the word of the Lord, and he buried him as he promised him. And the angels mourned at his death, and the lightnings and the torches and the arrows went all together before him. And in that day the hymn of the heavenly hosts was not sung because of the passing of Moses, nor was there such a day from the one on which the Lord made man upon the earth, nor shall there be such forever, that the hymn of the angels should stop on account of men; because he loved him very much. And he buried him with his own hands on a high place and in the light of all the world (*LAB* 19:16).

What is of note, and which represents a major narrative departure from the Biblical account itself, as well as other examples of the «rewritten Bible», is the cosmic mourning which accompanies the death of Moses. The Israelites have completely dropped from sight in the *LAB*, and in their place, the angels mourn by ceasing to offer the hymn of the heavenly hosts. The angelic mourning is in keeping, first of all, with the scale of the revelations which Moses has received here, and secondly, with the status of the one who has died.

## 1.3 *Theological analysis*

If, as we have seen, the literary conventions of the encomium served Philo's theological agenda by portraying Moses as a figure who is worthy of universal praise, the demands of catechesis likewise serve the theology of Pseudo-Philo. Like any work of catechesis, the *LAB* was designed to deepen the faith of its readers: it is not a speculative work, nor is it directed to an audience which has yet to be convinced of the central claim of the work, that God has chosen this people «so that [...] [he might] kindle among you an eternal light» (*ut [...] incendens in vobis sempiternam lucernam*: *LAB* 19:4). Consequently, Pseudo-Philo assumes a fundamental awareness on the part of his readers of the narrative of the history of salvation, of which his work may be seen as a handy summary. The *LAB* accomplishes its catechetical aims in two ways: it offers a theology of Moses by comparing him to other great figures from Israel's religious tradition, and it seeks to provide an explanation for the loss of the Temple.

Unlike the depiction of Moses in the works of Philo or Josephus, in which the great νομοθέτης is implicitly compared to great world-historical figures like Socrates, with the purpose of demonstrating the greatness of Moses to non-Jews, the portrait of Moses here in the *LAB* refrains from making any sort of comparison of Moses to such figures; instead, on those occasions when Moses is likened to any other person, he is compared to some other character from the Old Testament – Noah, for instance, or Solomon, or Amos. This is not to say that the comparison does not add lustre to the portrait of Moses; on the contrary, to present Moses in the likeness of a Noah is to suggest that in him, humanity enters into a new era of history: the human race gets a another chance with Moses and his covenant, just as it did with Noah. To portray Moses as a prototype of Solomon is to stress his authority over his people. Similarly, to depict Moses as a kind of Amos is to underscore his authority to speak for God.

The other great catechetical aim of Pseudo-Philo's portrait of Moses is to account for the loss of the Temple. It does so by asserting, through the authoritative means of a solemn revelation to Moses, that the destruction of the Temple as a privileged *locus* wherein God may be encountered does not mean that all hope of communion with the divine should be abandoned. On the contrary, God may be met here and now in other *loci*, even in the most improbable of places, like the land of Egypt. Moreover, the Temple itself continues to exist in the celestial realm, and may one day be restored to humanity. In this concern to account for the loss of the place may be seen affinities to Josephus, for whom the loss of the land, the city, and the Temple likewise demanded a theological justification. Unlike Josephus, however, who viewed the destruction of the Temple as a divine punishment for having mounted the revolt of 66-70, the author of the *LAB* sees the loss of the Temple as a punishment for the sin of idolatry: indeed, the reason Moses does not enter the Promised Land is to prevent him from seeing the idols to whom his people will soon start to pay homage[35].

These two catechetical aims are not unrelated: for the author of the *LAB* to have restricted himself to a comparison of Moses with figures who appear in the Scriptures is, in effect, for him to have claimed that only in the Scriptures are to be found figures worthy of such a comparison. Such a restriction implicitly devalues the world outside the community for which the *LAB* was written, a world which is rife with idolatry; such devaluation of the world is in perfect keeping with the polemic against idolatry which runs through the *LAB* as a motif.

## 2. The *Testament of Moses*

The *Testament of Moses*, like the other versions of the last words of Moses which have come down to us from the first century, purports to be instructions and predictions delivered to Joshua by Moses shortly before Moses dies. Like the *VM*, the *TM* takes as its primary focus the figure of Moses, and like the *LAB*, the predictive element in Moses' last words looms large. Indeed, one may make the claim that the last words of Moses in the *TM* are almost wholly predictive, serving to ratify the prophetic status of Moses within the community for whom the *TM* was originally written, since the future which he predicts will have been history with which they would have been familiar.

The *TM* has come under renewed scholarly scrutiny within the last twenty years, thanks largely to the efforts of George W. E. Nickelsburg[36]. The text of the *TM* is known from a single Latin palimpsest, discovered by A. M. Ceriani in Milan's Ambrosian Library in 1861 and later published as the *Assumption of Moses* with an English language translation by R. H. Charles[37]. That translation has now been superseded by new translations of the *TM* by John Priest[38] and Johannes

---

[35] See *LAB* 19:7.

[36] G. W. E. NICKELSBURG, *Resurrection, Immortality, and Eternal Life*, 29-30, 44-45; ID., ed., *Studies on the Testament of Moses*; ID., *Jewish Literature*, 80-82, 212-213.

[37] R. H. CHARLES, *The Assumption of Moses*; ID., «The Assumption of Moses: Introduction», 407-413.

[38] J. PRIEST, «The Testament of Moses», 919-934.

Tromp, who also presents a critical edition of the Latin text of the *TM*[39].

## 2.1 *Date, provenance, and original language*

Determining the date, the provenance, and the original language of the *TM* is no easy task, given the conditions under which the text survived. The same sorts of difficulties involved in analysing the *LAB* face anyone who wishes to understand the *TM*. The text of the *TM*, like the text of the *LAB*, survives only in its Latin translation and in an incomplete state, at that. The author of the *TM*, like the author of the *LAB*, is otherwise unknown; indeed, to speak of a single author of the *TM* is to misconstrue the process by which the text as we have it reached its final form, since current thinking about the *TM* sees it as a document which was finished only after some 150 years of composition.

### 2.1.1 Date of the *TM*

In 1986, John J. Collins summarised the current state of the question regarding the date of the *TM*: most scholars today accept Licht's thesis[40], later developed by George W. E. Nickelsburg[41] and Adela Yarbro Collins[42] that the *TM* is a composite document, having been written over the course of some 150 years[43]. Nickelsburg thinks that the earliest version of the *TM* was written sometime after the onset of persecutions during the reign of Antiochus Epiphanes IV, citing the similarity of *TM* 8 and 1 Macc 1:54-63[44]. According to this composite thesis, *TM* 6–7 were later inserted into the narrative since, in the text as it presently stands, there is a unmistakable reference to the campaign of Varus and the partial destruction of the Temple in 4 BC (*TM* 6:8-9) and a probable reference to the reign of Herod the Great (37-4 BCE) in *TM* 6:6: hence, as Collins notes, the latest redaction of the *TM* must be dated to around the turn of the era[45].

---

[39] J. TROMP, *The Assumption of Moses*; hereinafter *AM*.

[40] J. LICHT, «Taxo», 95-103.

[41] G. W. E. NICKELSBURG, «An Antiochan Date», 33-37.

[42] A. Y. COLLINS, «Composition and Redaction», 179-186.

[43] J. J. COLLINS, «The Testamentary Literature», 277.

[44] G. W. E. NICKELSBURG, «An Antiochan Date», 34.

[45] J. J. COLLINS, «The Testament (Assumption) of Moses», 148.

## 2.1.2  Provenance of the *TM*

Determining the provenance of the *TM* is a difficult endeavour, given the composite nature of the work, its status as a translation, and the incomplete state in which the manuscript has survived. These obstacles, however, have not prevented scholars from hazarding guesses respecting the original matrix out of which the *TM* emerged. While most scholars are agreed that the geographic provenance of the *TM* was Palestinian[46], the consensus evaporates in trying to affix the religious milieu to which the work belongs. R. H. Charles, for instance, thought that the author belonged to a branch of the Pharisees which he described as «quietistic»[47]. In a brief survey article, Charles De Santo proposed an Essene origin for the *TM*[48], and later, in a full-scale monograph, E. M. Laperrousaz made a similar suggestion[49], though the failure of anything to turn up so far in Qumran which may be identified as a version of the *TM* must be regarded as a serious blow to the thesis of Essene origins. At one point, Nickelsburg flirted with the possibility of an Essene origin for the *TM*[50], a position he later rejected[51]. John Priest prefers not to assign the *TM* to either a Pharisaic milieu or an Essene one, but thinks that the work «reflects the general outlook of the later Hasidic movement with a stress on apocalyptic motifs»[52]. Like Priest, Jonathan A. Goldstein thinks that the author of the *TM* belonged to the *Hasidim*, and bases his contention on the similarities between the figure of Taxo and the martyrs of 1 Macc 2:29-38 and 2 Macc 6:11[53]. In 1969, K. H. Haacker advanced the suggestion that the author of the *TM* was a Samaritan, given the exalted position Moses occupies in the *TM* as a *Religionsstifter*[54]. This position has been rejected by John D. Purvis, who has demonstrated that those elements which Haacker wanted to identify as specifically Samaritan are, in fact, part of the common heritage of both

---

[46] See *AM*, 117, for a handy summary for the evidence which points to the Palestinian origin of the *TM*.

[47] R. H. CHARLES, *The Assumption of Moses*, vii, xiv, liv.

[48] C. DE SANTO, «The Assumption of Moses», 305-310.

[49] E. M. LAPERROUSAZ, *Le Testament de Moïse*, 95.

[50] G. W. E. NICKELSBURG, *Resurrection, Immortality, and Eternal Life*, 45.

[51] G. W. E. NICKELSBURG, *Jewish Literature*, 82-83.

[52] J. PRIEST, «The Testament of Moses», 922.

[53] J. A. GOLDSTEIN, «The Testament of Moses», 48-50.

[54] K. H. HAACKER, «Assumptio Mosis» 385-405.

Judaism and Samaritanism[55]. John J. Collins admits that the work cannot be conveniently assigned to any of the religious groups within Judaism with which we are familiar, but nevertheless insists on the basis of the rejection of the Temple cult in *TM* 4:8 and the hatred of the Hasmonaean house in *TM* 6:1 that the work should be considered sectarian[56]. At one point, Johannes Tromp held that the author of the *TM* belonged to a group of schismatic Levites[57], a position he later retracted, preferring now to describe the work as «non-sectarian», since, first of all, the theology of the *TM* is unspecific, and second, our relatively limited knowledge of what differentiated one religious group within first century Judaism from another does not permit us to assign with any confidence the *TM* to a specific group, be it that of the Pharisees, the Sadducees, the Essenes, the Hasidim, or the Levites[58]. After reading through nearly a century's worth of such speculation, one is tempted to conclude that the *TM* is all things to all scholars.

### 2.1.3  Language of the *TM*

Like the *LAB*, the *TM* survives only in translation. Until fairly recently, the working hypothesis among scholars was that the extant text of the *TM* represented a Latin translation of a Greek translation of a Semitic original[59]. This hypothesis may be traced back to the pioneering efforts of R. H. Charles nearly a century ago, who was convinced that the *TM* was originally written in Hebrew[60]. By the mid-twentieth century, D. H. Wallace was somewhat more cautious in his attempt to fix the original language of the *TM*: the weight of historical probability is on the side of Charles' thesis of a Hebrew original, since this was the language reserved for what Wallace was pleased to call «holy writings»[61]; nevertheless, many of the examples which Charles had adduced as incontrovertible evidence of a Hebrew original turn out to have parallels in Aramaic, so the question was not definitively resolved for Wallace. Most recently, Johannes Tromp has argued that the so-called Hebraisms on the

---

[55] J. D. Purvis, «Samaritan Traditions», 93-117.

[56] J. J. Collins, «Date and Provenance», 31.

[57] J. Tromp, «Taxo», 209.

[58] *AM*, 109; 118-119.

[59] G. W. E. Nickelsburg, *Jewish Literature*, 83.

[60] R. H. Charles, *The Assumption of Moses*, xlii.

[61] D. H. Wallace, «The Semitic Origin», 323.

basis of which Charles had argued for a Hebrew original are, in actuality, style-figures, designed to lend a Biblical flavour to the style of the *TM*. Tromp concludes that while the evidence is strong that the Latin of the *TM* reflects a Greek *Vorlage*, «the evidence for assuming a Hebrew original is weak and unconvincing»[62]. In any case, any attempt to recover the original language of the *TM* is complicated by what must have been misunderstandings at the time the translation(s) were undertaken. Wallace's weary admission gets to the root of the linguistic problem: «It is clear that the Greek translator of the [*TM*] frequently misunderstood and thus improperly rendered the text [...] But the greatest difficulty is that the Greek translation was rendered into Latin by an individual who was obviously clumsy in his use of Latin, and deficient in his use of Greek»[63].

## 2.2 *Literary analysis*

A literary analysis of the *TM* involves many of the same issues and problems entailed in the analysis of Deuteronomy: the scholarly study of both narratives has been dominated by the methods of diachronic investigation, the aim of which has been to establish the process by which the texts as they presently exist came into being. Important as these studies have been for our understanding of the history of the composition of the narratives, my interest in the *TM*, like my interest in Deuteronomy, is not diachronic, but synchronic, which is to say that my intention here is to analyse those structures in the *TM* which are the result of the more than century-long process of composition, the elucidation of which G. W. E. Nickelsburg, J. J. Collins, A. B. Kolenkow, and others have devoted so much of their scholarly energy.

### 2.2.1 Genre of the *TM*

This literary analysis of the *TM* is complicated by the incomplete and fragmentary nature of the text as it has survived. Moreover, since the discovery of the *TM* in 1861, there has been some confusion over the nature of its genre: is the text as it survived substantially identifiable with the narrative which was known to the Fathers as the *Assumption of Moses*, and which survives today only in quotations in the Fathers?

---

[62] *AM*, 81-85.

[63] D. H. WALLACE, «The Semitic Origin», 328.

Charlesworth thought not, though he did allow in 1976 for the possibility that the *Assumption of Moses* and the *TM* did circulate together, and that the lost ending of the Latin manuscript contained an account of Moses' assumption[64]. Similarly, in 1984, John J. Collins held that the *TM* probably originally referred to the death of Moses[65]. By 1985, however, Charlesworth had altered his earlier position and cautioned against the presumption that the *TM* contained anything more than a brief statement of the death of Moses[66]. The majority opinion among scholars today is that the *TM* and the *Assumption of Moses* were two different documents.

Formally, the *TM* may be classified as a testament, as Charles recognised[67], and as E. von Nordheim has shown[68]. It manifests those characteristics which J. J. Collins recognised as typical of the testament: it is a first-person discourse delivered in anticipation of death; the speaker is, in this case, a leader addressing his successor; and the discourse proper is framed by a third-person narrative describing the situation in which the speech was delivered[69]. Kolenkow has attempted to categorize the *TM* as a blessing-revelation-testament[70], though a case can be made that such further refinements add little to our understanding. As what purports to be the last words of Moses, the *TM* possesses the same kind of authority with which Josephus invested his version of the last words of Moses: for Josephus, Moses' last words are to be trusted «because souls when on the verge of the end deliver themselves with perfect integrity» (διὰ τὸ τὰς ψυχὰς ἐπὶ τελευτῇ γιγνομένας μετ' ἀρετῆς πάσης ὁμιλεῖν: *JA* IV.179). Indeed, as J. J. Collins has recognised, the author's choice of Moses to narrate this prophecy of what is to come gives the *TM* a weight of authority which is indisputable[71].

From the perspective of content, the *TM* may be classified as a rewriting of Deut 31–34[72]. Harrington thinks that the author of the *TM* was

---

[64] J. H. CHARLESWORTH, *The Pseudepigrapha and Modern Research*, 161.

[65] J. J. COLLINS, *The Apocalyptic Imagination*, 102.

[66] J. H. CHARLESWORTH, *The Old Testament Pseudepigrapha*, 76-77.

[67] R. H. CHARLES, *The Assumption of Moses*, xlv-l.

[68] E. VON NORDHEIM, *Das Testament als Literaturgattung*, 194-207.

[69] J. J. COLLINS, *The Apocalyptic Imagination*, 102.

[70] A. B. KOLENKOW, «The Genre Testament», 58.

[71] J. J. COLLINS, *The Apocalyptic Imagination*, 105.

[72] J. J. COLLINS, *The Apocalyptic Imagination*, 103; D. J. HARRINGTON, «Interpreting Israel's History», 59-68; G. W. E. NICKELSBURG, *Resurrection, Immortality and Eternal Life*, 29.

particularly taken by the pattern of apostasy–punishment–vindication which characterises Deut 31-32, but modified the pattern in such a way that history now reveals a dynamic of apostasy–punishment–partial vindication–apostasy–punishment–eschatologicalvindication[73]. Harrington might better have described the pattern in the *TM* as a double sequence of apostasy-punishment-vindication, the second instance of which culminates in the eschatological vindication of those who have remained faithful to Israel's God[74].

## 2.2.2 Literary Structure of the *TM*

Originally, the *TM* was probably framed at its beginning and at its end by a narrative; only the introductory narrative survives, however, and consists of ten short verses:

> [...] which is the two thousand five hundredth year since the creation of the earth — but according to those who live in the East the number is the [...] and [...]th–, and the [...]th since the departure from Phoenicia, when the people left; after the departure that took place through Moses, until Amman over the Jordan; (*sc.* the book) of the prophecy which was given by Moses according to the book of Deuteronomy (*profetiae quae facta est a Moysen in libro Deuteronomio*), when he called unto him Joshua, the son of Nun, a man deemed worthy by the Lord, to be (*sc.* Moses') successor for the people and for the tabernacle of the testimony with all its holy objects, and to lead the people into the land that was given to their fathers, so that it would be given to them on account of the covenant and on account of the oath — the things he (*sc.* Moses) said in the tabernacle, namely that he (*sc.* God) would give it (*sc.* the land) through Joshua (*TM* 1:2-9).

The narrative framework accomplishes several purposes: it establishes the setting for the testament which follows; but, more importantly, it explicitly establishes the literary source, namely the *libro deuteronomio*, for what follows. Charles thought that *TM* 1:5 had to have been an interpolation, since «in a book of Hebrew origin, the phrase *libro deuteronomio* could not have been original»[75]. With respect to the putative Hebrew or Aramaic original of the *TM*, Charles may have been right; but with respect to its Greek version, he may not have had as great a reason for the rejection of the verse.

---

[73] D. J. HARRINGTON, «Interpreting Israel's History», 61.

[74] G. W. E. NICKELSBURG, *Jewish Literature*, 80.

[75] R. H. CHARLES, *The Assumption of Moses*, 55, n. 5.

What follows the introductory narrative may be outlined as follows:

1.    1:10-18        Instructions to Joshua
2.    2:1–10:10      Predictions of Israel's future
      A.   2:1–4:9      the future from the Conquest to the Exile
      B.   5:1–6:9      the future from the Return to the present
      C.   7:1–10:10   the eschatological scenario
3.    10:11-15       Instructions to Joshua
4.    11:1-17        Joshua's lament
5.    12:1-13        Moses' reply to Joshua

As the outline indicates, the majority of the *TM* (2:1–10:10) is taken up by predictions of Israel's future. These predictions are framed by instructions to Joshua respecting the preservation of the *TM*. Thus, in the first instruction, Moses charges Joshua in a particularly solemn fashion:

> You, however, receive this writing (*scribturam hanc*), which serves to acknowledge the trustworthiness of the books (*librorum*) I will hand to you, and you must order them, embalm them, and put them in earthenware jars in a place which he made from the beginning of the creation of the world, so that his name be invoked; until the day of repentance, in the visitation with which the Lord will visit them in the fulfillment of the end of days (*TM* 1:16-18).

At the conclusion of the predictions of Israel's future, Moses again instructs Joshua to preserve the *TM*:

> But you, Joshua son of Nun, keep these words (*verba haec*) and this book (*hunc librum*). For from my death, my being taken away, until his (*sc.* God's) advent, there will be 250 times that happen. And this is the course of events that will come to pass, until they will be completed. But I shall go to the resting-place of my fathers. Therefore you, Joshua son of Nun, be strong. It is you, whom God has chosen to be my successor to his covenant (*TM* 10:11-15).

These instructions respecting the preservation to the *TM* serve to stress the importance of the predictions of the future which they frame. Moreover, since much of the future envisioned in the *TM* is part of a past, both distant and recent, with which a first century Jewish reader would have been well aware, Moses' authority as a prophet is strengthened by the accuracy of his predictions. What yet remains to occur, namely the eschatological scenario, takes on a kind of inevitability in view of the precision of the historical predictions. In that sense, the author of the *TM* has organised these predictions in a fashion which Philo would have found congenial: «Some of these have already taken place, others are still looked for, since confidence in the future is assured by fulfillment in the past» (*VM* II.288).

What is «still looked for» in the *TM*, namely, the eschatological scenario of 7:1–10:10 contains several elements. The first element of this eschatological scenario is the description of «pestilent and impious men [...] who proclaim themselves to be righteous» (*homines pestilentiosi et impii docentes se esse justos*: *TM* 7:3).

> And they will excite their wrathful souls; they will be deceitful men, self-complacent, hypocrites in all their dealings, and who love to debauch each hour of the day, devourers, gluttons, [......] who eat the possessions of [...], saying they do this out of compassion [...] murderers, complainers, liars, hiding themselves lest they be recognised as impious, full of crime and iniquity, from sunrise to sunset saying, «Let us have extravagant banquets, let us eat and drink. And let us act as if we are princes». And their hands and minds will deal with impurities, and their mouth will speak enormities, saying in addition to all this: «Keep off, do not touch me, lest you pollute me [...] » (*TM* 7:4-10).

Tromp notes that while the description of these «pestilent and impious men» is drawn in the most stereotypical of terms, it probably refers, nevertheless, to specific people, contemporaries with whom the readers of the *TM* would have been familiar[76]. The derogatory language by which the «pestilent and impious men» are characterised may be compared with a similar vituperative language in 2 Tim, in which the would-be νομοδιδάσκαλοι are said to be

> lovers of self, lovers of money, proud, arrogant, abusive, disobedient to their parents, ungrateful, unholy, inhuman, implacable, slanderers, profligates, fierce, haters of good, treacherous, reckless, swollen with conceit, lovers of pleasure rather than lovers of God, holding the form of religion but denying the power of it (2 Tim 3:2-5).

Common to both attacks is the accusation of debauchery (φιλήδονοι in 2 Tim 3:4; *amantes convivia, devoratores, gulae* in *TM* 7:4), greed (φιλάργυροι in 2 Tim 3:2; *[...]rum bonorum comestores, dicentes se haec facere propter misericordiam* in *TM* 7:6), pride (ἀλαζόνες ὑπερήφανοι in 2 Tim 3:2; *Et putavimus nos tamquam principes erimus* in *TM* 7:8), and hypocrisy (ἔχοντες μόρφωσιν εὐσεβείας τὴν δὲ δύναμιν αὐτῆς ἠρνημένοι in 2 Tim 3:5; *ficti in omnibus suis* in *TM* 7:4, *celantes se, ne possent cognosci impii* in *TM* 7:7). I have noted before that R. J. Karris's

---

[76] *AM*, 207-208.

investigations into the polemic directed against the νομοδιδάσκαλοι in 2 Tim reveal that the stock character of many of these kinds of accusations may be traced back to the quarrel between the philosophers and the sophists dating back to the time of Plato. Such polemics are characterized by a fairly constant series of accusations against the opponent, including greed, deceit, hypocrisy, quibbling over words, and leading women astray[77]. That such accusations are of such hoary antiquity urges one to exercise caution before assigning any historical value to them, whether they be found in 2 Tim or in the *TM*.

Those cautions having been registered, such accusations in the *TM* may not be entirely devoid of historical value. Here, certain methodological considerations from historians of the early Christian traditions may be useful in the search for historical referents. M. Y. MacDonald has noted that while the struggle against false teaching is clearly of primary interest to the author of the Pastoral Epistles, «it does not appear to be primarily the doctrinal content of the false teaching which is of concern to the author of the Pastorals, but its implications for lifestyle»[78]. While one might object to her use of a term as vague and as imprecise as «lifestyle», her primary contention, namely, that the struggle against the false teachers was not simply a struggle of one idea against another, seems well-founded: as a practitioner of social history, she insists that doctrinal statements be seen in the context of the community's social setting. When one fails to attend to the social setting of doctrinal statements, «[w]hen the reciprocity between social realities and religious symbolism is ignored, distortion is inevitable»[79]. F. Wisse has pointed out the serious difficulties facing the historian of early Christianity in the attempt to reconstruct the inner diversity and conflicts within the church before 200 CE. Owing to the polemical nature of some of the literature which survives, the historian faces enormous problems in trying to reconstruct the position of the opponents: «[o]ne cannot expect that the position of the other side has been represented fairly and completely in the heat of controversy»[80]. He further argues that the nature of the conflicts during the third and fourth centuries mistakenly has been assumed to pertain to earlier periods, with the result that conflicts over

---

[77] R. J. KARRIS, «Background and Significance», 551-555.

[78] M. Y. MACDONALD, *The Pauline Churches*, 226.

[79] M. Y. MACDONALD, *The Pauline Churches*, 24.

[80] F. WISSE, «The Use of Early Christian Literature», 180.

practice and authority characteristic of the earlier periods have been (mis)interpreted as conflicts over doctrine characteristic of the later[81].

The implications for our understanding of the polemic against the «pestilent and impious men» of the *TM*, and of the Judaism of the first century, are two-fold. Following MacDonald's lead, we should try to relate the struggle against the «pestilent and impious men» in the *TM* to the social setting to which the *TM* sought to address itself. Secondly, in following Wisse's shrewd observation, we may be permitted to see the polemic in the *TM* as symptomatic of a struggle over who shall exercise authority within the community for which the *TM* was composed. Since these «pestilent and impious men» are said to rule over Israel (*TM* 7:3), the polemic may well have been directed against the priesthood. More-over, *TM* 7:10 (*Noli <ne me> tange, ne inquines me*) probably reveals a concern to maintain ritual purity[82], and seems plausibly to refer to the priestly fear of incurring uncleanness[83].

Whoever these «pestilential and impious men» were, their activities signal the advent of the time of persecution, the second element in the eschatological scenario. Here again, we find similarities to 2 Tim, in which the appearance of the νομοδιδάσκαλοι is one of the signs of the «last days» (ἐσχάταις ἡμέραις: 2 Tim 3:1) which will be «times of stress» (καιροὶ χαλεποί):

> And suddenly revenge and wrath will come over them, such as there will never have been over them since eternity until that time, in which he will raise for them the king of the kings of the earth, and a power with great might, who will hang upon the cross those who confess circumcision, but who will torture those who deny it. And he will lead them chained into captivity, and their wives will be divided among the Gentiles, and their sons will be operated on as children by physicians in order to put on them a foreskin. But they will be punished by torments, and with fire and sword, and they will be forced to carry publically their idols, that are defiled, just like those who touch them. And they will be forced by those who torture them to enter into their hidden place, and they will be forced by goads to disgracefully blaspheme the word. Finally, after these things (*sc.* they will

---

[81] F. WISSE, «The Use of Early Christian Literature», 178, 189-190.

[82] *AM*, 213.

[83] J. Tromp, however, rejects the contention that the *homines pestilentiosi et impii* might have been priests on the grounds that «such a concept of the Judean polity in this period assumes more of a regulated and institutionalised society than is probably warranted» (*AM*, 209-210).

be forced to blaspheme) also the laws through the things they will have on their altar (*TM* 8:1-5).

The similarities between the time of persecution envisioned in the *TM* and that under Antiochus Ephiphanes IV have persuaded scholars like Nickelsburg and J. J. Collins that this section of the *TM* should be dated to that time[84]. It should be noted that theirs is not a position which is universally held. J. Priest, for instance, thinks that the persecutions described here are deliberately evocative of any number of tragedies which had previously befallen Israel, from the fall of Jerusalem in 587 BCE, to the Antiochan persecution, to the capture of Jerusalem by Pompey in 63 BCE: «it seems better», he allows, «to assume that the author has put together many past events that he believes are about to be replicated in the end-time»[85]. Likewise, Tromp argues that while *TM* 8 represents a digest of the traditions underlying the legendary accounts of the Antiochan persecution found in 1, 2 and 4 Maccabees and in Josephus's *JA* XII, it does not necessarily date the composition of the work[86].

The disagreement between Nickelsburg and Collins, on the one hand, and Priest and Tromp, on the other, may be explained by their differing methods of analysis. Nickelsburg and Collins have tried to account for the process by which the text has reached its present state; their methods are traditionally historical-critical, and their approach, diachronic. Tromp and Priest, though they do not reject a historical-critical methodology, seem to be interested, at least in their reading of *TM* 8, in the present form of the work; their preoccupations here may be characterised as synchronic. Both approaches to the text are legitimate; though in view of my purpose in trying to recapture the way in which a first century reader might have read the *TM*, the second, synchronic approach would appear to be more useful.

The episode involving Taxo (*TM* 9:1-7) constitutes the third element in the eschatological scenario. Much scholarly ink has been spilled in the attempt to determine the identity of Taxo[87]. Given the fact that the

---

[84] G. W. E. NICKELSBURG, «An Antiochan Date», 34; J. J. COLLINS, *The Apocalyptic Imagination*, 103.

[85] J. PRIEST, «Testament of Moses», 931, n. A.

[86] *AM*, 122.

[87] *AM*, 124-128, includes a summary of the nearly thirty proposals which scholars have made since the publication of the manuscript in 1861, many of which involve attempts to identify Taxo with one or another figure (e.g., Judas the Galilean, Rabbi

story of Taxo occupies only seven verses of the entire work, the degree of scholarly energy which has been expended on what amounts to a relatively brief episode in the *TM* seems somewhat excessive.

From a literary perspective, the figure of Taxo functions in the *TM* as a counterweight to the *homines pestilentiosi et impii*; and just as their sins usher in the time of persecution, so his fidelity, along with that of his family – both his ancestors and his descendants – usher in the fourth and final element of the eschatological scenario, the vindication of Israel, which takes place in two stages. The first stage involves the destruction of the cosmos which Israel's enemies inhabit:

> For the Heavenly One will rise from his royal throne, and he will go out from his holy habitation with anger and wrath on account of his sons. And the earth will tremble until its extremes it will be shaken, and the high mountains will be made low, and they will be shaken, and the valleys will sink. The sun will not give off its light, and the horns of the moon will turn to darkness, and they will be broken; and (*sc.* the moon) will entirely be turned into blood, and the orbit of the stars will be upset. And the sea will fall back into the abyss, and the fountains of the waters will defect and the rivers will recoil. For the Highest God, the sole Eternal One, will rise, and he will manifest himself in order to punish the nations, and to destroy all their idols (*TM* 10:3-7).

The images of earthquakes and the levelling of mountains, of solar and lunar darkness, of disturbances among the stars and tumult of the waters is, of course, part of the apocalyptic stock-in-trade[88]. Here, the author of the *TM* marshalls such imagery in the service of his conviction that the vindication of Israel will be an event which will have cosmic implications: the very structure of the universe will be altered as a result of God's intervention on behalf of his people. That divine intervention has two purposes, according to the scheme set forth in the *TM*: God manifests himself to punish the nations (*et palam veniet et vindicet gentes*: *TM* 10:7) and to destroy idolatry (*et perdet omnia idola eorum*: *TM* 10:7).

---

Juda ben Baba, Rabbi Joshua ben Hananiah, Mattathias, and even Jesus Christ, to name but a few). See also E. M. LAPERROUSAZ, *Le Testament de Moïse*, 125-126, and G. W. E. NICKELSBURG, *Resurrection, Immortality and Eternal Life*, 97.

[88] For earthquakes, see Mark 13:8b; Rev 6:12; for the levelling of mountains, see Rev 6:14b; for solar and lunar darkness, see Mark 13:24; Acts 2:20; Rev 6:12b; 8:12; for disturbances in the orbit of the stars, see Mark 13:25a; Rev 6:13.

The second stage in Israel's vindication comes with what one may call Israel's astral elevation:

> Then you will be happy, Israel, and you will mount on the neck and the wings of an eagle, and they will be filled, and God will exalt you, and make you live in the heaven of the stars, the place of his habitation. And you will look down from above, and you will see your enemies on the earth, and you will recognise them. And you will rejoice, and you will thank and praise your Creator (*TM* 10:8-10).

A. Y. Collins has noted that the prediction of mounting on (or better, trampling on, if behind the Latin *ascendes* is the Greek ἐπιβήσῃ, as in Deut 33:29) the neck of an eagle is probably a reference to the *aquila* of silver or gold which each Roman legion possessed as its standard[89]. Hence, Israel's elevation to the stars comes at the expense of her enemies. The contrast between Israel's place among the stars and her enemies' place on earth below is equivalent to the contrast between blessedness and misery, salvation and damnation.

With Moses' statement of faith in the future blessedness of Israel, the eschatological scenario concludes. Moses' speech returns to the narrative present with his instructions to Joshua to preserve the *TM* and to serve the Israelites as his successor (*TM* 10:11-15). Joshua's response to the scenario as Moses has outlined it is to lament, posing a series of despairing questions. Tromp has divided these questions into three groups: 11:5-8, in which the problem of Moses' burial is addressed; 11:9-15, which deals with the care and feeding of the people; and 11:16-19, in which Joshua enunciates his fears of the Amorites in the absence of Moses' intercession[90]. Such a division is not entirely warranted: for one thing, Tromp's classification of the questions neglects Joshua's initial question in 11:4; and, secondly, the issue of how the Israelites will function in the absence of Moses' intercessory powers arises in 11:11 and 11:14, as well as 11:17. Indeed, one can claim that the overriding worry to which Joshua gives voice in these despairing questions is that the departure of Moses from the camp of the Israelites means that the people will be wholly bereft of an intercessor, upon the powers of whom their corporate existence depends. The implicit assumption behind Joshua's questions is that the death of Moses means the death of the people. Hence, Joshua's initial reaction upon hearing Moses' death notice and

---

[89] A. Y. COLLINS, «Composition and Redaction», 186.

[90] *AM*, 241-242.

the news of his succession is to perform the ritual act of mourning, the rending of his garments:

> And when Joshua had heard Moses' words as they were written in his writing, everything they foretold, he rent his clothes and fell at Moses' feet. And Moses comforted him and wept with him. And Joshua answered him and said: «Why do you terrify me, lord Moses, and how will I hide myself from what you have said with the bitter voice that comes from your mouth, and which is full of tears and sighs, because you will presently go away from this people?» (*TM* 11:1-4).

The Moses after whom Joshua feels unworthy to follow is so great that an ordinary funeral monument is insufficient:

> What place will receive you, or what will be the monument on your grave, or who, being human, will dare to carry your body from one place to another? For all who die when their time has come have a grave in the earth. But your grave extends from the East to the West, and from the North to the extreme South. The entire world is your grave (*TM* 11:5-8).

Here, the author of the *TM* proffers a solution to the problem of Moses' otherwise unknown burial place, a solution which is unique in the legends about the death of Moses in the «rewritten Bible». Rather than positing an assumption into heaven, as Philo and Josephus do, or a burial by the very hand of God «on a high place», as the author of the *LAB* does, the author of the *TM* proposes that the entire world (*omnis orbis terrarum*) constitutes the grave of Moses. Such a solution accomplishes two ends: first of all, it provides an identifiable resting place for the remains of *domine Monse*; and secondly, the scale of the grave – the entire world – elevates Moses' stature in such a way that he assumes a universal importance. Nothing less than the entire world itself is capable of sufficing as a funeral monument for «the holy and sacred spirit, the worthy one before the Lord, the versatile and inscrutable lord of the word, the trusted one in everything, the divine prophet for this world, the perfect teacher for this earth» (*TM* 11:16).

If the primary theme of Joshua's lament is to bewail the departure of Moses as a portent of the Israelites' destruction, its secondary theme is his own unworthiness to succeed Moses and his inability to intercede before God on behalf of his people:

> Lord, you are leaving. And who will feed this people, or who will be there to take mercy on them, and who will be their leader on the way, or who will pray for them, not omitting one single day (*aut quis orabit pro eis, nec*

*patiens ne uno quidem diem)*, so that I can lead them into the land of the Amorites? *(TM* 11:9-11).

By stressing his own inability to provide for his people's needs, Joshua thereby exalts the powers, especially the intercessory powers, of his predecessor:

> How will I be able to < guard > this people, like a father his only son, or like a woman her daughter — a virgin who is being prepared to be given to a man — and who is anxious to protect her *(sc.* daughter's) body from the sun and her feet from going unshod over the ground? And whence shall I procure for them the food and drink they urgently need? For their number was a hundred thousand, but now they have grown into this multitude here, only because of your prayers, lord Moses *(Nam isti in tantum qui creverunt in tuis orationibus, domine Monse)*. And what wisdom or understanding have I to administer justice or pronounce a verdict in accordance with the words of the Lord? *(TM* 11:12-15).

The future welfare of the Israelites is dependent upon Joshua's ability to provide food and drink for his people, about which he is apparently anxious, as the question at 11:13 demonstrates. Yet up until now, their growth from an initial hundred thousand to «this multitude here» came not from the simple provision of food and drink, but rather as the result of the prayers of Moses, a patent allusion to the episode of the manna and the quail (Ex. 16). The Biblical narrative, however, does not record any intercessory prayer on the part of Moses: the Israelites grumble against Moses and Aaron (Ex. 16:2-3), and the Lord, quite without any prompting from Moses, provides the «bread from heaven» (Ex. 16:4) and the quail (Ex. 16:13). Once again, we see in the *TM*, as in the other examples of the «rewritten Bible», a tendency to embroider the biblical narrative, thereby to enhance the stature of Moses.

The final series of questions betray Joshua's fear that in the absence of Moses' intercessory powers, the Israelites will fall prey to their enemies:

> Furthermore, the kings of the Amorites, after they have heard — whilst believing that they can defeat us — that the holy and sacred spirit, the worthy one before the Lord, the versatile and inscrutable lord of the word, the trusted one in everything, the divine prophet for this world, the perfect teacher for this earth, is no longer with them, will say: «Let us go at them. If the enemies will sin against their Lord once more, there is no longer an advocate for them, who will supplicate to the Lord for them, as Moses was, the great messenger, who bent his knees on earth every hour of the day and of the night, praying; and who could look at him who rules the entire world

with mercy and justice, reminding him of the covenant with the fathers, and placating the Lord with his oath«; surely they will say: «He is no longer with them. Let us go, then, and let us wipe them from the face of the earth». What then will happen to this people, Lord Moses? (*TM* 11:16-19).

Moses' intercessory powers are here understood in terms of his ability to secure pardon from God for the sins of the Israelites. It is clear now why the death of Moses threatens the death of the community of the Israelites. In the absence of an effective intercessor, Israel's sins will not be forgiven, and, as a consequence, she will be handed over to her enemies to be destroyed.

The *TM* does not end on this sombre note of inexorable destruction. On the contrary, Moses' reply to Joshua's lament, even though it survives in a fragmentary and incomplete state, serves to answer the objections raised in Joshua's lament. His reply is prefaced by a narrative sequence (*TM* 12:1-3) which recapitulates the preface to Joshua's lament in *TM* 11:1-2[91]. To Joshua's fear that he will be inadequate to the tasks set before him as Moses' successor, Moses reassures him by word and by gesture:

> And after Joshua finished speaking, he again fell at Moses' feet. But Moses took his hand and raised him up into the seat before him (*et Monse prendit manum ipsius et erexit illum in cathedra ante se*). And he answered and said to him: «Joshua, do not think too lightly of yourself (*te ne contemnas*), but show yourself free from care. And give heed to my words» (*TM* 12:1-3).

Whether one translates *te ne contemnas* as «do not despise yourself» or as «do not think too lightly of yourself», as Tromp does[92], the point of Moses' admonition seems to be that Joshua's worries are groundless. The real ground for confidence in the future will be outlined in the discourse which follows in *TM* 12:4-13.

Within the immediate narrative context of the *TM*, the gestures of taking Joshua by the hand, raising him, and seating him before Moses is meant to have a comforting effect. Joshua's bodily position corresponds to his interiour disposition, so that in being raised up (*erexit: TM* 12:2), Joshua's state of misery is transformed into one of equanimity. But something more than solace is at stake here. To have taken him by the hand and raised him from his prone position, and then to have placed him in a seat (*cathedra*) before Moses is, in effect, to have installed

---

[91] *AM*, 260.

[92] *AM*, 25, 261.

Joshua as the successor to Moses, and to have conferred upon him all the rights and obligations that were once proper to Moses. The Mosaic office does not die with Moses, in other words, since to occupy the seat (καθέδρα/*cathedra*) of Moses is to exercise his authority[93]. In contrast to the *homines pestilentiosi et impii* whose hypocritical pretentions to righteousness render them ineligible to rule over Israel, Joshua and those who succeed him represent the legitimate heirs of Moses: they alone deserve to rule over Israel.

The entirety of the discourse which follows, however truncated it may be, is meant to serve as comfort to Joshua: its primary thrust is that confidence in what will come is best placed in God, to whom the future is known beforehand:

> God has created all nations on earth, and he foresaw us, them as well as us, from the beginning of the creation of the earth until the end of the world. And nothing has been overlooked by him, not even the smallest detail, but he has seen and known everything beforehand. When he made them, the Lord saw beforehand all things that were to happen in this world (*TM* 12:4-5).

The Lord's foreknowledge of what is to come is meant to reassure Joshua, as well as the reader of the *TM*, that all the events of Israel's historical experience, tragic and triumphant alike, have a place in the divine plan. The classic problem of theodicy — how could God let these things happen to us? — is resolved here by an appeal to divine omniscience.

A secondary theme of Moses' reply to Joshua is that God's promises to his people are not predicated on that people's innate virtue, nor on the virtue of their intercessors, but rather on God's own divine power:

> The Lord has appointed me for them and for their sins, that I should pray and supplicate for them; yet not on account of my virtue or strength (*non enim propter meam virtutem aut in firmitatem*), but out of long-suffering his mercy (*misericordiae*) and his patience (*patientia*) have befallen me (*TM* 12:6-7).

These statements accomplish several ends. First of all, as one might expect, they glorify the rôle of Moses as the divinely appointed intercessor

---

[93] This understanding of the perpetuation of the Mosaic office is not unique to the community for which the *TM* was originally destined: in at least some Jewish communities of the first century, the scribes and the Pharisees were thought to occupy the seat of Moses (ἐπὶ τῆς Μωϋσέως καθέδρας ἐκάθισαν οἱ γραμματεῖς καὶ οἱ Φαρισαῖοι: Matt. 23:2). See *AM*, 261.

on behalf of the Israelites. At the same time, however, they relativise Moses' status in the face of the divine mercy (*misericordia*) and patience (*patientia*). The operative force in Israel's historical experience has not been Moses's virtue or strength, but rather those attributes of God by which he overlooks the shortcomings of the one he has chosen to lead his people. The emphasis in *TM* 12:6-7, then, is not so much on what Moses has done, but on what *God* has done through him. The *TM* never allows its «Moses-ology» to obscure its theology.

And just as God has not allowed Moses' imperfections to impede his plan for the Israelites, so he will not permit the failures of the Israelites under the leadership of Joshua to thwart his purposes:

> Therefore, I say to you, Joshua, not on account of the piety of this people (*non propter pietatem plebis hujus*) will you defeat the nations. All the firmaments of heaven and fundaments of the earth (*omnia caeli firmamenta < et fundamenta > orbis*) are made as approved of by God, and they are under the ring of his right hand (*TM* 12:6-9).

The promise of the defeat of the nations serves, of course, to reassure Joshua that his fears of annihilation in the absence of Moses are groundless. But victory will be granted Joshua by the same gratuitous act through which Moses' prayers on behalf of the Israelites have been heard, which is to say that God's actions are not dependent upon the virtue of the people (*pietatem plebis*: *TM* 12:8). By juxtaposing this guarantee of victory to a statement of God's sovereignty over *omnia caeli firmamenta et fundamenta orbis*, the *TM* seeks to provide a hope as secure as the physical structures of the universe.

The divine power operative in human history does not vitiate the human contribution to that history in such a way that the people may passively await the fulfillment of God's promises. They must bind themselves to obey the commandments of God:

> If they therefore do the commandments of God perfectly, they will grow and prosper. But the sinners and those who neglect the commandments (*peccantibus et neglegentibus mandata*) <must> miss the goods that have been foretold, and they will be punished by the nations with many torments. But it cannot happen that he will exterminate and leave them entirely. For God, who sees everything beforehand in eternity, will go out, and his covenant stands firm. And through the oath which [...] (*TM* 12:10-12).

The influence of Deuteronomy's covenantal theology may be felt here: prosperity comes as the result of obedience (Deut 30:16), and punishment follows upon disobedience (Deut 30:17-18). The *TM* understands

Israel's historical tragedies as the just punishment of sinners (*peccantibus*) and those who neglect the commandments (*neglegentibus mandata*). Nevertheless, even the disobedience of the sinners and the neglectful cannot frustrate the plan of God, whose covenant is stronger than the disobedience of sinners.

### 2.2.3  Moses as prophet in the *TM*

The prophetic claims which the *TM* advances on behalf of Moses are several. First of all, as in the other examples of the «rewritten Bible» which survive from the first century, Moses is implicitly presented as a prophet insofar as he displays an ability to foresee and foretell the future. In this respect, the dominant image of Moses in the *TM* is that of the prophet, since so much of the narrative is devoted to drawing a picture of what is to befall the Israelites.

Secondly, the *TM* itself is a prophecy, as *TM* 1:5 indicates. Clemen noted that while the first three lines of the manuscript are now lost, two elements were probably mentioned: the word *profetia* and the year of Moses' death, since the genitive *prophetiae* in *TM* 1:5 is resumptive, and since the four-fold synchronism of *TM* 1:2-4 specifies ways in which the death of Moses may be computed. Thus the missing lines probably read something like «the book of the prophecy of Moses, which was given in the 120th year of his life (*liber profetiae Moysis, quae facta est anno vita ejus Cmo et XXmo*)[94]. If Clemen was right – and his reconstruction of the missing lines certainly seems reasonable – then the status which is claimed for the *TM* redounds to its putative author: only a prophet can deliver himself of a prophecy. But in the *TM*, as in the *LAB*, Moses' prophetic functions are not exhausted by his ability to predict the future.

Curiously, it is when Moses is explicitly identified as a prophet that the *TM* presents an understanding of prophecy which goes beyond the predictive. The first instance comes in *TM* 11:16: Joshua calls Moses «the divine prophet for this world», (*divinum per orbem terrarum profetam*) not so much for his ability to foresee what is to come, as for his intercessory powers. Moses has just chosen Joshua to be his successor, who responds in mourning:

> Furthermore, the kings of the Amorites, after they have heard – whilst believing that they can defeat us – that the holy and sacred spirit, the worthy one before the Lord, the versatile and inscrutable lord of the word, the

---

[94] C. CLEMEN, *Die Himmelfahrt des Mose*, 4.

trusted one in everything, the divine prophet for this world, the perfect teacher for this earth, is no longer with them, will say: «Let us go at them. If the enemies will sin against their Lord once more, there is no longer an advocate for them, who will supplicate to the Lord for them, as Moses was, the great messenger, who bent his knees on earth every hour of the day and of the night, praying; and who could look on him who rules the entire world with mercy and justice, reminding him of the covenant with the fathers, and placating the Lord with his oath»; surely they will say: «He is no longer with them. Let us go, then, and let us wipe them from the face of the earth». What then will happen to this people, lord Moses? (*TM* 11:16-19).

Several observations respecting this passage might usefully be made here. As noted above, Moses is known by a variety of titles here. This variety of titles tends to stress, as Tromp recognises, Moses' relationship with God[95]. But any examination of the titles which the author of the *TM* applies to Moses must take under consideration the narrative context in which those titles appear. And that aspect of Moses' ministry before the Lord and on behalf of his people which receives the most attention in the narrative of Joshua's complaint is the intercessory functions which Moses performs. Joshua's fear, expressed in his lament, is that the Amorite kings will attack the Israelites, once they realise Moses is no longer with his people because they lack an intercessor who will be willing to «supplicate to the Lord for them», (*qui ferat pro eis praeces Domino*: *TM* 11:17).

The second instance in which Moses' prophetic office is presented in a way which goes beyond the predictive occurs in *TM* 3:10-13. Moses has foreseen the time when the Israelites will have been exiled to Babylon, and will have called upon God to restore them to the Promised Land. Moses tells Joshua that in their grief each one will say to the other:

Is it not this, the things which Moses formerly testified to us in his prophecies (*nonne hoc est quod testabatur nobis tum Moyses in profetis*)? Moses, who suffered many things in Egypt, and in the Red Sea, and in the desert, during forty years. And having testified (*testatus*), he also called upon heaven and earth to be witnesses, lest we should transgress his commandments, which he has mediated to us. But since then, these things have come over us, in accordance with his words and his solemn confirmation, which he testified to us in those days (*quomodo testatus est nobis temporibus illis*),

_____

[95] *AM*, 250-258.

and which have come true up to our expulsion into the land of the East (*TM* 3:11-13).

The most obvious way in which prophecy is understood here is the ability to describe with accuracy what lies in the future. So the Israelites in exile identify Moses as a prophet because he «testified» what would come of them – divisions, invasions, exile – should they fail to obey the commandments of the Lord. But Moses' prophetic functions include here more than prediction; Moses is said to have endured suffering (*qui multa passus est*: *TM* 3:11), and to have been the mediator (*arbiter*: *TM* 3:12) of the Law.

In this sense, any of the titles by which Moses is known here – *divinum per orbem terrarum profetem* or *arbiter* – are ways in which Moses' prophetic powers may be expressed. For the author of the *TM*, Moses' prophetic powers, his legislative powers, his intercessory powers – even his power to suffer – were all of a piece.

### 2.2.4 Moses as law-giver in the *TM*

In the *TM*, the image of Moses as a law-giver is a subsidiary function to his primary rôle of prophet. What law-giving functions exercised by Moses there are tend to be concentrated in the first two chapters. In the first chapter, Moses has appointed Joshua to be his successor, and has given him several directions, the first of which deals with the preservation of the *Testament* itself:

> You, however, receive this writing, which serves to acknowledge the trustworthiness of the books which I will hand to you and you must order them, embalm them, and put them in earthenware jars in the place which he made from the beginning of the creation of the world, so that his name be invoked; until the day of repentance, in the visitation with which the Lord will visit them in the fulfillment of the end of days (*TM* 1:16-18).

The concern for the preservation of a written text recalls Deut 31:9-13, though here, of course, what is being preserved is not the law but rather the *TM* itself. To have directed that the *TM* be preserved in earthenware jars recalls the command of Isaiah to seal up his teaching (τότε φανεροὶ ἔσονται οἱ σφραγιζόμενοι τὸν νόμον τοῦ μὴ μαθεῖν: Is 8:16) combined, perhaps, with Jeremiah's deposit of the deed of purchase in the earthenware jar (ἀγγεῖον ὀστράκινον: LXX Jer 39:14). Such a double-headed allusion to both Isaiah and Jeremiah accords well with the prophetic rôle which dominates the presentation of Moses in the *TM*.

The second set of directions Moses gives to Joshua deals with his duties once the Chosen People have entered the Promised Land:

> But now, they will enter through you into the land which he decided and promised to give to their fathers. And in it (*sc.* the land) you must give blessings, and you must give to each of them their share in it, and you must found for them a kingdom and arrange for them local rule according to their Lord's wish in justice and righteousness (*TM* 2:1-2).

Joshua's duties are four: first, he must bless the people; secondly, he must apportion the land among them; thirdly, he must establish a kingdom for them; and fourthly, he must see to the appointment of magistrates. One is tempted to see the second and fourth duties as concrete expressions of the first and third, which is to say that the people are blessed when they receive their tribal lands and the kingdom is established for them when the magistrates are appointed.

Typically for the *TM*, no sooner has Moses commanded Joshua to perform the four tasks of blessing, apportioning, establishing, and appointing, than he moves on to rehearse the sad history of his people:

> [...] however, after they will have entered into their land in the [...]th year, and afterwards, they will be ruled by princes and kings for eighteen years but in the nineteenth the ten tribes will break themselves loose. And the two tribes will separate themselves and transfer the tabernacle of testimony. The heavenly God will fasten the pole of his tabernacle and the tower of his sanctuary, and the two (*sc.* tribes) will be appointed as holy tribes. The ten tribes, however, will establish for themselves kingdoms according to their own ordinances. And they will offer sacrifices for twenty years. And in the seventh they will surround themselves with walls, and as the ninth will have elapsed they will also abandon the covenant of the Lord and defile the alliance the Lord made with them. And they will sacrifice their children to foreign gods and erect idols in the tabernacle and serve them and they will act disgraciously in the house of the Lord and sculpt many idols of all kinds of animals (*TM* 2:3-9).

The use of the future tense here is now no longer imperative; it has become predictive, and the *TM* moves on to its primary theme, the description of the reader's present from the vantage point of the past. Thus the law-giving functions of Moses are subordinated to his predictive/prophetic functions in the *TM*.

### 2.2.5  Moses as suffering intercessor in the *TM*

As we have seen, the suffering of Moses is explicitly acknowledged in *TM* 3:10, when the Israelites, having endured schism, invasion and exile, recall the prophecies of Moses:

> Then, on that day, they will remember me, each tribe saying to the other, and each man to his neighbour: «Is it not this, the things which Moses formerly testified to us in his prophecies? Moses, who suffered many things (*qui multa passus est*) in Egypt, and in the Red Sea, and in the desert, during forty years» *TM* 3:10-11).

The *loci* of Moses' sufferings are said to be three – Egypt, the Red Sea, and the desert. There does not appear to be in the identification of these three *loci* an attempt to fix a cause for the sufferings of Moses in such a way that, in Egypt, Moses suffered at the hands of Pharaoh, or in the Red Sea, he suffered at the hands of Pharaoh's armies; still less may we assume that Moses' sufferings in the desert were caused by the Israelites themselves. The audience of the *TM* would have seen the land of Egypt, the Red Sea, and the desert as venues in which the entire Israelite nation, Moses included, suffered many things. For the memory of Moses is recalled by the entire nation, «each tribe [...] to the other and each man to his neighbour» (*tribus ad tribum, et homo de proximo suo*: *TM* 3:10). The author of the *TM* may have intended to signify, in this acknowledgement of the sufferings of Moses, the same sense of solidarity between Moses and the nation signified by Josephus in *JA* III.1-9. What is crucial here is that those in the narrative who recall Moses' sufferings have themselves been subjected to suffering in the form of schism, invasion, and exile: moreover, these tragic experiences formed part of the historical experience of the audience for whom the *TM* was written. To remember Moses as one «who suffered many things in Egypt, and in the Red Sea, and in the desert for forty tears» (*qui multa passus est in Aegypto, in Mari Rubro, et in heremo annis XL*: *TM* 3:11) is to retroject onto this exemplary figure the national experience of loss, and to make of Moses a kind of symbol of the nation's adversity.

A related episode in which Moses demonstrates his solidarity with his people's grief comes at *TM* 11:2. Joshua has just heard the prophecies which comprise the majority of the *TM* and he reacts with grief, tearing his clothing and falling at the feet of Moses. So, «Moses comforted him and wept with him» (*Et hortatus est eum Monse et ploravit cum eo*: *TM* 11:2). By itself, this brief mention of Moses' tears cannot bear the weight of too much interpretation. Taken together with *TM* 3:10-13, however, it suggests that Moses was a figure ready to share the burdens of another, which, if it is not exactly suffering *per se*, is nevertheless a long way from Josephus' presentation of Moses in *JA* IV.329 as the master of his passions (παθῶν αὐτοκράτωρ).

### 2.3 *Theological analysis*

Since the manuscript of the *TM* breaks off abruptly, it is impossible to know how much longer Moses' testament would have gone on. It is clear, however, that in the manuscript as it presently survives, two inter-related theological themes predominate. The first theme, that of God's absolute sovereignty over the course of human history, serves to reassure the readers of the *TM* on two counts: (1) that despite the tragedies to which they have already been subjected, and which they have yet to undergo, their history and their future are under the control of God; and (2) that the divine plan will eventually work out in their favour. So though they may have to endure invasions by kings from the East (*TM* 3:1) and the West (*TM* 6:8), and though they may be ruled by the *homines pestilentiosi* (*TM* 7:3), yet will the Heavenly One «rise from his royal throne, and he will go out from his holy habitation with anger and wrath on account of his sons» (*TM* 10:3). The *TM*, as John Priest has written, «stands squarely within that tradition which affirms that God's promises to his covenant people will not fail and that their hope of ultimate vindication may be held with full assurance»[96].

The second theological theme, that of Moses' continuing rôle within the community of faith, is likewise meant to be doubly reassuring: first, the community is not wholly bereft of his presence, since it possesses his *Testament* which serves as a kind of textual surrogate for his actual comforting and reassuring presence; and second, the office of Moses continues to be exercised by legitimate successors who sit upon his *cathedra*, even if there are some whose illegitimate claim to exercise leadership over Israel temporarily displaces the rightful heirs of Moses. 2 Tim functions in a similar fashion within the community for which it was originally destined, since it purports to communicate Paul's last words relative to the future of that community[97], and like the *TM*, condemns those who lead the faithful astray, while at the same time identifying Paul's legitimate successors[98].

---

[96] J. PRIEST, «Some Reflections», 109.

[97] See 2 Tim 3:1-5, 12-13; 4:3-4.

[98] See 2 Tim 1:6; 2:2.

## CHAPTER V

## Images of Paul in 2 Timothy

In considering those first century stories of the last words and death of Moses, I have sought to situate the *testamentum Pauli* that is 2 Tim within a particular literary tradition. In an analysis of the legends of the dying Moses in the *VM*, the *JA*, the *LAB*, and the *TM*, I have attempted to show that despite the variety of treatments to which the figure of Moses is subject in each legend, and despite the variety of theologies of which he was made to serve as the vehicle, several points of commonality tie these legends to each other. To varying degrees, the figure of Moses is portrayed in each legend as a prophet, as a law-giver, and as a suffering intercessor. It is my contention that the figure of Paul in 2 Tim is similarly presented; indeed, I shall demonstrate in this section of the study that the Pastor deliberately paints a picture of Paul in such a way that Paul becomes a second Moses, and the fulfillment of the prophecies in Deut 18:15-19.

### 1. Paul as prophet in 2 Tim

The depiction of Paul as a prophet in 2 Tim is closely tied to the polemic in this letter against the Pastor's opponents, two of whom are explicitly identified in 2 Tim 2:17 as Hymenaeus and Philetus. In his capacity as prophet, the Pastor's Paul exercises the gift of *in*sight when he describes the reaction on the part of the opponents to his own mission and that of his heir, Timothy; he exercises the gift of *fore*sight when he describes what will come about as the result of the activity of these two who are «upsetting the faith of some» (2 Tim 2:18).

An intricate claim to Pauline authority on behalf of the Pastor is thereby established in this letter. Since the gift of insight is oriented to the present, it is used as a kind of diagnostic tool in 2 Tim, to the end of clarifying the meaning of the events which are taking place within the narrative present envisioned by the letter. Since the gift of foresight is oriented towards the future, it is used as a kind of prognostic tool in 2 Tim, to the end of predicting the narrative future envisioned by the letter. But, insofar as the narrative present is part of the readers' past, and the narrative future is part of the readers' present, the prophetic authority of the Pastor's Paul is vindicated in the same way as the authority of Deuteronomy's Moses is vindicated by the fulfillment of his words[1]. Moreover, the Pastor's readership, who identify with Timothy and those «faithful men who will be able to teach others also» (2 Tim 2:2) are likewise endowed with prophetic authority, inasmuch as they are the legitimate heirs of Paul, the second Moses.

## 1.1 Paul's prophetic insight in 2 Tim

The exercise of Paul's prophetic insight in 2 Tim is demonstrated primarily in his identification of the Pastor's opponents as those who engage in «profane chatter» (βεβήλους κενοφωνίας: 2 Tim 2:16), and «stupid, senseless controversies» (μωρὰς καὶ ἀπαιδεύτους ζητήσεις: 2 Tim 2:23). The consequence of this controversial chatter is to breed quarrels within the community (2 Tim 2:23), which the Pastor likens to disease: «their talk will eat its way like gangrene» (καὶ ὁ λόγος αὐτῶν ὡς γάγ-γραινα νομὴν ἕξει: 2 Tim 2:17).

There is no attempt here on the Pastor's part to refute the «profane chatter» or the «stupid, senseless controversies» of the opponents; rather, considerable invective is expended in the effort to attack their character. So they are accused of being the sorts of men who will exploit women: «For among them are those who make their way into households and capture weak women, burdened with sins and swayed by various impulses, who will listen to anybody and can never arrive at the knowledge of the truth» (2 Tim 3:6-7)[2]. And they are said to be «men of corrupt mind and counterfeit faith» (ἄνθρωποι κατεφθαρμένοι τὸν νοῦν, ἀδόκιμοι περὶ τὴν πίστιν: 2 Tim 3:8) whose «folly will be plain to all» (ἡ γὰρ ἄνοια αὐτῶν ἔκδηλος ἔσται πᾶσιν: 2 Tim 3:9). What counts, so to

---

[1] D. L. BARTLETT, Ministry, 163-164.

[2] Some (especially feminist) attempts to reconstruct the early history of the church have interpreted this and similar passages as pointing to the prominent rôle that women exercised in the communities which identified with the Pauline mission; see, for example, E. SCHÜSSLER FIORENZA, In Memory of Her, 309-315; J. DEWEY, «1 Timothy», 355-356. It would seem, however, that the point the Pastor is making reflects, rather, on the (bad) character of the διδάσκαλοι than it does on the women whose households the διδάσκαλοι infiltrate.

speak, as an expression of the prophetic insight of the Pastor's Paul is not any possible reply to the «profane chatter» or any refutation of the «stupid, senseless controversies;» the invective is employed here in the service of what, to the Pastor's mind, in any case, is simply an accurate description of the mischief Hymenaeus and Philetus have been breeding, and a diagnosis of its causes.

Paul's prophetic insight in 2 Tim is not confined to description and diagnosis. He also prescribes the remedy whereby Timothy, the «Lord's servant» (δοῦλος κυρίου), as well as his successors, might heal the disease of controversy:

> And the Lord's servant must not be quarrelsome but kindly to everyone, an apt teacher, forbearing, correcting his opponents with gentleness. God may perhaps grant that they will repent and come to know the truth, and they may escape from the snare of the devil, after being captured by him to do his will (2 Tim 2:24-26).

The set of characteristics appropriate to the δοῦλος κυρίου are the exact counterparts to those which identify the opponents. So where they engage in «stupid senseless controversies» (μωρὰς καὶ ἀπαιδεύτους ζητή σεις: 2 Tim 2:23) which eventuate in quarrels (μάχας: 2 Tim 2:23), the Lord's servant must not be quarrelsome (οὐ δεῖ μάχεσθαι: 2 Tim 2:24). Where the opponents wreak havoc with their teaching, whether by upsetting certain people's faith (2 Tim 2:18b), or by corrupting women (2 Tim 3:6), Timothy and his heirs must be «apt teachers» (διδακτικόν: 2 Tim 2:24), who are forbearing (ἀνεξίκακον: 2 Tim 2:24) and able to correct their opponents with gentleness (ἐν πραΰτητι παιδεύοντα τοὺς ἀντιδιατιθεμένους: 2 Tim 2:25).

The model for the δοῦλος κυρίου is, of course, Paul himself, whose teaching (διδασκαλία: 2 Tim 3:10) conduct (ἀγωγή: 2 Tim 3:10) and aim in life (πρόθεσις: 2 Tim 3:10) may be said to be characterised by faith (πίστις: 2 Tim 3:10), patience (μακροθυμία: 2 Tim 3:10), love (ἀγάπη: 2 Tim 3:10), and steadfastness (ὑπομονή: 2 Tim 3:10), not to mention persecutions (διωγμοί: 2 Tim 3:11) and sufferings (παθήματα: 2 Tim 3:11). Not only should Timothy and his heirs be faithful to Paul's teaching, they should also be faithful to his example.

This paradigmatic function of Paul in 2 Tim bears certain affinities to the way in which Moses functions in Philo's *VM*. Both the Sinai ascent in the *VM* as well as the death scene depict Moses in communion with God, and suggest thereby that all human beings are capable of a similar union with God, provided they adhere to the provisions of the law which

Moses handed down. Here, Paul's prophetic mission is characterised by what all people can recognise as virtues, namely, faith, patience, love, and steadfastness. Moreover, the persecutions and sufferings which Paul underwent – and which Timothy and his heirs are currently undergoing – are signs of his – and their – prophetic status. So Paul tells Timothy, «All who desire to live a godly life in Christ Jesus will be persecuted, while evil men and impostors will go on from bad to worse, deceivers and deceived» (2 Tim 3:12-13).

Yet unlike Philo's Moses, whose paradigmatic ascent/death may be said to have a universal significance insofar as all men and women must die, Paul's prophetic suffering seems to be directed to a more limited group, namely, those who suffer at the hands of evil men, or, in other words, the «faithful men who will be able to teach others also» (2 Tim 2:2) and whose authority to do so seems to have been challenged by the opponents. In this respect, the appeal to Paul in 2 Tim in order to condemn rival claimants to the same office resembles the appeal to Moses to condemn the *homines pestilentiosi et impii* in the *TM*. If Moses is employed in the *TM* to distinguish between the righteous and sinners within Israel, Paul is similarly employed in 2 Tim.

### 1.2 *Paul's prophetic foresight in 2 Tim*

Paul exercises his prophetic foresight in 2 Tim when he predicts what will take place in the «last days» (ἐσχάταις ἡμέραις):

> But understand this, that in the last days there will come times of stress. For men will be lovers of self, lovers of money, proud, arrogant, abusive, disobedient to their parents, ungrateful, unholy, inhuman, implacable, slanderers, profligates, fierce, haters of good, treacherous, reckless, swollen with conceit, lovers of pleasure rather than lovers of God, holding the form of religion but denying the power of it (2 Tim 3:1-5).

The resemblance of this description of the «times of stress» (καιροὶ χαλεποί) to the description of the *homines impii et pestilentiosi* in *TM* 7:3-9 has already been noted. The similarity does not permit us to argue a literary dependency, but it does point to an expectation common to both the author of the *TM* and the Pastor that struggles and conflicts within the community of faith will certainly usher in the «last days» when God will manifest his power on behalf of his elect.

One does not need to argue that the author of 2 Tim knew the *TM* in order to assert that he was influenced by an understanding of Moses as a prophet in his presentation of Paul. The depiction of Moses in the concluding encomium of Deuteronomy as a prophet whom the Lord knew πρόσωπον κατὰ πρόσωπον (Deut 34:10) and whose mighty works were made manifest before friend and foe alike seems to have provided the inspiration for the Pastor's portrait of Paul in 2 Tim. Just as Moses is incomparably great, first of all, because he wrought in Egypt «all the signs and prodigies» (πᾶσι τοῖς σημείοις καὶ τέρασιν: Deut 34:11), and secondly, because he displayed before all Israel «great wonders and the mighty hand» (τὰ θαυμάσια τὰ μεγάλα καὶ τὴν χεῖρα κραταιάν: Deut 34:12), so Paul exhibits a similar greatness, first of all, in his conduct before the Gentiles, and secondly, in his care for the churches.

That is why the final glimpse of Paul in the *testamentum Pauli* consists of two prophetic images. The first image is that of Paul, battling alone for the sake of the gospel, bereft of all companionship:

> At my first defense no one took my part; all deserted me. May it not be charged against them. But the Lord stood by me and gave me strength to proclaim the message fully, that the Gentiles might hear it. So I was rescued from the lion's mouth (ἐκ στόματος λέοντος). The Lord will rescue me from every evil and save me for his heavenly kingdom. To him be the glory forever and ever. Amen (2 Tim 4:16-18).

I do not agree with Dibelius – Conzelmann's assessment that this description of Paul need not necessarily be influenced by the language of the Old Testament[3]. On the contrary, the allusions to the Old Testament in this passage are manifold. While it is doubtless possible that the Pastor is quoting LXX Ps 21:22, as Lock[4], Spicq[5], and Hanson claim[6], the most obvious reference is to the story of Daniel, who was cast into the den of lions for having violated the decree of Darius forbidding prayer or petition to anyone other than himself (Dan 6:6-28), and who is delivered «from the mouth of the lions» (ἐκ στόματος τῶν λεόντων: Dan 6:21). Like Daniel, Paul is similarly delivered ἐκ στόματος λέοντος (2 Tim 4:17), though Daniel's lions are more numerous than the one from whom Paul was delivered. The deliverance of Daniel, however, is also mentioned in the testament of Mattathias (1 Macc 2:49-70): «Daniel for his innocence was delivered from the mouth of lions» (Δανιηλ ἐν τῇ ἁπλότητι αὐτοῦ ἐρρύσθη ἐκ στόματος λεόντων: 1 Macc 2:60) as part of

---

[3] Dibelius – Conzelmann, 124.

[4] W. LOCK, *Pastoral Epistles*, 116.

[5] C. SPICQ, *Saint Paul*, II, 810.

[6] A. T. HANSON, *The Pastoral Epistles*, 161-162.

an appeal to his sons before he dies to remember the great deeds of the
Israelite heroes. Implicitly, then, Paul is likened to the instigator of the
Maccabean Revolt. And like Moses in Egypt (Deut 34:11), Paul faces
down his adversaries on their own ground, thanks to the help of the
Lord.

What ties these seemingly disparate allusions together is the motif of
heroism in the face of a foreign adversary. Like Daniel before the sa-
traps of Darius, Mattathias before the officers of Antiochus Epiphanes,
or Moses before the sorcerers of Pharaoh, Paul stands unshaken before
his adversaries, relying on the strength given him by God and confident
in his eventual salvation. His witness here is heroic precisely because it
is manifested before a hostile audience.

The second of the two images with which the readers of the *testamentum Pauli* are left complements the first. If the image of Paul as a
Moses/Daniel/Mattathias, battling his adversaries on their own ground,
serves to illustrate his radical dependence upon God, in whose help he
has placed his trust and his hope of deliverance, this second image depicts a Paul busy about the work of the church, sending greetings, giving
information about persons, and laying plans for the future:

> Greet Prisca and Aquila, and the household of Onesiphorus. Erastus re-
> mained at Corinth; Trophimus I left ill at Miletus. Do your best to come
> before winter. Eubulus sends greetings to you, as do Pudens and Linus and
> Claudia and all the brethren (2 Tim 4:19-21).

Dibelius – Conzelmann posit five factors which account for the inclusion
of this section giving such specific information about various persons associated with the Pauline mission: (1) fidelity to a received tradition
about certain persons; (2) developing interest in the story of Paul's life
at the time of the composition of the letter, which interest is reflected in
apocryphal legends that may have exerted an influence on 2 Tim; (3)
creation of certain details by conjecture; (4) as a technique common
among pseudonymous writers to lend authenticity to the work; and (5)
to portray the special character of Paul himself and to highlight his
exemplary attitude[7]. This last fact is the one which best accounts for the
mention of Prisca and Aquila, Erastus, Trophimus, and the rest. Spicq

---

[7] Dibelius – Conzelmann, 127-128. Their approach to the problem of the information about persons accords with the position taken by L. R. DONELSON (*Pseudepigraphy*, 110) and D. G. MEADE (*Pseudonymity and Canon*, 124) that such details are
included for their paradigmatic value.

thought that these greetings gave evidence of Paul's supernatural love: «Consommé en charité, saint Paul ne peut séparer son amour de Dieu de celui de ses frères; son dernier regard se tourne vers ses meilleurs amis»[8]. Be that as it may, this dimension of Paul's prophetic rôle corresponds to the works of Moses on behalf of all Israel. Just as Moses' labours for his people's welfare serve to indicate his heroic status, so Paul's activities here, which may be described as community-building, are oriented towards the good of the Pauline communities, and serve to identify him as a prophetic hero.

## 2. Paul as law-giver in 2 Tim

Given the position the historical Paul had taken with respect to the «works of the law» (ἔργων νόμου), namely, that «no one is justified by the works of the law, but only through faith in Jesus Christ» (οὐ δικαι-οῦται ἄνθρωπος ἐξ ἔργων νόμου ἐὰν μὴ διὰ πίστεως Ἰησοῦ Χριστοῦ: Gal 2:16; see also Gal 3:2, 5, 10; Rom 3:20, 28), it would be ironic in the extreme if he should be depicted in 2 Tim as a law-giver. And, indeed, it must be admitted that nowhere in 2 Tim is Paul extolled as a νομο-θέτης, as Moses is in the *VM* or the *JA*. Nevertheless, the compelling appeal of which the law-giving activities proper to Moses may be said to be the proper function in the *VM*, the *JA*, the *LAB*, and the *TM* are not entirely absent from the portrait the Pastor gives his readers of the dying Paul.

For what is at issue here is the sort of persuasive appeal 2 Tim makes to its readership. Aristotle (*Rhetoric I.ii.3-6*) identified three means by which an audience might be persuaded to the speaker's point of view: (1) by an appeal to the reason (λόγος) of the audience, (2) by the appeal to their emotions (πάθος), or (3) by the appeal of the speaker's character or personality (ἦθος). The persuasive appeal of 2 Tim is of the second variety, the appeal to the emotions of the readers, specifically, the emotion of pity.

Aristotle (*Rhetoric* II.viii.2), defines pity as «a kind of pain excited by the sight of evil, deadly or painful, which befalls one who does not deserve it». We pity those, says Aristotle, who are most like ourselves: «men also pity those who resemble them in age, character, habits, position, or family; for all such relations make a man more likely to think that their misfortune may befall him as well» (*Rhetoric* II.viii.13).

---

[8] C. Spicq, *Saint Paul*, II, 822.

He singles out as an example of a situation especially worthy of pity «the words and everything else that concerns those who are actually suffering, for instance, at the point of death», particularly when the person who is dying shows himself undaunted (*Rhetoric* II.viii.16).

The depiction of the suffering, dying Paul who is nevertheless still faithful to his mission, both to the Gospel and to the elect for whose salvation he is willing to endure everything (2 Tim 2:9-10), is compelling precisely because it presents the readers of the *testamentum Pauli* with the portrait of a man who is dying but undaunted. The appeal here is not logical — no attempt is made to refute those who seek to displace Paul's legitimate heir, Timothy — rather, 2 Tim seeks to rouse the pity of its readers, so that they might be persuaded to the Pastor's programme, namely, to ensure that Timothy and the «faithful men who will be able to teach others also» (2 Tim 2:2) will be acknowledged as the sole and legitimate successors to Paul.

Thus, Paul does not so much lay down the law in 2 Tim as he exhorts. The effect, however, ends up being much the same, since those who are exhorted are compelled to undertake a certain set of actions just as surely as though they had been commanded by law, thanks to the emotional appeal of the exhortation. The grammatical sign whereby what passes for Paul's law-giving functions in 2 Tim may be recognised is the imperative mood[9].

Interestingly, all of these instances in which Paul uses the imperative are directed to Timothy. Some of the exhortations are general in nature: thus, for instance, Timothy is urged to «share in suffering» (συγκακοπάθησον: 2 Tim 1:8; 2:3), to «be strong» (ἐνδυναμοῦ: 2 Tim 2:1), to «be steady in everything» (νῆφε ἐν πᾶσιν: 2 Tim 4:5), to «suffer» (κακοπά-

---

[9] See 1:8 (συγκακοπάθησον: aorist imperative); 1:13 (ἔχε: imperative); 1:14 (φύλαξον: aorist imperative); 2:1 (ἐνδυναμοῦ: imperative passive); 2:2 (παράθου: second aorist imperative, middle voice); 2:3 (συγκακοπάθησον: aorist imperative); 2:7 (νόει: imperative); 2:8 (μνημόνευε: imperative); 2:14 (ὑπομίμνησκε: imperative); 2:15 (σπούδασον: aorist imperative); 2:16 (περιΐστασο: imperative); 2:22 (φεῦγε: imperative); 2:23 (παραιτοῦ: imperative); 3:1 (γίνωσκε: imperative); 3:5 (ἀποτρέπου: imperative); 3:14 (μένε: imperative); 4:2 (κήρυξον: aorist imperative); 4:2 (ἐπίστηθι: second aorist imperative); 4:2 (ἔλεγξον: aorist imperative); 4:2 (ἐπιτίμησον: aorist imperative); 4:2 (παρακάλεσον: aorist imperative); 4:5 (νῆφε: imperative); 4:5 (κακοπάθησον: aorist imperative); 4:5 (ποίησον: aorist imperative); 4:5 (πληροφόρησον: aorist imperative); 4:9 (σπούδασον: aorist imperative); 4:11 (ἄγε: imperative); 4:13 (φέρε: imperative); 4:15 (φυλάσσου: imperative, middle voice); 4:19 (ἄσπασαι: aorist imperative).

θησον: 2 Tim 4:5), to «do the work of an evangelist» (ἔργον ποίησον εὐ-αγγελιστοῦ: 2 Tim 4:5), and to «fulfill your ministry» (τὴν διακονίαν σου πληροφόρησον: 2 Tim 4:5). Other exhortations are rather more specific: these frequently forbid actions, activities, and attitudes which are characteristic of the opponents. These prohibitions seem to have the force of law. Thus, Timothy is told to «avoid such profane chatter» (τὰς δὲ βεβήλους κενοφωνίας περιΐστασο: 2 Tim 2:16), to «have nothing to do with stupid, senseless controversies» (τὰς δὲ μωρὰς καὶ ἀπαιδεύτους ζητήσεις παραιτοῦ: 2 Tim 2:23), and even to «avoid such people» (καὶ τούτους ἀποτρέπου: 2 Tim 3:5b).

When this second group of exhortations do not forbid certain attitudes and actions, they command others. So, for instance, Paul tells Timothy to «follow the pattern of the sound words which you have heard from me» (ὑποτύπωσιν ἔχε ὑγιαινόντων λόγων ὧν παρ' ἐμοῦ ἤκουσας: 2 Tim 1:13), to «guard the rich deposit» (τὴν καλὴν παραθήκην φύλαξον: 2 Tim 2:14), to «continue in what you have learned and have firmly believed, knowing from whom you have learned it» (σὺ δὲ μένε ἐν οἷς ἔμαθες καὶ ἐπιστώθης, εἰδὼς παρὰ τίνων ἔμαθες: 2 Tim 3:14), and «to preach the word, be urgent in season and out of season, convince, rebuke, and exhort, be unfailing in patience and in teaching» (κήρυξον τὸν λόγον, ἐπίστηθι εὐκαίρως ἀκαίρως, ἔλεγξον, ἐπιτίμησον, παρακάλεσον, ἐν πάσῃ μακροθυμίᾳ καὶ διδαχῇ: 2 Tim 4:2). These positive commands stress the bond between Paul and his heir.

To have presented Paul as a kind of law-giver, however much that depiction is softened by an emotional appeal to the Pastor's readership, is to have reworked the Pauline heritage in a considerable way. Set within the context of a religiosity in which the law was fundamentally important, however, the Pastor's strategy in so presenting Paul makes sense, insofar as he is depicting Paul in categories which would have been more readily understood by the opponents. We shall see, when we consider the polemic against the νομοδιδάσκαλοι in the Pastoral Epistles, that the law is one of those categories.

## 3. Paul as suffering intercessor in 2 Tim

The opening verse of the letter's message depicts Paul as an intercessor, who remembers Timothy constantly in his prayers (2 Tim 1:3). Yet the image of Paul as intercessor, as one who by his prayers serves as a mediator between God and his community, is here subordinated to the image of Paul as sufferer, which is to say that in 2 Tim, Paul mediates between God and his community by means of the suffering he undergoes.

The depiction of Paul's suffering in 2 Tim virtually dominates the Pastor's portrait of the great κῆρυξ καὶ ἀπόστολος καὶ διδάσκαλος: indeed, all the other dimensions of the Pastor's presentation of Paul are subordinated to his suffering. So, for instance, Paul's prophetic insight is closely allied to the question of his suffering, since the primary consequence of his mission as «preacher and apostle and teacher» is to suffer: «for this gospel I was appointed a preacher and apostle and teacher, and therefore I suffer as I do» (δι' ἣν αἰτίαν καὶ ταῦτα πάσχω: 2 Tim 1:11-12).

To preach the gospel must necessarily involve suffering, whether on the part of Paul or Timothy himself. In fact, the hallmark of the heir of Paul is the willingness to undergo suffering. That is why Paul urges Timothy: «Do not be ashamed then of testifying to our Lord, nor of me his prisoner, but share in suffering (συγκακοπάθησον) for the gospel in the power of God» 2 Tim 1:8). In the same way, Paul exhorts Timothy: «Share in suffering as a good soldier of Christ Jesus» (συγκακοπάθησον ὡς καλὸς στρατιώτης Χριστοῦ Ἰησοῦ: 2 Tim 2:3; see also 1:8 and 4:5). Suffering is not something one may choose to avoid if one wishes to remain faithful: «Indeed, all who desire to live a godly life in Christ Jesus will be persecuted» (2 Tim 3:12).

Just as Paul's prophetic rôle has a double focus — Paul witnesses to the Gentiles (2 Tim 4:17) and he continues to build up the community of faith (2 Tim 4:19-21) — so the suffering of Paul likewise exhibits a double purpose. The clearest expression of the double purpose of Paul's suffering comes in his exhortation to remember Jesus Christ as preached in his gospel,

> the gospel for which I am suffering (κακοπαθῶ) and wearing fetters like a criminal. But the word of God is not fettered. Therefore I endure everything for the sake of the elect, that they also may obtain salvation in Christ Jesus with its eternal glory (2 Tim 2:9-10).

Paul's suffering, the consequence of his call as a preacher, an apostle, and a teacher, is here linked to two realities, the gospel and the elect. The first reality, the gospel, represents the vertical purpose of Paul's suffering; the second reality, the elect, represents the horizontal purpose of his suffering. These twin purposes are united in the ἵνα clause of v. 10: «that they also may obtain salvation in Christ Jesus with its eternal glory» (ἵνα καὶ αὐτοὶ σωτηρίας τύχωσιν τῆς ἐν Χριστῷ Ἰησοῦ μετὰ δόξης αἰωνίου: 2 Tim 2:10b). In this respect, the Pastor's depiction of the suffering Paul who willingly endures his fetters bears more than a passing resemblance to Josephus' characterisation of Moses who suffers for the salvation (σωτηρίας: *JA* III.297; IV.42) of his people.

### 3.1 *Paul's suffering in the* homologoumena

The prominent rôle assigned to the suffering of Paul in 2 Tim, while it contributes to the Mosaic dimension of his portrait, is not included herein for paradigmatic reasons alone. Those communities which looked to Paul as their founder had as part of their Pauline patrimony, so to speak, the correspondence in which Paul's afflictions figure prominently. So, for instance, in 2 Corinthians, Paul boasts of his sufferings:

> Five times I have received at the hands of the Jews the forty lashes less one. Three times I have been beaten with rods; once I was stoned. Three times I have been shipwrecked; a night and a day I have been adrift at sea; on frequent journeys, in danger from rivers, danger from robbers, danger from my own people, danger from Gentiles, danger in the city, danger in the wilderness, danger at sea, danger from false brethren; in toil and hardship, through many a sleepless night, in hunger and in thirst, often without food, in cold and exposure. And, apart from other things, there is the daily pressure upon me of my anxiety for all the churches (2 Cor 11:24-28).

Self-presentation statements like 2 Cor 11:24-28 exercise a rhetorical function within the argumentative scope of the letter in which they may be found. Aristotle recommends περὶ αὑτοῦ remarks as a useful kind of digression (*Rhetoric* III.xvii.10-12). In addition to the illustrative value of such remarks, Aristotle claims that they serve an essential *ethical* function, which is to say that they demonstrate the character of the one who is speaking: «It is more fitting that a virtuous man should show himself good than that his speech should be painfully exact» (*Rhetoric* III.xvii.12). While hardly inexact and certainly painful, 2 Cor 11:24-28 serves to show to what (extraordinary) extent Paul was willing to risk his life that the Gospel might be preached.

Hendrikus Boers wants to compare this passage to others in the Pauline corpus, e.g., Rom 1:14-16a; 2 Cor 1:12 − 2:17; 7:5-16; Gal 1:10 − 2:21; 1 Thess 2:1-12, describing them as apostolic apologies, and holding that they serve to establish the authority of Paul and his proclamation[10]. But it seems that 2 Cor 11:24-28 might be compared more

---

[10] H. BOERS, «The Form-Critical Study», 140-158.

fruitfully to Rom 8:35, 1 Cor 4:9-13, and, elsewhere within 2 Corinthians, 4:8-9, 6:4c-5, and 12:10, as Victor Paul Furnish suggests[11]. To subsequent generations of Pauline Christians, for whom the authority of the Apostle to the Gentiles was indisputable, what would have been most notably striking is the painful catalogue of hardships Paul was forced to endure in the course of carrying out his mission. They preserved the memory of a man who, for their sake, was

> afflicted in every way, but not crushed; perplexed, but not driven to despair; persecuted, but not forsaken; struck down, but not destroyed; always carrying in the body the death of Jesus, so that the life of Jesus may also be manifested in our bodies (2 Cor 4:8-10).

Paul's Christological understanding of the purpose of his own suffering, also reflected in Phil 4:8-11, enabled him to make sense of his own experience, but, in addition, allowed subsequent generations of believers to see in him a likeness to Jesus himself.

The audience to whom the Pastor originally directed 2 Tim would doubtless have seen the resemblance between Paul and Jesus as primary. And, indeed, for a Christian congregation, such a similarity would have been compelling. Nevertheless, the Mosaic dimension of Paul's suffering cannot be ruled out, and would have contributed, in at least a secondary way, to the aura of authority which surrounds the Pastor's Paul.

## 4. Purposes of the testamentary genre in 2 Tim

The depiction of Paul in 2 Tim as a prophet, as a kind of law-giver, and a suffering intercessor is directly relevant to the literary form of the letter which is testamentary in character. To have cast the last words of such a prophet, law-giver, and suffering intercessor in the form of a testament is to have endued those words with a kind of authority which anyone — Timothy, the «faithful men who will be able to teach others», or the νομοδιδάσκαλοι — will recognise and to which everyone will sub-

---

[11] V. P. FURNISH, *II Corinthians*, 535-536. Furnish maintains that Paul is parodying in this passage two kinds of lists with which Paul's Corinthian congregation would have been familiar: (1) Cynic and Stoic lists of hardships that the wise person can recognise as trifling; and (2) catalogues of achievements publicly proclaimed by political notables like Augustus (e.g., the *Res Gestae Divi Augusti*). Paul's catalogue constitutes a parody of the first type inasmuch as his adversities are humiliating rather than ennobling; inasmuch as the list is a record of failures instead of accomplishments, it constitutes a parody of the second kind.

mit. The testamentary character of 2 Tim itself contributes to the Mosaic likeness according to which the Pastor depicts Paul as prophet, as law-giver, and as suffering intercessor.

Thus, what Kolenkow claims as a feature of Philo's depiction of Moses in the *VM*, namely, that Philo subscribed to the belief that the death of a great man is the time that he is particularly empowered with extraordinary prophecy[12], may with equal justification be said of the Pastor's portrait of Paul in 2 Tim: in the depiction of Paul on the eve, so to speak, of his martyrdom, the Pastor has constructed a scenario in which Paul may exercise those prophetic gifts which are his by virtue of his impending death.

And if, as we have seen, the law-giving functions of Paul in 2 Tim are muted, owing to the memory within the Pauline communities of Paul's own opposition to the «works of the law», something must replace the compelling function of the law in order for the pronouncements of 2 Tim to be authoritative. That compelling function is the appeal to the emotions which is ineluctably tied to the testamentary literary form. There is in 2 Tim an undeniable appeal to the emotions in the Pastor's depiction of a Paul on the verge of martyrdom. In this respect, I cannot agree with Michael Prior's contention that σπένδομαι in 2 Tim 4:6a as a liturgical metaphor refers not to Paul's impending death, but rather to the whole of his apostolic activity[13], and his claim that ἀνάλυσις in 2 Tim 4:6b refers to Paul's release from imprisonment at Rome, rather than his departure from this life[14]. The prospect of Paul's imminent release from imprisonment does not present the same sort of appeal to the emotions as the prospect of his impending death.

Finally, in the depiction of Paul as one who suffers, both for the sake of the gospel and for the salvation of the elect (2 Tim 2:9-10), the Pastor paints a portrait of Paul not unlike Josephus' portrait of Moses, who also underwent many hardships for the salvation of all (κοινῆς σωτηρίας: *JA* III.297). This resemblance does not assume any sort of literary relation-ship between Josephus and the Pastor: Josephus' depiction of Moses' suffering is founded, of course on the Biblical narratives, narratives to which the Pastor would have had access also. The similarity in presenta-

---

[12] A. B. KOLENKOW, «The Genre Testament», 60.

[13] M. PRIOR, *Paul the Letter-Writer*, 92-98.

[14] M. PRIOR, *Paul the Letter-Writer*, 98-110.

tion points to a common religious and literary tradition, and not a literary or theological influence.

As the testament of Paul, 2 Tim binds subsequent generations of believers in the same way that Deuteronomy 31 – 34 as the testament of Moses obliges subsequent generations of Israelites: it presents a series of final directives from a leader (Moses or Paul) to his companions (the Israelites of the wilderness generation or Timothy) and all who identify with the religious heritage inaugurated by the leader (succeeding generations of Israelites or the «faithful men who will be able to teach others»). And it does so through an emotional appeal to Pauline Christians: to oppose those final directives, is, in effect, to oppose the dying wishes of a great man.

### 4.1 *Implied narrative of the death of Paul in 2 Tim*

In fairness to Prior, however, it must be admitted that the death of Paul is nowhere directly presented in 2 Tim. This stands in marked contrast to the *VM*, in which Philo's Moses «prophesied with discernment while still alive the story of his own death» (ἐπιθειάσας ζῶν ἔτι τὰ ὡς ἐπὶ θανόντι ἑαυτῷ προφητεύει δεξιῶς: *VM* II.291), the *JA*, in which Moses is said to have «written of himself in the sacred books that he died» (γέγραφε δ' αὐτὸν ἐν ταῖς ἱεραῖς βίβλοις τεθνεῶτα: *JA* IV.326), and the *LAB*, in which Moses dies «in glory according to the word of the Lord» (*in gloria secundum os Domini*: *LAB* 19:16). In all three texts, the authors have made reference to the Sacred Scriptures from which their own versions of Moses' death derive, on which they are dependent, and to which the readers of the *VM*, the *JA*, and the *LAB* are at least implicitly directed, should they wish to pursue the matter further.

Alone of all the first century legends concerning the last words of Moses, the *TM* fails to depict directly the death of Moses, though, in view of the incomplete state of the text as it has come down to us, we cannot be certain that it did not originally do so. In any case, the death of Moses in the *TM* is foretold by Moses himself at *TM* 1:15, at 10:12, and 10:14; furthermore, Joshua alludes to the death of Moses at *TM* 11:9, 11:16, and 11:18. If, however, the death of Moses was never directly presented in the *TM*, it may well have been because the audience to whom the *TM* was originally directed may be presumed to have been so familiar with the story of Moses' death that a narrative presentation would have been unnecessary.

A similar contention may be advanced with respect to the death of Paul for the members of the community to which 2 Tim was directed. Naturally, as C. K. Barrett notes, «Paul's death cannot be described in documents purporting to have been written by his hand»[15]. But logical considerations imposed by the literary form of the testament may not have been as important as the fact that the Pastor did not need to narrate the death of Paul precisely because its circumstances were so well known within the community to which he addresses this testament. In fact, one may with justification claim that 2 Tim derives its compelling force precisely because its putative author was known to have suffered a martyr's death. An allusion to that death was enough, and in view of the prophetic rôle which Paul plays in 2 Tim, wholly appropriate. So Paul foretells his own death at 2 Tim 4:6-8, and alludes to it in the faithful saying of 2:11-13.

### 4.2  *Paul as the «prophet like Moses» of Deuteronomy 18:15*

The promise to raise up a prophet like Moses is referred to twice in the New Testament, both times in Acts. The first reference comes in Acts 3:22-23 in the speech of Peter (3:12-26) following the healing of the man crippled from birth (3:1-10). Peter's citation of the text from Deuteronomy is not exact, and it is in the differences between the text in the LXX and the text as it appears in Acts that the distinctive Christology of Acts presents itself. Robert O'Toole holds that the author of Acts has moved ἀναστήσει to its present position behind προφήτην ὑμῖν in v. 22 to serve his apologetic interests: as a result, the promise to «raise up *a prophet like Moses»* in Deut 18:15ff. becomes a promise to *«raise up* a prophet like Moses» in Acts 3:22-26; the prophet like Moses which God will «raise up» (ἀναστήσει) is Jesus himself[16].

The second instance in which the promise to raise up a prophet like Moses appears is in Acts 7:37. The citation occurs within the *Heilsgeschichte* speech of Stephen before the Sanhedrin (Acts 7:2-53). As in the case of Acts 3:22-23, the quotation is not exact; but unlike the earlier citation, the reference in Stephen's speech does not seem to serve any Christological *Tendenz*: it is one of two periods beginning with οὗτος (vv. 37 and 38) which identify Moses according to the speeches he makes. The verse seems to point no further than Moses himself.

---

[15] C. K. BARRETT, «Pauline Controversies», 240.

[16] R. O'TOOLE, «Some observations», 85-92.

Thus, there is nowhere in the New Testament an *explicit* reference to the promise to raise up a prophet like Moses which points to Paul. That does not mean that no such claims are made on Paul's behalf. On the contrary, the Pastor makes an *implicit* claim that Paul is the fulfillment of that promise. That is why he has taken such pains, as we have seen, to weave a web of references, both direct and indirect, in which Paul is compared to Moses, especially as a prophet, a law-giver, and a suffering intercessor.

At this point, it is necessary to consider why the Pastor should have so presented Paul. If Raymond Brown is correct that one aspect of the crisis facing the church as it separated itself from the matrix of Judaism is a crisis of authority[17], then one solution to that crisis is to re-present the new form of authority in such a way that it still appeals to those who still long for the good old days, and who may be seeking a way to turn back the clock. Paul becomes a second Moses in 2 Tim because Moses is the only authority who can command the respect of the νομοδιδάσ-καλοι.

## 4.3 *The preservation of the Pauline heritage and the polemic against the* νομοδιδάσκαλοι *in the Pastoral Epistles*

Like Moses, then, Paul delivers himself of his testament shortly before he dies, a testament which implicitly and explicitly presents him as a kind of latter-day Moses, the fulfillment of the ancient hope that God would raise up a «prophet like Moses» (Deut 18:15). The reasons for such a presentation of Paul on the part of the Pastor become clear when they are set in the context of the polemic against Hymenaeus and Phile-tus (2 Tim 2:17b). And since this polemic is common to all three Pastoral Epistles, it will be necessary at this juncture of the study to step beyond the *testamentum Pauli* that is 2 Tim and to consider 1 Tim and Tit as well.

### 4.3.1 «Myths and genealogies» in the Pastoral Epistles

Of all the accusations against Hymenaeus, Alexander, and Philetus, the one receiving most frequent mention in the scholarly literature is the charge that they concern themselves with «myths and endless genealogies which promote speculations rather than the divine training that is in

---

[17] R. E. BROWN, *The Churches*, 30.

faith» (μύθοις καὶ γενεαλογίαις ἀπεράντοις, αἵτινες ἐκζητήσεις παρέχουσιν μᾶλλον ἢ οἰκονομίαν θεοῦ τὴν ἐν πίστει: 1 Tim 1:4; see also 1 Tim 4:7; 2 Tim 4:4; Tit 1:14; 3:9). The coupling of the term *myths* with the term *endless genealogies* probably betrays some polemical intent: likewise, there seems to be some derisive insinuation behind the adjective «endless». Dibelius – Conzelmann have indicated some of the classical precedents for the disparaging use of the term myth[18], and have demonstrated how it is used to denote a false and foolish story[19]. The substantive term in this syntagm μύθοις καὶ γενεαλογίαις ἀπεράντοις is *genealogies*, and it is to this term that I will turn first in the effort to reconstruct the teachings of Hymenaeus, Alexander, and Philetus.

It is clear, even from a cursory reading of the Pastoral Epistles in general, and 2 Tim in particular, that the conflict reflected therein has something to do with the exercise of authority. One of the most methodologically provocative studies of the Pastoral Epistles which views the conflicts reflected therein within the social setting of early Christianity and analyses those conflicts precisely in terms of authority is that of D. C. Verner. His analysis of the conflict within the communities for which the Pastoral Epistles were written suggests that the «adherents of the false teaching, insofar as they can be identified, generally belonged to subordinate groups», and that such false teaching may have «appealed to ambitious men who were excluded from official leadership positions»[20]. Verner warns, however, that «nothing has emerged to suggest that the content of the false teaching as such would have held any special appeal for men excluded from official leadership positions»[21]. Yet, the language by which the Pastor refers to the myths and genealogies – they are called «endless» (γενεαλογίαις ἀπεράντοις: 1 Tim 1:4), «profane and silly» (βεβήλους καὶ γραώδεις: 1 Tim 4:7), and «stupid» (μωρὰς [...] γενεαλογίας: Tit 3:9) – is certainly scornful and dismissive, and thus may have been meant to exclude those who have a vested interest in such genealogies from exercising any authority in the community.

For there were those who had a vested interest in such genealogies and who were traditionally entitled to the exercise of authority: these

---

[18] See Epictetus, *Diss.* 3.24.18; Plutarch, *Mor.* 348a-b; cited in Dibelius – Conzelmann, 16; see also J. N. D. KELLY, *Commentary*, 44.

[19] Dibelius – Conzelmann, 16.

[20] D. C. VERNER, *The Household of God*, 179-180.

[21] D. C. VERNER, *The Household of God*, 180.

were the priests[22], whose official standing in the post-exilic community was directly dependent upon the evidence they could adduce proving the purity of their descent[23]. At least some priests were attracted to Chris-

---

[22] A comprehensive understanding of the Jewish priesthood is exceedingly complicated owing to the nature of the sources handed down to us. The Old Testament is not a treatise on religious ritual, though it does incorporate some of these into its texts; neither does it contain a systematic and organized study of the institutions associated with the religious life of the Chosen People, though it assumes their existence and makes frequent reference to them. Among the many book-length studies and scholarly monographs which have been written to extract what evidence the Old Testament does contain of such rituals and institutions, several directly address the question of priesthood: G. B. GRAY, *Sacrifice*, describes priestly activity in connection with the cult; A. CODY, *A History of Old Testament Priesthood*, traces the origins and development of the Israelite priesthood up until the early second century BCE; R. DE VAUX, *Ancient Israel*, considers the position and functions of Jewish priests up to the end of the Hasmonean dynasty; J. JEREMIAS, *Jerusalem*, devotes a chapter to the Jewish priesthood; A. VANHOYE, *Old Testament Priests*, compares the person and the activity of Jesus to what is known of Jewish priests from the Hebrew Scriptures and the Qumran literature, relying, for the most part on R. de Vaux and A. Cody. Neither A. Cody nor R. de Vaux, however, describe the rôle and purpose of the Jewish priesthood during the time of the Roman occupation of Judaea, and G. B. Gray's study focusses briefly on the office of the high priest during the period. Only J. JEREMIAS, *Jerusalem*, has collated what information there is on Jewish priests during the first century, and when he considers the ordinary priests, he tends to concentrate on the special functions they exercised when they came to Jerusalem for the three pilgrim festivals and their occasional weekly course (198-207).

[23] If, on the one hand, evidence regarding the precise origin and full extent of the priestly activities connected with the Torah is not completely clear, given the nature of the sources and the disagreement among the scholars, evidence from the Old Testament regarding the importance of priestly lineage is, on the other hand, unambiguous. A. CODY, *A History of Old Testament Priesthood*, notes that the hereditary nature of the Israelite priesthood was a feature it shared with the priesthoods of Phoenicia and Canaan, and that «the development of a hereditary priesthood is probably normal anywhere when sedentary life makes fixed sanctuaries possible and a family establishes itself at a sanctuary» (60). For R. DE VAUX, *Ancient Israel*, the hereditary priesthood of the ancient Near East, including that of Israel, «ensured that the sanctuaries were well looked after and kept in good repair, and that religious rites were left unchanged: the father would initiate his son into the skills required of him» (359). G. VON RAD (*Israel's Historical Traditions*, 244) thought that the demand made upon the priest was so great that «only one who had been brought up in the continuity of the tribal and family traditions could adequately meet its varied requirements». In actual fact, the Old Testament simply takes the hereditary character of the priesthood for granted: Exodus 29, ostensibly a ritual of priestly consecration, bears witness to the hereditary character of the Israelite priesthood: «Thus shall the priesthood be theirs by perpetual law, and

tianity: Acts preserves the tradition that «a great many of the priests were obedient to the faith» (πολύς τε ὄχλος τῶν ἱερέων ὑπήκουον τῇ πίστει: Acts 6:7). This notice of priestly conversion occurs in one of the summary statements which periodically punctuate Acts[24], and R. J. Dillon indicates that they are «important compositional strategems» which «idealize the period of the apostles' ministry in Jerusalem»[25]. As such, they resist historical verification[26]. F. F. Bruce, who holds that Acts is historically reliable, maintains that we cannot be sure whether these priests would have been forced to discontinue discharging their Temple duties after having joined the Christians[27].

Given the shrill polemic against the endless genealogies with which the opponents are said to have concerned themselves, and given the converging evidence stemming from an analysis of the other charges levelled against the opponents, a careful reading of the Pastoral Epistles suggests that these νομοδιδάσκαλοι may have been priests themselves, whose claim to exercise leadership in the communities for which the

---

thus shall you ordain Aaron and his sons» (Ex 29:9b). Leviticus 8 purports to be the chronicle of Aaron's ordination: apparently dependent upon the ritual prescribed in Exodus 29, it never mentions Aaron without at the same time mentioning his sons (Lev 8:1, 6, 13, 14, 18, 22, 24, 27, 30, 31a, 31b, 36). At the same time, however, God himself is said to have «chosen» certain men for the priesthood: Num 25:10-13 depicts God establishing «a covenant of perpetual priesthood» with the Aaronide Phineas and his descendants. Jesus ben Sira, himself most likely a priest, can speak early in the middle of the second century BCE of «an everlasting covenant for [Aaron] and for his descendants all the days of heaven to minister to [the Lord] and serve as priest and bless his people in his name» (ἐγενήθη αὐτῷ εἰς διαθήκην αἰῶνος καὶ τῷ σπέρματι αὐτοῦ ἐν ἡμέραις οὐρανοῦ λειτουργεῖν αὐτῷ ἅμα καὶ ἱερατεύειν καὶ εὐλογεῖν τὸν λαὸν αὐτοῦ ἐν τῷ ὀνόματι: Sir 45:15). Thus, throughout the history of the Israelite religion and early Judaism, priesthood was hereditary. E. SCHÜRER neatly sums up the importance of priestly lineage: «The priesthood was a community the boundaries of which were irremovable since they were laid down forever by natural descent. No one not belonging to this group could be admitted to it; and no one belonging to it by legitimate birth could be excluded from it» (History, II, 239).

[24] See also Acts 1:14, 2:42-47, 4:32-35, 5:11-16, 9:31, 12:24, 16:5, 19:20, 28:30-31.

[25] R. J. DILLON, «Acts of the Apostles», 724-725.

[26] L. T. JOHNSON (Acts of the Apostles, 107) says that the conversion of priests to Christianity is not inconsistent with what may be known about the status of priests in first century Jerusalem: their vast numbers, their marginalisation, even their disaffection from the ruling hierarchy may all have contributed towards the entry of at least some into the nascent Christian movement.

[27] F. F. BRUCE, Commentary on the Book of the Acts, 131.

Pastoral Epistles were written was based on their ancestry as demonstrated in their genealogical records. Many of the positions which may be reconstructed from the Pastor's polemic and which were apparently advanced by Hymenaeus, Philetus, and Alexander seem to be congruent with what we know of priestly concerns of late first century Judaism. The false teachers/priests challenged the current leadership of those communities to which the Pastoral Epistles were directed on the ground that they lacked the proper ancestral connections.

In presenting the polemic in the Pastoral Epistles as one which was directed against the claims of those who sought to exercise authority in the community for which the Pastoral Epistles were written, I do not mean to pose too sharp a dichotomy between the Pauline heritage and that of Alexander, Hymenaeus, and Philetus. Nor, in recognizing the Jewish origin, or at least the Judaizing tendencies behind their claim, do I intend to relegate the claims of the opponents to the category of Jewish Christianity and those of the Pastor to Hellenistic Christianity. M. Hengel has reminded us, in no uncertain terms, of the relative uselessness of this sort of categorization:

> [W]e must be concerned with the historical connections, which are more complicated and complex than our labels, clichés and pigeon-holes, but at the same time also with a real understanding and an evaluation which does justice to the past and is no longer one-sided and tendentious [...] We should therefore be more cautious in using the adjective «Hellenistic» in descriptions of earliest Christianity. *It says too much, and precisely because of that says too little.* In this matter of establishing the history of a small Jewish messianic sect with its roots in Palestine, which is so difficult, we need more precise differentiations for our reconstructions and understanding of the first hundred years[28].

In a similar fashion, R. E. Brown has argued against too facile a distinction between Jewish Christianity and Gentile Christianity: the identification of ethnic heritage with theological stance in first century Christianity plays false with what historical evidence we do possess[29], and the theo-

---

[28] M. HENGEL, *The Hellenization of Judaea*, 53-54. Emphasis in the original.

[29] To take the most notable example of a first century Christian whose ethnic heritage cannot be identified with his theological position vis-à-vis the Torah, Paul was «an Israelite, a descendant of Abraham, a member of the tribe of Benjamin» (καὶ γὰρ ἐγὼ Ἰσραηλίτης εἰμί, ἐκ σπέρματος Ἀβραάμ, φυλῆς Βενιαμίν: Rom 11:1b; see also 2 Cor 11:22, Phil 3:5); yet his attitude on the law which is reflected in his well-known position regarding the extent to which Gentile converts to Christianity should not have

logical distinction between Gentile Christianity and Jewish Christianity is imprecise and poorly designated[30]. Early Christian communities incorporated, virtually from their very beginnings, both those who had identified themselves as part of the covenant community of Judaism, as well as those whose religious background we would call pagan; and thus Brown identifies four types of first century Jewish/Gentile Christianity, each type embracing both Jews and their Gentile converts: (I) those who practised full observance of the Mosaic law, including circumcision, as necessary for salvation; (II) those who did not insist on circumcision as salvific for Gentile converts to Christianity but did require them to keep some Jewish observances, particularly the food laws; (III) those who insisted neither on circumcision nor on observance of the Jewish food laws for their Gentile converts; and (IV) those who did not insist on circumcision and Jewish food laws and saw no abiding significance in the cult of the Jerusalem Temple[31].

Brown's spectrum of theological stances can be extremely useful in describing in a more complete fashion the theological variety among first century Christians according to the position taken on three fundamental issues, circumcision, dietary restrictions, as well as the abiding significance of the cult of the Jerusalem Temple. It may be that there are other indicators of theological stance in the church of the first century which Brown neglects altogether, especially the issue of permissible marriages and intermarriages[32]. What is certain, however, is that his

---

been bound to the demands of the Torah placed him in an opposite corner from James, the brother of the Lord, whose putative ancestry was equally distinguished, but whose attitude towards the Torah seems to have varied considerably from that of Paul (see Gal 2:6-14).

[30] R. E. BROWN, «Not Jewish Christianity», 74-79; ID. – J. P. MEIER, *Antioch and Rome*, 1-9.

[31] R. E. BROWN, «Not Jewish Christianity», 77-78; ID. – J. P. MEIER, *Antioch and Rome*, 2-8.

[32] 1 Cor 5:1-13 records Paul's ire at hearing that a male member of the Corinthian church was either cohabiting with, or perhaps even married to, his father's wife. Orr – Walther hold that the scandal was not a simple case of sexual immorality: «the attitude of the church was involved, and Paul chided the church for indulgent pride. The implication is that they were proud in the assumption that their Christian freedom was enhanced by their sympathetic understanding of this unusual sexual relationship» (188). Among other things, the episode demonstrates that Paul's understanding of the permissibility of certain types of relationships differed widely from that of at least some of his converts.

taxonomy avoids the welter of confusing terminology suggested by S. K. Riegel[33]. And preliminary indications seem to show that Hymenaeus, Alexander, and Philetus probably belonged to either category (I) or (II). To verify this categorization, however, it will be necessary to examine more closely the several charges the Pastor levels against them.

### 4.3.2 The opponents as «those of the circumcision»

The evidence which, at first glance, seems to be most clearly indicative of the opponents' theological stance is their identification as «those of the circumcision» (οἱ ἐκ τῆς περιτομῆς: Tit 1:10). J. L. Houlden thinks that the phrase is «the clearest sign that the heresy in view in these writings is Jewish-Christian in origin»[34], and R. A. Wild[35], R. P. Martin[36] and Lock[37] all concur with this judgement. Oddly, the phrase οἱ ἐκ τῆς περιτομῆς in Acts does not occur in connection with the traditions about Paul's debates with those who thought circumcision should be obligatory for Gentile converts to Christianity (Acts 15:1): those who come to Antioch are said to be men from Judaea (τινες

---

[33] S. K. RIEGEL («Jewish Christianity») suggests that the term «Judaeo-Christianity» be reserved as a general term (415); that «Jewish Christianity» be used to refer to «Christianity expressed in Semitic-Jewish thought-forms, but limited to the traditions of the Jerusalem Church as contained largely in Jewish-Christian canonical works, and some extra-canonical [literature during] the apostolic age of the first Christian century»; he would reserve the term «Judaistic/Judaic Christianity» to heterodox varieties of Judaeo-Christianity which flourished mainly after 70 CE. The difficulties with Riegel's suggested taxonomy are manifold: I draw attention to only one here, and that is the variety of theologies presented in Jewish-Christian canonical works alone. The attitude towards the Mosaic law in Paul is vastly different than that represented in the Gospel according to Matthew. Both, however, would be subsumed under the term «Jewish Christianity» according to Riegel's suggested system of classification. A. F. J. KLIJN («The Study of Jewish Christianity») reminds us that it is impossible to compile «a» or «the» theology of Jewish Christianity: «[t]he many Jewish-Christian ideas which may be collectively called "Jewish-Christianity" cannot be confined into one clear-cut or well defined theology. We are dealing with isolated phenomena and can, therefore, only speak of the Jewish Christianity of a particular writing or of a particular group of Christians» (431). In the light of Klijn's analysis, Brown's grid allowing us to compare and to contrast the various theologies characteristic of what he would rather call «types of Jewish/Gentile Christianity» appears even more useful.

[34] J. L. HOULDEN, *The Pastoral Epistles*, 144.

[35] R. A. WILD, «The Pastoral Letters», 894.

[36] R. P. MARTIN, «1, 2 Timothy and Titus», 1243.

[37] W. LOCK, *Pastoral Epistles*, 132.

κατελθόντες ἀπὸ τῆς Ἰουδαίας), and later, during the deliberations in Jerusalem, some of those who spoke up in favor of compulsory circumcision are said to belong to the party of the Pharisees (τινες τῶν ἀπὸ τῆς αἱρέσεως τῶν Φαρισαίων: Acts 15:5).

The expression is found, however, in Acts 10:45 and 11:2, and refers to those Christians who are converts from Judaism. In the first instance (Acts 10:45), οἱ ἐκ τῆς περιτομῆς specifically refers to the group of believers who had accompanied Peter from Joppa to the house of Cornelius in Caesaria. They are amazed to see Cornelius and the other members of his household speaking in tongues and glorifying God. In the second instance (Acts 11:2), «those of the circumcision» are apparently from Jerusalem, and criticize Peter for having eaten with the uncircumcised, though once they hear of Peter's vision in Joppa, they are silenced. Thus, the phrase οἱ ἐκ τῆς περιτομῆς in the Acts of the Apostles, while denoting ethnic origin, seems also to connote a hesitation with regard to the entry of Gentiles into the Christian community and perhaps a certain inclination to restrict table-fellowship between Gentiles and Jews in the Christian community.

### a) «Those of the circumcision» and the Pauline letters

Paul's own letters reflect his opposition to those who decreed the necessity of circumcising Gentile converts to Christianity, even though the phrase οἱ ἐκ τῆς περιτομῆς does not itself occur in the indisputably Pauline corpus, nor even in Colossians or Ephesians. Galatians, written, perhaps, around 54 CE[38], expresses his opposition strongly, in terms which may even be considered violent (Gal 5:12). Philippians likewise expresses Paul's opposition to the practice of circumcision using strongly derogatory language (Phil 3:2 − 4:1). 1 Cor 7:18-20 is considerably calmer in tone, though it reiterates the fundamental contention of Gal regarding circumcision, namely, that «neither circumcision counts for anything nor uncircumcision, but keeping the commandments of God» (ἡ περιτομὴ οὐδέν ἐστιν, καὶ ἡ ἀκροβυστία οὐδέν ἐστιν, ἀλλὰ τήρησις

---

[38] See J. A. FITZMYER, «Galatians», 781. But H. D. BETZ (*Galatians*, 9-12) is rather more cautious than Fitzmyer in assigning so definite a date for the composition of Galatians: the difficulty in determining a date for the historical situation which gave rise to the letter, coupled with the difficulties involved in establishing an internal chronological order among Paul's extant letters, leads Betz to conclude that any date for the composition of Galatians must be, at best, approximate. He would posit the years between 50-55 CE as «a reasonable guess» (12).

ἐντολῶν θεοῦ: 1 Cor 7:19)[39]. The references to circumcision in Romans are numerous, and all but one reference (Rom 15:8) occur in the first four chapters of the letter, wherein περιτομή functions as a token for the Jewish religious heritage[40], just as ἀκροβυστία is a kind of shorthand for Gentile Christians: such references in Rom, then, do not seem to constitute any kind of polemic on Paul's part against circumcision imposed on Gentile converts. But Romans is an ambassadorial letter, according to R. Jewett[41], and Paul is at some pains in the letter to set forth his position in a diplomatic fashion to people whose acquaintance he has, for the most part, yet to make. If R. E. Brown is correct, and «the dominant Christianity at Rome had been shaped by the Jerusalem community associated with James and Peter, and hence was a Christianity appreciative of Judaism and loyal to its customs»[42], then it is no wonder that Paul's language in Romans is so diplomatic.

### b) *«Those of the circumcision» in the Pastoral Epistles*

Yet, for the Pastor to call the false teachers «those of the circumcision» is curious, insofar as the Pastoral Epistles do not otherwise depict Hymenaeus, Alexander or Philetus attempting either to restrict table-fellowship or to impose circumcision on Gentile converts. Thus, as Lock comments, the opponents here «do not correspond to the Pharisaic Jewish Christians denounced in Galatians [2:4, 12]»[43]. It may be that the classification of the false teachers in the Pastorals as οἱ ἐκ τῆς περιτομῆς is probably not so much an indication of their attitude towards table-fellowship nor the necessity of circumcision for Gentile converts as it is a derogatory epithet hurled at them by those who would make fun of their circumcised status. Joel Marcus has drawn attention to the metonymic use of the term περιτομή[44], and identifies it as an epithet of hostility commonly used in ethnically mixed communities in which «Jews

---

[39] See Gal 5:6: «in Christ Jesus neither circumcision nor uncircumcision is of any avail, but faith working through love» (ἐν γὰρ Χριστῷ Ἰησοῦ οὔτε περιτομή τι ἰσχύει οὔτε ἀκροβυστία, ἀλλὰ πίστις δι᾿ ἀγάπης ἐνεργουμένη).

[40] J. A. FITZMYER, «Romans», 837; J. ZIESLER, *Romans*, 93.

[41] R. JEWETT, «Romans as an Ambassadorial Letter», 8, 9.

[42] R. E. BROWN – J. P. MEIER, *Antioch and Rome*, 110.

[43] W. LOCK, *Pastoral Epistles*, 133.

[44] J. MARCUS, «The Circumcision», 76.

and Gentiles were thrown into close contact with one another»[45]. As an ethnic slur, then, the term refers to a cultural/religious/national heritage; the presence here in the Pastorals of such divisive language gives some indication of the mixed composition of the community for which the letters were intended, as well as the rifts within that community. Of itself, however, the phrase οἱ ἐκ τῆς περιτομῆς does not give a direct indication of the theological positions advocated by Hymenaeus, Alexander, and Philetus.

### 4.3.3  The opponents and abstinence from foods

The false teachers are accused of enjoining «abstinence from foods which God created to be received with thanksgiving by those who believe and know the truth» (1 Tim 4:3). Dibelius – Conzelmann connect this passage to the Pastor's exhortation to Timothy not to drink only water but to «use a little wine for the sake of your stomach and your frequent ailments» (1 Tim 5:23), though, as one might expect, they also see here a reference to Gnostic asceticism[46]. Lock notes that the prohibition of certain foods «finds an exact analogy in the Gnosticism of the second century»[47]. Towner sees in the injunction of 1 Tim 4:3 evidence of some sort of dualism, though he adds that «it is not certain that it was as radical as that of the later Gnostics nor that it had its basis in the belief that all matter was inherently evil because of an evil creator»[48].

The reference here, however, need not necessarily be to forms of Gnostic asceticism; instead, the opponents may have attempted to impose the dietary restrictions of Judaism on their followers. The dietary laws so characteristic of Judaism constituted part of the larger system of cleanness and uncleanness, according to which certain persons, foods, places and objects are susceptible to physical, ritual, or moral impurity[49]. For de Vaux, the laws governing ritual purity served to separate Israel from the pagan world around it[50]. G. von Rad indicates that within ancient Israel, creation itself was divided into clean and unclean,

---

[45] J. MARCUS, «The Circumcision», 79.

[46] Dibelius – Conzelmann, 65; see also R. P. MARTIN, «1, 2 Timothy and Titus», 1239; R. A. WILD, «The Pastoral Letters», 898.

[47] W. LOCK, *Pastoral Epistles*, 47.

[48] P. H. TOWNER, «Gnosis and Realised Eschatology», 107.

[49] L. E. TOOMBS, «Clean and Unclean», 641.

[50] R. DE VAUX, *Ancient Israel*, 464.

holy and secular, blessing and curse, and that the unclean was the most basic form in which Israel encountered what was displeasing to God[51]. Here, then, in the system of cleanness and uncleanness reappear one of L. Hoffmann's variations on the fundamental diadic opposition between the holy and the profane which is so basic to Judaism[52]. Thus Towner is right to see a kind of dualism in the position attributed to the false teachers in 1 Tim 4:3, though it need not necessarily be attributed to incipient forms of Gnosticism. The habits of thought characteristic of first century Judaism were themselves capable of providing plenty of occasion for sharp oppositions.

Lev 11:2-47 and Deut 14:3-21 list those foods which were permitted and those which were prohibited to members of the covenant community: cloven-hoofed, cud-chewing animals were allowed to serve as food (Lev 11:3; Deut 14:6), whereas animals like the camel (Lev 11:4; Deut 14:7), the rock-badger (Lev 11:5; Deut 14:7), the hare (Lev 11:6; Deut 14:7), and the pig (Lev 11:7; Deut 14:8) were excluded from human consumption because either they were cloven-hoofed but not ruminant, like the pig, or else because they were thought to be ruminant, even though were not cloven-hoofed, like the camel, the rock-badger, and the hare. Certain birds (Lev 11:13-19; Deut 14:12-18), perhaps because they were perceived as scavengers, all winged insects (Lev 11:20-23; Deut 14:19) and any water creature without scales or fins (Lev 11:9-12; Deut 14:10) were likewise excluded from human consumption.

R. J. Faley suggests that the exclusion of certain animals like the pig was based originally on their use in pagan worship, though, he adds, that «it is not unlikely that other reasons, such as hygiene and natural abhorrence, also affected Hebrew custom and legislation»[53]. Whatever the original motive governing the exclusion of certain foods, the violation of these laws was ultimately regarded as a direct affront to the very holiness of God himself since the Israelites were enjoined to be holy even as God is holy (Lev 11:45). The literary form of these laws indicates that while they were directed to the priests, their content was intended for oral transmission to the laity; hence, the responsibility for teaching what was prohibited and what was permitted as food seems to have been that of the priests[54].

---

[51] G. VON RAD, Israel's Historical Traditions, 272, 273.

[52] L. A. HOFFMANN, Beyond the Text, 37.

[53] R. J. FALEY, «Leviticus», 68.

[54] O. EIßFELDT, Introduction, 31; M. NOTH, Leviticus, 91-92.

### a) *Acts, the Council of Jerusalem and dietary restrictions*

Controversies over food laws, particularly those which forbade eating meat previously sacrificed to idols (εἰδωλόθυτον) were not unfamiliar to Paul, and are reflected both in Acts and in his own letters. The traditions preserved in Acts indicate that the Council of Jerusalem was convened to address the dissension caused by some men who had come down from Judaea to Antioch and who were teaching the necessity of circumcision (Acts 15:1): the issue is further sharpened in Acts 15:5, when some believers who belonged to the party of the Pharisees are reported to have demanded that the Gentiles be compelled both to circumcision, and to the full observance of the law of Moses. Presumably food laws were not absent from the concerns of these Pharisees, and indeed, may have been at the forefront of their misgivings, since the stipulations of the Council required Gentile converts to observe certain restrictions in their diet, though they were bound only to refrain from eating «what had been sacrificed to idols, and from blood, and from what is strangled» (εἰδωλοθύτων καὶ αἵματος καὶ πνικτῶν: Acts 15:29).

As a term referring to what had previously been sacrificed to idols, εἰδωλόθυτον appears relatively late in the literature of Judaism, not until 4 Macc 5:2[55], in an episode describing the outrages of Antiochus Epiphanes against the inhabitants of Jerusalem:

> And so the tyrant Antiochus took his seat with his counselors on a certain high place, with his fully armed troops around him, and he ordered his guards to drag along every single one of the Hebrews and compel them to eat swine's flesh and food sacrificed to idols [εἰδωλοθύτων]. Whoever refused to eat the defiled food was to be tortured and put to death (4 Macc 5:1-3).

The strict prohibition against eating food previously sacrificed to idols is reflected in the later rabbinical literature, and represents not only the «resolute resistance of Judaism to any kind of religious syncretism», as Büchsel would have it[56], but its real horror at anything which would

---

[55] The manner in which the author of 4 Maccabees refers to the Temple and its services presupposes that the Second Temple is still standing, according to H. ANDERSON, («4 Maccabees», 533). But the author's eagerness to explain in 4:1 that in the days of Seleucis IV, the high priest Onias held his office for life indicates a period after the collapse of the Hasmonean dynasty. Thus Anderson holds that 4 Maccabees was written outside of Palestine by an unknown author sometime between 63 BCE and 70 CE.

[56] F. BÜCHSEL, «εἰδωλόθυτον», 378-379.

impugn its central tenet, the doctrine of the one God. Presumably similar kinds of concerns underlay the prohibition in Acts.

The second and third stipulations of the Council of Jerusalem prohibited eating blood or meat with the blood still in it[57]. But unlike the case of εἰδωλόθυτον, the dietary restrictions regarding blood are amply witnessed in the Hebrew Scriptures. If the prohibition against eating blood is an allusion to the Noachic covenant found in Genesis 9:4, it probably represented in the view of those who were convened in Jerusalem an obligation binding upon the whole of humanity[58]. R. J. Dillon has suggested, however, that the prohibition against eating blood may be founded on the laws governing the conduct of sojourners (גֵּרִים) recorded in Lev 17:10-12; in that case, it was binding only on those who wished to gain access to the sacred terrain of the Chosen People[59]. Yet the decision of the Council seemingly bound Christians living in Antioch. If the dietary restrictions of the Council of Jerusalem were founded on the laws governing the conduct of the גֵּרִים, then it does not seem as though Christians living outside the Promised Land would have been obliged to observe the prohibition.

Implicit in the laws governing the conduct of the גֵּרִים as they are found in Leviticus 17 is the sense of Israel as a land specially consecrated to God. The prohibition in Leviticus against eating blood, even by the גֵּרִים, thus perpetuated the sharp distinctions between the sacred and the profane, the clean and the unclean, Israel and the nations so characteristic of first century Jewish thought. Yet the gist of Peter's speech in Acts 15:7-11 seems to eliminate the exclusivist interpretation of the Council's dietary restrictions: God «made no distinction between us and them, but cleansed their hearts by faith» (καὶ οὐθὲν διέκρινεν μεταξὺ ἡμῶν τε καὶ αὐτῶν, τῇ πίστει καθαρίσας τὰς καρδίας αὐτῶν: Acts 15:9). Moreover, the joyful reception of the decision in Antioch seems to argue against exclusivism. Thus it appears to be more likely that the Council of Jerusalem's prohibition against eating blood was founded on a principle conceived to be universally binding, namely the Noachic covenant.

---

[57] J. MUNCK (Acts, 141) holds that the prohibition against strangulation (πνικτόν) ensured that the animal would have been slaughtered in such a way that all the blood would have been drained from it.

[58] C. WESTERMANN, Genesis 1 – 11, 469.

[59] R. J. DILLON, «Acts of the Apostles», 752.

## b) *Dietary restrictions in the Pauline letters*

Disputes over the binding force of the dietary restrictions of the Mosaic law were ones into which Paul himself had entered, both in Corinth (1 Cor 8 – 10)[60] and in Rome (Rom 14:1-23)[61]. Yet the disputes in Rome and in Corinth had to do with the propriety of eating the εἰδωλόθυτον: the question of eating blood or meat with its blood still in it seems not to have been a concern to these early Christian communities. There were good reasons for this: the eating of the εἰδωλόθυτον was bound to raise some serious questions regarding the depth of one's commitment to the one God in a way that the consumption of blood would not. In Corinth, Paul had urged those who possessed the «knowledge» that idols enjoyed no real existence, and for whom, therefore, the consumption of the εἰδωλόθυτον implied no allegiance to any idol, to defer to the conscience of those who did not possess this «knowledge» (1 Cor 8:1-7), and whose faith might thereby be weakened. Orr and Walther summarize Paul's position: «To be the cause of another's downfall [...] is a sin *against Christ* inasmuch as Christ's purpose toward that person is love»[62]. In Rome, Paul had urged «the strong» to be mindful of the scruples of «the weak:» and while Paul very clearly identified himself with «the strong» (Rom 15:1), he nevertheless used language which accentuated the link with those who constituted «the weak», primarily through the use of the term «brother» (ἀδελφός: Rom 14:10a, 10b, 13, 15, 21), thereby stressing the horizontal ties which bound the Roman Christians each to each. The weak were not simply brothers in some sort of abstract sense; they were Paul's brothers, and he did not wish to injure them[63].

---

[60] Orr – Walther, 228; G. D. FEE, «Εἰδωλόθυτα Once Again», 172-197.

[61] J. ZIESLER, *Romans*, 324.

[62] Orr – Walther, 235.

[63] We note here the claim of E. P. SANDERS (*Paul, the Law, and the Jewish People*, 101) to detect a fundamental consistency in Paul with regard to circumcision and the dietary laws, though he claims that Paul offered no theoretical basis for his opposition to these two practices. Sanders maintains, instead, that circumcision and the dietary restrictions, along with Sabbath observance, created a social distinction between Jews and other races in the Graeco-Roman world, drawing the ridicule of pagans; and that Paul's theological conviction that all are saved on the same basis (Rom 3:23) caused him unconsciously to delete those elements from the law – circumcision, dietary restrictions, and the Sabbath – which were most apt to create divisions (103). The ridicule which circumcision, dietary restrictions and the Sabbath observance attracted is amply re-

c) *The argument in the Pastoral Epistles in favour of liceity*

Yet here in the Pastoral Epistles the argument in favor of the liceity
of any and all foods is not based on the fear of offending a brother in
the faith; here, the argument is more strictly theological: the Pastor refers to the creation of foods «to be received with thanksgiving by those
who believe and know the truth» (1 Tim 4:3). And if the seeming slogan
«All things are pure to those who are pure, but to the corrupt and
unbelieving nothing is pure» (πάντα καθαρὰ τοῖς καθαροῖς· τοῖς δὲ με-
μιαμμένοις καὶ ἀπίστοις οὐδὲν καθαρόν: Titus 1:15) is also a reference
to the dispute over the liceity of any and all foods, as Dibelius –
Conzelmann think[64], then the refusal to eat what is set before one is
evidence of one's unbelief, and represents, in effect, a failure to
recognize God as creator[65].

Elements of the Pastor's argument in favor of the liceity of all foods
are not un-Pauline; indeed, the argument is reminiscent of that in 1 Cor
10:23-30 in which Paul quotes Ps 24:1. And the apparent slogan of Tit
1:15 may be a conscious echo of another apparent slogan in 1 Cor
10:23: «All things are lawful but not all things are helpful» (πάντα ἔξεσ-
τιν, ἀλλ᾽ οὐ πάντα συμφέρει), and, more remotely, to the first half of
Paul's statement in Rom 14:14: «I know and am persuaded in the Lord
Jesus that nothing is unclean in itself; but it is unclean for anyone who
thinks it is unclean» (οἶδα καὶ πέπεισομαι ἐν κυρίῳ Ἰησοῦ ὅτι οὐδὲν
κοινὸν δι᾽ ἑαυτοῦ. εἰ μὴ τῷ λογιζομένῳ τι κοινὸν εἶναι, ἐκείνῳ κοινόν).
But if the Pastor is making reference to Rom 14:14, it seems as though
he is reading Paul a little selectively: the opponents here apparently hold
that some foods are unclean, and thus, according to Paul's own argument, such foods are unclean to them.

However, the Christological dimension of the argument in favor of the
liceity of all foods, so typical of Paul, seems at first glance to be nearly
absent altogether. Dibelius – Conzelmann see a cultic motif in the Pas-

---

flected in the literature of Romans like Cicero, Seneca, and Petronius, and widely recognised by contemporary scholars. (See J. J. COLLINS, *Between Athens and Jerusalem*, 5-6; J. L. DANIEL, «Anti-Semitism».) But Sanders' assertion that Paul *unconsciously* deleted from the law circumcision, the dietary laws, and the obligation to observe the sabbath seems to me to be unduly speculative and unsupported by the data.
Furthermore, Sanders' analysis of Paul's position fails to appreciate the specifically
Christological element in Paul's thought.

[64] Dibelius – Conzelmann, 137-138.

[65] See J. L. HOULDEN, *The Pastoral Epistles*, 145.

tor's argument: εὐχαριστία in 1 Tim 4:3,4 is equivalent to ἔντευξις in 1 Tim 4:5[66]; and the λόγος θεοῦ in 1 Tim 4:5 refers to table prayers using Biblical expressions[67]. While they would attribute such language to the liturgical traditions of Judaism[68], one might as easily see in such vocabulary allusions to the Christian celebration of the Eucharist. Thus the Christological rationale in favor of the liceity of all foods is introduced through the use of the language of Christian cult.

Thus the abstinence from food which Alexander, Hymenaeus, and Philetus enjoin may be seen as an endeavor to impose the dietary restrictions of Judaism on the communities to which the Pastoral Epistles were written. Yet they may have done so not so much in the attempt to put «a yoke on the neck of the disciples» (Acts 15:10) as in the effort to discharge their traditional priestly obligations to distinguish between the clean and the unclean, the holy and the secular, the sacred and the profane. Seen in this light, the Pastor's refutation of their attempt which charges them with unbelief seems highly ironic: those who prided themselves on the punctilious observance of their faith (Rom 2:17-24) have become, in the view of the Pastor, and precisely as a result of that punctilious observance of the law, no better than unbelievers.

### 4.3.4  The opponents as teachers of the law

In the Pastor's charge that the opponents want to be «teachers of the law» (νομοδιδάσκαλοι: 1 Tim 1:7), there seems to be a fairly clear indication of their theological position. The term νομοδιδάσκαλος in the NT is attested only two other times besides 1 Tim 1:7, namely, in Luke 5:17, where it refers to those with the Pharisees who witness the healing of the paralytic and who later in the pericope are called γραμματεῖς (Lk 5:21), and in Acts 5:34 where it refers to Gamaliel as an influential teacher of the law. But these two Lucan usages do not provide sufficient information to indicate a distinctive theological stance proper to a νομοδιδάσκαλος. And K. H. Rengstorf does not think that the term is Jewish in origin, but is «rather a Christian construction designed to mark off Jewish from Christian teachers at a decisive point, namely, the absolutizing of the νόμος»[69]. Here perhaps, as with the denomination

---

[66] Dibelius – Conzelmann, 64, n. 5.

[67] Dibelius – Conzelmann, 64.

[68] Dibelius – Conzelmann, 30, 64.

[69] K. H. RENGSTORF, «νομοδιδάσκαλος», 159.

of the opponents as οἱ ἐκ τῆς περιτομῆς, the language may be polemical and divisive; it certainly seems designed to establish boundaries and demarcate differences.

### a) *Law, «covenantal nomism», and first century Judaism*

The centrality of the law to Judaism is well attested, both in the canonical literature[70], and in the works of first century Jewish authors. Josephus, for instance, devotes more than half of the second book of *Against Apion* to praise of the law:

> What could one alter in it? What more beautiful one could have been discovered? What improvement imported from elsewhere? Would you change the entire character of the constitution? Could there be a finer or more equitable polity than one which sets God at the head of the universe, which assigns the administration of its highest affairs to the whole body of priests, and entrusts to the supreme high priest the direction of other priests? (*Against Apion* II.184-186).

Here, in Josephus' encomium of the law, he portrays the priests as the ones under the law to whom the administration of the highest legal affairs has been entrusted, an arrangement which, presumably, illustrates the excellence of the law. For Josephus, the law is essential to Judaism, and priests are essential to the administration of the law.

But identifying the law as essential does not explain its function within the religious world first century Jews inhabited. E. P. Sanders has devoted much of his professional life to the study of the relationship between Judaism and Christianity during the late first and early second centuries, concentrating on the vexed question of the place of the law in first and second century Judaism[71]. Reacting against the scholarly caricature of Judaism as a religion of legalistic works-righteousness[72], Sanders perceives a basic pattern which he denotes by the phrase «covenantal nomism», and which he describes as «the view that one's place in God's plan is established on the basis of the covenant and that the covenant requires as the proper response of man his obedience to the com-

---

[70] See J. BLENKINSOPP, *Wisdom and Law*; W. D. DAVIES, «Law in first-century Judaism»; P. GRELOT, «Law»; W. J. HARRELSON, «Law in the OT».

[71] See, for instance, E. P. SANDERS, *Paul and Palestinian Judaism*; ID., *Paul, the Law, and the Jewish People*.

[72] E. P. SANDERS, *Paul and Palestinian Judaism*, 33-59.

mandments, while providing means of atonement for transgression»[73].
In the religious pattern of covenantal nomism, God initiates the relationship with Israel, and through the provisions of the law, Israel responds
to God. Thus, the function of the law in the Judaism of the late first and
early second centuries is to enter into a kind of dialogue with God, a
grateful acknowledgment of God's mercy for having chosen Israel, for
having established a covenant with them, and for continuing to dwell
among them[74]. Moreover, this view of the law was not confined to one
or another religious group within the Judaism of the first century:
Sanders' investigations into Tannaitic literature, the Dead Sea Scrolls,
and the Apocrypha and Pseudepigrapha lead him to conclude that
covenantal nomism was pervasive in Palestine from early in the second
century BCE to late in the second century CE: it was, therefore, the
pattern of religiosity known to Jesus and, presumably, to Paul and to the
Pastor[75].

Seen in the light of Sanders' scholarship, first century Judaism can no
longer be viewed as a religion of the self-righteous, and the works of the
law as the means by which first century Jews earned their way into the
favor of the Almighty[76].

b) *The law in the Pauline* homologoumena

Part of the difficulty in trying to establish Paul's own understanding
of the law hinges on the precise meaning of the term νόμος in the *homologoumena*: Heikki Räisänen observes that nowhere in any of Paul's
letters does he define the term νόμος, presumably because he presupposes his readers will know what he is talking about[77]. If that is so, then
at least some of his readers, namely those familiar with the Hebrew
Scriptures, would have understood the term νόμος as the Torah, since

---

[73] E. P. SANDERS, *Paul and Palestinian Judaism*, 75.

[74] E. P. SANDERS, *Paul and Palestinian Judaism*, 82-83.

[75] E. P. SANDERS, *Paul and Palestinian Judaism*, 426.

[76] «The supposed legalistic Judaism of scholars [...] serves a very obvious function.
It acts as the foil against which superior forms of religion are described. One must note
in particular the projection on to Judaism of the view which Protestants find most
objectionable in Roman Catholicism [...] We have here the retrojection of the
Protestant-Catholic debate into ancient history, with Judaism taking the rôle of
Catholicism and Christianity the rôle of Lutheranism». E. P. SANDERS, *Paul and
Palestinian Judaism*, 57.

[77] H. RÄISÄNEN, *Paul and the Law*, 16.

νόμος was the usual way in which תּוֹרָה was translated in the LXX[78]. W. D. Davies holds, on the other hand, that the term νόμος in Paul seems to indicate not just the law of Moses, but an «inexorable necessity», an internal governing principle[79]. According to M. Black, Paul identified the law as holy (ἅγιος, Rom 7:12), spiritual (πνευματικός, Rom 7:14) and good (καλός, Rom 7:16) in order to answer the question: «What then shall we say? That the law is sin?» (τί οὖν ἐροῦμεν; ὁ νόμος ἁμαρτία: Rom 7:7). Paul's answer, that the law is holy, spiritual, and good, constituted a reply to his critics for whom his position would have been perceived as antinomian, in Black's estimation; thus it is not the law which Paul indicted here, but rather human weakness overcome by sin[80]. Similarly, Sanders says that since Paul had come perilously close to identifying the law with sin in Rom 6:15 − 7:6, he must now explicitly deny the implied equation[81].

Admittedly, much of Paul's theology as presented in his letters was occasioned by the community controversies in which he found himself embroiled; yet here in Romans, Paul's stance vis-à-vis the law seemed to depend less on theological polemics and more on his deeply held convictions regarding the meaning of Christ's coming with respect to the law[82]. As Bornkamm says:

---

[78] W. Gutbrod, «νόμος», 1046. He adds that «the use of νόμος in Paul is not wholly uniform, for he can sometimes employ the term when he does not have the OT law in view. Nevertheless, he does not start with a general sense which is then predominantly used for the Mosaic law. His starting point is the traditional use of νόμος for the specific OT law. Hence it is self-evident what νόμος means, and usually no more precise definition is given» (1069).

[79] W. D. Davies, «Law in the NT», 99. I think, however, that Davies fails to attend to the nuanced uses to which Paul puts the term νόμος: in Rom 7:21, 23 and 25, Paul mentions «another law» (ἕτερος νόμος), a «law of sin» (νόμῳ τῆς ἁμαρτίας; νόμῳ ἁμαρτίας) to which he is made captive. In these cases, the term νόμος indicates the claim or will which comes from the source indicated by the *genitive auctoris* (W. Gutbrod, νόμος», 1071): it is this sense of νόμος which carries the burden of inexorable necessity, and not the «holy», «spiritual», and «good» law with which it is at war.

[80] M. Black, *Romans*, 104-106.

[81] E. P. Sanders, *Paul, the Law, and the Jewish People*, 73.

[82] For a spirited discussion regarding the purpose and occasion of Romans, see K. P. Donfried, «False Presuppositions in the Study of Romans»; R. J. Karris, «The Occasion of Romans»; and W. Wuellner, «Paul's Rhetoric of Argumentation», all of which have now been reprinted, along with more recent contributions to the ongoing discussion, by K. P. Donfried, ed., *The Romans Debate*.

To say what is perfectly correct historically, that the meaning of Christ's coming was deducible from the law, was, in [Paul's] view, not enough. Put in such general terms, the statement was true for all the first Christian converts from Judaism. For Paul, however – and for him alone – it also held true when put the other way around: only in the light of Christ could one deduce the status of the law. The law was the basis of, and the limitation put upon, the unredeemed existence of all men, both Jew and Gentile[83].

Sanders corroborates Bornkamm's view: Paul's understanding of the way to salvation, that only by belonging to Christ can one achieve salvation, preceded his understanding of the place of the law. Thus he formulated his arguments in Romans regarding the place of the law on the conclusions he had previously reached regarding the place of Christ, rather than formulating his conclusions about Christ on his arguments regarding the place of the law[84].

*Since* salvation is only in Christ, *therefore* all other ways to salvation are wrong, and attempting to follow them has results which are the reverse of what is desired. What is wrong with following the law is not the effort itself, but the fact that the observer of the law is not seeking the righteousness which is given by God through the coming of the Christ (Rom 10:2-4)[85].

Thus Paul's position with regard to the law was founded on two convictions: on the one hand, Paul affirmed that the law is holy, spiritual, and good; on the other hand, he was absolutely convinced that salvation is only by faith in Christ, and that in the light of Christ, everything else, the law included, pales.

c) *The law in the Pastoral Epistles*

Given the paradoxical status of the law in Romans – that it is holy, spiritual, and good, while at the same time, wholly inadequate to justify humanity – there is little wonder that subsequent generations of Christians have wrestled with the implications of Paul's position. Indeed, the Pastoral Epistles display that struggle over the Pauline legacy. For my contention in this study is that the opponents do not simply represent the latest generation of Judaizers, seeking to impose the yoke of the law on Timothy's Ephesian congregation and Titus's Cretans: instead, they were

---

[83] G. BORNKAMM, *Paul*, 120-121.

[84] E. P. SANDERS, *Paul, the Law, and the Jewish People*, 35, 125, 150.

[85] E. P. SANDERS, *Paul and Palestinian Judaism*, 482.

conscientious men, most likely from priestly families, who sought to integrate their own heritage as they understood it with the Pauline legacy. The Pastor, likewise, was not simply Paul *redivivus*, but a conscientious man in his own right who sought to preserve the Pauline heritage as he understood it in the face of a challenge Paul himself had never faced and thus had never addressed.

Thus criticisms like that of Heikki Räisänen who holds that «there are no signs in the Pastorals of Paul's view that the law convicts humanity of sin, let alone of the views that it leads to sin or that it cannot be fulfilled»[86] are ultimately irrelevant. Like Räisänen, Dibelius – Conzelmann note a departure from the specifically Pauline teaching about the law: in the Pastoral Epistles, «the law does not serve to disclose the paradoxical situation of man without faith»[87]. But their objections to the Pastor's supposed lack of fidelity to the Pauline legacy rest on the assumption that the Pastor's purpose in writing the Pastoral Epistles was identical to that of Paul, namely, to convict humanity of sin (Räisänen) or to disclose the paradoxical situation of man without faith (Dibelius – Conzelmann). Leaving aside the question of whether these were, in fact, Paul's own purposes in Romans, we must examine the Pastor's purpose in writing these letters. That purpose may be deduced, at least in part, by an analysis of the polemic against those who sought to discharge their obligations as νομοδιδάσκαλοι.

Unlike the identification of the opponents as «those of the circumcision» in Tit 1:10, the identification of the opponents as «teachers of the law», does indicate something about the theological positions of the opponents, at least from the point of view of the Pastor. From his perspective, the νομοδιδάσκαλοι do not understand what they themselves are saying, «nor the things about which they make assertions» (μήτε περὶ τίνων διαβεβαιοῦνται: 1 Tim 1:7). What they misunderstand, according to the Pastor, is the place of the law, which is not laid down for the just, among whom, presumably, the Pastor would number the Christian community, but for

the lawless (ἀνόμοις) and disobedient, for the ungodly and sinners, for the unholy and profane, for murderers of fathers and murderers of mothers, for manslayers, immoral persons, sodomites, kidnappers, liars, perjurers, and whatever else is contrary to sound doctrine (1 Tim 1:9-10).

---

[86] H. RÄISÄNEN, *Paul and the Law*, 206.

[87] Dibelius – Conzelmann, 22.

I do not agree with J. L. Houlden's estimation that the law in this passage from the Pastoral Epistles refers to the general moral law or the law of the state[88]. Nor do I think, along with H. Räisänen, that the Pastor's view of the character of the law is one which

> simply guarantees the order of society by holding sinners and criminals in check; the loyal citizen, who lives in the proper way anyhow, does not really need this law[89].

The law to which the Pastor refers here in 1 Tim 1:9-10 is the Mosaic law, the Torah, the observance to which the opponents are obliged, and to which they would like to oblige the members of the communities to which the Pastoral Epistles were written. The law they want to teach, were it the sort to which Houlden and Räisänen refer, is hardly the kind to which the Pastor would object: after all, he urges that «supplications, prayers, intercessions, and thanksgivings be made for all men, for kings and all who are in high positions, that we may lead a quiet and peaceable life, godly and respectable in every way» (1 Tim 2:1-2). Dibelius − Conzelmann are doubtless right when they argue that the Pastoral Epistles exhibit an ideal of good Christian citizenship[90], but the evidence for that bourgeois ideal is not found in 1 Tim 1:8-11.

Clearly, the Pastor is engaging in polemics here: if the opponents wish to live under the law, he implies, they are virtually admitting that they are ungodly, sinful, murderous, and so on, since it is for these that the law has been instituted. It seems clear, in view of the force and the bitterness of the polemic against Hymenaeus, Alexander, and Philetus, that the Pastor thinks that the community is directly threatened by their attempt to set themselves up as teachers of the law. Yet the Pastor does not seem to object to what the would-be teachers attempt to propound as much as he objects to their aspirations to exercise authority in the community. Negatively, this struggle over authority is reflected in the language used to describe the would-be teachers: they engage in stupid, senseless controversies (μωρὰς καὶ ἀπαιδεύτους ζητήσεις: 2 Tim 2:23); they are

> lovers of self, lovers of money, proud, arrogant, abusive, disobedient to their parents, ungrateful, unholy, inhuman, implacable, slanderers, profligates, fierce, haters of good, treacherous, reckless, swollen with conceit,

---

[88] J. L. HOULDEN, *The Pastoral Epistles*, 53, 58.

[89] H. RÄISÄNEN, *Paul and the Law*, 206.

[90] Dibelius − Conzelmann, 39-41.

lovers of pleasure rather than lovers of God, holding the form of religion but denying the power of it (2 Tim 3:2-5).

But if the attack on the character of the νομοδιδάκαλοι is, in reality, a defense of the Pastor's authority, the Pastor does so because he sees his authority as being rooted in the Pauline legacy. He preserves the memory of a community organized according to the promptings of the Spirit, in which «God has appointed in the church first apostles, second prophets, third teachers, then workers of miracles, then healers, helpers, administrators, speakers in various kinds of tongues» (καὶ οὓς μὲν ἔθετο ὁ θεὸς ἐν τῇ ἐκκλησίᾳ πρῶτον ἀποστόλους, δεύτερον προφήτας, τρίτον διδασκάλους, ἔπειτα δυνάμεις, ἔπειτα χαρίσματα ἰαμάτων, ἀντιλήμψεις, κυβερνήσεις, γένη γλωσσῶν: 1 Cor 12:28). This is not to say that the Pauline communities lacked structure: on the contrary, as M. Y. Mac-Donald notes, «Paul's ranking of apostles, prophets, and teachers suggests that some formalization is taking place»[91]. But it seems clear that what community structures did emerge in the communities Paul founded were based on the needs of the community, the talents of the individual, and perhaps, his or her socio-economic status[92]. In any case, genealogical credentials do not seem to have recommended a person for a particular rôle.

### 4.3.5 The opponents and marriage

Another accusation against the opponents is the charge that they forbid marriage (1 Tim 4:3). Karris sees in this charge an indication of the opponents' «gnostic and world-hating perspective»[93]. Dibelius – Conzelmann note that continence, both in marriage and in diet, would have been especially congenial for a man of the Hellenistic age on anti-materialistic grounds[94]. Lock traces the prohibition of marriage to a Gnostic belief in the evil of matter[95].

Yet it is equally plausible that the opponents' objection to marriage might have been founded on a very different set of grounds; indeed, it may not be marriage *per se* which Hymenaeus, Alexander, and Philetus prohibited, but rather exogamous marriages. According to the Pharisees,

---

[91] M. Y. MacDonald, *The Pauline Churches*, 57.

[92] M. Y. MacDonald, *The Pauline Churches*, 58.

[93] R. J. Karris, *The Pastoral Epistles*, 28.

[94] Dibelius – Conzelmann, 65.

[95] W. Lock, *Pastoral Epistles*, xvii.

even an ordinary Jew in the first century was obliged, as A. Segal reminds us, «to behave as if he had to keep the laws of priestly purity», including the injunction to enter into an endogamous marriage[96]. Intermarriage is forbidden for the same reason that table fellowship is restricted: a people set apart from the nations expresses its election through symbolic segregation. Purity laws, Segal goes on to say, were the concrete expression of this symbolic separation, «and though impurity need not necessarily express immorality, the ambiguity inherent in the concept was often exploited»[97]. Thus, an exogamous marriage would have been viewed by Hymenaeus, Alexander, and Philetus as immoral, and therefore to be shunned.

### a) *Paul and marriage*

Paul himself had prohibited certain types of sexual relationships in 1 Cor 5:1-13 and, in very strong language, he upbraided the members of the Corinthian community for their acceptance of an irregular sexual union among two of their number. Apparently, a member of the Corinthian congregation had entered into a sexual relationship with his father's wife. It is not clear from Paul's account whether the woman in question was divorced from the man's father, or whether she was his widow[98]. Neither is it clear whether the two were married, though the present of ἔχειν «to have» in 1 Cor 5:1 points to some lasting state, according to Conzelmann, either marriage or concubinage[99]. What is clear, however, is that the Corinthian community at least tolerated the relationship, and may well have given its approval to it in the name of Christian freedom[100].

Paul felt compelled to write to disabuse the community of their misapprehension, repeating an earlier admonition from a letter now lost[101] and telling them «not to associate with immoral men» (Ἔγραψα ὑμῖν ἐν τῇ ἐπιστολῇ μὴ συναναμίγνυσθαι πόρνοις: 1 Cor 5:9). At the same time, he presented his own convictions on permissible kinds of marriage through a complicated set of allusions to the Book of Deuteronomy:

---

[96] A. SEGAL, *Rebecca's Children*, 125-126.

[97] A. SEGAL, *Rebecca's Children*, 125, 178.

[98] H. CONZELMANN, *1 Corinthians*, 96; Orr – Walther, 187.

[99] H. CONZELMANN, *1 Corinthians*, 96.

[100] Orr – Walther, 188.

[101] H. CONZELMANN, *1 Corinthians*, 99; Orr – Walther, 18, 120, 190.

Deut 17:7, Deut 22:22, and Deut 22:30, instructing the Corinthians to purge the evil from among them (ἐξάρατε τὸν πονηρὸν ἐξ ὑμῶν αὐτῶν: 1 Cor 5:13). The first reference to Deuteronomy (Deut 17:7) provided Paul with the citation; the second reference (Deut 22:22) outlawed adultery, and the third reference (Deut 22:30) specifically excluded sexual relations with one's father's wife; furthermore, the penalty for adultery provided for in Deut 22:22 is death, the imposition of which purges the evil from Israel. Paul did not go so far as to impose the death penalty: he did, however, instruct the Corinthian Christians that they were not to associate «with anyone who bears the name of brother if he is guilty of immorality or greed» (1 Cor 5:11). The instruction was tantamount to a decree of excommunication, since Paul specifically excluded even table-fellowship.

### b) *The opponents and the prohibition of exogamous marriage*

It may be objected that the situation at Corinth which warranted so extreme a response on Paul's part as excommunication of the offending parties did not involve exogamous marriage, but rather a relationship between a man and his father's wife. But, to men of a generation or two later, like Hymenaeus, Philetus, and Alexander for whom, presumably, the entirety of the law was perceived as binding, and for whom the distinction between immorality and impurity would have been nugatory, Paul's position in Corinth could have been cited in support of their own position regarding exogamous marriage. Thus, the struggle between the opponents and the Pastor for the Pauline legacy involves a struggle over the interpretation of Paul's own words.

Here again, however, the Pastor does not respond directly by offering, for instance, reasons why marriage should not be forbidden. Instead, he is content to brand the teaching of his opponents as «the pretensions of liars whose consciences are seared» (ἐν ὑποκρίσει ψευδολόγων, κεκαυ-στηριασμένων τὴν ἰδίαν συνείδησιν: 1 Tim 4:2). The attack on their integrity is sufficient to brand their teaching as unreliable.

### 4.3.6 The opponents and resurrection

Of all the accusations against the opponents, the most vexing one the Pastor makes, at least for the twentieth century interpreter, is the accusation that Hymenaeus and Philetus «have swerved from the truth by holding that the resurrection is past already» (οἵτινες περὶ τὴν ἀλήθειαν ἠστό-χησαν, λέγοντες [τὴν] ἀνάστασιν ἤδη γεγονέναι: 2 Tim 2:17b). J. N. D.

Kelly holds that this denial amounted to a spiritualizing of the resurrection, tantamount «to denying that the body participated in salvation»[102]. Dibelius – Conzelmann declare that «the thesis which is opposed here is best explained as a spiritualized teaching of Gnostics»[103]. Lock adduces several passages from Irenaeus, Tertullian, and Justin Martyr in support of the Gnostic character of the opponents[104].

But one must ask: can one retroject late second and early third century controversies into late first or early second century disputes without thereby distorting the nature of the earlier disputes? Along with F. Wisse, I think not. Thus, methodological considerations urge caution before the opponents' stance regarding resurrection is attributed to some sort of proto-Gnosticism thought to have presaged the full-blown Gnosticism against which Irenaeus, Tertullian, and Justin Martyr later inveighed.

Another methodological difficulty inheres in the phenomenon that here, too, as in the charges that the opponents try to impose the law or to forbid marriage, is the absence of any explicit attempt at rebuttal: aside from claiming that Hymenaeus and Philetus «are upsetting the faith of some» (καὶ ἀνατρέπουσιν τήν τινων πίστιν: 2 Tim 2:18b), the Pastor seemingly makes no attempt to refute them. Thus, the usual expedient of piecing together the opponents' position from the polemics the Pastor wages against it fails us here.

a) *The opponents and the resurrection of the faithful*

Setting methodological scruples aside for the moment, we turn to consider the specific reference in the accusation that the resurrection is already past. It is not apparent from the immediate context the specific reference of the accusation, but it seems as though the resurrection which Hymenaeus and Philetus claim is already past is that of the baptized. The references to resurrection and faithlessness in the sure saying of 2 Tim 2:11-13 seem to indicate that the hope of resurrection on the part of believers is under attack:

If we have died with him, we shall also live with him (καὶ συζήσομεν);
if we endure, we shall also reign with him (καὶ συμβασιλεύσομεν);
if we deny him, he also will deny us (κἀκεῖνος ἀρνήσεται ἡμᾶς);

---

[102] J. N. D. KELLY, *Commentary*, 11.

[103] Dibelius – Conzelmann, 112.

[104] W. LOCK, *Pastoral Epistles*, 99.

if we are faithless, he remains faithful – for he cannot deny himself (ἐκεῖνος πιστὸς μένει, ἀρνήσασθαι γὰρ ἑαυτὸν οὐ δύναται).

The series of conditions followed by verbs in the future tense is bipartite in structure: the first two conditions («if we have died [...] we shall also live» and «if we endure [...] we shall also reign») constitute the first part of the saying, and present the hope of Christians positively; the last two conditions (if we deny [...] he also will deny» and «if we are faithless, he remains faithful») constitute the second half of the saying and are more ominous in tone, and probably refer to the claims of Hymenaeus and Philetus. The charge to Timothy to «remember Jesus Christ, risen from the dead, descended from David, as preached in my gospel, the gospel for which I am suffering and wearing fetters like a criminal» (Μνημόνευε Ἰησοῦν Χριστὸν ἐγηγερμένον ἐκ νεκρῶν, ἐκ σπέρματος Δαυίδ, κατὰ τὸ εὐαγγέλιόν μου· ἐν ᾧ κακοπαθῶ μέχρι δεσμῶν ὡς κακοῦργος: 2 Tim 2:8-9), with its emphasis on the Lord's resurrection, probably does not indicate that the resurrection of Jesus was a point of contention between the Pastor and the opponents so much as it provides the reason for the Christian hope in a future life.

### b) *Sources for the opponents' position*

We do know that one of the issues in first century Judaism which divided Pharisees from Sadducees was the issue of resurrection[105]. Matt 23:22, Mark 12:18, Luke 20:27, Acts 23:6 and Sanhedrin 10:1[106] testify to the Sadducean disbelief that the resurrection of the dead is stated in the Torah. And Segal points to evidence from the Palestinian Talmud which indicates that people leading services in the synagogue, probably Sadducees, sometimes wanted to leave out prayers mentioning resurrection[107]. Yet it does not seem very likely that Hymenaeus and Philetus would have been Sadducees, if only because of the unlikelihood that those who in principle disbelieved in the resurrection should have been attracted to a movement which proclaimed that Jesus had risen. In addition, with the dissolution of the Sanhedrin following the destruction

---

[105] S. J. D. COHEN, *From the Maccabees*, 147; E. P. SANDERS, *Paul and Palestinian Judaism*, 149, 151-152.

[106] The relevant passage from the Mishnah dates from before 70 CE, and is anti-Sadducean; see E. P. SANDERS, *Paul and Palestinian Judaism*, 149, n. 13.

[107] j. Ber. 9c; cited in A. SEGAL, *Rebecca's Children*, 150.

of the Temple in 70, the base of Sadducean influence was eliminated: the Sadducees thereupon vanish from history[108].

It does not seem possible to trace the accusation that Hymenaeus and Philetus hold that the resurrection is past already to any Jewish doctrine preserved in the sources which have been handed down. It may well be in this accusation, as in the accusation that the opponents want to be teachers of the law (1 Tim 1:7), that an issue over authority is presented here in the guise of an issue over doctrine. Certainly, what purports to be a reply on the part of the Pastor in 2 Tim 2:19 gives credence to this speculation.

### c) *The Pastor's reply*

I have already had occasion to examine in the first part of this study the purpose of the allusion to Numbers 16:5 in the Pastor's reply[109]. He likens the opponents to Korah, Dathan, and Abiram, figures who once opposed Moses, and who came to a bad end because of their opposition. The irony in the allusion is, of course, that in Numbers the authority of the hereditary Aaronide priesthood is vindicated by the miraculous death of the rebels (Num 16:31-35). Yet here, the Pastor puts the story to precisely the opposite use: he wishes to undermine the claims of those who wish to exercise authority on the basis of their genealogical credentials. At the same time, the analogous relationship between Moses and Aaron on the one hand, and Timothy and those who hold to the faithful word on the other, serves to underscore the latters' divine right to exercise authority in the community.

### 4.3.7 Conclusions

If it is true that the Pastoral Epistles constitute a partial record of a conversation which transpired about 1900 years ago, it is equally true that we can understand what survives of that conversation only by trying to reconstruct what was said by the other partners to the dialogue. My concern throughout this examination of the polemic against Hymenaeus, Philetus, and Alexander in the Pastoral Epistles has been to ascertain the specific positions these teachers advanced, in the effort to understand

---

[108] E. SCHÜRER, *History*, I, 523. S. J. D. COHEN, *From the Maccabees*, adds that the numbers of the Sadducees were reduced both by the Romans and by the revolutionaries (226).

[109] See above, Ch 1, § 1.2.1.

better the Pastor's response. The underlying issue in the complexus of specific positions to which the Pastor raises such strenuous objections is the opponents' claim to exercise leadership in the community to which the Pastoral Epistles were directed, a claim which they attempted to demonstrate by advancing their genealogical credentials as members of priestly families.

The Pastor's response to this claim to exercise leadership is to compose a letter in which Paul, the authority *par excellence* for this community, might express his views on the matter, in a manner which is unmistakably authoritative. The manner by which the Pastor's Paul exercises his authority is by means of the testament, the theological implications of which shall now be the focus of attention.

## 5. Theological implications of the testamentary genre in 2 Tim

Just as the literary conventions of the encomium served Philo's three-pronged theological agenda, so the literary conventions of the testament serve the Pastor's theological agenda. By choosing to cast in the form of a testament what he believes Paul's attitude towards these priestly claimants to the teaching office would be, the Pastor constructs an argument which is well-nigh unimpeachable. Indeed, J. D. Quinn notes that

> the irrefutable, incontestable character of parenesis reaches its highest pitch when it takes the form of a will. The last words of the apostle to his legitimate child (1 Tim 1:2; cf. 1:18; 2 Tim 1:2; 2:1) admit of no refutation. The heir cannot argue with the patriarchal will. He may indeed ignore or reject his inheritance, but there is no escaping the terms on which it comes to the one who does accept it, the responsibilities he assumes, the goods for which he must answer[110].

And if the heir cannot argue with the patriarchal will, those who have been disinherited, namely the νομοδιδάσκαλοι, have even less room to manoeuvre. They have been shut out of the will altogether.

But something more than winning an argument with rivals is at issue here. The ability of a theological tradition to address contemporary problems, the relationship between the past and the present, the capacity of an institution to respond to a pastoral challenge are all at stake in the Pastor's reply to the νομοδιδάσκαλοι. To have employed a testament, as the Pastor has, as the means by which the tradition is brought to bear

---

[110] J. D. QUINN, «Parenesis», 499.

on the contemporary scene is to have asserted the continuing relevance of the past.

## 5.1 *Pseudonymity and the presence of the past*

Implicit in the Pastor's effort to compose a reply in Paul's name to the priestly claimants to authority within this Pauline community is the assumption that the Pauline heritage, as he understands it, has something to contribute to the controversies which have divided this community. The phenomenon of pseudepigraphy is a tribute to the one in whose name the work is written, since it testifies to his status. R. Collins thinks that the emergence of a set of letters written in the name of Paul came about as result of an emerging Pauline hagiography:

> The image of the Paul which [the Pauline pseudepigrapha] project is an image of Paul about to be placed on the pedestal of sainthood. The pseudepigrapher's Paul is one whose life and ministry were considered to be exemplary. He is a revered figure from the past who deserves to be imitated in the present, and imitation, it is said, is a form of praise[111].

The second assumption which governs the Pastor's effort to compose a letter in Paul's name is that the will of Paul as it is expressed in this testament will be respected by the likes of Hymenaeus and Philetus. In effect, to have written in Paul's name is to have constructed an argument from authority. «Paul forbade us to dispute about words, to engage in profane chatter, to wander into myths», the Pastor claims, «and here is the letter in which he so forbade us».

Donelson is content to admit that the practice of writing a document in someone else's name is deceitful, and that such practice was common in the first few centuries of the Christian era[112]. Few other scholars have been so willing to characterise the practice as deceitful, and most have sought a theological justification for the practice. Thus Aland maintained that the attribution of apostolic authorship was simply the result of a logical conclusion that the Spirit was the author of the work in question[113]. R. F. Collins views the deutero-Pauline literature in general and the Pastoral Epistles in particular as implicit tributes to the memory of Paul, and attempts to re-embody his teachings in new cir-

---

[111] R. F. COLLINS, *Letters*, 251.

[112] L. R. DONELSON, «The Structure of Ethical Argument», 110.

[113] K. ALAND, «The Problem of Anonymity», 45.

cumstances[114]. Meade holds that in pseudonymous or pseudepigraphic literature, «literary attribution is primarily an assertion of authoritative tradition, not literary origin», by which he means that the intent of the Pastor was not to deceive, as Donelson would have it, but to provide a *Vergegenwärtingung* (actualisation) of the Pauline tradition[115].

To attribute deceit to the author of the Pastoral Epistles is, in my opinion, to confuse a literary issue with a moral one. Meade's approach to the phenomenon of pseudonymity and pseudepigraphy, as well as that of Collins, seems to be more fruitful, inasmuch as the approach attempts to relate the phenomenon not to the motive of the author, but to the needs of the community to which the author directs his efforts. The community to which the Pastor directs his efforts was one which was beset by competing claims to exercise authority. What better way to adjudicate those competing claims than to allow the one in whose name the claim is made to speak for himself?

## 5.2 *Tradition as a source of renewal in the Pauline communities*

In having raised Paul from the dead, so to speak, and having let this great figure from the past address contemporary problems, the Pastor does not simply apply ancient solutions to new problems. Tradition in the Pastoral Epistles is not a dead weight imposed by the dead on the living; on the contrary, the Pauline tradition is deployed here in the service of innovation.

W. Kurz claims that the primary function of the farewell address is to promote transition from the original religious leader – Moses, David, Jesus, Paul – to their successors: «it is especially concerned with maintaining community tradition and the authority to preserve that tradition for later generations»[116]. But Kurz further maintains that the very genre of the farewell address is conservative: «it is not primarily concerned with the progressive unfolding of the tradition nor with adapting it to changing circumstances»[117]. While this may be true of some of the examples of the *discours d'adieu* that Kurz has in mind, his contention cannot be sustained with respect to the Pastoral Epistles in general, nor with 2 Tim in particular. Far from being content to reapply the words

---

[114] R. F. COLLINS, *The Birth of the New Testament*, 190.

[115] D. G. MEADE, *Pseudonymity and Canon*, 105.

[116] W. S. KURZ, *Farewell Addresses*, 50.

[117] W. S. KURZ, *Farewell Addresses*, 50.

of the historical Paul to the situation facing his community, the Pastor seeks to preserve the Pauline freedoms in the face of a conservative retrenchment. He accomplishes this task in two ways: by enjoining a set of virtues appropriate for the successor to Paul, and by the innovation (or renovation) of institutional offices within this deutero-Pauline community.

## 5.2.1 Personal criteria of the Pauline leader

Even a casual reading of the Pastoral Epistles reveals that when the Pastor speaks of the ἐπίσκοπος, the πρεσβύτερος, or the διάκονος that he has precious little to say about their duties, but a great deal to say about what kind of people they should be. Thus, the ἐπίσκοπος is supposed to be

> above reproach, the husband of one wife, temperate, sensible, dignified, hospitable, an apt teacher, no drunkard, not violent but gentle, not quarrelsome, and no lover of money. He must manage his own household well, keeping his children submissive and respectful in every way; for if a man does not know how to manage his own household, how can he care for God's church? He must not be a recent convert, or he may be puffed up with conceit and fall into the condemnation of the devil; moreover he must be well thought of by outsiders, or he may fall into reproach and the snare of the devil (1 Tim 3:2-7).

What specific duties are mentioned in this passage (e.g., household management) are not so much ones which the ἐπίσκοπος discharges as part of his official duties; rather, they are qualifying factors which, if he is able to perform them suitably, allow him to advance to the office of the ἐπίσκοπος.

A similar set of personal qualities are demanded of the διάκονος:

> Deacons likewise must be serious, not double-tongued, not addicted to much wine, not greedy for gain; they must hold the mystery of the faith with a clear conscience. And let them also be tested first; then if they prove themselves blameless let them serve as deacons [...] Let deacons be the husband of one wife, and let them manage their children and their households well, for those who serve well as deacons gain a good standing for themselves and also great confidence in the faith which is in Christ Jesus (1 Tim 3:8-10, 12-13).

In the struggle over the exercise of authority, which is to say the struggle for self-definition within the communities for which the Pastoral Epistles were written, the genealogical criterion for authority was ruled out, and a set of what might be called personal and moral virtues was substituted, virtues which, as R. E. Brown notes, were appropriate for an organization with a familial tone: «stability and close relationship similar to that of a family home will hold the church together against the disintegrating forces that surround and invade it»[118]. In this respect, the injunction that the «Lord's servant must not be quarrelsome, but kindly to everyone, an apt teacher, forbearing, correcting his opponents with gentleness» (δοῦλον δὲ κυρίου οὐ δεῖ μάχεσθαι, ἀλλὰ ἤπιον εἶναι πρὸς πάντας, διδακτικόν, ἀνεξίκακον, ἐν πραΰτητι παιδεύοντα τοὺς ἀντιδια-τιθεμένους: 2 Tim 2:24-25a; see also 1 Tim 6:11) outlines a set of personal characteristics which are not simply the opposite of those possessed by the opponents; the «Lord's servant» is enjoined to develop those moral qualities which will bring peace to a community and cause it to flourish.

### 5.2.2 Institutional innovations in the Pastoral Epistles

But the personal virtues of the «Lord's servant» are not the only means by which the Pauline tradition shall be preserved within this community to which the Pastor directs 2 Tim. His desire to preserve the Pauline heritage moves him to describe a set of qualifications for what were probably the already existing if fluidly defined structures of the presbyterate-episcopate and the diaconate[119].

Spicq identified the πιστοῖς ἀνθρώποις of 2 Tim 2:2 to whom Timothy is supposed to entrust what he has heard from Paul so that they can teach others also with the presbyter-bishops of Tit 1:6-9, who are supposed to be able to «hold firm to the sure word as taught, so that he may be able to give instruction in sound doctrine and also to confute those who contradict it» (ἀντεχόμενον τοῦ κατὰ τὴν διδαχὴν πιστοῦ λόγου, ἵνα δυνατὸς ᾖ καὶ παρακαλεῖν ἐν τῇ διδασκαλίᾳ τῇ ὑγιαινούσῃ καὶ τοὺς ἀντιλέγοντας ἐλέγχειν: Tit 1:9; see also 1 Tim 3:2; 5:17)[120]. Knight

---

[118] R. E. BROWN, *The Churches*, 34. See also J. SÁNCHEZ BOSCH, «Le charisme des Pasteurs», 370-371.

[119] See G. BORNKAMM, *Paul*, 183; R. E. BROWN, *Priest and Bishop*, 63-73; B. BYRNE, «Philippians», 793; M. Y. MACDONALD, *The Pauline Churches*, 217; M. R. VINCENT, *The Epistles to the Philippians and to Philemon*, 41. H. VON LIPS (*Glaube – Gemeinde – Amt*, 111-113) holds that the episcopate derives from Hellenistic circles and that the presbyterate originated in the synagogue, a position that has not won universal approval.

[120] C. SPICQ, *Saint Paul*, II, 739.

makes a similar identification[121], though Kelly and Hanson both think that the emphasis here is on the succession of orthodox teaching than on ministerial office[122].

To distinguish between the teaching and the one who teaches, as Kelly and Hanson do, however logical it may seem, is anachronistic when applied to the Pastoral Epistles in general and 2 Tim in particular. The «faithful men» of 2 Tim 2:2 are ἱκανοί (qualified, competent, able)[123] to teach precisely because they are faithful; indeed, it is their fidelity which so equips them to undertake the office of teaching. Consequently, Spicq and Knight are right to have identified these «faithful men» of 2 Tim 2:2 with the presbyter-bishops of Tit 1:6-9 whose primary responsibilities include teaching.

It may be possible that the Pastor has encouraged the growth of the presbyterate-episcopate and the diaconate precisely because he is attempting to preserve the Pauline heritage from forces which would otherwise destroy it. In fact, M. Y. MacDonald claims that «the need to protect the community against the destructive forces of false teaching seems to have been the major factor providing impetus for the institutionalization process»[124]. In the light of this understanding of the purpose of these church offices, a good case can be made that the Pastor's initiative with respect to the qualifications for presbyter-bishop and deacon should be seen as an inspired and creative attempt to preserve the freedom of the Christian in the face of those who seek to restrict it in the name of tradition and genealogy.

## 5.3 Frühkatholizismus *and the Pauline heritage*

It no longer seems possible, then, to maintain the position enunciated by Käsemann that the emergence of what he called *Frühkatholizismus* must be attributed to the delay of the parousia. For Käsemann, «early catholicism means [...] the transition from earliest Christianity to the so-called ancient Church, which is completed with the disappearance of the imminent expectation» of the Lord's return[125]. *Frühkatholizismus* be-

---

[121] G. W. KNIGHT, *The Pastoral Epistles*, 391-392.

[122] J. N. D. KELLY, *Commentary*, 174; A. T. HANSON, *The Pastoral Epistles*, 128-129.

[123] G. W. KNIGHT, *The Pastoral Epistles*, 392.

[124] M. Y. MACDONALD, *The Pauline Churches*, 220.

[125] E. KÄSEMANN, «Paul and Early Catholicism», 236-237.

comes, in this understanding of the history of the early Church, an accommodation to the world as well as a departure from the apostolic faith in such a way that Spirit-driven spontaneity is replaced by hierarchical structure, and faith as an on-going response to the call of the Gospel is transformed into a «deposit» which exists to be preserved and handed on intact.

Yet, in the light of MacDonald's investigations into the place of institutionalisation in the churches which Paul himself founded, Käsemann's understanding of the emergence of *Frühkatholizismus* seems to be somewhat naïve. Far from being a simple response to the delay of the Lord's return, the phenomenon of institutionalisation is a function of the growth of the early church. MacDonald describes the dynamic of growth and institutionalisation in the Pauline churches:

> As groups grow, they require greater organisation. The multiplication of tasks involves a division of labour. A segmentation of the institutional order occurs with only certain individuals performing certain rôles. In the Pauline sect, the multiplication of tasks and differentiation of rôles is clearly present. There are apostles, fellow workers, local leaders and members of communities. There are also powerful figures in Jerusalem to whom Paul and his churches are somehow connected[126].

MacDonald has identified the «authority structures» in Pauline churches, the foremost among which is Paul's own authority as an apostle[127]. D. L. Bartlett maintains that Paul's associates, Timothy especially, functioned as «apostles from the apostle». His reading of Phil 2:19-22, in which Timothy is described as Paul's son, asserts that Paul cannot simply assume that the Philippians will accept Timothy as Paul's surrogate; instead, Paul must argue for it on the basis of Timothy's interest in the welfare of the Philippian church, and his devotion to Paul[128].

Beyond the personal apostolic authority of Paul himself and his surrogates, however, there are other positions of authority within the churches that he founded: 1 Cor 12:28 testifies to the variety of those positions and their relative importance, at least in the eyes of Paul. Meeks would characterise these as local leaders, and in comparing the lists and functions of 1 Cor 12:28-30, 1 Cor 12:8-10, Rom 12:6-8, and Eph 4:11, con-

---

[126] M. Y. MacDonald, *The Pauline Churches*, 46.

[127] M. Y. MacDonald, *The Pauline Churches*, 46-51. See also W. A. Meeks, *The First Urban Christians*, 131-133.

[128] D. L. Bartlett, *Ministry*, 40.

cludes that there was considerable local variation in the way in which these offices configured themselves[129]. Both MacDonald and Meeks agree that the lists indicate that some degree of formalisation has already taken place, even within the lifetime of Paul himself[130].

To imagine, then, that the Pauline church was prompted solely by the impulses of the Spirit and lacked altogether any sort of enduring structures whereby the Gospel might be preached within the community is to play false with human nature and the evidence that has been preserved in the *homologoumena*. And thus, what has been called «emerging Catholicism» in the Pastoral Epistles, and too often looked upon as a betrayal of the Pauline legacy, may well have been intended by the Pastor as a way precisely to preserve a Pauline understanding of ministry in the face of a conservative retrenchment. If that is the case, I cannot agree with the negative assessment typical of scholars like James D. G. Dunn:

> [W]e must note [...] that the finely tuned balance Paul had achieved between prophecy and teaching, that is between new revelations of the ever-present eschatological Spirit and the passing on and interpretation of established tradition, seems to have gone. Wholly dominant is the concern to preserve the doctrinal statements of the past — the «sound teaching/doctrine», «the faithful sayings», «the sound words», «the faith». The Spirit has become the power to guard the heritage of tradition handed on from the past [...] And even Paul himself is depicted more as the keeper of tradition than as its author [...] Clearly then the vision of charismatic community has faded, ministry and authority have become the prerogative of the few. The experience of the Christ-Spirit has lost its vitality, the preservation of the past has become more important than openness to the present and future. *Spirit and charisma have become in effect subordinate to office, to ritual, to tradition* — early Catholicism indeed[131]!

Dunn's assessment of the move towards institutionalization is largely if not wholly negative, and grounded in the sense that since the «authentic» Pauline churches lacked any structures beyond what the Spirit directed, any movement in the direction of institutionalization must be, by definition, a departure from the Pauline heritage. I do not think the data, either with respect to the Pauline churches, or with respect to the deutero-Pauline churches, can support such a contention.

---

[129] W. A. MEEKS, *The First Urban Christians*, 135.

[130] W. A. MEEKS, *The First Urban Christians*, 135; M. Y. MACDONALD, *The Pauline Churches*, 57.

[131] J. D. G. DUNN, *Jesus and the Spirit*, 348-349. Emphasis in the original.

## 5.4 *Conclusions*

If the Pastor's aim was to bring the Pauline tradition as he understands it to bear on the crisis facing the Pastor's church, he may be judged to have accomplished his goal: his opponents have been branded by none other than Paul himself as «men of corrupt mind and counterfeit faith» (ἄνθρωποι κατεφθαρμένοι τὸν νοῦν, ἀδόκιμοι περὶ τὴν πίστιν: 2 Tim 3:8) and their positions have been dismissed as so much «profane chatter» (βεβήλους κενοφωνίας: 2 Tim 2:16). And, if my analysis of the polemic in the Pastoral Epistles is correct, and the Pastor has sought to thwart the claims of those who sought to exercise leadership in this deutero-Pauline community on the grounds of their genealogical credentials, then the Pastor's programme may be termed a complete success. With all the authority of a dying Moses, the Pastor's Paul bestows his spirit on his successor, Timothy, who in his turn, like Joshua, is thereby empowered to lead his people henceforth. As the legitimate successor to Paul, Timothy will then pass on to «faithful men who will be able to teach others also» what he has heard from Paul. Thanks to the work of the Pastor, there will be a chain of continuity which links one generation to the next in the Church, but it will not be forged of something so fragile as flesh.

# ABBREVIATIONS

| | |
|---|---|
| AnBib | Analecta Biblica |
| AncB | Anchor Bible |
| *AncBD* | *The Anchor Bible Dictionary*, ed. D. N. Freedman, New York 1992 |
| AncBRL | Anchor Bible Reference Library |
| ACNT | Augsburg Commentary on the New Testament |
| ALGHL | Arbeiten zur Literatur und Geschichte des hellenistischen Judentums |
| *AM* | *Assumption of Moses* |
| *ANRW* | *Aufstieg und Niedergang der römischen Welt* |
| ATD | Das Alte Testament Deutsch |
| *AUSS* | *Andrews University Seminary Studies* |
| BCE | before the Common Era |
| BEThL | Bibliotheca Ephemeridum Theologicarum Lovaniensium |
| BEvTh | Beiträge zur evangelischen Theologie |
| *BHS* | *Biblica Hebraica Stuttgartensia* |
| *Bib* | *Biblica* |
| *BJRL* | *Bulletin of the John Rylands Library* |
| BJSt | Brown Judaic Studies |
| BNTC | Black's New Testament Commentaries |
| *BR* | *Bible Review* |
| *BiTod* | *Bible Today* |
| *BTB* | *Biblical Theology Bulletin* |
| CB | The Computer Bible |
| CBC | Cambridge Bible Commentary |
| *CBQ* | *Catholic Biblical Quarterly* |
| CBQMS | CBQ Monograph Series |
| CE | Common Era |
| ColBibCom | Collegeville Bible Commentary |
| CRINT | Compendia Rerum Iudicarum ad Novum Testamentum |
| *CTR* | *Catholic Theological Review* |
| DBI | *A Dictionary of Biblical Interpretation*, ed. R. J. Coggins -- J. L. Houlden, London – Philadelphia 1990 |
| Diss | dissertation |

| | |
|---|---|
| *EDNT* | *Exegetisches Wörterbuch zum Neuen Testament*, ed. H. Balz – G. Schneider, Stuttgart 1978-1981; Eng: *Exegetical Dictionary of the New Testament*, Grand Rapids 1990-1993 |
| *EEC* | *Encyclopedia of Early Christianity*, ed. E. Ferguson, New York – London 1990 |
| *EJMI* | *Early Judaism and Its Modern Interpreters*, ed. R. A. Kraft – G. W. E. Nickelsburg, Philadelphia – Atlanta 1986 |
| EKKNT | Evangelisch-Katholischer Kommentar zum Neuen Testament |
| *ER* | *Encyclopedia of Religion*, ed. M. Eliade – C. Adams, New York 1987 |
| Eng | English translation |
| *ET* | *Expository Times* |
| FRLANT | Forschungen zur Religion und Literatur des Alten und Neuen Testaments |
| Fs. | *Festschrift* |
| *FV* | *Foi et Vie* |
| GNS | Good News Studies |
| *HBC* | *Harper's Bible Commentary*, ed. J. L. Mays, San Francisco 1988 |
| *HBD* | *Harper's Bible Dictionary*, ed. P. Achtemeier, San Francisco 1985 |
| HNTC | Harper's New Testament Commentaries |
| *HThR* | *Harvard Theological Review* |
| HThS | Harvard Theological Studies |
| *IBSt* | *Irish Biblical Studies* |
| ICC | International Critical Commentary |
| *Interp* | *Interpretation* |
| *IDB* | *Interpreter's Dictionary of the Bible*, ed. G. A. Buttrick, New York – Nashville 1962 |
| *IDB* Sup | *IDB Supplementary Volume*, ed. K. Crim, Nashville 1976 |
| *IThQ* | *Irish Theological Quarterly* |
| *JA* | *Jewish Antiquities* |
| *JAAR* | *Journal of the American Academy of Religion* |
| *JBL* | *Journal of Biblical Literature* |
| *JCPW* | *Jews and Christians: The Parting of the Ways*, ed. J. D. G. Dunn, Tübingen 1992 |
| *JETS* | *Journal of the Evangelical Theological Society* |
| *JJS* | *Journal of Jewish Studies* |
| *JQR* | *The Jewish Quarterly Review* |
| *JR* | *Journal of Religion* |
| *JSHRZ* | *Jüdisches Schriften aus hellenistisch-römischer Zeit* |
| *JSJ* | *Journal for the Study of Judaism* |
| *JSNT* | *Journal for the Study of the New Testament* |
| *JSNT.S* | *Journal for the Study of the New Testament* Supplement Series |
| *JSOT* | *Journal for the Study of the Old Testament* |
| JSOT.S | *Journal for the Study of the Old Testament* Supplement Series |

| | |
|---|---|
| *JSP* | *Journal for the Study of the Pseudepigrapha* |
| *JThS* | *Journal of Theological Studies* |
| KEK | Kritisch-Exegetischer Kommentar über das Neue Testament |
| *LAB* | *Liber Antiquitatum Biblicarum* |
| LCL | Loeb Classical Library |
| LEC | Library of Early Christianity |
| *LTP* | *Laval Theologique et Philosophique* |
| MSSNTS | Monograph Series: Society for New Testament Studies |
| NAC | New American Commentary |
| NCeBC | New Century Bible Commentary |
| NICNT | New International Commentary on the New Testament |
| NICOT | New International Commentary on the Old Testament |
| NIGTC | New International Greek Testament Commentary |
| *NJBC* | *New Jerome Biblical Commentary*, ed. R. E. Brown − J. A. Fitzmyer − R. E. Murphy, Englewood Cliffs 1990 |
| *NT* | *Novum Testamentum* |
| NTM | New Testament Message |
| NT.S | Supplements to *Novum Testamentum* |
| NTD | Das Neue Testament Deutsch |
| *NTS* | *New Testament Studies* |
| ÖBS | Österreichische Biblische Studien |
| *OCD* | *The Oxford Classical Dictionary*, ed. N. G. L. Hammond − H. H. Scullard, Oxford 1970$^2$ |
| *OJRS* | *Ohio Journal of Religious Studies* |
| OTL | The Old Testament Library |
| OTM | Old Testament Message |
| *OTPs* | *The Old Testament Pseudepigrapha*, ed. J. H. Charlesworth, New York 1983-1985 |
| *PIBA* | *Proceedings of the Irish Biblical Association* |
| PNTC | Pelican New Testament Commentaries |
| *PerRS* | *Perspectives on Religious Studies* |
| *RB* | *Revue Biblique* |
| *RivBib* | *Rivista Biblica Italiana* |
| RNT | Regensburger Neues Testament |
| *RevSR* | *Revue des sciences religieuses* |
| rprnt | reprint |
| SBi | Sources bibliques |
| SBL | Society of Biblical Literature |
| SBLDS | SBL Dissertation Series |
| SBLMS | SBL Monograph Series |
| SBLSCS | SBL Septuagint and Cognate Studies |
| SBLSBS | SBL Sources for Biblical Study |
| SBT | Studies in Biblical Theology |
| SC | Sources chrétiennes |

| | |
|---|---|
| *ScEs* | *Science et ésprit* |
| *Schol* | *Scholastik* |
| Sem. | Semitica |
| *SP* | *Studia Philonica* |
| *SPA* | *Studia Philonica Annual* |
| *STM* | *Studies on the Testament of Moses*, ed. G. W. E. Nickelsburg, Cambridge 1973 |
| *TDNT* | *Theologisches Wörterbuch zum Neuen Testament*, ed. G. Kittel – G. Friedrich, Stuttgart 1933-1973; Eng: *Theological Dictionary of the New Testament*, Grand Rapids 1964-1976 |
| *TDOT* | *Theologisches Wörterbuch zum Alten Testament*, ed. G. Booterweck – H. Ringgren, Stuttgart 1970-1982; Eng: *Theological Dictionary of the Old Testament*, Grand Rapids 1974-1990 |
| *Theol* | *Theology* |
| *ThLZ* | *Theologische Literaturzeitung* |
| *TM* | *Testament of Moses* |
| TNTC | Tyndale New Testament Commentaries |
| TOTC | Tyndale Old Testament Commentaries |
| TPINTC | Trinity Press International New Testament Commentaries |
| *USQR* | *Union Seminary Quarterly Review* |
| *VigChr* | *Vigiliae Christianae* |
| VigChr.S | Supplements to *Vigiliae Christianae* |
| *VM* | *Vita Mosis* |
| *VT* | *Vetus Testamentum* |
| WBC | Word Biblical Commentary |
| WMANT | Wissenschaftliche Monographien zum Alten und Neuen Testament |
| WUNT | Wissenschaftliche Untersuchungen zum Neuen Testament |
| ZBK | Zürcher Bibelkommentar |
| *ZNW* | *Zeitschrift für die neutestamentliche Wissenschaft* |

# SELECTED BIBLIOGRAPHY

## 1. Texts and Translations

ALAND, K. – BLACK, M. – MARTINI, C. M. – METZGER, B. M. – WIKGREN, A., ed., *Novum Testamentum Graece*, Stuttgart 1986²⁶.

ANDERSON, H., «4 Maccabees: A New Translation and Introduction», *OTPs* II, 531-564.

ARISTOTLE, *Rhetoric*, trans. J. H. Freese, LCL 193, London – Cambridge, MA 1926; rprnt 1991.

———, *Poetics*, trans. W. H. Fyfe, LCL 199, Cambridge, MA 1932; rprnt 1991.

CHARLES, R. H., ed., *The Assumption of Moses, translated from the Latin Sixth Century MS*, London 1897.

CHARLESWORTH, J. H., ed., *The Old Testament Pseudepigrapha*, Garden City 1983-1985.

CONFRATERNITY OF CHRISTIAN DOCTRINE, *The New American Bible*, New York 1970, 1986.

*De Ratione Dicendi (Rhetorica Ad Herennium)*, trans. H. Caplan, LCL 403, London – Cambridge, MA 1954; rprnt 1989.

DIVISION OF CHRISTIAN EDUCATION OF THE NATIONAL COUNCIL OF THE CHURCHES OF CHRIST IN THE UNITED STATES OF AMERICA, *The Holy Bible*, Revised Standard Version, New York 1973.

ELLIGER, K. – RUDOLPH, W., ed., *Biblica Hebraica Stuttgartensia*, Stuttgart 1977.

FLAVIUS JOSEPHUS, *Jewish Antiquities: Books I–XX*, trans. H. St. J. Thackeray – R. Marcus – L. H. Feldman, LCL 242, 281, 326, 365, 456, London – Cambridge, MA 1930-1965; rprnt 1967-1987.

———, *The Life and Against Apion*, trans. H. St. J. Thackeray, LCL 186, Cambridge, MA 1966.

HARRINGTON, D. J., «Pseudo-Philo: A New Translation and Introduction», *OTPs* II, 298-377.

———— – CAZEAUX, J. – PERROT, C. – BOGAERT, P. M., *Pseudo-Philon: Les Antiquités Bibliques*, SC 229-230, Paris 1976.

KIRCH, C., *Enchiridion Fontium Historiae Ecclesiasticae Antiquae*, ed. L. Ueding, Barcelona 1965.

LAPERROUSAZ, E. M., *Le Testament de Moïse (généralement appelé «Assomption de Moïse»): Traduction avec introduction et notes*, Sem. 19, Paris 1970.

MALHERBE, A. J., *The Cynic Epistles*, SBLSBS 12, Atlanta 1977; rprnt 1986.

PHILO JUDAEUS, *De Legatione*, trans. F. H. Colson, LCL 379, London – Cambridge, MA 1962; rprnt 1971.

————, *De Virtutibus*, trans. F. H. Colson, LCL 341, Cambridge, MA 1939; rprnt 1989.

————, *De Vita Mosis*, trans. F. H. Colson, LCL 289, London – Cambridge, MA 1935; rprnt 1984.

————, *Hypothetica (Apologia Pro Iudaeis)*, trans. F. H. Colson, LCL 363, Cambridge, MA 1941; rprnt 1985.

————, *In Flaccum*, trans. F. H. Colson, LCL 363, London – Cambridge, MA 1941; rprnt 1985.

————, *Quaestiones et Solutiones in Exodum*, trans. R. Marcus, LCL 401, London – Cambridge, MA 1953; rprnt 1987.

————, *Quaestiones et Solutiones in Genesin*, trans. R. Marcus, LCL 380, London – Cambridge, MA 1953; rprnt 1993.

PIETERSMA, A. – LUTZ, R. T., «Jannes and Jambres: A New Translation and Introduction», *OTPs* II, 427-442.

PLATO, *Phaedo*, trans. H. N. Fowler, LCL 36, London – Cambridge, MA 1914; rprnt 1990.

————, *The Republic*, trans. P. Shorey, LCL 237, 276, London – Cambridge, MA 1930-1935; rprnt 1982-1987.

PRIEST, J., trans., «The Testament of Moses: A New Translation and Introduction», *OTPs* I, 919-934.

PSEUDO-PHILO, *The Biblical Antiquities of Philo*, trans. M. R. James, with a prolegomenon by L. J. Feldman, London – New York 1971.

QUINTILIANUS, MARCUS FABIUS, *Institutio Oratoria*, trans. H. E. Butler, LCL 124-127, London – Cambridge, MA 1966-1969.

RAHLFS, A., ed., *Septuaginta*, Stuttgart 1935; rprnt 1979.

TROMP, J., *The Assumption of Moses: A Critical Edition with Commentary*, Leiden 1993.


## 2. The Pastoral Epistles: Commentaries and Monographs

ALAND, K., «The Problem of Anonymity and Pseudonymity in Christian Literature of the First Two Centuries», *JThS* 12 (1961) 39-49.

ALLEN, J. A., «The "In-Christ" Formula in the Pastoral Epistles», *NTS* 10 (1963) 115-121.

BARNETT, A. E., *Paul Becomes a Literary Influence*, Chicago 1941.

BARRETT, C. K., *The Pastoral Epistles*, Oxford 1963.

————, «Pauline Controversies in the Post-Pauline Period», *NTS* 20 (1973-1974) 235-245.

BASSLER, J. M., «The Widow's Tale: A Fresh Look at 1 Tim 5:3-16», *JBL* 103 (1984) 23-41.

BEKER, J. C., *Heirs of Paul: Paul's Legacy in the New Testament and in the Church Today*, Minneapolis 1992.

BETZ, H. D., «Review of *The Function of Personal Example in the Socratic and Pastoral Epistles* by Benjamin Fiore», *JBL* 107 (1988) 335-337.

DE BOER, M. C., «Images of Paul in the Post-Apostolic Period», *CBQ* 42 (1980) 359-380.

BROWN, R. E., *The Churches the Apostles Left Behind*, New York 1984.

————, «Not Jewish Christianity and Gentile Christianity, but Types of Jewish/Gentile Christianity», *CBQ* 45 (1983) 74-79.

BROX, N., *Die Pastoralbriefe*, RNT 7, Regensberg 1969.

BUSH, P. G., «A Note on the Structure of 1 Timothy», *NTS* 36 (1990) 152-156.

COLLINS, R. F., *Letters That Paul Did Not Write: The Epistle to the Hebrews and the Pauline Pseudepigrapha*, GNS 28, Wilmington 1988.

————, «The Image of Paul in the Pastorals», *LTP* 31 (1975) 147-173.

COLSON, F. H., «"Myths and Genealogies" – A Note on the Polemic of the Pastoral Epistles», *JThS* 19 (1918) 268.

DALTON, W. J., «Pseudepigraphy in the New Testament», *CTR* 5 (1983) 29-35.

DEWEY, J., «1 Timothy, 2 Timothy, Titus», *WBC*, 353-361.

DIBELIUS, M .– H. CONZELMANN., *Die Pastoralbriefe*, Tübingen 1955[4]; Eng: *The Pastoral Epistles*, trans. P. Buttolph – A. Yarbro, Hermeneia, Philadelphia 1972.

DONELSON, L. R., *Pseudepigraphy and Ethical Argument in the Pastoral Epistles*, Hermeneutische Untersuchungen zur Theologie 22, Tübingen 1986.

———, «The Structure of Ethical Argument in the Pastorals», *BTB* 18 (1988) 108-113.

DORNIER, P., *Les Épîtres Pastorales*, SBi, Paris 1969.

ELLIOTT, J. H., «A Catholic Gospel: Reflections on "Early Catholicism" in the New Testament», *CBQ* 31 (1969) 312-323.

———, «Ministry and Church Order in the New Testament», *CBQ* 32 (1970) 367-391.

ELLIS, E. E., «The Pastorals and Paul», *ET* 104 (1992) 45-47.

FABRIS, R., *Le Lettere Pastorali*, Brescia 1986.

———, «Il Paolinismo nelle Lettere Pastorali», *RivBib* 34 (1986) 451-470.

FEE, G. D., *1 & 2 Timothy, Titus*, San Francisco 1984.

———, «Reflections on Church Order in the Pastoral Epistles, with Further Reflections on the Hermeneutics of Ad-Hoc Documents», *JETS* 28 (1985) 141-151.

FIORE, B., *The Function of Personal Example in the Socratic and Pastoral Epistles*, AnBib 105, Rome 1986.

FORD, J. M., «Proto-Montanism in the Pastoral Epistles», *NTS* 17 (1970-71) 338-346.

FULLER, R., «The Pastoral Epistles», *Ephesians, Colossians, 2 Thessalonians, The Pastoral Epistles*, Philadelphia 1978, 97-121.

GUTHRIE, D., *The Pastoral Epistles*, TNTC, Grand Rapids 1982.

HANSON, A. T., *Studies in the Pastoral Epistles*, London 1968.

———, *The Pastoral Epistles*, NCeBC, Grand Rapids 1982.

———, «The Domestication of Paul: A Study in the Development of Early Christian Theology», *BJRL* 63 (1981) 402-418.

———, «The Use of the Old Testament in the Pastoral Epistles», *IBSt* 3 (1981) 203-219.

HARRISON, P. N., *The Problem of the Pastoral Epistles*, London 1921.

HASLER, V., *Die Briefe an Timotheus und Titus: Pastoralbriefe*, ZBK 12, Zurich 1978.

HOLTZ, G., *Die Pastoralbriefe*, THKNT 13, Berlin 1972².

HOULDEN, J. L., *The Pastoral Epistles*, PNTC, Harmondsworth 1976.

HULTGREN, A. J., *I – II Timothy, Titus*, ACNT, Minneapolis 1984.

JEREMIAS, J. – STROBEL, A., *Die Briefe an Timotheus und Titus. Die Brief an die Hebraer*, NTD 9, Göttingen 1975.

JOHNSON, L. T., «II Timothy and the Polemic Against False Teachers: A Re-Examination», *OJRS* 6-7 (1978-79) 1-26.

————, «Review of *Paul the Letter-Writer and the Second Letter to Timothy* by Michael Prior», *CBQ* 53 (1991) 339-341.

KARRIS, R. J., *The Pastoral Epistles*, Wilmington 1979.

————, «Review of *The Function of Personal Example in the Socratic and Pastoral Epistles* by Benjamin Fiore», *CBQ* 50 (1988) 134-135.

————, «The Background and Significance of the Polemic of the Pastoral Epistles», *JBL* 92 (1973) 549-564.

KÄSEMANN, E., «Paul and Early Catholicism», *New Testament Questions of Today*, Philadelphia 1969, 236-251.

KELLY, J. N. D., *A Commentary on the Pastoral Epistles: I Timothy, II Timothy and Titus*, BNTC, London 1963; rprnt 1986.

KIDD, R. M., *Wealth and Beneficence in the Pastoral Epistles*, SBLDS 122, Atlanta 1990.

KITTEL, G., «Die *Genealogiai* der Pastoralbriefe», *ZNW* 20 (1920-21) 49-69.

KNIGHT, G. W., *The Pastoral Epistles: A Commentary on the Greek Text*, NIGTC, Grand Rapids 1992.

KNOCH, O., *Die «Testament» des Petrus und Paulus*, Stuttgart 1973, 44-64.

LEA, T. D. – GRIFFIN, H. P., *1, 2 Timothy and Titus*, NAC 34, Nashville 1992.

LEMAIRE, A., «Pastoral Epistles: Redaction and Theology», *BTB* 2 (1972) 25-42.

DE LESTAPIS, S., *L'Énigme des Pastorales de St. Paul*, Paris 1976.

LOCK, W., *A Critical and Exegetical Commentary on the Pastoral Epistles*, ICC, Edinburgh 1952.

MACDONALD, M. Y., *The Pauline Churches: A Socio-historical Study of Institutionalization in the Pauline and Deutero-Pauline Churches*, MSSNTS 60, Cambridge 1988.

MALHERBE, A., «In Season and Out of Season: 2 Tim 4:2», *JBL* 103 (1984) 235-243.

MALONEY, E. C., «Biblical Authorship and the Pastoral Letters: Inspired and Anonymous», *BiTod* 24 (1986) 119-123.

MARSHALL, I. H., «"Early Catholicism" in the New Testament», *New Dimensions in New Testament Study*, ed. R. Longenecker – M. Tenney, Grand Rapids 1974, 217-231.

———, «Review of *Luke and the Pastoral Epistles* by Stephen G. Wilson», *JSNT* 10 (1981) 69-74.

MARTIN, R. P., «1, 2 Timothy and Titus», *HBC*, 1237-1244.

MCELENEY, N. J., «Vice Lists in the Pastoral Epistles», *CBQ* 36 (1974) 204.

MEIER, J. P., «Presbyteros in the Pastoral Epistles», *CBQ* 35 (1973) 323-245.

MERKEL, H. *Die Pastoralbriefe*, NTD 9/1, Göttingen 1991.

METZGER, B. M., «Literary Forgeries and Canonical Pseudepigrapha», *JBL* 91 (1972) 3-24.

MORTON, A. Q. – MICHAELSON, S. – THOMPSON, J. D., *A Critical Concordance to the Pastoral Epistles*, CB 25, Wooster, OH 1982.

MOTT, S. C., «Greek Ethics and Christian Conversion: the Philonic Background of Titus ii 10-14 and iii 3-7», *NT* 20 (1978) 22-48.

MUNCK, J., «Discours d'adieu dans le Nouveau Testament et dans la littérature biblique», *Aux sources de la tradition chrétienne*, Fs. Maurice Goguel, Neuchâtel – Paris 1950.

MURPHY-O'CONNOR, J., «2 Timothy Contrasted with 1 Timothy and Titus», *RB* 98 (1991) 403-418.

NEILSEN, C. M., «Scripture in the Pastoral Epistles», *PerRS* 7 (1980) 4-23.

NEYREY, J., *First Timothy, Second Timothy, Titus, James, First Peter, Second Peter, Jude*, ColBibCom 9, Collegeville 1983.

OSIEK, C., «Women's Rôle in the Pastorals», *BiTod* 24 (1985) 246-247.

PADGETT, A., «Wealthy Women at Ephesus: 1 Tim 2:8-15 in Social Context», *Interp* 41 (1987) 19-31.

PRIOR, M., *Paul the Letter-Writer*, JSNT.S 23, Sheffield 1989.

QUINN, J. D., *The Letter to Titus*, AncB 35, New York 1990.

QUINN, J. D., «On the Terminology for Faith, Truth, Teaching and the Spirit in the Pastoral Epistles: A Summary», *Teaching Authority and Infallibility in the Church*, ed. P. Empie, Minneapolis 1980, 232-237.

————, «Parenesis and the Pastoral Epistles», *De la Tôrah au Messie*, Fs. Henri Cazelles, Paris 1981.

————, «The Last Volume of Luke: the Relation of Luke – Acts to the Pastoral Epistles», *Perspectives on Luke – Acts*, ed. C. H. Talbert, Edinburgh 1978.

————, «The Pastoral Epistles», *BiTod* 23 (1985) 228-238.

————, «The Pastoral Epistles on Righteousness», *«Righteousness» in the New Testament: «Justification» in the United States Lutheran – Roman Catholic Dialogue*, ed. J. Reumann, Philadelphia – New York 1982, 231-238.

————, «Timothy and Titus, Epistles to», *AncBD* VI, 560-571.

REISER, M., «Bürgerliches Christentum in den Pastoralbriefen?», *Bib* 74 (1993) 27-44.

RENGSTORF, K. H., «νομοδιδάσκαλος», *TDNT* II, 159.

RIECKE, B., «Chronologie des Pastoralbriefe», *ThLZ* 101 (1976) 81-94.

ROBINSON, T. A., «Grayston and Herdon's "C" Quantity Formula and the Authorship of the Pastoral Epistles», *NTS* 30 (1984) 282-288.

ROGERS, P., «The Few in Charge of the Many», Diss. Pontifical Gregorian University 1970.

————, «The Pastoral Epistles as Deutero-Pauline», *IThQ* 45 (1978) 248-260.

SCHLOSSER, J., «La didascalie et ses agents dans l'épîtres pastorales», *RevSR* 59 (1985) 81-94.

SCHWARTZ, R., *Burgerliches Christentum im Neuen Testament: Eine Studie zu Ethik, Amt, und Recht in den Pastoralbriefen*, ÖBS 4, Klosterneuberg 1983.

SCOTT, E. F., *The Pastoral Epistles*, London 1936.

SPICQ, C., *Saint Paul: Les Épîtres Pastorales*, 2 vols., Paris 1969[4].

TAYLOR, W., «1 – 2 Timothy, Titus», *The Deutero-Pauline Letters: Ephesians, Colossians, 2 Thessalonians, 1-2 Timothy, Titus*, Minneapolis 1993[2], 59-93.

TOWNER, P. H., *The Goal of Our Instruction: The Structure of Theology and Ethics in the Pastoral Epistles*, JSNT.S 34, Sheffield 1989.

TOWNER, P. H., «Gnosis and Realised Eschatology in Ephesus (of the Pastoral Epistles) and the Corinthian Enthusiasm», *JSNT* 31 (1987) 95-124.

————, «The Present Age in the Eschatology of the Pastoral Epistles», *NTS* 32 (1986) 427-448.

TRUMMER, P., *Die Paulustradition der Pastoralbriefe*, BEvTh, Frankfurt 1978.

VERNER, D., *The Household of God: The Social World of the Pastoral Epistles*, SBLDS 71, Chico 1983.

VIVIANO, B. T., «The Genres of Matthew 1–2: Light from 1 Timothy 1:4», *RB* 97 (1990) 31-53.

VON LIPS, H., *Glaube – Gemeinde – Amt: Zum Verstandnis der Ordination in den Pastoralbriefen*, FRLANT 122, Göttingen 1979.

WHITE, J. L., «Saint Paul and the Apostolic Letter Tradition», *CBQ* 45 (1983) 433-444.

WILD, R. A., «The Image of Paul in the Pastoral Epistles», *BiTod* 23 (1985) 239-245.

————, «The Pastoral Letters», *NJBC*, 891-902.

WILSON, S. G., *Luke and the Pastoral Epistles*, London 1979.

WOLTER, M., *Die Pastoralbriefe als Paulustradition*, Göttingen 1988.

WUEST, K. S., *The Pastoral Epistles in the Greek New Testament*, Grand Rapids 1952.

YOUNG, F., «The Pastoral Epistles and the Ethics of Reading», *JSNT* 45 (1992) 105-120.

## 3. Other Works Consulted

ABBA, R., «Priests and Levites», *IDB* III, 876-889.

ACHTEMEIER, E., *Deuteronomy, Jeremiah*, Philadelphia 1978.

ACHTEMEIER, P. J., gen. ed., *Harper's Bible Dictionary*, San Francisco 1985.

ACKROYD, P. R. – EVANS, C. F., ed., *The Cambridge History of the Bible: From the Beginnings to Jerome*, Cambridge 1970.

ALBRIGHT, W. F., «Some Remarks on the Song of Moses in Deuteronomy XXXII», *VT* 9 (1959) 339-346.

ALEXANDER, P. S., «Targum, Targumim», *AncBD* VI, 320-331.

ALETTI, J. N., *Comment Dieu est-il juste? Clefs pour interpréter l'epître aux Romains*, Paris 1991.

ALETTI, J. N., «La présence d'un modèle rhétorique en Romains: son rôle et son importance», *Bib* 71 (1990) 1-24.

————, «Rom 1:18–3:30: Incohérence ou cohérence de l'argumentation paulinienne?», *Bib* 69 (1988) 54-61.

ALLISON, D. C., *The New Moses: A Matthean Typology*, Minneapolis 1993.

ALONSO SCHÖKEL, L., *A Manual of Hebrew Poetics*, Rome 1988.

ALTER, R., *The Art of Biblical Narrative*, New York 1981.

————, *The Art of Biblical Poetry*, Edinburgh 1990.

———— – KERMODE, F., ed., *The Literary Guide to the Bible*, London 1989.

ANDERSON, B. W. – HARRELSON, W., ed., *Israel's Prophetic Heritage*, Fs. James Muilenburg, New York 1962.

APPLEBAUM, S., «Jews in North Africa», *AncBD* III, 1072-1073.

ARGYLE, A. W., «Philo: the Man and His Work», *ET* 85 (1974) 115-117.

ASTIUS, D. F., *Lexicon Platonicum sive Vocum Platonicarum Index*, Leipzig 1835.

ATTRIDGE, H. W., *The Interpretation of Biblical History in the* Antiquitates Judaicae *of Flavius Josephus*, Missoula 1976.

————, «Josephus and His Works», *Jewish Writings of the Second Temple Period*, ed. M. E. Stone, CRINT II/2, Assen – Philadelphia 1984, 185-232.

————, trans., «The Ascension of Moses and the Heavenly Jerusalem», *STM*, 122-125.

AUERBACH, E., *Moses*, Detroit 1975.

AULD, A. G., *Joshua, Moses and the Land: Tetrateuch, Pentateuch, Hexateuch in a Generation Since 1938*, Edinburgh 1980.

AUNE, D. E., *The New Testament in Its Literary Environment*, LEC 8, Philadelphia 1987.

AUS, R., *II Thessalonians*, ACNT, Minneapolis 1984.

BACON, B. W., «The Five Books of Moses Against the Jews», *Expositor* 15 (1918) 56-66.

BAILEY, J. L. – VANDER BROEK, L. D., *Literary Forms in the New Testament*, London – Louisville 1992.

BALCH, D. L., *Let Wives Be Submissive: The Domestic Code in 1 Peter*, SBLMS 26, Atlanta 1981.

BALTZER, K., *Das Bundesformular*, WMANT 4, Neukirchen-Vluyn 1964²; Eng: *The Covenant Formulary in the Old Testament, Jewish, and Early Christian Writing*, trans. D. E. Green, Philadelphia – Oxford 1971.

BALZ, H. – SCHNEIDER, G., ed., *Exegetisches Wörterbuch zum Neuen Testament*, Stuttgart 1978-1981; Eng: *Exegetical Dictionary of the New Testament*, Grand Rapids 1990-1993.

BARRETT, C. K., *A Commentary on the Epistle to the Romans*, HNTC, New York 1957.

———, *A Commentary on the First Epistle to the Corinthians*, HNTC, New York 1968.

———, «The Interpretation of the Old Testament in the New», *The Cambridge History of the Bible: From the Beginnings to Jerome*, ed. P. R. Ackroyd – C. F. Evans, Cambridge 1970, 377-411.

BARTH, M., *Ephesians 1–3*, AncB 34, Garden City 1974.

———, *Ephesians 4–6*, AncB 34A, Garden City 1974.

BARTLETT, D. L., *Ministry in the New Testament*, Minneapolis 1993.

BARTON, J., «Prophets and Prophecy», *DBI*, 556-559.

BARZANO, A., «Tiberio Giulio Alessandro, Prefetto d'Egitto (66/70)», *ANRW* II.10.1 (1988) 518-580.

BARZEL, H., «Moses: Tragedy and Sublimity», *Literary Interpretations of Biblical Narratives*, ed. K. R. R. Gros Lewis *et al.*, Nashville 1974.

BAUCKHAM, R., *Jude and the Relatives of Jesus in the Early Church*, Edinburgh 1990.

———, «Pseudo-Apostolic Letters», *JBL* 107 (1988) 469-494.

BAUER, W. – ARNDT, W. F. – GINGRICH, F. W. – DANKER, F., ed., *A Greek-English Lexicon of the New Testament and Other Early Christian Literature*, Chicago 1979².

BECKWITH, R., «The Ancient Attitude to Pseudonymity», *The Old Testament Canon of the New Testament Church: and its Background in Early Judaism*, Grand Rapids 1985, 346-358.

BEEGLE, D. M., «Moses: Old Testament», *AncBD* IV, 909-918.

———, *Moses, the Servant of Yahweh*, Grand Rapids 1972.

BEGG, C. T., «The Literary Criticism of Deut 4, 1-40: Contributions to a Continuing Discussion», *ETL* 56 (1980) 10-55.

———, «The Significance of the *Numeruswechsel* in Deuteronomy: the "Prehistory" of the Question», *ETL* 55 (1979) 116-124.

BEGG, C. T., «The Tables (Deut X) and the Lawbook (Deut XXXI)», *VT* 33 (1983) 96s.

BENKO, S., *Pagan Rome and the Early Christians*, Bloomington 1984.

BERCHMAN, R. M., «Philo of Alexandria», *EEC*, 726-727.

BERTHOFF, W., «Fiction, History, Myth: Notes Toward the Discrimination of Narrative Forms», *Fiction and Events*, New York 1971, 30-55.

BETZ, H. D., *Galatians: A Commentary on Paul's Letter to the Churches in Galatia*, Hermeneia, Philadelphia 1979.

————, «In Defense of the Spirit: Paul's Letter to the Galatians as a Document of Early Christian Apologetics», *Aspects of Religious Propaganda in Judaism and Early Christianity*, ed. E. Schüssler Fiorenza, Notre Dame 1976, 99-114.

BICKERMAN, E. J., *The Jews in the Greek Age*, Cambridge, MA 1988.

BLACK, E., *Rhetorical Criticism: A Study in Method*, Madison 1979.

BLACK, M., *Romans*, NCeBC, Grand Rapids – London 1973.

————, *The Scrolls and Christian Origins: Studies in the Jewish Background of the New Testament*, BJSt 48, Chico 1983.

BLASS, F. – DEBRUNNER, A., *A Greek Grammar of the New Testament and Other Early Christian Literature*, trans. R. W. Funk, Chicago 1961.

BLENKINSOPP, J., *The Pentateuch: An Introduction to the First Five Books of the Bible*, AncBRL, New York 1992.

————, *Wisdom and Law in the Old Testament*, Oxford 1983.

————, «Deuteronomy», *NJBC*, 94-109.

BOADT, L., *Reading the Old Testament: An Introduction*, New York 1984.

BOERS, H., «The Form-Critical Study of Paul's Letters: 1 Thess as a Case-Study», *NTS* 22 (1976) 140-158.

BOGAERT, P. M., «Histoire et prophétie dans la composition des Antiquités bibliques du Pseudo-Philon», *À cause de l'Évangile: Études sur les Synoptiques et les Actes*, Fs. Jacques Dupont, Paris 1985.

BOOTERWECK, G. J. – RINGGREN, H., ed., *Theologisches Wörterbuch zum Alten Testament*, Stuttgart 1970-1982; Eng: *Theological Dictionary of the Old Testament*, trans. J. T. Willis – G. W. Bromiley – D. E. Greene, Grand Rapids 1974-1990.

BORGEN, P., «Judaism in Egypt», *AncBD* III, 1061-1072.

————, «Philo of Alexandria», *AncBD* V, 333-342.

BORGEN, P., «Philo of Alexandria», *Jewish Writings of the Second Temple Period*, ed. M. E. Stone, CRINT II/2, Assen – Philadelphia 1984, 233-282.

————, «Philo of Alexandria: A Critical and Synthetical Survey of Research since World War II», *ANRW* II.21.1, 98-154.

BORNKAMM, G., *Paulus*, Stuttgart 1969; Eng: *Paul*, trans. D. M. G. Stalker, New York 1971.

————, BARTH, G. – HELD, H. J., *Überlieferung und Auslegung im Matthäusevangelium*, WMANT 1. Neukirchen 1960; Eng: *Tradition and Interpretation in Matthew*, trans. P. Scott, London 1963.

BOSCH, J. S., «Le charisme des Pasteurs dans le corpus paulinien», *Paul de Tarse: apôtre du notre temps*, ed. L. de Lorenzi, Rome 1979, 363-397.

BOSSMAN, D. M., «Authority and Tradition in First Century Judaism and Christianity», *BTB* 17 (1987) 3-9.

————, «Images of God in the Letters of Paul», *BTB* 18 (1988) 67-76.

BOSTON, J. R., «The Wisdom Influence upon the Song of Moses», *JBL* 87 (1968) 198-202.

BOTTE, B., «La vie de Moïse par Philon», *Moïse, l'homme de l'alliance*, ed. H. Cazelles – A. Gelin *et al.*, Tournai 1955, 55-62.

BRANDENBURGER, E., *Himmelfahrt Moses*, JSHRZ 5.2, ed. W. G. Kümmel, *et al.*, Gütersloh 1976.

BRAULIK, G., *Deuteronomio: il testamento di Mosè*, Assisi 1987.

BRECK, J., «Biblical Chiasmus: Exploring Structure for Meaning», *BTB* 17 (1987) 70-74.

BRIGHT, J., *A History of Israel*, London 1972.

BROOTEN, B. J., *Women Leaders in the Ancient Synagogue: Inscriptional Evidence and Background Issues*, BJSt 36, ed. J. Neusner – W. Dietrich – E. Frerichs – A. Zuckerman, Chico 1982.

BROWN, P., *The Body and Society: Men, Women and Sexual Renunciation in Early Christianity*, London 1988.

BROWN, R. E., *Priest and Bishop: Biblical Reflections*, Paramus 1970.

———— – MEIER, J. P., *Antioch and Rome: New Testament Cradles of Catholic Christianity*, New York 1983.

———— – Fitzmyer, J. A. – MURPHY, R. E., ed., *The New Jerome Biblical Commentary*, London – Englewood Cliffs, NJ 1990.

BRUCE, F. F., *Commentary on the Book of Acts*, London 1954.

—————, *New Testament History*, London 1969.

BÜCHSEL, F., «εἰδωλόθυτον», *TDNT* II, 378-379.

BUDD, P. J., *Numbers*, WBC 5, Waco 1984.

BURKERT, W., *Ancient Mystery Cults*, Cambridge, MA 1987.

BURKITT, F. C., «Assumption of Moses», *Hastings' Dictionary of the Bible*, New York 1901.

BURNS, R. J., *Has the Lord Indeed Spoken Only Through Moses? A Study of the Biblical Portrait of Miriam*, SBLDS 84, Atlanta 1987.

BUTTRICK, G. A., ed., *The Interpreter's Dictionary of the Bible*, New York – Nashville 1962.

BYRNE, B., «The Letter to the Philippians», *NJBC*, 791-797.

CAHILL, P. J., «The Unity of the Bible»,

CANEVET, M., «Remarques sur l'utilisation du genre littéraire historique par Philon d'Alexandrie dans la Vita Moysis, ou Moïse général en chef-prophète», *RevSR* 60 (1986) 189-206.

CARMICHAEL, C. M., *Law and Narrative in the Bible*, Ithaca 1985.

—————, *The Laws of Deuteronomy*, Ithaca 1974.

CARLSON, D. C., «Vengeance and Angelic Mediation in Testament of Moses 9 and 10», *JBL* 101 (1982) 85-95.

CASTELOT, J. J. – CODY, A., «Religious Institutions of Israel», *NJBC*, 1254-1259.

CAZEAUX, J., «Philon d'Alexandrie, exégète», *ANRW* II.21.1, 156-226.

CAZELLES, H., A. GELIN, *et al.*, *Moïse, L'homme de l'alliance*, Paris 1955.

CHARLES, R. H., «The Assumption of Moses: Introduction», *The Apocrypha and Pseudepigrapha of the Old Testament In English*, Vol II: *Pseudepigrapha*, Oxford 1913, 407-413.

CHARLESWORTH, J. H., *Jesus Within Judaism*, AncBRL, New York 1988.

—————, *The Old Testament Pseudepigrapha and the New Testament*, MSSNTS 54, Cambridge 1985.

—————, *The Pseudepigrapha and Modern Research with a Supplement*, SBLSCS 7S, Missoula 1976.

—————, «Biblical Interpretation: The Crucible of the Pseudepigrapha», *Text and Testimony*, Fs. A. F. J. Klijn, Kampen 1988, 66-78.

CHRISTENSEN, D. L., *Deuteronomy 1–11*, WBC 6A, Dallas 1991.

———, «Two Stanzas of a Hymn in Deuteronomy 33», *Bib* 65 (1984) 382-389.

———, ed., *A Song of Power and the Power of Song: Essays on the Book of Deuteronomy*, Winona Lake, IN 1993.

CIPRIANI, S., *Le Lettere di Paolo*, Assisi 1991[7].

CLARK, D. L., *Rhetoric in Greco-Roman Education*, New York 1957.

CLEMENTS, R. E., *Deuteronomy*, Sheffield 1989.

———, *God's Chosen People: A Theological Interpretation of the Book of Deuteronomy*, London 1968.

CLIFFORD, R., *Deuteronomy, with an Excursus on Covenant and Law*, OTM 4, Wilmington 1982.

COATS, G. W., «Healing and the Moses Traditions», *Canon, Theology, and Old Testament Interpretation*, Fs. Brevard S. Childs, Philadelphia 1988, 131-146.

———, «Legendary Motifs in the Moses Death Reports», *CBQ* 39 (1977) 34-44.

———, *Moses: Heroic Man, Man of God*, JSOT.S 57, Sheffield 1988.

———, «The Moses Narratives as Heroic Saga», *Saga, Legend, Tale, Novella, Fable: Narrative Forms in Old Testament Literature*, ed. G. W. Coats, JSOT.S 35, Sheffield 1985; rprnt 1989, 33-44.

CODY, A., *A History of Old Testament Priesthood*, AnBib 35, Rome 1969.

COGGINS, R. J. – HOULDEN, J. L., ed., *A Dictionary of Biblical Interpretation*, London 1990.

COHEN, S. J. D., *From the Maccabees to the Mishnah*, LEC 7, Philadelphia 1987.

———, «Was Timothy Jewish (Acts 16:1-3)? Patristic Exegesis, Rabbinic Law, and Matrilinear Descent», *JBL* 105 (1986) 251-268.

COLLINS, A. Y., «Composition and Redaction of the Testament of Moses», *HThR* 69 (1976) 179-186.

———, «The Political Perspective of the Revelation to John», *JBL* 96 (1977) 241-256.

COLLINS, J. J., *The Apocalyptic Imagination: An Introduction to the Jewish Matrix of Christianity*, New York 1985.

———, *Between Athens and Jerusalem: Jewish Identity in the Hellenistic Diaspora*, New York 1986.

COLLINS, J. J., «Some Remaining Traditio-Historical Problems in the Testament of Moses», *STM*, 38-43.

———, «Testaments», *Jewish Writings of the Second Temple Period*, ed. M. E. Stone, CRINT II/2, Assen – Philadelphia 1984, 325-355.

———, «The Date and Provenance of the Testament of Moses», *STM*, 15-32.

———, «The Testament (Assumption) of Moses», *Outside the Old Testament*, ed. M. de Jonge, Cambridge 1985, 145-158.

———, «The Testamentary Literature in Recent Scholarship», *EJMI*, 268-286.

COLLINS, R. F., *The Birth of the New Testament: The Origin and Development of the First Christian Generation*, New York 1993.

CONLEY, T. M., «Philo's Rhetoric: Argumentation and Style», *ANRW* II.21.1, 343-371.

CONZELMANN, H., *Das erste Brief an die Korinther*, KEK, Göttingen 1969; Eng: *1 Corinthians*, trans. J. W. Leitch, Hermeneia, Philadelphia 1975.

CORTÈS, E., *Los discursos de Adiós de Gen 49 a Jn 13–17: Pistas para la historia de un género literario en la antigua literatura judía*, Barcelona 1976.

CRAIGIE, P., *The Book of Deuteronomy*, NICOT, Grand Rapids 1976.

CRANFIELD, C. E. B., *A Critical and Exegetical Commentary on the Epistle to the Romans*, ICC, Edinburgh 1975-1979.

CRIM, K., gen. ed., *The Interpreter's Dictionary of the Bible*, Supplementary Volume, Nashville 1976.

CROSS, F. M., *Canaanite Myth and Hebrew Epic: Essays in the History of the Religion of Israel*, Cambridge, MA 1973.

——— – FREEDMAN, D. N., «The Blessing of Moses», *JBL* 67 (1948) 191-210.

CULLEY, R. C., *Studies in the Structure of Hebrew Narrative*, Philadelphia – Missoula 1976.

DAHOOD, M., «Chiasmus», *IDB* Sup, 145.

DALTON, W. J., «Pseudepigraphy in the New Testament», *CTR* 5 (1983) 29-35.

D'ANGELO, M. R., *Moses in the Letter to the Hebrews*, SBLDS 42, Missoula 1979.

DANIEL, J. L., «Anti-Semitism in the Hellenistic-Roman Period», *JBL* 98 (1979) 45-65.

DANIELOU, J., *Philon d'Alexandrie*, Paris 1958.

DAVIES, W. D., «Law in first century Judaism», *IDB* III, 89-95.

———, «Law in the NT», *IDB* III, 95-102.

———, *The Setting of the Sermon on the Mount*, Cambridge 1964

DE JONGE, M., ed., *Outside the Old Testament*, Cambridge 1985.

DE LORENZI, L., ed., *Paul de Tarse: apôtre du notre temps*, Rome 1979.

DE ROBERT, P., «La fin de Moïse», *Le monde de la Bible* 44 (1986) 20-23.

———, «Le récit de Deutéronome», *Le monde de la Bible* 44 (1986) 25ff.

———, «Les traditions samaritaines», *Le monde de la Bible* 44 (1986) 24.

DE SANTO, C., «The Assumption of Moses and the Christian Gospel», *Interp* 16 (1962) 305-310.

DE VAUX, R., *Les institutions de l'Ancien Testament*, Paris 1960; Eng: *Ancient Israel: Its Life and Institutions*, trans. J. McHugh, London 1965[2].

DENIS, A. M., OP., *Concordance grecque des pseudépigraphes d'Ancien Testament*, Louvain-la-Neuve 1987.

DEY, L. K. K., *The Intermediary World and Patterns of Perfection in Philo and Hebrews*, SBLDS 25, Missoula 1975.

DIÉTERLÉ, C., «Le Livre des Antiquités Bibliques: regard sur quelques textes», *FV* 89 (1990) 49-60.

DIETZFELBINGER, C. «Pseudo-Philo: *Antiquitates Biblicae*», JSHRZ 2 (1975) 96.

DI LELLA, A., «Sirach», *NJBC*, 496-509.

DILLON, R. J., «Acts of the Apostles», *NJBC*, 722-767.

DOGNIEZ, C. – HARL, M., *Le Deutéronome*, La Bible d'Alexandrie 5, Paris 1992.

DONALDSON, T. L., «Moses Typology and the Sectarian Nature of Early Christian Anti-Judaism: A Study in Acts 7», *JSNT* 12 (1981) 27-52.

DONFRIED, K. P., «False Presuppositions in the Study of Romans», *CBQ* 36 (1974) 332-355.

———, ed., *The Romans Debate*, Peabody, MA 1991[2].

DORAN, R., «T. Mos 4:8 and the Second Temple», *JBL* 106 (1987) 491-492.

DOTY, W. G., *Letters in Primitive Christianity*, Philadelphia 1973.

DRIVER, S. R., *A Critical and Exegetical Commentary on Deuteronomy*, ICC, Edinburgh 1895[3]; rprnt 1973.

DUFF, J. W., *A Literary History of Rome*, New York 1960.

DULING, D. C., «"[Do not swear. . .] by Jerusalem because it is the city of the Great King" (Matthew 5:35)», *JBL* 110 (1991) 291-309.

DUNN, J. D. G., *Jesus and the Spirit*, London 1975.

————, *Jesus, Paul and the Law: Studies in Mark and Galatians*, London 1990.

————, ed., *Jews and Christians: The Parting of the Ways, A.D. 70-135*, WUNT 66, Tübingen 1992.

————, «Paul's Epistle to the Romans: An Analysis of Structure and Argument», *ANRW* II.25.4, 2842-2890.

————, *Romans 1–8*, WBC 38A, Dallas 1988.

————, *Romans 9–16*, WBC 38B, Dallas 1988.

————, *Unity and Diversity in the New Testament: An Inquiry into the Character of Earliest Christianity*, London – Philadelphia 1990².

DUPONT, J., ed., *Jésus aux origines de la christologie*, BEThL XL, Leuven 1989².

EIßFELDT, O., *Einleitung in das Alte Testament*, Tübingen 1964³; Eng: *The Old Testament: An Introduction*, trans. P. R. Ackroyd, Oxford 1965; rprnt 1974.

ELLIS, E. E., *Paul's Use of the Old Testament*, Edinburgh – London 1957.

————, *Pauline Theology: Ministry and Society*, Grand Rapids – Exeter 1989.

FALEY, R. T., «Leviticus», *NJBC*, 61-79.

FALLON, F. T., *2 Corinthians*, NTM 11, Wilmington 1980.

FEE, G., *The First Epistle to the Corinthians*, NICNT, Grand Rapids 1987.

————, «εἰδωλόθυτα Once Again: An Interpretation of 1 Corinthians 8–10», *Bib* 61 (1980) 172-197.

FELDMAN, L. H., «Josephus», *AncBD* III, 981-998.

————, «Josephus' *Jewish Antiquities* and Pseudo-Philo's *Biblical Antiquities*», *Josephus, the Bible and History*, ed. L. H. Feldman – G. Hata, Leiden 1989, 59-80.

————, «Josephus' Portrait of Moses», *JQR* 82 (1992) 285-328.

————, «Josephus' Portrait of Moses: Part Two», *JQR* 83 (1992) 7-50.

————, «Josephus' Portrait of Moses: Part Three», *JQR* 83 (1993) 301-330.

FELDMAN, L. H. – HATA, G., ed., *Josephus, the Bible, and History*, Leiden 1989.

————, ed., *Josephus, Judaism, and Christianity*, Detroit 1987.

FENTON, J. C., «Pseudonymity in the New Testament», *Theol* 58 (1955) 51-56.

FERCH, A. J., «The Two Aeons and the Messiah in Pseudo-Philo, 4 Ezra, and 2 Baruch», *AUSS* 15 (1977) 135-151.

FERGUSON, E., ed., *Encyclopedia of Early Christianity*, New York – London 1990.

FISCH, H., *Poetry with a Purpose: Biblical Poetics and Interpretation*, Bloomington – Indianapolis 1988.

FITZER, G., «Μωϋσῆς», *EDNT* II, 450-452.

FITZMYER, J. A., *The Gospel according to Luke I–IX*, AncB 28, Garden City 1981.

————, *The Gospel according to Luke X–XXIV*, AncB 28A, Garden City 1985.

————, «Glory Reflected on the Face of Christ (2 Cor 3:7–4:6) and a Palestinian Jewish Motif», *TS* 42 (1981) 630-644.

————, «The Letter to the Galatians», *NJBC*, 780-790.

————, «The Letter to the Romans», *NJBC*, 830-868.

————, *Romans*, AncB 33, New York 1993.

————, *A Wandering Aramean: Collected Aramean Essays*, SBLMS 25, Chico 1979.

FORD, D. F., «Narrative Theology», *DBI*, 491-493.

FOX, R. L., *Pagans and Christians*, New York 1987.

FRAADE, S. D., «Palestinian Judaism», *AncBD* III, 1054-1061.

FRANK, H. T. – REED, W. L., ed., *Translating and Understanding the Old Testament*, Fs. Herbert Gordon May, Nashville – New York 1970.

FREEDMAN, D. N., ed., *The Anchor Bible Dictionary*, New York 1992.

————, «The Poetic Structure of the Framework of Deuteronomy», *The Bible World*, Fs. Cyrus H. Gordon, New York 1980, 25-46.

FREYNE, S., *Galilee from Alexander the Great until Hadrian, 323 BCE to 135 CE: A Study of Second Temple Judaism*, Wilmington – Notre Dame 1980.

FRIEDMAN, R. E., «The Biblical Expression *mastir panim* [Dt. 31,17]», *Hebrew Annual Review* 1 (1977) 139-148.

FRYE, N., *The Great Code: The Bible and Literature*, New York – London 1982.

FURNISH, V. P., *II Corinthians*, AncB 32A, Garden City 1984.

GAFNI, I., «The Historical Background», *Jewish Writings of the Second Temple Period*, ed. M. E. Stone, CRINT II/2, Assen – Philadelphia 1984, 1-31.

————, «The Historical Background», *The Literature of the Sages*, ed. S. Safrai, CRINT II/3, Philadelphia 1987.

GAGER, J. G., *Moses in Greco-Roman Paganism*, SBLMS 16. Nashville 1972.

GARLAND, D. E., «The Composition and Unity of Philippians», *NT* 27 (1985) 141-173.

GELIN, A., «Moïse dans l'Ancien Testament», *Moïse, l'homme de l'alliance*, ed. H. Cazelles – A. Gelin, *et al.*, Paris 1955, 29-52.

GILLMAN, J., «Epaphroditus», *AncBD* II, 533-534.

GILLMAN, F. M., «Moses: New Testament», *AncBD* IV, 918-920.

GOLDBERG, M., *Theology and Narrative*, Nashville 1982.

GOLDSTEIN, J. A., «The Testament of Moses: Its Content, Its Origin, and Its Attestation in Josephus», *STM*, 44-52.

GOODENOUGH, E. R., «Philo Judeus», *IDB* III, 796-799.

————, «Philo's Exposition of the Law and his *De Vita Mosis*», *HThR* 26 (1933) 109-125.

————, «The Political Philosophy of Hellenistic Kingship», *Yale Classical Studies*, ed. A. M. Harmon, New Haven 1928, 55-102.

———— – GOODHART, H. L., *The Politics of Philo Judaeus: Practice and Theory*, New Haven – London 1938.

GOODMAN, M., «Diaspora Reactions to the Destruction of the Temple», *JCPW*, 27-38.

GRABBE, L. L., «Josephus», *DBI*, 366.

GRANT, M., *The Jews in the Roman World*, New York 1973.

————, *A Social History of Greece and Rome*, New York 1992.

GRANT, R. M., *Gnosticism and Early Christianity*, New York 1960.

————, *Gods and the One God*, LEC 1, Philadelphia 1986.

GRAY, G. B., *A Critical and Exegetical Commentary on Numbers*, ICC, Edinburgh 1903; rprnt 1965.

GRAY, G. B., *Sacrifice in the Old Testament: Its Theory and Practice*, Oxford 1925; New York 1971.

GREENFIELD, J. C., «Smitten by Famine, Battered by Plague (Deuteronomy 32:24», *Love and Death in the Ancient Near East*, Fs. Marvin H. Pope. Guilford, CT 1987, 151-153.

GREENSPAHN, F. E. – HILGERT, E. – MACK, B. L., ed., *Nourished with Peace*, Fs. Samuel Sandmel, Chico 1984.

GREENWOOD, D., «Jesus as Hilasterion in Rom 3:25», *BTB* 3 (1973) 316-322.

GREENWOOD, D., «Rhetorical Criticism and Formgeschichte: Some Methodological Considerations», *JBL* 89 (1970) 418-426.

GRELOT, P., «Law», *DBT*, 301-307.

GROS LEWIS, K. R. R., ed., *Literary Interpretations of Biblical Narratives*, Nashville 1974.

GUNDRY, R. H., *The Use of the Old Testament in St. Matthew's Gospel, with Special Reference to the Messianic Hope*, NT.S, Leiden 1967.

GUTBROD, W., «νόμος», *TDNT* IV, 1046.

HAACKER, K. H., «Assumptio Mosis – eine samaritanische Schrift?», *TZ* 25 (1969) 385-405.

HAASE, W., ed., *Hellenistisches Judentum in Römischer Zeit: Philon und Josephus*, ANRW II.21.1. Berlin – New York 1984.

HACHLILI, R., «Synagogue», *AncBD* VI, 251-263.

HADOT, J., «Le milieu d'origine du "Liber antiquitatum biblicarum"», *La littérature intertestamentaire: Colloque de Strasbourg*, ed. A. Caquot, Paris 1985, 153-171.

HAFEMANN, S. J., «Moses in the Apocrypha and Pseudepigrapha: A Survey», *JSP* 7 (1990) 79-104.

HAÏK-VANTOURA, S., *La musique de la bible révélée*, Paris 1976; Eng: *The Music of the Bible Revealed*, trans. D. Weber, Berkeley 1991.

HALL, D. R., «Romans 3:1-8 Reconsidered», *NTS* 29 (1983) 183-197.

HALPERIN, D., *Heavenly Ascension in Ancient Judaism: the Nature of the Experience*, SBL Seminars 1987, 218-232.

HALS, R. L., «Legend: A Case Study in OT Form-Critical Terminology», *CBQ* 34 (1972) 166-176.

HAMMOND, N. G. L. – SCULLARD, H. H., ed., *The Oxford Classical Dictionary*, Oxford 1970$^2$.

HANSON, A. T., «The Domestication of Paul: A Study in the Development of Early Christian Theology», *BJRL* 63 (1981) 402-418.

————, «The Midrash in II Corinthians 3: A Reconsideration», *JSNT* 10 (1980) 2-28.

HARAN, M., *Temples and Temple Service in Ancient Israel*, Oxford 1978.

HARL, M. – DORIVAL, G., – MUNNICH, O., *La Bible greque des Septante. Du judaïsme hellénistique au christianisme ancien*, Paris 1988.

HARRELSON, W. J., «Law in the OT», *IDB* III, 77-89.

HARRINGTON, D. J., «The Biblical Text of Pseudo-Philo's *Liber Antiquitatum Biblicarum*», *CBQ* 33 (1971) 1-17.

————, «A Decade of Research on Pseudo-Philo's Biblical Antiquities», *JSP* 2 (1988) 3-12.

————, *The Gospel of Matthew*, Sacra Pagina 1, Collegeville 1991.

————, «Interpreting Israel's History: The Testament of Moses as a Rewriting of Deut 31–34», *STM*, 59-68.

————, «The Original Language of Pseudo-Philo's *Liber Antiquitatum Biblicarum*», *HThR* 63 (1970) 503-514.

————, «Palestinian Adaptations of Biblical Narratives and Prophecies: The Bible Rewritten (Narratives)», *EJMI*, 239-247.

————, «Philo, Pseudo-», *AncBD* V, 344-345.

————, «Pseudo-Philo, Liber Antiquitatum Biblicarum», *Outside the Old Testament*, ed. M. de Jonge, Cambridge 1985, 6-25.

HARTDEGAN, S. J., gen. ed., *Nelson's Complete Concordance of the New American Bible*, Collegeville 1977.

HARVEY, J., «Le "Rib-pattern", réquisitoire prophétique sur la rupture de l'alliance», *Bib* 43 (1962) 172-196.

HATCH, E. – REDPATH, H. A., *A Concordance to the Septuagint*, Graz 1954.

HAWTHORNE, G. F. – MARTIN, R. P. – REID, D. G., ed., *Dictionary of Paul and His Letters*, Downers Grove 1993.

HAYS, R. B., «"Have We Found Abraham to be Our Forefather according to the Flesh?" A Reconsideration of Rom 4:1», *NT* 27 (1985) 75-98.

HAYS, R. B., *Echoes of Scripture in the Letters of Paul*, New Haven – London 1989.

HAYWARD, C. T. R., «Rewritten Bible», *DBI*, 595-598.

————, «Targum», *DBI*, 671-673.

HEARD, W. J., «Maccabean Martyr Theology: Its Genesis, Antecedents and Significance for the Earliest Soteriological Interpretation of the Death of Jesus», Diss. University of Aberdeen (1987).

HEDWICK, C. W. – HODGSON, R., ed., *Nag Hammadi, Gnosticism and Early Christianity*, Peabody, MA 1986.

HEIL, J. P., *Paul's Letter to the Romans: A Reader-Response Commentary*, New York 1987.

HENGEL, M., *Between Jesus and Paul*, trans. J. Bowden, London 1983.

————, *Earliest Christianity*, trans. J. Bowden, London 1986; rprnt: *Zur urchristlichen Geschichtsschreibung*, Stuttgart 1979; Eng: *Acts and the History of Earliest Christianity*, London 1979 and *Eigentum und Reichtum in der frühen Kirche*, Stuttgart 1973; Eng: *Property and Riches in the Early Church*, London 1974.

————, *Judentum und Hellenismus, Studien zu ihrer Begegnung unter besonderer Berücksichtigung Palästinas bis zur Mitte des 2 Jh.s v. Chr*, WUNT 10, Tübingen 1973; Eng: *Judaism and Hellenism*, trans. J. Bowden, Minneapolis 1974.

————, *The Pre-Christian Paul*, London – Philadelphia 1991.

————, *Zum Problem der «Hellenisierung» Judäas im 1. Jahrhundert nach Christus*; Eng: *The «Hellenization» of Judaea in the First Century after Christ*, trans. J. Bowden, London – Philadelphia 1989.

HILGERT, E., «Bibliographia Philoniana 1935-1981», *ANRW* II.21.1, 47-97.

HILLERS, D. R., *Covenant: The History of a Biblical Idea*, Seminars in the History of Ideas. Baltimore – London 1969; rprnt 1982.

HIMMELFARB, M., *Ascent to Heaven in Jewish and Christian Apocalypses*, New York – Oxford 1993.

HOCK, R. F., «Paul's Tentmaking and the Problem of his Social Class», *JBL* 97 (1978) 555-564.

HOFFMAN, L. A., «Havdalah: A Case of Categories», *Beyond the Text: A Holistic Approach to Liturgy*, Bloomington – Indianapolis 1987, 20-45.

HOOKER, M. D., «Pistis Christou», *NTS* 35 (1989) 321-342.

HORBURY, W., «The Benediction of the *Minim* and the Early Jewish-Christian Controversy», *JThS* 33 (1982) 19-61.

HOUSTON, M. V., «The Identification of Torah as Wisdom: A Traditio-critical Analysis of Dt 4:1-8 and 30:11-20», Diss. University of Iowa (1987).

HUBBARD, M. E., «Tiberius Julius Alexander», *OCD*, 1072.

HUFFMON, H. B., «The Covenant Lawsuit in the Prophets», *JBL* 78 (1959) 285-195.

HUTTON, R. R., «Korah», *AncBD* IV, 100-102.

HYATT, J. P., «Were There an Ancient Historical Credo in Israel and an Independent Sinai Tradition?», *Translating and Understanding the Old Testament*, Fs. Herbert C. May. Nashville – New York 1970, 152-170.

INSTITUTE FOR NEW TESTAMENT TEXTUAL RESEARCH AND THE COMPUTER CENTER OF MÜNSTER UNIVERSITY, *Concordance to the Novum Testamentum Graece*, Berlin – New York 1987³.

ISENBERG, S. R., «On the Non-Relationship of the Targumim to the Testament of Moses», *STM*, 79-85.

JACOBSON, H., «Biblical Quotation and Editorial Function in Pseudo-Philo's *Liber Antiquitatum Biblicarum*», *JSP* 5 (1989) 47-64.

JAEGER, W., *Early Christianity and Greek Paideia*, Cambridge 1961.

JANZEN, J. G., «The Yoke that Gives Rest», *Interp* 41 (1987) 256-268.

JEREMIAS, J., «ἄνθρωπος, ἀνθρώπινος», *TDNT* I, 364.

———, *Jerusalem zur Zeit Jesu*, Göttingen 1962; Eng: *Jerusalem in the Time of Jesus*, trans. F. H. – C. H. Cave, London 1969.

JEWETT, R., «Law and the Coexistence of Jews and Gentiles in Romans», *Interp* 39 (1985) 341-356.

———, «Romans as an Ambassadorial Letter», *Interp* 36 (1982) 5-20.

JOHNSON, L. T., *The Acts of the Apostles*, Sacra Pagina 5. Collegeville 1992.

———, «Romans 3:21-26 and the Faith of Jesus», *CBQ* 44 (1982) 77-90.

JOHNSON, M. D., *The Purpose of the Biblical Genealogies*, MSSNTS 8, Cambridge 1969.

JOHNSON, R. F., «Moses», *IDB* III, 440-450.

JOHNSTONE, W., «Moses», *DBI*, 467-469.

JUEL, D., *Messiah and Temple*, SBLDS 31, Missoula 1977.

KARRIS, R. J., «The Occasion of Romans», *CBQ* 36 (1974) 356-358.

———, «Rom 14:1–15:13 and the Occasion of Romans», *CBQ* 35 (1973) 155-178.

KECK, L. E., *Paul and His Letters*, Philadelphia 1988.

KENNEDY, G. A., *Classical Rhetoric and Its Christian and Secular Tradition from Ancient to Modern Times*, Chapel Hill 1980.

————, *New Testament Interpretation through Rhetorical Criticism*, Chapel Hill 1984.

KINNEAVY, J. L., *Greek Rhetorical Origins of Christian Faith*, New York 1987.

KINZIG, W., «"Non-Separation": Closeness and Cooperation between Jews and Christians in the Fourth Century», *VigChr* 45 (1991) 27-53.

KITTEL, G. – FRIEDRICH, G., ed., *Theologisches Wörterbuch zum Neuen Testament*, Stuttgart 1933-1973; Eng: *Theological Dictionary of the New Testament*, trans. G. W. Bromiley, Grand Rapids 1964-1976.

KLEIN, R. W., «The Text of Deuteronomy Employed in the Testament of Moses», *STM*, 78.

KLEINKNECHT, H. – GUTBROD, W., «νόμος», *TDNT* IV, 1022-1091.

KLIJN, A. F. J., «The Study of Jewish Christianity», *NTS* 20 (1974) 419-431.

———— – REININK, G. J., *Patristic Evidence for Jewish Christian Sects*, NT.S 36, Leiden 1973.

KNOCH, O., *Die «Testament» des Petrus und Paulus*, Stuttgart 1973, 44-64.

KNOWLES, M. P., «"The Rock, his work is perfect": Unusual Imagery for God in Deuteronomy XXXII», *VT* 39 (1989) 307-322.

KOESTER, H., *Einführung in das Neue Testament*, Berlin 1980; Eng: *Introduction to the New Testament*, Vol 1: *History, Culture and Religion of the Hellenistic Age*, Vol 2: *History and Literature of Early Christianity*, Berlin 1982.

————, «Philippians, Letter to», *IDB* Sup, 665-666.

————, «The Purpose of the Polemic of a Pauline Fragment (Phil III)», *NTS* 8 (1961-1962) 317-332.

KOLENKOW, A. B., «The Assumption of Moses as a Testament», *STM*, 71-77.

————, «The Genre Testament and Forecasts of the Future in the Hellenistic Jewish Milieu», *JSJ* 6 (1975) 57-71.

————, «The Literary Genre "Testament"», *EJMI*, 259-267.

KRAELING, C. H., «The Jewish Community at Antioch», *JBL* 51 (1932) 130-160.

KRAFT, R. A., «Philo and the Sabbath Crisis: Alexandrian Jewish Politics and the Dating of Philo's Works», *The Future of Early Christianity*, Fs. Helmut Koester, Minneapolis 1991, 131-141.

KRAFT, R. A. – NICKELSBURG, G. W. E., ed., *Early Judaism and Its Modern Interpreters*, Atlanta – Philadelphia 1986.

KRAUS, H. J., *Psalmen*, Neukerchen-Vluyn 1978⁵; Eng: *Psalms 1–59: A Commentary*, trans. H. C. Oswald, Minneapolis 1988; *Psalms 60–150*, trans. H. C. Oswald, Minneapolis 1989.

KRIEG, R. A., *Story-Shaped Christology: The Role of Narratives in Identifying Jesus Christ*, New York 1988.

KUGEL, J. L. – GREER, R. A., *Early Biblical Interpretation*, LEC 3, Philadelphia 1986.

KURYLOWICZ, J., *Studies in Semitic Grammar and Metrics*, London – New York 1973.

KURZ, W. S., *Farewell Addresses in the New Testament*, Zacchaeus Studies: New Testament, Collegeville 1990.

————, «Luke 22:14-38 and Greco-Roman and Biblical Farewell Addresses», *JBL* 104 (1985) 251-268.

LAMBRECHT, J., «Structure and Line of Thought in 2 Cor 2,14–4,6», *Bib* 64 (1983) 344-380.

————, «Transformation in 2 Cor 3,18», *Bib* 64 (1983) 243-254.

LAPORTE, J., «Philo in the Tradition of Biblical Wisdom Literature», *Aspects of Wisdom in Judaism and Early Christianity*, ed. R. L. Wilken, Notre Dame – London 1975.

LATTEY, C. J., «The Messianic Expectation in "The Assumption of Moses"», *CBQ* 4 (1942) 9-21.

LAUSBERG, H., *Handbuch der literarischen Rhetorik: Eine Grundlegung der Literaturwissenschaft*, München 1960.

LEIMAN, S. Z., «Josephus and the Canon of the Bible», *Josephus, the Bible and History*, ed. L. H. Feldman – G. Hata, Leiden 1989, 50-58.

LÉON-DUFOUR, X., «Jésus devant sa mort, à la lumière des textes de l'institution eucharistique et des discours d'adieu», *Jésus aux origines de la christologie*, ed. J. Dupont, BEThL XL, Leuven 1989², 141-168.

LÉON-DUFOUR, X., ed., *Vocabulaire de théologie biblique*, Paris 1968²; Eng: *Dictionary of Biblical Theology*, trans. P. J. Cahill – E. M. Stewart, New York 1973².

LEVENSON, J. D., «The Jerusalem Temple in Devotional and Visionary Experience», *Jewish Spirituality: From the Bible to the Middle Ages*, ed. A. Green, London 1989, 32-57.

LEVENSON, J. D., *Sinai and Zion: An Entry into the Jewish Bible*, San Francisco 1967.

LEVINE, B. A., *Numbers 1–20*, AncB 4, New York 1993.

————, «Priests», *IDB* Sup, 687-690.

L'HEUREUX, C., «Numbers», *NJBC*, 80-93.

LICHT, J., «Taxo, or the Apocalyptic Doctrine of Vengeance», *JJS* 12 (1961) 95-103.

LIDDELL, H. G. – SCOTT, R., *A Greek-English Lexicon*, Oxford 1940[9]; rprnt 1958.

LIEBERMAN, S., *Hellenism in Jewish Palestine: Studies in the Literary Transmission, Beliefs, and Manners of Palestine in the Ist Century BCE–IVth Century CE*, New York 1962.

LIEU, J. M., «Pharisees and Scribes», *DBI*, 537-539.

LOEWENSTAMM, S. E., «The Death of Moses», *STA*, 185-217.

————, «The Testament of Abraham and the Texts Concerning Moses' Death», *STA*, 219-225.

LOHFINK, N., *Das Deuteronomium: Entstehung, Gestalt, und Botschaft*, Louvain 1983.

————, *Das Hauptgebot: eine Untersuchung literarischer Einleitsfragen zu Dtn. 5–11*, AnBib 20, Rome 1963.

————, *Studien zum Deuteronomium und zur deuteronomistischen Literatur I*, Stuttgart 1990.

————, «Die deuteronomistische Darstellung des Übergangs der Führung Israels von Moses auf Josua», *Schol* 37 (1962) 32-44.

LOHSE, E., «χείρ», *TNDT* IX, 424-439.

LONGENECKER, R. N., «Ancient Amanuenses and the Pauline Epistles», *New Dimensions in New Testament Study*, ed. R. N. Longenecker – M. C. Tenney, Grand Rapids 1974, 281-297.

LONGMAN, T., «A Critique of Two Recent Metrical Systems», *Bib* 63 (1982) 230-254.

LUEDEMANN, G., *Paulus der Heidenapostel*, Band 2: *Antipaulinismus im frühen Christentum*, FRLANT 130, Göttingen 1983; Eng: *Opposition to Paul in Jewish Christianity*, trans. M. E. Boring, Minneapolis 1989.

LUND, N., *Chiasmus in the New Testament: A Study in Formgeschichte*, Chapel Hill 1942.

LUZ, U., *Das Evangelium nach Matthäus. 1. Teilband, Mt 1-7*, EKKNT. Zurich, Einsiedeln – Köln – Neukirchen-Vluyn 1985; Eng: *Matthew 1-7: A Commentary*, trans. W. C. Linss, Minneapolis 1989.

LYONS, G., *Pauline Autobiography: Toward a New Understanding*, SBLDS 73, Atlanta 1985.

MACDONALD, D. R., *The Legend and the Apostle*, Philadelphia 1983.

MACK, B. L., «*Imitatio Mosis*: Patterns of Cosmology and Cosmology in the Hellenistic Synagogue», *SP* 1 (1972) 27-55.

MACK, B. L., «Philo Judaeus and Exegetical Traditions in Alexandria», *ANRW* II.21.1, 227-271.

———, *Rhetoric and the New Testament*, Minneapolis 1990.

MALHERBE, A., *Ancient Epistolary Theorists*, Atlanta 1988.

———, «Ancient Epistolary Theorists», *OJRS* 5 (1977) 3-77.

———, *Moral Exhortation: A Greco-Roman Sourcebook*, LEC 4, Philadelphia 1986.

MANN, T. W., «Theological Reflections on the Denial of Moses», *JBL* 98 (1979) 481-494.

MARCUS, J., «The Circumcision and the Uncircumcision in Rome», *NTS* 35 (1989) 67-81.

MARTIN, J., *Antike Rhetorik: Technik und Methode*, München 1974.

MARTIN, R. P., *Carmen Christi: Philippians ii. 5-11 in Recent Interpretation and in the Setting of Early Christian Worship*, MSSNTS 4, Cambridge 1967.

MARTYN, J. L., «Paul and His Jewish-Christian Interpreters», *USQR* 42 (1988) 1-15.

MARXSEN, W., *Einleitung in das Neue Testament*, Gütersloh 1964; Eng: *Introduction to the New Testament*, trans. G. Buswell, Oxford 1968.

MASON, S. N., «Priesthood in Josephus and the Pharisaic Tradition», *JBL* 107 (1988) 657-661.

MATERA, F. J., *Galatians*, Sacra Pagina 9. Collegeville 1992.

MAYES, A. D. H., *Deuteronomy*, NCeBC, London – Grand Rapids 1979.

———, «Deuteronomy», *DBI*, 177-178.

———, «Deuteronomy 4 and the Literary Criticism of Deuteronomy», *JBL* 100 (1981) 23-51.

———, «Deuteronomy: Law of Moses or Law of God», *PIBA* 5 (1981) 36-54.

MAYES, A. D. H., «On Describing the Purpose of Deuteronomy», *JSOT* 58 (1993) 13-33.

MAYS, J. L., gen. ed., *Harper's Bible Commentary*, San Francisco 1988.

MCARTHUR, H., «Celibacy in Judaism at the Time of Christian Beginnings», *AUSS* 25 (1987) 163-181.

MCBRIDE, S. D., «Polity of the Covenant People: The Book of Deuteronomy», *Interp* 41 (1987) 229-244.

MCCARTHY, D. J., *Institution and Narrative: Collected Essays*, AnBib 108, Rome 1985.

————, *Treaty and Covenant: A Study of Form in the Ancient Oriental Documents and in the Old Testament*, AnBib 21A, Rome 1981[2].

MCCONVILLE, J. G., *Law and Theology in Deuteronomy*, JSOT.S 33, Sheffield 1984.

MCDONALD, J. I. H., «Rhetorical Criticism», *DBI*, 599-600.

MCEVENUE, S. E., *The Narrative Style of the Priestly Writer*, AnBib 50, Rome 1971.

MCNAMARA, M., *Intertestamental Literature*, OTM 23, Wilmington 1983.

————, «Targums», *IDB* Sup, 856-861.

MEADE, D. G., *Pseudonymity and Canon: An Investigation into the Relationship of Authorship and Authority in Jewish and Earliest Christian Tradition*, Tübingen 1986; Grand Rapids 1987.

MEEKS, W. A., *The First Urban Christians: The Social World of the Apostle Paul*, New Haven – London 1983.

————, «Judgement and the Brother: Romans 14:1–15:13», *Tradition and Interpretation in the New Testament*, Fs. E. Earle Ellis, Grand Rapids 1987.

————, *The Moral World of the First Christians*, LEC 6, Philadelphia 1986.

————, «Moses as God and King», *Religions in Antiquity: Essays in Memory of Erwin Ramsdell Goodenough*, Leiden 1970, 354-371.

————, *The Prophet-King: Moses Traditions and the Johannine Christology*, NT.S 14, Leiden 1967.

———— – WILKEN, R. A., *Jews and Christians in Antioch in the First Four Centuries of the Common Era*, SBLSBS 13, Missoula 1978.

MEIER, J. P., *Matthew*, NTM 3, Wilmington 1981.

MENDELSON, A., *Philo's Jewish Identity*, BJSt 161, Atlanta 1988.

MENDENHALL, G. E., *The Tenth Generation: The Origins of the Biblical Tradition*, Baltimore – London 1973.

———, «Covenant», *IDB* I, 714-723.

———, «Covenant Forms in Israelite Tradition», *BA* 17 (1954) 50-76.

———, «Samuel's "Broken Rib": Deuteronomy 32», *No Famine in the Land*, Fs. John L. McKenzie, Missoula 1975, 63-74.

——— – HERION, G. A., «Covenant», *AncBD* I, 1179-1202.

METZGER, B. M., *The Canon of the New Testament: Its Origin, Development, and Significance*, Oxford 1987.

———, *The Text of the New Testament: Its Transmission, Corruption and Restoration*, Oxford 1968[2].

MEYER, B. F., «The Pre-Pauline Formula in Rom 3:25-26a», *NTS* 29 (1983) 198-208.

MILLER, P., «The Many Faces of Moses: A Deuteronomic Portrait», *Bible Review* 4, 5 (1988) 30-35.

———, «"Moses My Servant": The Deuteronomic Portrait of Moses», *Interp* 41 (1987) 245-255.

MITCHELL, M. M., «New Testament Envoys in the Context of Greco-Roman Diplomatic and Epistolary Conventions: The Example of Timothy and Titus», *JBL* 111 (1992) 641-662.

MOESSNER, D. P., «Paul and the Pattern of the Prophet like Moses in Acts», *SBL 1983 Seminar Papers*, ed. K. H. Richards, Chico 1983, 203-212.

MONDÉSERT, C., ed., *Le monde grec ancien et la Bible*, Paris 1984.

MOULE, C. F. D., *An Idiom Book of New Testament Greek*, Cambridge 1959[2]; rprnt 1986.

MOULTON, H. K., ed., *The Analytical Greek Lexicon Revised*, Grand Rapids 1978.

MOULTON, J. H. – MILLIGEN, G., *The Vocabulary of the Greek Testament*, Grand Rapids 1930.

MOULTON, W. F. – GEDEN, A. S., *A Concordance to the Greek Testament*, Edinburgh 1926[3].

MORRIS, J., «The Jewish Philosopher Philo», in E. Schürer, *A History of the Jewish People in the Time of Jesus Christ*, III.2, ed. G. Vermes – F. Millar – M. Black, Edinburgh 1973-1987, 851-853.

MUILENBERG, J., «The Form and Structure of the Covenantal Formulations», *VT* 9 (1959) 347-365.

MUNCK, J., *The Acts of the Apostles*, AncB 31, Garden City 1967.

————, «Discours d'adieu dans le Nouveau Testament et dans la littérature biblique», *Aux sources de la tradition chrétienne*, Fs. Maurice Goguel. Neuchâtel – Paris 1950.

————, *Paulus und die Heilsgeschichte*, Copenhagen 1954; Eng: *Paul and the Salvation of Mankind*, trans. F. Clarke, Atlanta 1959; rprnt 1977.

MUNRO, W., *Authority in Paul and Peter: The Identification of a Pastoral Stratum in the Pauline Corpus and I Peter*, MSSNTS 45, Cambridge 1983.

MURPHY, F. J., «Divine Plan, Human Plan: A Structuring Theme in Pseudo-Philo [Biblical Antiquities]», *JQR* 77 (1986s) 5-14.

————, «The Eternal Covenant in Pseudo-Philo», *JSP* 3 (1988) 43-57.

————, «God in Pseudo-Philo [Biblical Antiquities]», *JSJ* 19 (1988) 1-18.

————, *Pseudo-Philo: Rewriting the Bible*, New York – Oxford 1993.

————, *The Religious World of Jesus: An Introduction to Second Temple Judaism*, Nashville 1991.

————, «Retelling the Bible: Idolatry in Pseudo-Philo», *JBL* 107 (1988) 275-287.

MURPHY-O'CONNOR, J., *1 Corinthians*, NTM 10, Wilmington 1979.

NASUTI, H. P., «The Woes of the Prophets and the Rights of the Apostle: The Internal Dynamics of 1 Corinthians 9», *CBQ* 50 (1988) 246-264.

NELSON, R. D., «Deuteronomy», *HBC*, 209-234.

NEUSNER, J., *First Century Judaism in Crisis*, Nashville 1975.

————, *Judaism in the Beginning of Christianity*, Philadelphia 1984.

————, *Method and Meaning in Ancient Judaism*, BJSt 10, Chico 1979.

———— – FRERICHS, E. S., ed., *New Perspectives on Ancient Judaism*, Vol 3: *Judaic and Christian Interpretation of Texts: Contents and Contexts*, Lanham – New York – London 1987.

NEWSOM, C. A. – RINGE, S. H., ed., *The Women's Bible Commentary*, London – Louisville 1992.

NICHOLSON, E. W., *Deuteronomy and Tradition*, Oxford – Philadelphia 1967.

NICKELSBURG, G. W. E., «An Antiochan Date for the Testament of Moses», *STM*, 33-37.

————, «The Decalogue as the Direct Address of God», *VT* 27 (1977) 422-433.

NICKELSBURG, G. W. E., «Good and Bad Leaders in Pseudo-Philo's *Liber Antiquitatum Biblicarum*», *Ideal Figures in Ancient Judaism: Profiles and Paradigms*, ed. J. J. Collins – G. W. E. Nickelsburg, Chico 1980, 49-65

―――, *Jewish Literature between the Bible and the Mishnah: A Historical and Literary Introduction*, Philadelphia 1981.

―――, *Resurrection, Immortality and Eternal Life in Intertestamental Judaism*, HTS 26, Cambridge, MA 1972.

―――, ed., *Studies on the Testament of Moses*, SBLSCS 4, Cambridge, MA 1973.

NIGOSIAN, S. A., «Moses As They Saw Him», *VT* 43 (1993) 339-350.

NOLL, S. F., *The Intertestamental Period: A Study Guide*, Madison 1985.

NORTON, D., *A History of the Bible as Literature*, Vol I: *From Antiquity to 1700*, Cambridge 1993.

NOTH, M., *Das dritte Buch Moses, Leviticus*, ATD 6, Göttingen 1962; Eng: *Leviticus: A Commentary*, trans. J. E. Anderson, OTL, London 1965.

―――, *Das vierte Buch Mose, Numeri*, ATD 7, Göttingen 1966; Eng: *Numbers, A Commentary*, trans. J. D. Martin, OTL, London 1968.

―――, *Überlieferungsgeschichte des Pentateuch*, Stuttgart 1948; Eng: *A History of Pentateuchal Traditions*, trans. B. W. Anderson, Englewood Cliffs 1972.

OLSON, D. T., *The Death of the Old and the Birth of the New: The Framework of the Book of Numbers and the Pentateuch*, BJSt 71, Chico 1985.

―――, «Numbers», *HBC*, 182-208.

OLSON, S. N., «Epistolary Uses of Expressions of Self-Confidence», *JBL* 103 (1984) 585-597.

OLYAN, S. M., «The Israelites Debate Their Options at the Sea of Reeds: LAB 10:3, Its Parallels, and Pseudo-Philo's Ideology and Background», *JBL* 110 (1991) 75-91.

―――, «Problems in the History of the Cult and Priesthood in Ancient Israel», Diss. Harvard University (1985).

ORR, W. F. – WALTHER, J. A., *I Corinthians*, AncB 32, Garden City 1976.

O'TOOLE, R., «Some observations on anístēmi "I raise" in Acts 3, 22.26», *ScEs* 31 (1979) 85-92.

OVERMAN, J. A. – GREEN, W. S., «Judaism in the Greco-Roman Period», *AncBD* III, 1037-1054.

OWEN, J. J., *Analytical Key to the Old Testament*, Grand Rapids 1989-1990.

PEARSON, B. A., «Jewish Sources in Gnostic Literature», *Jewish Writing of the Second Temple Period*, ed. M. E. Stone, CRINT II/2, Assen – Philadelphia 1984, 443-481.

PENNA, R., «Judaism in Rome», *AncBD* III, 1073-1076.

PERRIN, N. – DULING, D., *The New Testament: An Introduction*, New York 1982[2].

PÉTER, R., «L'imposition des mains dans l'Ancien Testament», *VT* 27 (1977) 48-55.

PETERSEN, D. L. – RICHARDS, K. H., *Interpreting Hebrew Poetry*, Minneapolis 1992.

PHILLIPS, A., *Deuteronomy*, CBC, Cambridge 1973.

POLZIN, R., *Moses and the Deuteronomist: A Literary Study of the Deuteronomic History*, Part I: *Deuteronomy, Joshua, Judges*, New York 1980.

———, «Deuteronomy», *The Literary Guide to the Bible*, ed. R. Alter – F. Kermode, London 1987, 92-101.

PORTER, J. R., *Moses and Monarchy: A Study in the Biblical Tradition of Moses*, Oxford 1963.

———, «The Succession of Joshua», *Proclamation and Presence*, Fs. Gwynne Henton Davies, London 1970, 102-132.

PRICE, B. J., «"Paradeigma" and "Exemplum" in Ancient Rhetorical Theory», Diss. University of California at Berkeley (1975).

PRIEST, J. F., «Moses, Testament of», *AncBD* IV, 920-922.

———, «Some Reflections on the Assumption of Moses», *PerRS* 4 (1977) 92-111.

PURVIS, J. D., «Samaritan Traditions on the Death of Moses», *STM*, 93-117.

RADICE, R. – RUNIA, D. T., *Philo of Alexandria: An Annotated Bibliography 1937-1986*, VigChr.S 8, Leiden 1988.

RAHTJEN, B. D., «The Three Letters of Paul to the Philippians», *NTS* 6 (1959-1960) 167-173.

RÄISÄNEN, H., *Paul and the Law*, Philadelphia 1986.

RAMSEY, G. W., «Joshua», *AncBD* III, 999-1000.

RENGSTORF, K. H. *A Complete Concordance to the Works of Flavius Josephus*, Leiden 1973.

RENGSTORF, K. H., «δοῦλος», *TDNT* II, 261-279.

RHOADS, D. M., «The Assumption of Moses and Jewish History: 4 B.C. – A.D. 48», *STM*, 53-58.

————, *Israel in Revolution: 6-74 CE*, Philadelphia 1976.

RIEGEL, S. K., «Jewish Christianity: Definition and Terminology», *NTS* 24 (1978) 410-415.

RIST, M., «Assumption of Moses», *IDB* III, 451.

RIST, M., «Pseudepigrapha and the Early Christians», *Studies in New Testament and Early Christian Literature*, ed. D. E. Aune, NT.S 33, Leiden 1972, 75-91.

RIVKIN, E., *A Hidden Revolution*, Nashville 1978.

ROBERTS, C. H., «Books in the Graeco-Roman World and in the New Testament», *The Cambridge History of the Bible: From the Beginnings to Jerome*, ed. P. R. Ackroyd – C. F. Evans, Cambridge 1970, 48-66.

ROETZEL, C. J., *The World that Shaped the New Testament*, Atlanta 1985.

ROSSANO, P. – RAVASI, G. – GIRLANDA, A., *Nuovo Dizionario di Teologia Biblica*, Milano 1989.

ROWLAND, C., *Christian Origins: An Account of the Setting and Character of the Most Important Messianic Sect of Judaism*, London 1985.

ROWLEY, H. H., *The Relevance of Apocalyptic*, New York 1963.

————, «The Figure of "Taxo" in the Assumption of Moses», *JBL* 64 (1945) 141-143.

RUIZ, J. P., *Ezekiel in the Apocalypse: The Transformation of Apocalyptic Language in Revelation 16,7–19,10*, Frankfurt-am-Main 1989.

RUNIA, D. T., *Philo of Alexandria and the* Timaeus *of Plato*, Leiden 1986.

RUSSELL, D. S., *The OT Pseudepigrapha: Patriarchs and Prophets in Early Judaism*, London 1987.

SAFRAI, S., «Home and Family», *The Jewish People in the First Century*, ed. S. Safrai – M. Stern, CRINT I/2, Amsterdam – Philadelphia 1976. 753.

————, «Religion in Everyday Life», *The Jewish People in the First Century*, ed. S. Safrai – M. Stern, CRINT I/2, Amsterdam – Philadelphia 1976. 815.

SAILHAMMER, J. H., *The Pentateuch as Narrative: A Biblical-Theological Commentary*, Grand Rapids 1992.

SALDARINI, A., *Pharisees, Scribes, and Sadducees in Palestinian Society*, Wilmington 1988.

————, «Pharisees», *AncBD* V, 289-303.

SAND, A., «ἄνθρωπος», *EDNT* I, 100-104.

SANDERS, E. P., *Paul and Palestinian Judaism*, London 1977.

————, *Paul, the Law, and the Jewish People*, London 1985.

SANDMEL, S., *Judaism and Christian Beginnings*, New York 1978.

————, *The First Christian Century in Judaism and Christianity: Certainties and Uncertainties*, New York 1969.

————, «Philo Judaeus: An Introduction to the Man, his Writings, and his Significance», *ANRW* II.21.1, 3-46.

————, *Philo of Alexandria: An Introduction*, New York – Oxford 1979.

————, *Philo's Place in Judaism: A Study of Conceptions of Abraham in Jewish Literature*, New York 1971.

SCAGLIONE, A., *The Classical Theory of Composition from Its Origins to the Present: A Historical Survey*, Chapel Hill 1972.

SCHNACKENBURG, R., *Das Johannesevangelium*, Part III. HTKNT IV/I. Freiburg im Breisgau 1975; Eng: *The Gospel according to St. John*, Vol 3. trans. David Smith – G. A. Kon, HTCNT, New York 1982.

SCHRENK, G., «ἱερεύς», *TDNT* III, 257-265.

SCHULER, P. L., «Philo's Moses and Matthew's Jesus», *SPA* 2 (1990)

SCHULTZ, J. P., «Angelic Opposition to the Ascension of Moses and the Revelation of the Law», *JQR* 61 (1971) 282-307.

SCHÜRER, E., *Geschichte des jüdischen Volkes im Zeitalter Jesu Christi*; Eng: *History of the Jewish People in the Age of Jesus Christ*, rev. and ed. G. Vermes – F. Millar – M. Black, Edinburgh 1973-1987.

SCHUSSLER FIORENZA, E., *In Memory of Her: A Feminist Theological Reconstruction of Christian Origins*, New York 1984.

SCHWARTZ, D. R. *Studies in the Jewish Background of Christianity*, WUNT 60, Tübingen 1992.

————, «Philo's Priestly Descent», *Nourished With Peace*, ed. F. E. Greenspahn – E. Hilgert – B. L. Mack, Chico 1984, 155-171.

SEEBASS, H., «Die Stämmeliste von Dtn. XXXIII», *VT* 27 (1977) 158-169.

SEGAL, A. F., *Rebecca's Children: Judaism and Christianity in the Roman World*, Cambridge, MA 1986.

SENIOR, D., *What Are They Saying About Matthew?* New York 1983.

SHARPE, J. L., «The Second Adam in the Apocalypse of Moses», *CBQ* 35 (1973) 35-46.

SHERWIN-WHITE, A. N., *Roman Society and Roman Law in the New Testament*, Grand Rapids 1992.

SHULER, P. L., «Philo's Moses and Matthew's Jesus: A Comparative Study in Ancient Literature», *SPA* 2 (1990) 86-103.

SIKER, J. S., *Disinheriting the Jews: Abraham in Early Christian Controversy*, Louisville 1991.

SIMON, M., *Verus Israel*, Paris 1964; Eng: *Verus Israel: A Study of the Relations between Christians and Jews in the Roman Empire (AD 135-425)*, trans. H. McKeating, Oxford 1986.

SKA, J. L., *«Our Fathers Have Told Us:» Introduction to the Analysis of Hebrew Narratives*, Rome 1990.

SKEHAN, P. W., «The Structure of the Song of Moses in Deuteronomy (Deut. 32:1-43)», *CBQ* 13 (1951) 153-163.

SLY, D., *Philo's Perception of Women*, BJSt 209, Atlanta 1990.

SMALLWOOD, E. M., *The Jew Under Roman Rule*, Leiden 1976.

————, «High Priests and Politics in Roman Palestine», *JThS* 13 (1962) 14-34.

SMITH, M., «Pseudepigraphy in the Israelite Literary Tradition», *Pseudepigrapha I: Pseudopythagorica – Lettres de Platon – Littérature pseudépigraphique juive*, ed. K. von Fritz, Genève 1971, 194-198.

SORDI, M., *The Christians and the Roman Empire*, trans. A. Bedini, London 1986.

STANLEY, C. D., *Paul and the Language of Scripture: Citation Technique in the Pauline Epistles and Contemporary Literature*, MSSNTS 74, Cambridge 1992.

STAUFFER, E., *New Testament Theology*, New York 1955, 344-377.

STENDAHL, K., «The Bible as Classic and the Bible as Holy Scripture», *JBL* 103 (1984) 3-11.

STERN, M., «Aspects of Jewish Society: The Priesthood and Other Classes», *The Jewish People in the First Century*, ed. S. Safrai – M. Stern, CRINT I/2, Amsterdam – Philadelphia 1976, 561-630.

STERNBERG, M., *The Poetics of Biblical Narrative: Ideological Literature and the Drama of Reading*, Bloomington 1985.

STOCK, A., «Chiastic Awareness and Education in Antiquity», *BTB* 14 (1984) 23-27.

STOCKHAUSEN, C. K., *Moses' Veil and the Glory of the New Covenant: The Exegetical Substructure of II Cor. 3,1–4,6*, AnBib 116, Rome 1989.

STONE, M. E., *Scriptures, Sects, and Visions: A Profile of Judaism from Ezra to the Jewish Revolt*, Philadelphia 1980.

———, «Three Armenian Accounts of the Death of Moses», *STM*, 118-121.

STOWERS, S. K., *The Diatribe and Paul's Letter to the Romans*, Chico 1982.

———, «Diatribe», *AncBD* II, 190-193.

———, «Epistle», *DBI*, 197-198.

———, *Letter-Writing in Greco-Roman Antiquity*, LEC 5, Philadelphia 1986.

———, «Paul's Dialogue with a Fellow Jew in Romans 3:1-9», *CBQ* 46 (1984) 707-722.

———, «Social Status, Public Speaking and Private Teaching: The Circumstances of Paul's Preaching Activity», *NT* 26 (1984) 59-82.

SURBURG, R. F., *Introduction to the Intertestamental Period*, St. Louis – London 1975.

TANNEHILL, R. C., «Narrative Criticism», *DBI*, 488-489.

TAYLOR, J. E., «The Phenomenon of Early Jewish-Christianity», *VigChr* 44 (1990) 313-334.

THEISSEN, G., *The Social Setting of Pauline Christianity*, Philadelphia 1982.

THOMPSON, J. A., *Deuteronomy*, TOTC, London 1974.

THOMPSON, R. W., «Paul's Double Critique of Jewish Boasting: A Study of Rom 3:27 in Its Context», *Bib* 67 (1986) 520-531.

THYLEN, H., *Der Stil der Judisch-hellenistisch Homilie*, Göttingen 1955.

TIEDE, D. L., «The Figure of Moses in the Testament of Moses», *STM*, 86-92.

DE TILLESSE, G. M., «Sections "tu" et sections "vous" dans le Deutéronome», *VT* 12 (1962) 29-87.

TOOMBS, L. E., «Clean and Unclean», *IDB* I, 641.

TOWNER, P. H., «Gnosis and Realised Eschatology in Ephesus (of the Pastoral Epistles) and the Corinthian Enthusiasm», *JSNT* 31 (1987) 95-124.

TREBILCO, P., *Jewish Communities in Asia Minor*, MSSNTS 69, Cambridge 1991.

TREVES, P., «Philon», *OCD*, 684

TROMP, J., «Taxo, the Messenger of the Lord», *JSJ* 21 (1990) 200-209.

VANHOYE, A., *Prêtres Anciens, Prêtre Nouveau, selon le Nouveau Testament*, Paris 1986; Eng: *Old Testament Priests and the New Priest*, trans. J. B. Orchard, Petersham, MA 1986.

VANNI, U., *L'Apocalisse: ermeneutica, esegesi, teologia*, Bologna 1988.

———, «Liturgical Dialogue as a Literary Form in the Book of Revelation», *NTS* 37 (1991) 348-372.

———, «Un esempio di dialogo liturgico in Ap 1, 4-8», *Bib* 57 (1976) 453-467.

VERMES, G., *Scripture and Tradition in Judaism: Haggadic Studies*, Leiden 1973².

———, «A Summary of the Law by Flavius Josephus», *NT* 24 (1982) 289-303.

———, «La figure de Moïse au tournant des deux testaments», *Moïse: l'homme de l'alliance*, ed. H. Cazelles – A. Gelin, *et al.*, Tournai 1955, 63-92.

VEYNE, P., ed., *Histoire de la vie privée*, Vol 1: *De l'Empire romain à l'an mil*, Paris 1985; Eng: *A History of Private Life: From Pagan Rome to Byzantium*, trans. A. Goldhammer, Cambridge, MA 1987.

VINCENT, M. R., *A Critical and Exegetical Commentary on the Epistles to the Philippians and to Philemon*, ICC, Edinburgh 1897.

VISOTSKY, B. L., «Prolegomena to the Study of Jewish-Christianity in Rabbinic Literature», *AJS Review* 14 (1989) 47-70.

VON NORDHEIM, E., *Die Lehre von Alten*, Vol I: *Das Testamente als Literaturgattung im Judentum der hellenistisch-römischen Zeit*, ALGHL 13, Leiden 1980.

VON RAD, G., «Das formgeschichtliche Problem des Hexateuch», *Gesammelte Studien zum Alten Testament*, München 1958, 9-86; Eng: «The Form-Critical Problem of the Hexateuch», *The Problem of the Hexateuch and Other Studies*, trans. E. W. T. Dicken, Philadelphia 1967, 1-27.

———, *Das erste Buch Mose, Genesis*, Göttingen 1956; Eng: *Genesis*, OTL, Philadelphia 1961.

———, *Das fünfte Buch Mose, Deuteronomium*, Göttingen 1964; Eng: *Deuteronomy*, trans. D. Barton, OTL, Philadelphia – London 1966.

———, *Deuteronomium-Studien*, Göttingen 1948²; Eng: *Studies in Deuteronomy*, trans. D. M. G. Stalker, SBT 9, London 1953; rprnt 1956.

———, «Deuteronomy», *IDB* I, 831-838.

VON RAD, G., *Moses*, London 1960.

————, *Old Testament Theology*, Vol I: *The Theology of Israel's Historical Traditions*, trans. D. M. G. Stalker, Edinburgh 1970.

————, *Weisheit in Israel*, Neukirchen-Vluyn 1970; Eng: *Wisdom in Israel*, trans. J. D. Martin, London 1972.

WADSWORTH, M., «The Death of Moses and the Riddle of the End of Time in Pseudo-Philo», *JJS* 28 (1977) 12-19.

WALLACE, D. H., «The Semitic Origin of the Assumption of Moses», *TZ* 11 (1955) 321-328.

WATSON, D. F., ed., *Persuasive Artistry*, Fs. George A. Kennedy, JSNT.S, Sheffield 1991.

WEINFELD, M., *Deuteronomy 1–11*, AncB 5, New York 1991.

————, *Deuteronomy and the Deuteronomic School*, Oxford 1972.

————, «Deuteronomy – The Present State of Inquiry», *JBL* 86 (1967) 249-262.

————, «Deuteronomy, Book of», *AncBD* II, 168-182.

————, «Traces of Assyrian Treaty Formulae in Deuteronomy», *Bib* 46 (1965) 417-427.

WEISER, A., «δουλεύω», *EDNT* I, 349-352.

————, *Die Psalmen*, ATD 14/15, Göttingen 1959[5]; Eng: *The Psalms*, trans. H. Hartwell, OTL, London 1962.

WELCH, J. W., «Chiasmus in the New Testament», *Chiasmus in Antiquity: Structures, Analysis, Exegesis*, Hildesheim 1981.

WENGST, K., *Pax Romana: Anspruch und Wirklichkeit. Erfahrungen und Wahrnehmungen des Friedens bei Jesus und im Urchristentum*, München 1986; Eng: *Pax Romana and the Peace of Jesus Christ*, trans. J. Bowden, London 1987.

WESTERMANN, C., *Grundformen prophetischer Rede*, München 1960; Eng: *Basic Forms of Prophetic Speech*, trans. H. C. White, Cambridge – Louisville 1991.

WHITE, J., *The Form and Function of the Body of the Greek Letter: A Study of the Letter Body in the Non-literary Papyri and in Paul the Apostle*, SBLDS 2, Missoula 1972.

————, *Light from Ancient Letters*, Philadelphia 1986.

————, «Saint Paul and the Apostolic Letter Tradition», *CBQ* 45 (1983) 433-444.

WIDENGREN, G., «What do we know about Moses?», *Proclamation and Presence*, Fs. Gwynne Henton Davies, London 1970, 21-47.

WILDER, A. N., *The Language of the Gospel: Early Christian Rhetoric*, New York 1964.

————, «Scholars, Theologians, and Ancient Rhetoric», *JBL* 75 (1956) 1-11.

WILLIAMSON, R., «Philo», *DBI*, 542-544.

————, *Jews in the Hellenistic World: Philo*, Cambridge 1989.

————, *Philo and the Epistle to the Hebrews*, ALGHL 4, Leiden 1970.

WILLIS, W., «An Apostolic Apologia? The Form and Function of 1 Corinthians 9», *JSNT* 24 (1985) 33-48.

WILSON, R. R., *Genealogy and History in the Biblical World*, New Haven – London 1977.

————, «Old Testament Genealogies in Recent Research», *JBL* 94 (1975) 169-189.

WINSTON, D., «Judaism and Hellenism: Hidden Tensions in Philo's Thought», *SPA* 2 (1990) 1-19.

————, «Two Types of Mosaic Prophecy According to Philo», *JSP* 4 (1989) 49-67.

WINTER, P., «Philo, Biblical Antiquities of», *IDB* III, 795-796.

WISSE, F., «The Use of Early Christian Literature as Evidence for Inner Diversity and Conflict», *Nag Hammadi, Gnosticism, and Early Christianity*, ed. C. W. Hedrick – R. Hodgson, Jr., Peabody, MA 1986, 177-190.

WITHERINGTON, B., *Women and the Genesis of Christianity*, Cambridge 1990.

WOLFSON, H. A., *Philo: Foundations of Religious Philosophy in Judaism, Christianity, and Islam*, Cambridge, MA 1947.

WRIGHT, G. E., «Deuteronomy», *Interpreter's Bible*, 311-537.

————, «The Lawsuit of God: A Form-Critical Study of Deuteronomy 32», *Israel's Prophetic Heritage*, Fs. James Muilenburg, New York 1962, 26-67.

WUELLNER, W., «Paul's Rhetoric of Argumentation in Romans: An Alternative to the Donfried-Karris Debate over Romans», *CBQ* 38 (1976) 330-351.

————, «Where is Rhetorical Criticism Taking Us?», *CBQ* 49 (1987) 448-463.

YOUNG, F., «Rhetoric», *DBI*, 598-599.

ZAHAVY, T., «Judaism in the Mishnaic Period», *AncBD* III, 1083-1089.

ZEITLIN, S., «The Assumption of Moses and the Bar Kochba Revolt», *JQR* 38 (1947/48) 1-45.

ZERWICK, M. – GROSVENOR, M., *A Grammatical Analysis of the Greek New Testament*, Rome 1988³.

ZIESLER, J., *Paul's Letter to the Romans*, TPINTC, London – Philadelphia 1989.

ZIMMERLI, W. – JEREMIAS, J., *The Servant of God*, trans. H. Knight, SBT 20, London 1957.

# INDEX TO LITERATURE

## Biblical Literature

# INDEX TO AUTHORS

# TABLE OF CONTENTS

# TESI GREGORIANA

Since 1995, the series «Tesi Gregoriana» has made available to the general public some of the best doctoral theses done at the Pontifical Gregorian University. The typesetting is done by the authors themselves following norms established and controlled by the University.

## Published Volumes [Series: Theology]

1. NELLO FIGA, Antonio, *Teorema de la opción fundamental.* Bases para su adecuada utilización en teología moral, 1995, pp. 380.

2. BENTOGLIO, Gabriele, *Apertura e disponibilità.* L'accoglienza nell'epistolario paolino, 1995, pp. 376.

3. PISO, Alfeu, *Igreja e sacramentos.* Renovação da Teologia Sacramentária na América Latina, 1995, pp. 260.

4. PALAKEEL, Joseph, *The Use of Analogy in Theological Discourse.* An Investigation in Ecumenical Perspective, 1995, pp. 392.

5. KIZHAKKEPARAMPIL, Isaac, *The Invocation of the Holy Spirit as Constitutive of the Sacraments according to Cardinal Yves Congar*, 1995, pp. 200.

6. MROSO, Agapit J., *The Church in Africa and the New Evangelisation.* A Theologico-Pastoral Study of the Orientations of John Paul II, 1995, pp. 456.

7. NANGELIMALIL, Jacob, *The Relationship between the Eucharistic Liturgy, the Interior Life and the Social Witness of the Church according to Joseph Cardinal Parecattil*, 1996, pp. 224.

8. GIBBS, Philip, *The Word in the Third World.* Divine Revelation in the Theology of Jen-Marc Éla, Aloysius Pieris and Gustavo Gutiérrez, 1996, pp. 448.

9. DELL'ORO, Roberto, *Esperienza morale e persona.* Per una reinterpretazione dell'etica fenomenologica di Dietrich von Hildebrand, 1996, pp. 240.

10. BELLANDI, Andrea, *Fede cristiana come «stare e comprendere».* La giustificazione dei fondamenti della fede in Joseph Ratzinger, 1996, pp. 416.

11. BEDRIÑAN, Claudio, *La dimensión socio-política del mensaje teológico del Apocalipsis*, 1996, pp. 364.

12. GWYNNE, Paul, *Special Divine Action. Key Issues in the Contemporary Debate (1965-1995)*, 1996, pp. 376.

13. Niño, Francisco, *La Iglesia en la ciudad*. El fenómeno de las grandes ciudades en América Latina, como problema teológico y como desafío pastoral, 1996, pp. 492.

14. Brodeur, Scott, *The Holy Spirit's Agency in the Resurrection of the Dead*. An Exegetico-Theological Study of 1 Corinthians 15,44b-49 and Romans 8,9-13, 1996, pp. 300.

15. Zambon, Gaudenzio, *Laicato e tipologie ecclesiali*. Ricerca storica sulla «Teologia del laicato» in Italia alla luce del Concilio Vaticano II (1950-1980), 1996, pp. 548.

16. Alves de Melo, Antonio, *A Evangelização no Brasil. Dimensões teológicas e desafios pastorais*. O debate teológico e eclesial (1952-1995), 1996, pp. 428.

17. Aparicio Valls, María del Carmen, *La plenitud del ser humano en Cristo*. La Revelación en la «Gaudium et Spes», 1997, pp. 308.

18. Martin, Seán Charles, *«Pauli Testamentum». 2 Timothy and the Last Words of Moses*, 1997, pp. 308.

Riproduzione anastatica: 21 marzo 1997
Tipografia Poliglotta della Pontificia Università Gregoriana
Piazza della Pilotta, 4 – 00187 Roma